Olga Childs

What Russians Think

Everything you should know, but didn't bother to ask

Miami
2021

Other books by Olga Childs

Аквариум 1972-1992 (1992)

Это "Родина" моя (2004)

Автобиография аферистки (2008)

World of Borders (2022, upcoming)

What Russians Think. Everything you should know, but didn't bother to ask
ISBN 978-1-0879-7573-3
Library of Congress Control Number: 2021916729
Printed in the United States of America for Giraffe Books
Available through IngramSpark
First hardcover edition – September 2021
Cover art by Darya Kurlyandtseva
olgachilds.com
giraffe-books.com

For Clyde, who always remembers
that he is a Russian dog

"You are a microscopic cog in his catastrophic plan,
designed and directed by his Red Right Hand"
Nick Cave and the Bad Seeds

PROLOGUE

*"Why would someone from a country full of ponies
come to a non-pony country?"
Seinfeld, "The Pony Remark"*

In her famous account of the expansion of the British Empire, Heaven's Command, the late Jan (previously James) Morris writes: "[The Imperial] impulses were by no means always altruistic, and were often brutal. If my book seems to display a certain sympathy for them, that is because I am a child of my times."

I, too, am a child of my times – and I am also a child of an empire, which is no more. I, too, have sympathy for the Soviet Union. My Soviet childhood was quite privileged, and my memories of it are idyllic. The last thirty years have done nothing to help me resolve the fundamental question of my life: was the Soviet Union really as great as I remember it, or do I miss it simply because we all miss the carefree time of our childhood, when the sun was always shining, all of our parents and grandparents were alive, and large families, with all of their friends, gathered around tables laden with food and drink to mark every conceivable occasion? As children, we cannot place our lives into a greater context – whatever happiness we have, is ours to cherish.

Perhaps, my own sympathy for the Soviet Union is simply due to my family's relative privilege within it. In fact, none of my life as an adult anywhere in the United States or the United Kingdom – the two places where I spent most of my adulthood – has ever approached, in its level of comfort, the life I had growing up (even though I remain, so to speak, in a "professional" class).

One vivid memory of my childhood is eating black caviar with a spoon out of a glass jar for breakfast before school, and lamenting lack of bread to put it on. My mother, may she rest in peace, was against bread: carbs were bad for you, and bread was something that *proles* ate. (Yes, my parents had a typewritten *samizdat* copy of Orwell's *1984*, and actually used the word *proles*, which, just like *proletariat*, is the same in Russian as it is in English). Worse: unlike the rest of our food, which came in special parcels, called *payok* (an allowance), bread had to be procured at a local bakery, and that was where proles *went*. We didn't go there. To this day, when an umpteenth commentator on American TV brings

7

up an anti-Soviet trope of proverbial "breadlines", I chuckle – for many reasons at once. Were there "breadlines" in Moscow of the late-stagnation era? I don't think so, but I also probably wouldn't know.

As for the rest of the country, I didn't know it existed at all – I was raised with a firm notion that there was only darkness and uncivilized wilderness beyond the *MKAD* (the capital beltway). As a child, I have met numerous visiting foreigners, but never any Russians that weren't from Moscow. When I encountered the first ones at the age of 12, they were only from Leningrad (present day St.Petersburg), which was, as we then thought, a sort of "Moscow light". Between the ages of 0 and 12, I left Moscow a total of four times, to go to the seaside: twice to Crimea in summer, and twice to Latvia in winter. We took night trains and didn't get off until the final destinations, which were both resorts, full of vacationing Muscovites. I assume the help were probably locals, but they didn't count.

The only other places we went to, were our two *dachas* – summer homes – which were both only a few miles outside the MKAD, and everyone there was also from Moscow. That is, unless they were a Western diplomat or a foreign correspondent. One of our dachas, all the way down the now famous Rublevo-Uspenskoye shosse ("*Rublevka*"), was in *Nikolina Gora* – the only place that the USSR allowed foreigners to visit unsupervised, for the purpose of enjoying its beach on the Moskva river. The locals still call the beach "dip", short for "diplomatic".

Entire lived experiences of the people who grew up in the Soviet Union were shaped by their place of origin. Geographic mobility was negligible. All Russians from either Moscow or St. Petersburg can immediately recognize one of their own and each other, and most Russians, generally, can immediately tell if someone is from Moscow. In my case, the latter tends to hold true even before I open my mouth to say anything – and it holds true to this day, even though I spent most of the last 25 years overseas.

In my high school, we did have one girl whose family moved to Moscow from another city. They were easy to spot from the distance – the girl had a brother, even though they were ethnic Russians. For some reason, all Russian families in Moscow had only one child – this is not scientific but was certainly true in our social stratum. The families that we knew who had two children, were Jewish. If anyone had two children but was not Jewish, chances were, they were

8

not from Moscow. When I was 3 years old, my parents asked me, guardedly, whether I wanted a little brother or sister. "What nonsense!" – I exclaimed.

Twenty-seven years later, as my mother lay dying of lung cancer, I learned that she had been pregnant again, and had an abortion as a result of my alleged intervention. My mother later became a well-known TV personality and a celebrated art critic. Television vans reported live from outside her apartment building when she died, and hundreds of strangers attended her funeral. The abortion was, in the end, her only regret – and she promptly blamed me for it. Yet, I do not blame my 3-year-old self at all. I simply told my parents what they already knew: among the Muscovites, a second child would be a scandal.

In 2010, when my 85-year-old paternal grandmother died and I was arranging her funeral, I discovered that she was not, actually, from Moscow. The news shocked me, but on some level it made sense: after all, it was her who had brought all the caviar and filet mignon upon us. A knack for upward mobility was a prerequisite to moving laterally from elsewhere to Moscow. Grandma Tonya studied Chinese at Moscow State University and spent her early career as a translator with the *Pravda* newspaper bureau in China. When she died, we removed the entire works of Karl Marx, translated into Chinese, from her room.

She met my Grandpa Boris, a Japanologist, at the faculty of Oriental Studies. He later worked for the Soviet Union trade mission to Japan. I only met him once, the day I turned 12. He never had children besides my father, and did not have any idea what children liked, or were like. He gave me a 100-rouble bill to spend "on sweets". I do not think he knew how much that was – my father's monthly salary as a line editor at a social science magazine, at the time, was 195 roubles. I had never held a 100-rouble bill in my hands before. I am guessing Grandpa Boris didn't do too badly. The next time I heard of him, years later, was a call telling me a date and place of his funeral.

Things did not work out between Grandma Tonya and Grandpa Boris – and it was my grandmother's journalism career that lead her into the arms of her eventual husband, my father's stepfather. A son of a prominent Soviet academic (Konstantin Ostrovityanov, for whom a street is named in Moscow), my step-grandfather, whom I called Uncle Yuri, was, before long, the editor of *Communist* magazine, published for the benefit of the Soviet Bloc countries in Eastern Europe, and a candidate for the membership in the Central Committee of the Communist party (this is what I was always told, but cannot verify now).

Grandma Tonya and Uncle Yuri had been adamantly opposed to my father's 1974 marriage to my mother, which they considered a *mésalliance*. When he went ahead with it for reasons of honor (her pregnancy with me), they broke off all contact with the young family. Grandma Tonya and Uncle Yuri were, however, getting the coveted food distribution – "*payok*" – parcels from both the Communist Party and the Academy of Sciences, and, otherwise childless, they could not manage to consume both, so they had my father come pick one of them up. If our – the more humble, from the Academy of Sciences – *payok* had black caviar and filet mignon, I can only guess what was in the Communist Party *payok* that they kept. I still think about that sometimes.

My paternal grandparents occupied the decidedly upper-class world in every respect: their apartment was two-level, located in a tower of a building on the banks of the Moskva River. They had black *Volga* limousines, chauffeurs, housekeepers, and a massive leafy dacha in the aforementioned part of the suburbs, that became the most expensive land in all of Russia in later years. I guess it makes sense, in the end, that they were a product of whatever geographic mobility there was in the USSR. Communist leaders have all had come from somewhere – they consistently failed to emerge from the inert ranks of Muscovite *intelligentsia*.

The family on my mother's side have been in Moscow since time untold. One of my ancestors, the family legend has it, sailed with the explorer Adam Johann von Krusenstern as an artist, in order to document the voyage. A tiny painting, allegedly by said ancestor, was, in my childhood, on permanent exhibition in the Tretyakov gallery. It was not a remarkable painting, and it was eventually moved to storage. My maternal grandfather's family were not aristocrats, but certainly *bourgeoisie* – before the 1917 Revolution, they and their various relations were traders and prominent landlords throughout Moscow.

After the Revolution, they all demonstrated amazing dexterity and conformity, and, within 20 years, my grandfather's uncles and aunts were Communist Party officials and other important members of society in Moscow and across the reaches of now-Soviet Russia. Grandpa Georgiy was 16 when his mother died of tuberculosis in 1940. In his older years, he recalled how they had already known of the advent of antibiotics at the time, but it was impossible to come by them yet. Family photos show my grandfather and his brother Evgeny, with their father, standing over their mother's coffin, which is covered by a pile of

10

flowers from well-wishers. Her name was Olga, and it was after her that my mother later named me. My great-grandfather Sergey, grief stricken at his wife's death, was taken by a heart attack just months later.

Grandpa Georgiy pulled himself together and entered the competition for admission into the specialized high school for the future officers of the Soviet Navy. The school had just opened, with the first intake of students in 1940, and, according to Grandpa Georgiy himself, it was the most prestigious high school in the Soviet Union. September 1941 was going to be its second intake, and competition was 7 young men for 1 seat. In early June 1941, Grandpa Georgiy was exalted to learn that he got in.

As it happens, the quest also saved his life. When the USSR was forced to enter World War II two weeks later, the newly recruited cadets, who were meticulously selected for future military command, and included among them offspring of high-ranking Soviet military officials, were evacuated far away from the front – initially to Siberia, then Kuibyshev (present-day Samara) and eventually Baku. In Baku, Grandpa Georgiy went straight on to Caspian Naval Academy[1]. Since he was already, technically, in the Armed Forces, Grandpa Georgiy was never drafted, and didn't take part in the War – which, over the next 4 years, took the lives of everyone else whom he had known until that point.

My Great Uncle Evgeny, who was two years older, did end up drafted but survived the War, serving in the Air Defense forces. His life went downhill afterward: a habitual drunk, he eventually killed himself in 1977. At that point it transpired that my grandfather had previously enabled his career in the Soviet Navy by reporting on all of the paperwork that he had no surviving relatives, so we never talked about Great Uncle Evgeny. In fact, it turned out that he had a daughter and a granddaughter (who is my second cousin). They lived in Moscow. In the late 1970s, my mother and I met with them once, but quickly realized that there was nothing to talk about. I have never seen them again, and do not even know their names. Ethnic Russians aren't very big on extended family. To us, the blood of the covenant was always thicker than the water of the womb.

Years later, in 2005, I had security at the Moscow House of Journalism detain a couple of women I had never seen before, who were trying to steal my

---

1 Presently, Azerbaijan Higher Naval Academy.

mother's official framed portrait after her memorial service. Upon questioning, they introduced themselves as Great Uncle Evgeny's relations.

It is worth mentioning that I had been told a very different story of my grandfather's life when I was a child. My mother, may she rest in peace, rebelled against all things having to do with her parents and the State, in the typical fashion of the baby boomer bohemians. She was ashamed of her clean Soviet pedigree, and always tried to make up stories of persecution. For example, she insisted that we must have come from Lithuania, and constantly insinuated to people around her that she was Jewish. (I only realized the extent of this years later, when strangers approached me after her death, to ask why she was having a Christian funeral.) In respect of Grandpa Georgiy, she had always told me that my great grandparents were "repressed" for political reasons and perished in the labor camps of the GULAG, that he had grown up in an orphanage and was forced to join the military against his will.

I realize now that it was important for my mother to raise me as a dissident, and she had told me these things in order to dissuade me from forming what would otherwise be a logical emotional attachment to the State that fed me filet mignon and black caviar, and had me chauffeured between *dachas*. Perhaps she eventually convinced herself that some of it was true. For his part, Grandpa Georgiy was so terrified of his daughter's ire, that he only gathered the courage to set the record straight after she died. By then, it was 2005, and the State that my mother so elaborately disparaged was long gone. Concerned that I would not believe him, Grandpa used photos of my great grandmother Olga's posh funeral, and the Navy specialized high school admission paperwork that he kept for 64 years, to prove the point.

Grandpa Georgiy was not a pauper, as my snotty paternal grandparents would have everyone believe. He rose quickly to Captain 1st rank – a colonel – in the Soviet Navy. He worked for the Navy Central Command for most of his military career, had received a Masters degree in physics, in addition to his degree from the Naval Academy, and invented a method of neutralizing naval mines. He and my grandmother had the use of a pool of seats reserved for the officers of the Navy Central Command at the Bolshoi theater. They mostly only had red caviar in their house, their *dacha* was smaller than that of my paternal grandparents, and Grandpa Georgiy drove his own car – but they were certainly not *proles*. Grandpa Georgiy was also paid enough to have actually bought their

12

apartment – a co-op, a rarity by Soviet standards – and then splashed out for another one, in the same building, to give to my newlywed parents as a gift on the occasion of my birth. He was the ultimate Soviet *bourgeois*.

Grandpa Georgiy 's passion was the sea, even though he lived incurably far away from it for most of his life. Throughout my childhood, he relentlessly taught me the rules of sailing and navigating the sea by wind. He particularly took care that I, aged 8, knew how to sail a schooner into the wind. They even sent me to sailing school (yes, Moscow is landlocked, but then, you wouldn't let 10-year-olds into sailboats alone on an open sea, would you? So we did it in an artificial water reservoir).

I was massively into pirate books at the time, and only realized much later that the Soviet Navy no longer had any vessels under sails in its command. The Navy Day – last Sunday in July – was the biggest holiday of the year in my maternal grandparents' summer home. They always had 3-4 families, fellow Navy officers or fellow military physicists, over for a *shashlyk* (a sort of open-fire barbecue). Yours truly, dressed in a sailor's outfit, ceremonially raised makeshift flags of the Soviet Navy and (bafflingly) the blue cross of the Russian Imperial Navy. There was no Soviet flag. Years later, my middle daughter Sophia had tried to inquire of her aging great grandfather, what his job had been when he was younger. "My job was to give orders", – he said, after much deliberation. Sophia challenged him for details, but none came.

My maternal grandmother Clara's name was actually Klavdiya, but, as a teenager in the 1930s, she styled herself after the German feminist Klara Zetkin. Both of Grandma Clara's brothers died during World War II – one went missing in the Battle of Moscow, another died in a non-combat incident in the Navy. She graduated from Moscow State University with an equivalent of a Master's in history, but only ever worked occasionally: as a daycare teacher, primary school teacher and camp counselor. It was all so that she could hover over my mother, her only child, as my mother progressed between those institutions. Grandma Clara invented helicopter parenting in the 1950s USSR, and took to it fervently.

After my mother went on to the history department at Moscow State herself, Grandma Clara took to consumer activism. She *did* go to the same food stores *where proles went*, but only so that she could expose their shortcomings. Everyone in our part of Moscow feared her. She was the only person I ever heard of in the Soviet Union, who could return the half-eaten *kielbasa* to the store on the grounds of unsatisfactory taste, and get her money back. Grandma Clara, as it turned out, wasn't that much for *me* mixing with the populace, though. In the early 1980s, I was usually dropped off at school by a black *Volga,* a Soviet limo which had come to collect our neighbor, a junior agricultural minister – but I had to make my own way back home afterward. Grandma Clara would constantly give me money so that I would take the *marshrutka* – a shared minicab – instead of traveling two stops on a city bus. I took the bus anyway, and used the money for ice-cream and bubble gum (which, yes, we did have in the USSR).

A typical occasion in our family in the mid-1980s (and there were occasions all the time) included my parents, my maternal grandparents and me, gathered around a dining table. My grandparents served a lot of food, in formal Soviet style, and Grandma Clara notoriously insisted that everyone finish all of it, which no one ever wanted to do. Exasperated, she would then throw her utensils down and embark on an indictment of contemporary morals, which usually went like this: "If only Stalin was around, who thankfully, in his wisdom..." Hearing Stalin mentioned, my mother would shriek and run out, and my father would run after her, pretending to want to bring her back, but actually using this as a pretext to get out of having to finish the food. Every meal I ever remember ended exactly like this, leaving me one on one with the Stalin-approving grandparents and all of the remaining food. Thankfully, I had fast metabolism as a child.

My late mother was the only adult of employable age that I knew in the Soviet Union who did not work. She stayed at home with me throughout my childhood, until I was 11. I did not know any other children whose mothers stayed at home. Ergo, there were no other stay-at-home mothers for my mother to hang out with. Her solution was to spend all of her time hanging out at the Pushkin Museum of Fine Art, where she had worked as a junior curator and a tour guide before I was born (her Master's thesis at Moscow State was on Dutch Renaissance). Most of my mother's friends still worked at the cursed museum, and so it became the bane of my childhood. Not only was I forced to aimlessly wander its halls for hours on end, almost every day, but I was also forced to attend every enrichment activity they had on site for children of different ages – an art school, a young art historians society, you name it. I lived through it all, and I hated it. I can still tell a Monet from a Manet, but the lifelong resentment of fine art that I developed still persists.

They told me that I must be ashamed of myself for not loving fine art. "Goebbels hated art", – my mother would tell me. "Goebbels said that he had wanted to reach for his pistol the moment he heard the word *culture*". Our country's collective identity was based primarily around having defeated fascism in World War II. Every Soviet child knew who Joseph Goebbels was, and most certainly, one would avoid being compared to Goebbels at any cost. It was only later that I learned that Goebbels was, actually, very much into arts and culture, which he thought to be a huge factor in Nazi propaganda. The phrase so often quoted to me is actually attributed to playwright Hanns Johst. (Johst was also a Nazi, but I had never heard of him and would not be nearly as impressed). Yet there I was, a little girl desperately hating fine art, but not telling anyone for fear of being deemed a Goebbels sympathizer.

When I was 11, at the start of the era of *Glasnost*, my mother mercifully decided to embark on a career as a curator of underground Soviet Art, which I found considerably more fun. Among my mother's close friends at the time was Victoria Mochalova, the then-wife of the legendary conceptual artist Ilya Kabakov, whose installations went a long way to shape my idiosyncratic adolescent worldview. Mother's early career, which paved the way to her later fame, was based around guiding visiting foreigners through the hidden world of contemporary art galleries. From 1986 onward, our tiny 2-room apartment was constantly, daily, filled with visiting foreigners who had arrived to study the Soviet culture. I am straining but cannot remember most of them – except, perhaps, the now well-known author Andrew Solomon. In retrospect, Andrew was the first openly gay person that I ever met.

It was 1986 when *Moskovskaya Pravda* commissioned my mother to write a small story about the burgeoning open-air art market in the city's Izmailovo district. My mother saw the place as an epitome of kitsch and the assignment as unworthy, but it did pay, so she simply asked me to do it. I took the subway to the market, stared at it for a few minutes, then shrugged and wrote... something. My mother turned it in without checking it. To my astonishment, it was promptly published, and that was how I made my first ever money. *Moskovskaya Pravda*, clearly, had no clue that their stories were being written by 11-year-olds.

If this was not at all how you always imagined the Soviet Union, this book is for you. Whatever you think you know of the Evil Empire, you probably

15

know from the accounts of the Soviet era dissidents, political asylees, former "refuseniks", as well as intelligence analysts and "experts" who have never actually been to the Soviet Union at all. I pity the latter, but in no way mean to devalue the lived experience of the former, who are entitled to their own interpretations of it. However, I am also entitled to mine – the overwhelming majority of us, whether it was by choice or not, stayed in the Soviet Union until the end, and we defend the right to recall our past lives fondly.

I am, of course, most certainly aware now that the USSR wasn't all caviar and sailing. Yet, you will find today that most Russian adults who came of age before it all collapsed, no matter where they were in the Soviet Union and what their lived experience was, are nonetheless nostalgic for it. Even without the ridiculous privilege of my origins, the Soviet Union was, empirically, not at all what it is still painted to have been.

Yes, it did house people in expropriated "communal apartments", a whole family to a room – but it housed them with 100% efficiency. No one in the Soviet Union was homeless. No one begged, or slept under a bridge. If you have seen the endless tent cities in 2020 San Francisco, you would want to close your eyes and wake up in the Soviet Union the next instance. In the United Kingdom today (where a better job is done housing the homeless overall, than in most of the United States), many families classed as "homeless" or eligible for emergency homelessness aid, are housed in dilapidated motel rooms – also a family to a room. As a lawyer, I had a client who lived in a motel room, courtesy of Birmingham city council, with her two small children, for three years. Is it time for "regime change" in Birmingham then?

No one in the Soviet Union was unemployed. In fact, throughout most of my childhood, it was illegal to be unemployed. You could get arrested and prosecuted for not having a job. It was called *tuneyadstvo* (loitering), and it was a crime. You would then be sentenced to getting a job, and required to do it. If you wanted to be a poet or a rock musician, you had to join the government-sponsored union of poets or composers, and if the union wouldn't have you, you had to have a "real" job, and pursue your creative vocations outside of it. Abridgment of freedom? Yes, it was. Nobel Prize laureate Joseph Brodsky, whose poetry defined my life as a teenager, infamously fell foul of the employment requirement and was expelled from the Soviet Union after he failed to get a "proper" job. Even then, curiously, he absolutely did not want to leave.

16

This abridgment of freedom, however, worked quite well for the rest of the 200 million Soviet citizens, who weren't anywhere near winning a Nobel Prize. They all had jobs, and those jobs paid them steady salaries. Many of those were ridiculous, made-up jobs – the government came up with all sorts of jobs that did not need doing, just so that people could have them. The government believed it was key to social stability – and, in that, it was not wrong.

Most of my parents' friends, soon to be famous – but, as of the mid-80s, still underground – rock musicians and artists, had ludicrous nominal jobs, such as "a night guard at a library". Who on Earth needs to have a library guarded 24/7? There was virtually no crime in the Soviet Union anyway, and I certainly never heard of a library being robbed. But, in its quaint way, it worked. Think about it next time you deride the Soviet Union's unsustainable economic model, its 5-year plans and its non-convertible currency. Yes, all of it could not last forever. But it was not all bad while it lasted.

Some time around "Mr. Gorbachev, tear down that wall" and all such nonsense, the *payok* food parcels stopped. It would be years until I ate black caviar again. Pretty soon, shopping for any food at all became a hunting sport, and once you got hold of some, you certainly did not take it back, no matter the taste. Many of my friends' families left abruptly for Israel. My father's social science magazine closed down. Crimea, where Grandpa Georgiy had spent most of the 1980s conducting his naval de-mining exercises, was soon to be given to the newly independent Ukraine, forcing him into retirement from the Institute of Physics, to which he had migrated from the Navy.

The Western narrative nowadays tells us that the Soviet Union was unsustainable and thus collapsed, while nudged, only ever so lightly, by the Western powers that be. I do not dispute, for the sake of the exercise, that the Soviet economic model was not sustainable and would eventually collapse. But it certainly did not collapse by itself at the time that it did – it was methodically, and systematically, destroyed, from the outside as well as from within. To all of us, the cause and effect looked absolutely the opposite form what the rest of the world was led to believe it was. Everything was fine, and then the Western intervention came, and then the food disappeared and the economy crashed, and our country was torn at the seams.

Millions of former Soviet citizens, to this day, blame the vanity of Mikhail Gorbachev – arguably, the most hated Russian that ever lived – for

17

destroying their lives and taking away their livelihoods. There were no serious shortages of food; everything was working, the sun was shining, and people were employed, when Gorbachev came to power in 1985. That summer, Moscow hosted the International Festival of Students, and USSR started to license and produce its own Fanta and Pepsi-Cola in advance of it. A new city park, with statues and rowboats to rent, was laid in our neighborhood. It was all good, except that I got thrown out of the sailing school for hitting the instructor's barge head-on (never set out to single-handedly sail a boat built to be manned by two people, and especially not if you are 10 years old).

Of course, there were problems. Lack of transparency and isolation from the rest of the world were top among them, and intolerance for dissent, such as it was, had been an issue (even though, as it relates to the post-Stalin era, one also somewhat exaggerated by those who made asylum claims in the West having ostensibly fled persecution for such dissent). One must never forget, however, that a person cannot miss that which he never had, nor desire that which he knows not of. Insular and quaint, the Soviet world was, to its inhabitants, more tolerable than what came next.

Gorbachev's ascent in 1985, Glasnost in 1986 (after Chernobyl), Perestroika in 1987, "Mr Gorbachev, tear down that wall" in 1988, all led to 1989, when they did tear down the Wall, and in Moscow, it brought the "food cards" limiting how much cheese we could buy at once (have you ever bought 2 kilograms of cheese at once? I have, because this was how much it said I *could* buy). The food staple of the time were the "Bush legs", awful frozen chlorinated chicken legs shipped from America by way of humanitarian aid. We hated them, for they were fatty, tasteless and humiliating (some of us nostalgically longed for filet mignon). No Soviet citizen thought this was good food, nor was grateful to America whatsoever for sending us this crap in order to solve the crisis that the Americans, as most people believed and still do, deliberately caused.

That was all followed by the introduction of "market pricing" for consumer goods, which emptied the shelves entirely, and the devaluation of the currency, in which millions lost their life savings. By the time the USSR finally collapsed in late 1991, there was hardly anything left to salvage. It didn't happen all at once, but unfolded over the course of 6 years, and therefore it is very difficult to perceive the timeline, through which we all lived, as supporting any Western-approved theory of cause and consequence in the matter.

18

One day at the dawn of the 1990s, the day the Soviet system of set consumer pricing was to end, and market-based pricing was to take effect the next morning, every shelf of every store in Moscow that sold anything at all, was empty. I had not seen anything like this ever before, and have not since. Soviet citizens, who did not have a lot of faith in the idea of market-based pricing, bought up everything. In the evening on that day, two girls from my high school and I somehow found our way into a near-empty food store in a remote residential neighborhood, in the last hour that it was open.

All that remained in it, inexplicably, were a couple of dozen or so bottles of 777 – the USSR's awful and cheap, but iconic port wine. We bought them all, the last ever to be sold at the nominal Soviet price, and the staff carried them out for us and locked the doors, grateful that they got to go home early. There we stood, three teenage girls in the bitter cold of the Moscow spring, realizing that we absolutely cannot carry all this alcohol across the city on public transport in our hands, without any bags or a crate, yet unwilling to leave any of the loot behind ("a burden to carry, a pity to drop", goes an apt Russian proverb). Thus ended our collective childhood, and started the greatest adventure of our lives. That adventure still goes on.

Such was the lived experience of the Soviet people. When the formidable empire that housed and employed every citizen, invented space travel and defeated Hitler, was reduced to feeding its population that fatty chlorinated frozen humanitarian aid chicken, I was there. So were Vladimir Putin, Roman Abramovich, Alexey Navalny and every other Russian over the age of 45, of whom you are notionally aware. Tens of millions of citizens of present-day Russia were there, and we all remember. We all came from different walks of life and ended up in very different places. But without understanding what it was like to once stand on the ruins of our world, you will never understand us. And it is because you do not understand us, that you fear us.

I have now lived in the West for 25 years, mostly split between the United States and the United Kingdom. I recently relinquished my Russian citizenship, but my reasons for doing so were not political, and I visit often. I sometimes take part in Russian public life, idiosyncratically, and have published books there. While I was a Russian citizen, I never voted for Vladimir Putin. I worked in politics and media a lot, and prefer to vote for people that I personally know, no matter how much I disagree with them. I have never met Putin.

19

That being said, if there was ever a concern that Putin could lose an election, I probably would have voted for him. I never had a problem with Putin. Under his rule, Russia became a stable and civilized country, which it certainly wasn't in the mid-1990s, when I left it. In the Putin era, people stopped leaving – which is to say, they stopped leaving permanently. There are two tales of one Russia abound in the world now. The well promoted and paraded, but very small clique of "Russians in exile", that capitalize – in a literal and metaphorical sense – on peddling the tales of Russia's evil, is the only one that the Western media and political class choose to see, because its proclamations fit their narrative.

Meanwhile, many thousands of Russians live and work today in Western countries but refuse to denounce Russia, or to stand for having it disparaged any longer. These people are better integrated into the receiving communities than the self-styled exiled dissidents will ever be. They move because they want to see and learn things, and gain experience of other societies, not because they had to run from somewhere or something. Many of them credit Russia, and specifically Putin's Russia, with skills and funds that enabled them to roam the world, and most never stray too far from home. I call them *Global Russians.*

I spent years practicing immigration law in London and doing community work in the Russian-speaking immigrant diaspora in both the United Kingdom and the United States. Over the last ten years, just as vicious Russophobia and anti-Russian paranoia grew in the West, not just the recent exports, but even those who left 30 years ago, are less and less willing to tolerate it. Many of those Americans and Brits who paid little attention to *the Putin doctrine* before, have now come to see it as their only refuge. The architects of Russiagate have shot themselves in both feet – and, as a British citizen and an American resident, I'd say they created more geopolitical and national security issues for these two countries than they solved.

On some days – mostly in England – I wake up and see in this a global anti-Russian conspiracy, in which political emigres join with opportunistic European leaders and self-righteous hypocritical British MPs in their attempts to destroy Russia by destabilizing it, so that it is no longer a global power that they have to put up with in their backyard.

On some days – mostly in America – I stare at the TV screen in disbelief, and see that Russia is just an abstract notion, a cartoon to most of those spewing all that ear-destroying nonsense about it; about *us*. "OMG", – I then say to myself.

"None of these people has even the remotest idea of what Russia is really like, or how Russians – let alone *the Russians* – actually think.

While we most certainly don't, as the hawks would have you believe, all receive signals from some giant alien mother ship, our collective experience as former Soviet citizens, and our modern experience as Russians, leads most of us to independently draw the same conclusions from the same shared facts and observations. I do not need to have met Vladimir Putin to know what he thinks: in all likelihood, I think the same thing, and so do many, if not most, of the educated Russians above a certain age.

In this book, I will tell you what we really think.

PART ONE. WE

It sank

Helsinki, Finland, July 16, 2018. It's more than halfway through the now infamous Putin-Trump press-conference, when its most oft-repeated exchange takes place. Most Americans perceived it through the version that was broadcast on CNN. The video is still available on its official YouTube channel, and I use timestamps from that version, which runs at 45 minutes 58 seconds in total.[2]

[32:17] Jeff Mason, Reuters: Mr. President, did you want President Trump to win the election...

[32:19] Female voice (in Russian): "President..." [immediately cuts out]

[32:20] Mason: ...and did you direct any of your officials to help him do that"[32:23]?

[32:23] Putin (in Russian): "Да, я хотел. Я хотел, чтобы он выиграл... " [This means, literally: "Yes, I wanted. I wanted him to win..."]

[32:26] Translator (in English): "Yes, I did. Yes, I did."

At this moment, the most frequently broadcast fragment of the wretched press-conference cuts abruptly. If you roll the tape further, you can hear Putin explain that he wanted Trump to win, because Trump spoke passionately during the campaign about the improvement in the relations between Russia and the United States.

There is a word for *doing something* in the Russian language, such as you would use in "what are you doing?". But there is no "to do" and, therefore, no "I did". A Russian speaker is forced to use a verb indicating, specifically, what it is that they have, or haven't, *done*. In Putin's original answer, there was no ambiguity as to which part of the question he was answering. "Yes, I wanted," – he literally said. "I wanted him to win."

By expediently substituting a general response of "Yes, I did" for the specific answer actually given, the translator inadvertently led some native English speakers to believe that it was the most recent question that they heard – i.e, the second part – that was being answered (or, at least, both parts at once).

Needless to say, all hell broke loose on American TV. The initial reaction on the political left in the United States was, of course, to claim that Putin

---

2 https://youtu.be/cwxqOoIyWm0

admitted to election interference. They called it a "smoking gun moment". Lawrence O'Donnell on MSNBC went farther than most. "Yes, I did. Yes, I did" was plastered in giant letters across his "green screen". O'Donnell himself, in a clip posted to the official MSNBC YouTube account the next day, can be heard questioning Putin's intelligence: "Vladimir Putin proved today that he is not nearly as smart as any other G7 leader, when he confirmed that he wanted Trump to win, and that he directed his government to help Trump win, the Presidency".

It didn't help that there were further problems, too. The White House stenographer was given a tape that cuts in and out, and the whole fragment, initially, ended up not appearing in the official transcript at all (I speculate that someone there knew Russian and figured out that it makes no sense, so they edited the entire exchange out – but the official answer was, it seems, that parts of the tape were missing in the version provided to them).

For a few days, confusion reigned. It was fascinating to watch all of the alleged "intelligence experts" on CNN and MSNBC, people who made their entire careers blaming Russia for everything, going back endlessly to the "yes, I did". Why don't any of these people speak even basic Russian, anyway? Or do they simply hope that the viewers don't?

The first 48 hours were a maddening vacuum. Where were all the Russian-speaking darlings of the left-wing media, explaining that Putin didn't say anything of the sort? Where was Masha Gessen? Julia Ioffe? Anna Nemtsova? I disagree with Gessen a lot, but I know her, and she, at least, would certainly not stand for a mistranslation. It took a couple of days for Russian speakers to stop (presumably) throwing shoes at the TV screens and get through to someone to explain what happened.

Some liberal media outlets, to their credit, published specific explainers. On Wednesday, July 18th, The Atlantic ran a story titled unambiguously: "Russian Speakers Explain What Putin Actually Said About Trump. In Helsinki, the Russian president didn't confess to meddling. But he left no doubt about who he wanted to win the U.S. election." Axios' Jonathan Swan was in Helsinki himself, and probably checked with Russians on the scene. In his initial report, filed on July 16th, Putin's answer was given as " Yes I did [prefer Trump]".

It wasn't everyone that took advantage of the mistranslation. But most did. And, of course, you can't quite put things in square brackets on TV, so they just kept playing and playing it, usually cutting after the second "Yes I did". I am

23

absolutely convinced that the mistranslation of that one answer was the best thing that happened to the architects of Russiagate, it was their pivotal moment – and it was owed entirely to human error. The error was not Putin's.

The Russia haters were quite reluctant to let go of it. Once they corrected the record in future publications and segments, many still never pointed out the original error. A few days after the event, Rachel Maddow on MSNBC opened her show with a promise of a great revelation about the Helsinki press-conference. "Thank God", – I thought – "they have realized that there was a mistranslation!"

Nope, it wasn't about that at all. Even though Maddow indicated correctly, at that point, that Putin admitted to merely having a preference for Trump (rather than helping him win), the scandal she touted had been the alleged editing of the transcript by the White House. Maddow appeared to imply that the question from Reuters was edited out at Putin's behest. She did not, at any time, indicate that there had been any mistranslation of the dialogue involved.

This made no sense. If Maddow knew, by then, that there had been a mistranslation, why imply that the White House edited it out for evil reasons? Without the mistranslation, there was nothing sinister about the answer actually given. It was merely a repetition. By that late time in the press-conference, Putin had already elaborated at length on wanting Trump to win, and explained that he was entitled to having a preference, just like everyone else in the world. There was no reason for anyone to want that specific question redacted.

I switched to watching Fox News after that, so I wouldn't know whether Lawrence O'Donnell, who isn't nearly as smart as any other TV talk show host, ever acknowledged or corrected his mistake, or apologized for insulting the intelligence of the President of Russia.

"I hope you are fired" was a pre-Internet version of a hashtag. Helsinki was certainly one of those moments, and I feel bad for the translator involved. I can tell from his accent, that he is Russian. The Western media didn't do a lot of autopsy on this (and the Russian media, of course, never knew there was a problem, because they had the original feed of Putin speaking).

If you listen to the whole 46 minutes, you get a sense of what led to this. It was a long and complex press-conference. Several translators were translating for different feeds, there were technical difficulties involved. Putin had, by that point, answered a number of the same or very similar questions in detail, and was

24

visibly losing patience. He spoke faster and faster. The fateful Reuters question was an exact repeat of one or two previous questions – or, at least, I can see how it would have seemed to Putin that it was. By then, he probably felt as if he was forced to keep saying the same thing over and over.

The translation from Russian into English was far behind – so much so that, in the preceding 10 minutes, Putin's entire expressions and sometimes whole sentences were left out. In fact, just before he uttered the infamous "Yes, I did", the translator was gravely out of time, and was forced to fumble and abort the translation of Putin's previous answer (he was, by that point, speaking over Jeff Mason, who was already asking the first part of his question, but can barely be heard on the tape). I assume the translator said "Yes, I did", because he did not actually hear Mason's question, and needed that one saved second to figure out what was being talked about.

Mason takes from approximately [32:17] to [32:20] to ask the first part of his question. At [32:19] on the CNN tape, a female voice is suddenly heard saying, in Russian, "President...", and then it cuts out of the public feed. I speculate that it may have been the translation into Russian, for Putin's benefit. We can see him adjusting his earpiece at that moment. She probably became audible to him when she cut out of our feed. It would then take her about 3 seconds to ask the first part of the question, and by [32:23] she'd be done. While doing so, she would be speaking over the Reuters guy, who was still talking.

Putin interjects with his answer at [32:23], impatiently – this is probably as soon as the female Russian translator finished speaking the first part into his ear. By then, Mason has already spoken the second part, but it is clear that Putin, even though he understands English, was listening to the Russian translation during those same three seconds, and could not have been aware that there was a second part to the question at all. Since Putin's speech in Russian was unintelligible to most of the foreign press, to them the dialogue was simple. At [32:23], Mason finishes the second part of his question. Three seconds later, the Russian to English translator's hopeless, ungrammatical "Yes, I did" lands where it wasn't intended.

I am 100% bilingual in English and Russian, but it is, by far, not the same thing as live interpretation. In fact, I found that the better you know each language, the more you are aware that words and phrases routinely used as

25

translations of one another have subtly different meaning or usage, and the harder you are pressed to misuse them. In live translation of VIP events, compromises are made all the time, because there is no time to think – and being able to forgo what you know for the sake of expediency is also a skill; one that I, for my part, do not possess.

There was a moment once, during the Crimea conundrum in 2014, when I was nearly forced to translate a feed of Putin speaking live, for Sky in the UK. I found myself drafted in, ad hoc, to help with production in their Moscow bureau one day, once the regular crew had gone off to Ukraine. There was a technical problem with the interpretation and no one else around spoke both Russian and English fluently enough. My absolution came about five seconds before Putin started speaking – thank you, Vladimir Vladimirovich, for always being late! Had it not come, I would have probably started a nuclear war.

For that reason, I do not begrudge the interpreter. I hope he wasn't fired. After all, if the first part of the question had been the only question asked, the fateful phrase wouldn't have been a mistranslation ("Did you want President Trump to win the election?" – "Yes, I did").

If I were Putin, however, I would, by now, either ditch the translation and switch to English myself, or start insisting on having my own interpreter translate both ways, and on the interpretation being consequential, so that one person is finished before the other starts talking. After all, Helsinki was not Putin's first mistranslation gaffe, and, for all its infamy, it was not his biggest.

In Soviet schools, pupils learned one foreign language; the most common options were English and German. Proactive parents of better students engaged in machinations to ensure their offspring were placed onto the English track. Depending on the type of school, sometimes they learned a lot, sometimes barely any. Vladimir Putin, by his own admission a *hooligan* at school, was probably one of those kids who were always stuck in the less popular German – it is well-known that he is fluent in it. At the time when he was elected to his first term as President of Russia in the spring of 2000, Putin did not speak any English at all.

He does now, and his English isn't even bad. His accent is not inspiring, but he does not seem to struggle. Putin spoke publicly in English at UEFA twice in connection with Russia being awarded the 2018 World Cup, and, in Oliver Stone interview tapes, he could be heard competently making small talk with

26

Stone's wife off camera. I cannot claim to know what exactly possessed Putin to take the important time off being the world's biggest villain in order to broaden his language skills, but I can venture a guess. If I were Putin, this is what I myself would have done, after "it sank".

In the August of 2000, Putin's young presidency was marred by one of Russia's biggest ever maritime disasters – the sinking of the Kursk submarine and loss of 118 lives onboard. The Russians seemed to be unable to breach the hull with their own technology, and were reluctant to avail themselves of foreign help offered, due to national security concerns. This was, of course, based on the Russian military assessment that the crew had died in the initial explosion that sunk the submarine. After foreign help was eventually accepted and rescue teams entered the hull, it was discovered that some of the crew survived for days after the sinking, leaving diaries behind. They could have been rescued if help was accepted sooner. For Russia, it was an unspeakable humanitarian tragedy, and an even greater PR disaster. Especially so because Putin, just weeks after the tragedy, found himself in New York, interviewed live by the late Larry King.

At the time, I lived in New York myself, and did not follow Russian politics (my mind was entirely consumed by the Gore-Bush 2000 election, in which I volunteered passionately for Gore). I had only heard of Putin once before. My then-husband, who had visited from Russia during the time of the Russian presidential election in the spring of 2000, insisted that I take him to the Russian embassy so that he could vote. The embassy didn't let him vote, because he was a Russian resident without an absentee ballot. Unexpectedly, they said that I could, however, because I was still Russian, and I was on their expatriate rolls. I took the ballot.

My husband then suggested that I vote for some guy I had never heard of, named Vladimir Putin. "Our client", – he explained. My husband worked for the Effective Politics Fund, a consultancy that ran Putin's campaign. In my world, this was not particularly impressive. Everyone I knew in Russia back then ran election campaigns all the time. I shrugged and voted for a guy that I knew instead. By the time, in early September, when I sat in front of the TV watch the new Russian President on Larry King, I had never seen Putin or heard him speak.

It's been 21 years since that fateful day, and "она утонула" – "it sank" – is still widely used in colloquial Russian as shorthand for a PR disaster. The West remembers, too. The Independent in the UK included it in a 2017 list of "9

27

Vladimir Putin quotes that offer terrifying insights into his mind", and Russia's own RT had even managed to put a positive spin on it in its 2011 piece on Larry King and Putin: *"It's become a famous statement – one Larry King called "a great television moment" and a "brilliant way to answer a difficult question. It was a combination of being new and being direct," – King told RT.*

My deepest respect both to the late Larry King and to RT (for purposes of disclosure, I was briefly employed by RT in 2020, when I was stuck in Moscow at the start of the COVID-19 pandemic), but it was not a great television moment at all. It was the world's most atrocious instance of mistranslation. To the viewers watching on CNN in English, it simply went as follows. Having mentally prepared for the most difficult part of the conversation, Larry King asked, solemnly: "The submarine, Mr. President. What happened?!" To which Putin, after a second or two, answered: *Она утонула.* It was correctly translated into English as, "It sank". That's it.

As English speakers, when we ask, "what happened", it is usually not because we do not know, literally, what took place. It certainly wasn't in this case. Larry King knew very well that *it sank*, and so did the whole world. When the question "what happened" is asked in English, what is really meant is – *why* did it happen. *What led to it.* It calls for an autopsy of an already known unfortunate outcome. Such as, when Hillary Clinton titled her post-2016 book *What happened?*, it can be safely assumed that she already knew, by then, that she had lost the presidential election. The book aimed to explain, *how* it happened. Perhaps, even, analyze what could have been done differently to prevent it from happening (although I hear there isn't much of self-reflection in Clinton's book).

When the Russian President, pressed passionately for reasons behind an unspeakable tragedy, answered dejectedly "it sank", and seemingly failed to elaborate, a lot of things happened at once. The Americans assumed that he was a heartless man who had nothing to say for himself, diabolically trying to get out of answering a difficult question. In Russia, where the dialogue was played as it was broadcast in English, with ad hoc Russian translations added by each broadcaster, there was variety of opinion – but, to the extent that those translations were competent, Putin's detractors at home had managed to cultivate and propagate a lifelong image of a man who does not care. *Not caring* is a cardinal sin in Russia – see, they said, he showed his true face.

28

To anyone who has ever been exposed to simultaneous translation, however, it was immediately – in the moment – clear, well, *what happened*. Putin had King's questions translated to him on the earpiece – by whom, I do not know, but I would certainly have that person taken out back and shot. None of us – no one ever, actually, other than Putin himself at that moment – heard that translation. From what I can surmise, it was not being recorded. One can be pretty certain that Larry King's *"what happened?"* was mistranslated to Putin – and that is one question which is very easy to mistranslate.

If you go with, most literally, *что произошло [с подводной лодкой]*, you would be asking, literally, to be told what took place, and no more. This is probably what Putin heard – in fact, when he gave his answer, there was some confusion on his face, as if he'd well expect King to know by now, *what took place,* and was unsure why the question was being asked. In order for such a question to be understood by a Russian speaker appropriately, you would need to ask *что случилось* (that's something closer to *what happened* as we use it, or even, *transpired)* or, even better, *в чем там дело* (what's the deal), or finally, to leave no room for doubt at all, you need to ask *как так получилось* (how/why did it happen). If Putin was asked any of those versions of the question, there would have been no *it sank*, and, I think, much of his presidency would have turned out differently. This was the mother of all mistranslations, all the more infuriating because most people, no matter which language they speak, missed it.

After *it sank*, Putin learned English, but that didn't help him avoid the *yes, I did*. The morale of these two tales is, I think, that translation is never perfect, and there will always be things lost in it. In recent years, just as language skills became more ubiquitous, they became a commodity, and translation of geopolitically pivotal events and conversations is often left to people not particularly well qualified for it. This doesn't apply just to Putin – it's everywhere, and I personally saw people submitting hundreds of pages of Google Translate interpretations, which are often awful and incomprehensible, as evidence in courts and in immigration cases. Trust me, a bad translation is infinitely more harmful than none at all.

Yet, in the Anglo-American narrative, it often feels as if no one is particularly aware that Putin is, in fact, speaking a different, and poorly understood, language. As it already happened and cannot be undone, Putin's image as a heartless, diabolical, uncaring person (2000) who easily admits to all sorts of misdeeds because he doesn't care what people would think (2018), was cultivated by the enemies of Russia on the basis of a *Google Translate-like* version of what he had to say each time.

People change as they get older, and they certainly change in the course of life experience. I am not at all the same person that I was in 2000, and I would hardly want to have anything to do with the then-me. Over the course of 20 years that would be true of most people – especially people who were subjected to extraordinary, unique life experiences that the rest of us cannot fathom. One can see with the naked eye that it most certainly happened to Vladimir Putin. He is not at all the same person as 20 years ago, and he is most certainly more knowledgeable, experienced and wiser, and more comfortable speaking in public. Yet, he remains lost in translation.

Watching the present-day narrative of Russia unfold in the Western media, however, I think that Russia as a country and we all, as the native speakers of its official language, remain misunderstood on a fundamental level. We are constantly lost in translation of not just the speech, but of also the shared knowledge, the emotions, the cultural norms that guide us and shape our worldview. I have this persistent, nagging feeling that everyone else can't read us. We are simply not coming through. In this book, I will try to explain the starting points of our system of belief, and, as it happens, our discontent.

Grandchildren of War

In 2008, I was working as a special correspondent for *RIA Novosti*, a Russian newswire. I had been tasked with covering the environment and the work of international NGOs, and, in June that year, found myself aboard an expedition vessel cruising around Spitsbergen archipelago in the Arctic. The ship had been chartered by the World Wildlife Fund, and aboard it were delegations from its different international chapters. We were there to see for ourselves that the glaciers were melting, and that the polar bears were getting hungry (to drive the latter point home, back in Svalbard they made us all sign undertakings that we were not, at any time in this vast icy emptiness, to walk more than 6 feet away from someone with a rifle).

Being me, I managed, of course, to cause an international incident when I was there. Our vessel sailed under the Russian flag. The flag was massive, and sometimes people took pictures of themselves with that flag. I, too, took pictures. Multimedia reporting was all the rage, and I had been given a digital camera and ordered to supplement my writing with photos and videos for the agency's website. At one point, a prominent environmentalist from the WWF's German chapter grabbed the flag and attempted to pose with it, asking me to take a picture. "Thanks", – I replied, – "but I don't think it will go down well with Russian readers." To his befuddlement, mock or not, I explained: "lots of folks back home still haven't gotten over the War yet, and having a German hold a Russian flag could be insensitive". All hell broke loose then, but I stand by what I said. I would absolutely not, even today, publish a photo of a grinning German citizen posing with a Russian flag. A child of baby boomers, I am two generations removed from first-hand memory of the War, but there is a level on which that picture offends me.

You cannot understand Russia, or any individual Russian of Generation X or older, without a full understanding of how much World War II affected our country. There is a great chasm between East and West on this understanding, and it widens with the passage of time. To us, the War was always so fundamental to our life and existence, so profound in our thoughts, and so important to our identity as a people, that we assumed that its role and influence on us – as well as, crucially, our role in the War and our defining contribution to its outcome – would be obvious to everyone else in the world. Turns out, not necessarily.

To Russians, this was the Great Patriotic War. When all was said and done, it killed, by various accounts, between 22 and 27 million Soviet citizens. That loss is comparable to the entire present-day population of Texas. Of those, up to 9 million were combat deaths – mostly young conscripts or older, drafted and volunteer civilians, fathers, brothers and sons without any aptitude for, or experience of, war. The rest, to the tune of up to 20 million people, were civilian deaths – a total of around 10% of the population of the Soviet Union at the time (approximately 200 million).

Of the generation affected most by the War – those born in the early 1920s – many, like my Grandpa Georgiy, now 96, are still alive – or, at least, they have been alive until recently, for long enough, in large enough numbers, to have passed on the pain, anguish and trauma of their experience and their loss, both to their children – the baby boomers, like Vladimir Putin and my parents – and their grandchildren, the Gen X-ers, like me. Russians usually have children in their early to mid-twenties, so we have a generation in every demographic cohort. When I was a child, my grandparents were only in their fifties. My world was shaped by the War just as much as theirs had been.

I have never met anyone of my generation in Russia whose family hadn't lost someone in the War. Grandma Clara lost both of her brothers. One of them died directly in combat, in the War's most defining battle, the Battle of Moscow in late 1941. It was there that the hitherto victorious march of the Axis forces was finally reversed, but the human cost was incomprehensible (by most historic accounts, Soviet military losses in defense of Moscow were over 650,000 troops, and then more died in the subsequent counteroffensive). The aftermath was so brutal that the bodies of the fallen, in many cases, could not be adequately recovered or identified. They never found anything left of my great uncle Konstantin, then 18 years old, and he was never buried. His older brother, my great uncle Anatoly, died from internal bleeding due to a ruptured hernia aboard a Navy vessel, also around the same time. My great grandmother passed shortly thereafter, unable to cope with the grief of losing both of her sons. At the end of the War, only Grandma Clara and her father, my great grandfather Alexey, survived, out of a family of five.

Grandpa Georgiy was luckier, because his enrollment in various elite military officer training institutions consistently kept him away from the front. His brother survived the War, and both of their parents had died prior to the start

32

of it. But Grandpa Georgiy lost all of his childhood friends and classmates. He still keeps his closest friend's letters from the front, and often points out the last one, written hours before its writer was killed. Grandpa Georgiy says the trauma of that experience was overwhelming – a Muscovite in his early twenties, coming back to the city after the War and suddenly realizing that he does not know anyone, because they are all dead. The experience, to him, was like a protagonist of a science fiction movie, frozen in nitrogen and thawed a hundred years later. He could no longer even visit his parents' graves, because, in the immediate aftermath of the massive wartime losses, the cemetery was expanded, reorganized, and burials that had not been hitherto tended to, were simply bulldozed over (I cannot verify those claims, and therefore will not name the cemetery, but they ring true).

The deaths of my relatives and their close friends were military deaths – my maternal grandparents were both from Moscow, which, owing to the success of the battle in its defense, was never taken by the Germans, and did not experience substantial civilian loss (and, in the face of the imminent advance of the Wehrmacht, most of its civilian residents, along with its key institutions, were evacuated to regions far away from the front lines anyway). It is important, however, to put the scale of even that military loss into perspective.

The United States – from whose territory the War was quite far away, except for the attack on Pearl Harbor, which was a military base – lost only military personnel in the War (except 68 civilians in Pearl Harbor). Total U.S. losses stand at around half a million people. That is a lot of people, and no one in Russia ever sought to diminish the loss that their families experienced – we all know that, in many cases, entire sets of brothers died in the War, having made a choice to go to Europe and help liberate it. But the total number of U.S. servicemen lost in World War II is fewer than those the Soviet Union lost just in defense of Moscow alone (the Battle of Moscow having principally concluded before the United States even entered the War on December 9, 1941).

The total loss of British citizens in World War II is comparable to that of the United States, and stands also at around half a million people. Britain was never occupied, so the overwhelming majority of this number are also military deaths – although, of course, a number of Britain's civilians did die as a result of bombing campaigns over its territory.

33

Combat deaths or circa 5 to 9 million people, meanwhile, were no more than 30% percent of the 27 million total Soviet deaths, nor are they the main reason for lingering anguish that any mention of the War still brings. Almost 20 million dead were civilians – and, in case of the Soviet Union, this means that, by definition, they were women, children, the elderly and the infirm, because all able-bodied males of combat age were on the front lines with the Army, either via the draft or by having volunteered.

For reasons that are beyond the scope of this book, most of Continental Europe surrendered to Nazi Germany quickly, lingering resistance having been limited to guerrilla fighting and insurrection on the already occupied territory. In Continental Europe, the most depraved German atrocities were ultimately wreaked on civilians under occupation (as well as Germany's own citizens of Jewish descent, and a number of others whom the Nazi government saw as misfits). Millions of Europeans were herded into ghettos, treated inhumanely and shipped to concentration camps, where more than 6 million of them, including women, children, the elderly and the infirm, were brutally exterminated.

By contrast, when the Wehrmacht forces breached the territory of the Soviet Union at 4 am on June 22, 1941, they were met with fierce resistance – and the civilian resistance was almost as fierce as the military one. Without delving into WWII history, of which I am not a scholar, it seems as if the axe fell particularly hard on civilians from the get-go, because the Soviet military did not anticipate, and did not prepare for, an offensive, and was not present at the Western border in sufficient combat-ready numbers to mount an initial defense. Something may also be said for the Soviet notion of patriotism, stoked by Joseph Stalin's iron fist rule and personality cult, that signaled that failure to resist was a crime for which your own people would shoot you. Whatever the reason, Soviet civilians resisted defiantly, and most of them, in the march of the Axis forces to Moscow on all fronts, were brutally slaughtered.

There was, of course, some cooperation and *collaborationism* – especially in the confusion of the early days, and mostly in the present-day Baltic states, which were aggrieved to have been annexed to the USSR earlier (one of the main cultural reasons underlying the present-day animosity between Russia and the Baltic states, particularly Latvia, is the perceived exaltation there of the wartime Nazi *collaborationists*). In Lithuania, as well as in present-day Belarus and Ukraine, there were substantial Jewish populations that were targeted by the

German army and their local *collaborationists*. Jewish civilians were immediately slaughtered or shipped to the camps.

Going eastward, where most of the population were Slavs, the Germans initially hoped for peaceful occupation, but were quickly disabused of that notion. As the tale of their atrocities preceded them, the resistance only became fiercer. From then on they were, for the most part, on an extermination march, treating every old man, woman and child, of any ethnicity, as an enemy combatant. Their common extermination methods, among others, included making parents watch their children stripped naked and freeze to death in the snow, before being themselves buried alive.

While most of the Germans who were guards and employees at the concentration and extermination camps were eventually prosecuted, most of the rank and file Wehrmacht soldiers were not. Numbers of those nice German fellas that laughed as they forced our naked women, children and the elderly freeze to death in the snow and buried the rest alive, went back to Germany and lived out the rest of their lives in peace after the capitulation. Perhaps a father or a grandfather of that environmentalist guy in my Arctic expedition, who wanted to pose with the Russian flag, was among them. The "I was just following orders", or "if I did not participate, I would have been killed" defense seems to have worked for most German soldiers who survived the campaign, even though their atrocities in the USSR exceeded any imaginable definition of war crimes, and, of course, duress is not a defense to murder.

I have spent a lot of time in Germany, and I love Berlin – but I have always shuddered at the sight of German men my grandfather's age. That's because I know what they – each one of them, more or less – did. One of my friends had moved to Germany in the post-Soviet period, and, one day, one such nice elderly gentleman turned out to have been her downstairs neighbor. She lived in an apartment just above him for years. When she finally spoke to him for the first time, and told him she had lived in Leningrad, he reacted with recognition and excitement. "I hear it's a great city" – he said. "Unfortunately, I never got to see it when I was in Russia". "Oh, when was that?" – she asked innocently. "1944", – he answered casually, as if it wasn't a big deal. She was face to face with a former Wehrmacht soldier – and one, no less, that took part in the Siege of Leningrad.

The Siege of Leningrad, the complete blockade of Russia's second largest city by the Wehrmacht from September 1941 to January 1943 (the siege continuing until January 1944), was the greatest single atrocity of World War II, a close second only to the Holocaust itself. The original Soviet figures reported just under 700,000 dead in the siege. By modern estimates, as many as 1.5 million civilians died (for context, just under 400,000 people died in the nuclear attacks on Hiroshima and Nagasaki combined). This is, broadly, at least half of the population that remained in the city at the start of the siege.

Almost all of them starved to death, and some of the residents, as researchers now believe, resorted to eating their dead. The very cold winter in 1941-1942 played a key part. The unusual cold killed many malnourished civilians, but the Red Army maintained control of a strip of shore across Lake Ladoga, and was able to eventually lay a roadway into the city over its frozen ice. Some provisions were brought in, and up to half a million residents were evacuated over the 5 months that *дорога жизни* – the Road of Life – was in operation; yet, many died during the attempt, under enemy fire or of previous starvation. The intervention, while it undoubtedly saved lives, was insufficient to effect cardinal change before the ice melted.

Attempts to bring in provisions or evacuate residents over water, using the few available vessels on the lake, were only intermittently successful. Among those evacuated in April 1942 was Maria Volpert, an accountant, and her 2-year-old son Iosif. The toddler had been named by his parents, apparently, in honor of Iosif Stalin, usually called Joseph by Westerners. The toddler's father, Alexander Brodsky, was Captain 3rd rank in the Soviet Navy at the start of the War, in which, unlike my Grandpa Georgiy, he valiantly fought, eventually taking part in ending the Siege of Leningrad. The boy himself would also one day be called Joseph in the West, where he would go on to win the Nobel Prize in literature and define poetry for several generations of Russian speakers.

A single roadway into the city was finally laid along the shore of the lake in January of 1943, allowing for a steady supply of provisions, even as the siege remained in place for another year. By that time, large numbers of the survivors were orphaned children, to whom dying parents had given their last bits of food.

The son of other local residents, a man named Vladimir Putin and his wife Maria, was not so lucky – at the start of the siege he had been, along with many other children, turned over to the local government's ad hoc children's home. The parents, who had already lost another child in infancy, thought, at the time, that the government would be able to provide him with better care and nutrition than that which was available to the starving general population. This did not prove true for long, and the boy died. The Putins both survived, although only barely – the father had been already crippled by a combat injury in the days leading up to the siege, and the mother was, on the day the blockade was lifted, so near death that she could no longer walk.

When they both eventually recovered after the War, the grief of their loss was still too much to bear. And so, they decided to try for a child for the third time. The future President of Russia was born and raised in the ruins of this unspeakable atrocity, inflicted on our country by the Germans[3]. There was not a single person in the Soviet Union at the time, who wasn't born ready to take any kind of revenge on the bastards. As little kids, even in the late 1970s and early 1980s, our only game was "war", and, looking back, it was rather a schizophrenic game: the enemy was imaginary, because no one ever agreed to be "the Germans". In that context, perhaps, Vladimir Putin Jr.'s later choice of a career as an intelligence officer in Germany makes a lot of sense.

For my part, I always break down in tears wherever the Siege of Leningrad is brought up. I still do, even as I write this.

Every Soviet child knew of the Holocaust, and the liberation of Auschwitz in 1945 by the Red Army – our army – was the major source of our collective pride. We were, in the end, not just the people who defended their homeland and thus reversed the course of World War II, we were the liberators of Europe. It was us – and us alone, the Allies still way out West at that time – that took Berlin and erected the red Soviet flag on the Reichstag, forcing the final capitulation of the Wehrmacht.

Imagine our collective surprise, one day in 2020, when one Facebook user was informed that the famous photo of a Red Army soldier installing the Soviet Flag on the Reichstag was banned from the platform. The original photo was black and white, of course – and, in the days leading to the 75th anniversary

---

3 For any insight into Putin's family and childhood, I draw on "The Man Without a Face", a biography by Masha Gessen. While by no means an account friendly to its subject, the book is engaging, and I do not have reasons to doubt the veracity of the underlying research.

of Victory Day, someone had edited it, to color in the flag. Exactly as it was in reality – the Soviet flag. Red. The photo, shared in this version, was promptly banned by social media censors as disinformation. The decision was reversed after the outcry, and an apology issued. Yet, it was unmistakable: Facebook employs as fact-checkers people who did not know, and apparently did not believe, that it was the Soviets who took Berlin at the end of World War II. They thought this was Russian propaganda.

And why wouldn't they? Yes, it's been 75 years – and in recent years, the memory of World War II has been fading from public conscience. Holocaust denialism became a problem, and ignorant Millennial neo-fascists are on the rise across Europe. An increase in antisemitism is being seen all over the world, partly as a result of the coddling of unprecedented numbers of Muslim immigrants in Western communities. Thankfully, most Anglo-Americans would not stand for Holocaust deniers: at best, they are out there with flat-Earthers and alien abductees, and, at worst, they are universally condemned and abhorred.

Why, then, do Anglo-Americans not equally condemn the widespread revisionism of World War II, to the effect of downplaying, or virtually excluding, the role played in it by the country that sustained most of the casualties, and took in battle the capital city of the common enemy? Increasingly, American children are growing up without being taught at all that Russia and the United States were allies in World War II. Implicitly, they tend to believe the opposite – drawing on knowledge of the Cold War, they assume that the preceding actual war must have been waged against the same enemy. Whether true or not (most Russians believe it), a memorial coin reportedly was minted in the United States in 2020, celebrating the Allied forces without the Soviet Union at all. From what I see, it very well may have been true.

Things are somewhat better in the United Kingdom. My middle daughter, who studied WWII in her GCSE history course in a British school, reported that the role of the Soviet Union was, somewhat adequately, covered. When ex-Soviet adult parents of British children look at the syllabus, we find it, nonetheless, distorted. Yes, the Soviet Union is mentioned, and the losses it sustained, albeit sometimes but a footnote, are there. But one can very well surmise, from the general narrative taught, that the United Kingdom was the principal victor of World War II, Winston Churchill was its main commander, and the Blitz was its chief atrocity.

It is not just our wounded pride as liberators-in-chief, or the mild annoyance at having the lives of 27 million of our fellow citizens being rendered unworthy of commemoration. The main problem is, that the failure of the new generations to adequately see the historic role of the Russian people in the greatest calamity of modern times, reflects on how they see Russia, and the Russians, now. They are being told every day that Russia is evil – but fewer would be ready to believe so, if they realized, at the same time, that the Soviet Union was the principal ally of the United States and the United Kingdom in the deadliest war in human history, and that the Russians were instrumental in defeating the Nazi Germany in that war.

When they are deliberately not told that, the present narrative of the evil Russians stands unchallenged by common sense. And that narrative, as we will see later, does not reflect poorly only on Vladimir Putin, upon whose family one of the War's greatest atrocities was perpetrated directly, by the country that failed to prosecute most of the rank and file perpetrators, and is now leading the anti-Russian crusade. It reflects poorly on every one of us, Russians abroad, every day.

Unsurprisingly, the Victory in the Great Patriotic War was the cornerstone of the Soviet patriotic narrative, the main substance that bound our society together. This was not just our source of pride, the very reason for our existence as a world power – after all, it was also the one thing we could all agree on. The War has been written about, and sung about, and performed about, and painted about, countless millions of times – and it was for a good reason. Victory Day on May, 9 (VE Day plus the time zone difference) was our main holiday. Schoolchildren, dressed in their Sunday best, girls with braids and sashes, sang and recited poems about Victory, as veterans, who were our ostensibly most celebrated citizens, looked on. Although they were otherwise respectable communists and patriots of the highest order, being left out of that class (as a result of having not been to war) was my grandparents' shame.

The military awarded Grandpa Georgiy most of the medals related to Victory and its periodic commemorations, and even one of the medals related to the Battle of Moscow – rather baffling, considering that he was in the Navy, and Moscow is very far from the sea[4]. However, the small issue of not having

---

4 When I challenged him on the provenance of the award, Grandpa Georgiy said that it was issued

actually *been* to war, prevented him from being counted as a veteran and availing himself of the corresponding honors and social benefits. It seemed understandable, but he was upset. After all, he reasoned, he was *in the military* and there was war, so whose fault was it that they did not send him to the front? He eventually grew annoyed to have been spared. At one point in the 1970s, he was awarded a medal as an "international combat veteran" for taking part in some shady *coup d'etat* in some obscure country. He henceforth maintained that it ought to be just as good, but no one took him seriously.

War-related patriotic sentiment stood the test of time well, and was, for the most part, just as prevalent when the Berlin Wall fell in 1989. By the late 1980s, however, the then-ongoing war in Afghanistan, which was pointless and very unpopular, eventually brought all things military into relative disrepute, for the first time since the War. Meanwhile, independence movements in the Baltic States were based on the narrative of the Soviet Union as the occupying force, and that occupation was traced back to the 1939 Molotov-Ribbentrop pact.

Suddenly more self-aware and self-conscious than ever, the more enlightened citizens started to struggle reconciling the cult of Victory with the atrocities perpetrated by the Soviet wartime leader Joseph Stalin. Discredited on the point of his "excesses" and domestic political repressions after his death in 1953, Stalin nonetheless remained an icon to the war generation (Grandma Clara was just one of his many admirers). His perceived achievement as the commander-in-chief and the ultimate victor of World War II, stood thus far untarnished. Once it became apparent to the post-war generations that Stalin's personal vanity and incompetence may have contributed to the initially disastrous course of the War and high Soviet casualties in it, Victory became harder and harder to parse.

Had Stalin not been a tyrant, adorned by a *personality cult*, Soviet citizens would not be sacrificing themselves in his name, or resisting fiercely in

---

to all cadets in his specialized Naval High School, who had been sent to build fortifications for the anticipated defense of Moscow, in September 1941, prior to being evacuated to Siberia. He had previously told me that they were sent to Siberia as early as summer of 1941, and now says it was early October 1941 - but either way, it was well in advance of the Wehrmacht's arrival, and the cadets, aged 16 and 17 at the time, did not take part in any actual defense.

fear of being executed for surrendering. And, had he not been willing to use hundreds of thousands of Soviet children as cannon fodder, the War would, perhaps, not have been won.

A part of these sacrifices, on the other hand, had only become necessary because of the inexcusable errors that were made by Stalin himself at the start of the War (the view expressed valiantly, among others, by the venerated Marshal Georgiy Zhukov, the commander-in-chief of the Soviet forces as of June 1941). Overall, Stalin remains a controversial figure, but challenging the devotion of the remnants of the war generation to him is still considered undesirable. You piss on Stalin – you piss on the War, and you absolutely do not want to do that. That is why Death of Stalin movie was banned in Russia recently, even though it was, as everyone agreed, funny – and, in a caricature sense, somewhat historically accurate. I do not have any sympathy for Stalin personally, and I enjoyed it.

There is an extra layer as to why the issue of Stalin, and hence the unfortunate movie, was more sensitive in Russia that many in the West anticipated. In recent years, a new tendency emerged – mostly within Russia, but among Russia-haters overseas as well – to describe Stalin as if he were *just as bad as Hitler*. This is a vile attempt at a narrative – Stalin was, of course, a dictator, a madman and, directly and indirectly, caused many deaths and a lot of suffering. But he was, by a long shot, not Hitler – and, he actually rid the world of Hitler.

Losing the understanding of that, or peddling a version of reality in which the two are comparable, does much more damage than simply offend the notions of the dwindling devotees of Stalin's *personality cult*. It trivializes the magnitude of Hitler's evil and demeans the memory of his victims – more than 20 million of whom died with Stalin's name on their lips, and having never heard of his sins. In many ways, that narrative is not unlike Holocaust denialism. You do not hear it as much in the West, but some feeble-minded Russian opposition figures and demented Soviet-era dissidents do peddle it in Russia – therefore, anything Stalin related is taken defensively and causes debate, and sometimes unrest. The attempt to quell it by banning the movie was a knee-jerk reaction.

The 1990s were chaos and ruin in Russia, and patriotic education was haphazard at best. Older Millennials grew up without any significant sentiment about the War. On top of that, they all went to Germany for a vacation, and saw

41

that it was good. By the time Vladimir Putin took office as President at the turn of the century, lack of shared values among Russians had been a problem for a while. The country was being torn apart, devastated by the brain drain, the flight of capital and the then-ongoing war in Chechnya. The war generation, its ceremonial elders no longer buoyed by excessive adulation, was quickly dying off. In Russia, life expectancy is lower than in the West, and most of the World War II combat veterans died by 2000, when they would have been about 80.

The patriotic songs of my childhood still referred to "our fathers" going to war, but for the generation of children that were now growing up in Putin's Russia, those songs became disastrously unsuitable. In most cases, it had been their great-grandfathers that went to war, and, for the first time in post-war history, most of those children were growing up without any elderly relatives still around to tell the story of their first-hand experience of it.

To Putin's credit, in the scramble for a unifying idea, in the last 20 years he has managed to reboot the Victory franchise to enormous success. The ranks of veterans were swiftly replenished. Pretty much everyone who was still alive that had been alive and breathing during the War, was now counted as a veteran. Grandpa Georgiy, finally in receipt of his little red *veteran's book*, took to walking around in full medals, humbly shaking the hand of everyone who came up to thank him for his service. He never bothered telling anyone that he hadn't served *in the war*, and eventually, it seems, he had himself forgotten. Living past the age of 90 was a job well done, by Russian standards, so he figured that the adulation was long overdue.

At traditional school Victory Day concerts, Grandpa Georgiy was now flanked by veterans who seemed, at most, in their seventies – the child survivors of the Siege of Leningrad. The songs and poems had been written anew, telling stories of the War and Victory entirely in the third person, or with the use of properly distant generational pronouns. Presentations by the children were now supplemented by video and multimedia presentations to the audience, educating the students, as well as their Millennial parents, on the history of the War and its horrors. Victory Day marches by veterans, who were now too small in numbers and too frail to march, were replaced by *Eternal Regiment* marches by the post-war generations, carrying the portraits of their parents and grandparents who fought in the war. The President himself marched at the front.

Initially, this had all been admirable and in good taste. War-related patriotism was on the rise. As one of her fondest memories of visiting Russia, my middle daughter once recalled Victory Day in 2014. We were on a city tram in Moscow that evening, just as the fireworks started. The driver stopped in the middle of a bridge, and an old Soviet-era Victory Day song was playing. All passengers got out, and stood on that bridge, watching the fireworks and sharing the moment. It was uplifting, like the 4th of July in America in the best of times. I

As the Putin years went on, and the veterans kept dying, War-related patriotism started to take a somewhat weird turn. Since 2014, militant sentiment has been on the rise, due to the conflict in Ukraine and the perceived isolation of Russia in the world. Previously the least patriotic generation – the Millennials – blended their new, militaristic vision of patriotism with their rather simplistic understanding of World War II. Where previous generations saw tragedy, suffering and survival, of the kind that we still cannot fully recover from and definitely do not want to ever see happen again, this generation started to see a victorious march to Berlin, jubilation and singing.

The War was never celebrated in the Soviet Union – it was commemorated by the people who were still under the spell of deep collective PTSD, and those commemorations were led personally by those who were never able to move on from their personal loss. Now that those people aren't around anymore, the memory of the War is turning into mindless triumphalism. Russia's 30-somethings are acutely aware of Western revisionism, in which Russia's role in the War is now being constantly undermined, and perceive this not as a historic debate, but a new, ongoing conflict.

You can now often see Millennials decorating their cars to look as tanks, adorned with handmade signs that read "To Berlin!". Seeing as how excited they are about the journey, it seems that they don't know that the road to Berlin, for the Soviet Army, led through Auschwitz. To this generation, Putin's joke about the possibility of "taking Kiev in three days", and a faint notion that we have taken Berlin once, lie somewhere on the same reality pane. Many have taken to a weird idea of dressing their children up in what they think are WWII-period military uniforms (for the most part, they are not even the correct uniforms, but that is beside the point).

In the Russian-speaking diasporas in Europe (less so in the United States), *avtoprobeg* car rallies in May have become a tradition, in which they all get together and drive in procession through the Shires of England, with their "to Berlin" signs and Soviet flags, leaving the locals in sleepy villages utterly befuddled. In the diasporas, as far as I can see, this movement is often fueled, strictly speaking, not by Russians, but by Russian-speaking immigrants from other Soviet states. Given the recent animosity and discord in Eastern European geopolitics, this is seen by all of them as a proxy way of reuniting the former Soviet citizens – or, in most cases, their descendants – back into a community bound by one unifying idea.

It is also, without doubt, a symbolic way to show approval of Putin, and support for Russia, for many expats from those ex-Soviet states where a different sentiment, perhaps, prevails back home. Overseas, they feel more connected to the wider Russian-speaking diaspora, in which all Russian-speaking immigrants, especially of the working class, are often interdependent for mutual assistance and social networking. This phenomenon, dubbed *победобесие* – "Victory mongering" – gives them a sense of brotherhood that they otherwise lack.

Yet this "victory mongering" is, without a doubt, weird. No ex-Soviet citizen of older generations would rejoice in the idea of going "to Berlin" through rural Oxfordshire in a tank-attired BMW. Our Soviet-era war patriotism was a way to recover from a lasting tragedy and deal with collective pain. It is not, as we can now see, a suitable device for uniting the generations that have no memory of the War, and who appear to think that this was a wonderful experience, worthy of endless jubilation and an odd encore.

It *has*, after all, been more than 75 years. We are in dire need of a new unifying idea. And we are more vulnerable than ever to discord and unrest, until we find it. This makes for dangerous times, and this is a vulnerability that our enemies, old and new, are frantically looking to exploit.

At the time of writing, Grandpa Georgiy is 96 years old. Three years ago, after the third time he set his apartment building on fire, we finally moved him to a retirement home. The industry is not too well developed in Russia, but, I assure you, this one is no worse than your own home. It is a special home, in a lush part of Moscow, for the veterans of the War – but, since they have almost all died, Grandpa Georgiy, who has never been to war, is now its most celebrated resident.

44

He is also their oldest resident ever. He has his own little apartment, thankfully without a kitchen. He is no longer transportable to school concerts, but delegations of children and adults are brought before him on Victory Day. Grandpa Georgiy can no longer hear them and can barely see them, but he speaks to them. Since dementia set in, he took to telling everyone that he provided security for the Tehran conference. Aged 18 at the time, he wasn't anywhere near it, of course – and I told everyone at the home so, but no one there takes *me* seriously[5].

5 I was unable to verify the veracity of Grandpa Georgiy's new claim to military glory, and am skeptical because I have never heard it before. I consider it a false memory, such as are common to dementia patients. At the time of Tehran Conference, Grandpa Georgiy was a cadet at the Naval Academy in Baku. It is plausible that the Navy would seek to provide patrol of the event at sea, and that cadets may have been the only personnel available in the region. Yet, I could not find any records of Naval Academy cadets from Baku dispatched there. And even if they were, this was, of course, still thousands of miles from the front, and made one not a participant in the War.

The Capital of Peace

When the Bolsheviks took power in Russia in the Revolution of 1917, one of their first orders of business was to simplify the written Russian language, so as to facilitate the education of the masses. (The Russian Empire of the early 20th century was still mostly an agricultural country, and the peasants were usually illiterate). The Orthographic Reform of 1918 got rid of what were thought of as duplicate letters. The side effect of it was the inadvertent creation of new homonyms – and, by far the most confusing one was the word *мир*. Depending on the context, it can mean either *peace* or *the world*.

The word for "the world" always sounded the same as the word for "peace", but used to be spelled differently at the time when Lev Tolstoy wrote *War and Peace*. Controversy still surrounds the title of the great novel in Russia – or, rather, its translation into English as *War and Peace*. Most scholars now seem to agree that Tolstoy meant *peace*, but at least one of the book's pre-reform editions apparently featured the title spelled as if to mean *War and the World*. Mercifully, Tolstoy did not live to see the Orthographic Reform of 1918, or, for that matter, the Revolution. But it is possible, of course, that he anticipated some ambiguity around the title, since both versions of *мир* already sounded the same. Later-age Soviet propaganda had a lot of fun with the word play, too – for example, "world peace" in Russian is *миру – мир,* which is simply the same word twice. Thank God for conjugation.

The neighborhood in which Grandpa Georgiy bought himself, and my parents, co-op apartments in the early 1970s, was a new subdivision at the far North of Moscow, where the march of urbanization was swallowing up dilapidated villages still remaining inside the *MKAD*. The new subdivisions were built just a few kilometers from Sheremetyevo airport, the Soviet Union's gateway to the world – since 1967, regular flights from Sheremetyevo connected Moscow with New York. Our neighborhood was the first Russian neighborhood that visitors from all over the world would see on arrival, as they would be driving through it on their way into the city.

A giant sign greeting visitors driving into the city from Sheremetyevo on Leningradsky highway was erected, and it read "Moscow is the capital of peace and labor". It was clear which *мир* was meant by it, because *peace and labor* were two words often used together. They were the topmost values of the

46

Soviet society, after all. As their morale dwindled in the late 1980s, Muscovites had a lot of fun with the sign, and words *and labor* eventually went missing for good. *Moscow is the capital of the world,* read the amended sign, rather ambitiously. For me, this symbolized the process by which what we, Russians, had actually intended, turns into what the rest of the world *assumes* that we meant. The sad story of the Cold War is full of such examples.[6]

By most historical accounts (and I shall not pretend to write one myself, for my mission is to tell you what I, and many other Russians, *think*), Stalin was very fond of Franklin Roosevelt. Stalin was put upon to deal with Churchill, and did not trust him – but he did admire, and trust, FDR. The *new deal* policies could be understood in terms of the socialist narrative, and are still widely admired by many Russians today. Roosevelt himself did not seem to see Stalin as a threat, and understood, unlike many of his excitable fellow statesmen, that the Soviets had no geopolitical ambitions that extended to America.

I am aware that FDR's true feelings and post-war intentions toward Stalin are subject to some debate in the United States, into which I shall not delve. Whether or not he was mistaken, Stalin thought that FDR was a friend of the Soviet Union, or, at least, definitely not an enemy. The two men, by all accounts, discussed the post-war future of Europe in the aftermath of anticipated Allied victory, and their agreement on future zones of influence was almost settled. (I draw, from memory, on Oliver Stone's excellent *The Untold History of the United States*, which I emphatically recommend. While different interpretations of the Yalta summit and other informal negotiations between the two leaders exist, the view that many Russians hold on post-war agreements regarding Europe and their fate, is broadly the one expressed by Stone).

Stalin was absolutely crushed by FDR's death. At that time, the Soviet Army was on the march of liberation across Europe, and final Victory was just a matter of weeks. Victory was to be our greatest triumph, but it was dampened by the brutal murder of some 20 million of our fellow citizens. Many of our cities lay in ruins. One named after himself, Stalingrad – present-day Volgograd – had been completely razed to the ground.

---

6 The signs that read " Москва- столица мира и труда", *Moscow is the capital of peace and labor*, were later erected at different entrances to the city and some, I think, still stand.

With Roosevelt's' death, Victory was to be even more bittersweet: there was no mistaking that all of the FDR's agreements with Stalin were to be immediately abandoned. The Soviet Union, more misunderstood – and now, also, more feared – than ever, was to stand, once again, alone, and claiming a zone of influence at its immediate borders in Europe was going to be a challenge. An alliance and understanding with Roosevelt, which was to establish our firm place in the world, was supposed to be the only tiny sliver of silver lining that was to come of the whole horrid thing. Now, it was not to be.

Franklin Delano Roosevelt was from New York; he attended Harvard University and Columbia University Law school, and had been Governor of New York before running for President. Whatever you think of him, the man was highly intelligent, well-informed, worldly and certainly capable of independent thought. In his wake rose Harry S. Truman, a semi-literate tailor from rural Missouri, who barely managed to graduate from high school. He was a hillbilly moron with an amenability to persuasion of a 5-year-old, and he was surrounded by the vicious lobby of war mongers and military industrialists, who incessantly pandered to his vanity. What could go wrong?

A man of no international experience and no ability to think for himself, Truman was easily scared into believing that, having taken Berlin, the vicious Reds, who had turned out to be mighty enough to defeat the Wehrmacht, were coming straight after him. According to brochures given to tourists in Hiroshima, dedicated to the 1945 nuclear bombing, the only reason Japan did not surrender to the Allies after the Potsdam conference in June 1945, was that the Americans wouldn't let it keep the Emperor. By all accounts, Japan was otherwise on the verge of total and complete defeat by August 1945.

When you consider that, it seems as if Truman's decision to try out newly invented nuclear bombs on Hiroshima and Nagasaki was an act of pure stupidity, but it was actually worse than that. It was vicious, paranoid stupidity, predicated on vanity. By that time, the Soviet Union had gathered together all the troops it could spare after Victory in Europe, and managed to assemble them in the Far East (in furtherance of the Yalta accord). In the days leading up to Hiroshima, the USSR was about to enter Japan, in order to assist the Allies there.

Rumors of the Soviets' impending entry into the theater were causing panic in Japan, and most agree that it would immediately surrender unconditionally when that happened. Thus, the final victory of World War II, the

48

Victory against the very country that attacked the United States at Pearl Harbor, would be left to the Soviet Union. Harry Truman's war-mongering handlers, in their hatred of the Russians, convinced him that this would be a dangerous result. Their solution was to burn alive almost 400,000 civilians in a nuclear Holocaust, so as to avenge 2,403 people (only 68 of them civilians) lost at Pearl Harbor.[7]

The world's only use of nuclear weapons on a population to date, was thus driven purely by a public relations objective. Harry Truman, whose only excuse was that he was too stupid to understand what he was doing, murdered almost a half a million people in order to save face, and to lay the ground for a new world war that he was about to start: the Cold War.

In my leftist days, I always thought Franklin D. Roosevelt to be one of the best ever Presidents of the United States. I still think of FDR fondly; what I am definitely sure of, however, is that Harry S. Truman was one of the most despicable, disgusting human beings ever to have lived. This man invented and defined the vicious post-War anti-Sovietism in every form. I never quite figured out, nor do I really care, whether he was just this docile in the face of the military industrial complex, or he truly believed, against all common sense, that his greatest enemy was now the country that had just won a world war in an alliance with the United States. One would also do well, of course, to remember that Russia was in alliance with the United Kingdom, France and the United States in World War I, as well. The Anglo-American world had fought – and won – every 20th century war until that point alongside the Russians. Then Harry Truman came to town, and suddenly, overnight, the Russians were evil.

Considering all the hell that his vitriol launched at home and abroad, starting with McCarthyism (for which, I am sure, no one in the United States is particularly grateful in hindsight), I have always asked myself: what was *so* scary about the Soviet Union? What had it done – other than signed up for an Alliance

---

7 I defer to the account in Oliver Stone's Untold History of the United States on that, but it chimes with many other accounts that I am familiar with, including my friend Owen Matthews' biography of Richard Sorge, and what I myself was told in Hiroshima. More broadly, one must also note that an appearance of apparently no longer needing Soviet help in the Pacific gave Truman, in his own understanding, moral ground to renege on other agreements, both formal, in Yalta, and informal, that may have existed between FDR and Stalin.

with the United States and the UK, and won the War together with them – that was so wrong, that FDR's agreements with Stalin could not be honored? Why could not the USSR have been treated by its former allies with the respect it deserved after the War?

I think I am starting to understand it now. Whether he realized it or not, Harry Truman was probably at his most uncomfortable with the realization that the Soviet Victory in WWII laid bare: neither democracy, nor freedom, were prerequisites for superiority. No definitive proof emerged that free, capitalist societies were any good at winning wars at all. In fact, it was Stalin's evil, and the reverence and fear that he instilled in his own people, that led the USSR to victory. I am not even sure that today's Russia could, or would, have done the same. A repressive, totalitarian state was the only one in which the Nazi Germany met its match.

No free, capitalist society would bear the human cost that the Soviet Union did in World War II. Your average democratic European state would, and ultimately did, opt to save its cities and most of its population, even, as it were, at the uncomfortable price of having the Jews among them shipped to extermination camps. France was a free democratic society, and so were the Netherlands, and Austria. If the geographic location of the United Kingdom as an island did not ultimately protect it from invasion, we do not know that it would have done any better. Neville Chamberlain, as we do know, thought that Hitler was lovely, and so did several members of the Royal Family.

The fear of Soviet Union in the wake of World War II had very, very big eyes. I will even grant the present-day fans of Harry Truman this: Joseph Stalin was a diabolical and unpredictable fellow. Yet, Stalin's madness, as that of most dictators (Hitler being the notable exception), was inward-facing, directed onto that which he could control. He craved recognition from other states, and increased influence in nearby countries, but he never, exactly, betrayed anyone on the world stage. Stalin trusted Hitler, and was betrayed. As far as he was concerned, in 1945 he was then betrayed again, this time by the Americans. In all likelihood, this precipitated his final descent into madness at home, where he managed to wreak a lot of further grief on his own people before dying in 1953, mad and discontented.

Any suggestion that the Soviet Union in the immediate aftermath of the War was a threat to anyone at all was, however, bizarre. Crazy or not, Stalin presided over a country in ruins, one that it would take years to rebuilt. A huge part of its male population of combat age was wiped out or crippled. To suggest that the Truman Doctrine, an elaborate and extremely hostile strategy of "containment" of Soviet influence, was anything other than a deliberate insult to the fellow victors of WWII, would be absurd. There was never any real threat. What it really was, of course, was a strategy to contain ideas – to wit, socialism – on which the Soviet Union was founded. Those ideas were popular, and Harry Truman was not a fan of ideas.

The Marshall Plan, which is still deceptively peddled as a plan to "rebuild Europe", was the original framework that established the United States as the meddler-in-chief in international affairs, a country that made everyone's business its own, and still does. The distribution of funds under the Marshall Plan established the original system of funneling U.S. money for the purchase of political influence in small states. Its most recent iteration was the "color revolutions" in the former Soviet countries, including *maidan* uprisings in Ukraine and attempts to destabilize the situation in Russia.

And then, of course, came NATO, the military arm of the Truman Doctrine. Stalin was a madman, they said. It was necessary. Maybe it was, maybe it wasn't – but Stalin died in 1953, two months after Harry Truman left office. Whatever you can say about the Soviet rulers that came after, none of them was a madman. Yet, the madness of Harry Truman, who started the Cold War like Don Quixote, fighting against *red* windmills, lived on in his successors. And the Soviet Union, if anything, was definitely not up for losing any wars.

Nikita Khrushchev was not a madman. He was an affable guy, a class clown. In Soviet politics, he was the original Trump. He knew how to put on a show. He banged the shoe on the lectern at the UN. He had eccentric ideas, such as the planting of corn everywhere – an idea he picked up in the Americas. This idea was not necessarily mad, but tragically unsuited for the climate in which Khrushchev proposed to do it. He was the butt of many jokes, too. One was a tale of a newspaper photo picturing Khrushchev with pigs on a farm. *"Khrushchev, third from left",* – read the caption. The other had him write a draft of a letter to Kennedy and show it to an aide, who replied: *"It's awesome, Nikita Sergeevich, but "f**k you" are two separate words, and "motherf**ukers" should be one word".* A welcome change from Stalin, GenSec Khrushchev was a lot of fun.

51

He had populist policy ideas, too. Khrushchev made enormous strides in home building, and thousands upon thousands of rapidly constructed 5-story apartment buildings that we still call *khrushchevki* went up all around the country. They were begrudged for their cheap design, toilets combined with bathrooms, and lack of hallways in flats – but they provided separate accommodation for families that used to be housed in "communal" apartments, and served their purpose well. Many of them still stand.[8]

There was one idea, however, that Khrushchev absolutely never had. The man could be flustery and grumpy, but he was not at all homicidal. He was entirely benign. As certain as day, Nikita Khrushchev would never, ever bomb anyone, let alone start a nuclear war. And I mean, *anyone*. And most certainly not the United States in October of 1962.

The Cuban Missile Crisis represents the most acute example of the collective madness of the Americans. To this day, it is treasured in the United States as a genuine military crisis that saw the world on the brink of a nuclear war. Otherwise reasonable people still believe that. Apparently, Robert McNamara personally believed it. The Kennedys milked the "brink of war" narrative for all it was worth, and kept riding on the idea of having saved the world for years after JFK and RFK were both dead. How can anyone take seriously the country whose best of the best genuinely believed, in October 1962, that the world was about to end?

The Soviets knew that they were feared beyond reason and seen as unpredictable and unreasonable. Such was the legacy of Joseph Stalin, and, for all of their obsession with the Red Scare, the Americans never fully realized that he had been one of a kind. Not only was Khrushchev not diabolical, he also didn't govern alone – never again did anyone govern the Soviet Union alone. Gromyko, Mikoyan, the young Leonid Brezhnev and other members of the Politburo of the time were not madmen, either. They were having a bit of fun with the gullible Americans, to try and, perhaps, make them see how American missiles in Turkey felt to us. It was never supposed to be a crisis at all.

Every decision in the course of the *Caribbean Crisis*, as it became known in Russia, was collegial (except the one letter that Khrushchev wrote to

---

8 If only we knew then, when we begrudged the *khrushchevki*, that all apartments in the supposedly more developed Western countries lack hallways and combine toilets with bathrooms!

Kennedy by himself, as commemorated in the joke). Members of the Politburo voted to move the weapons to Cuba, they voted to end the crisis, and they voted on every decision in the course of it. Some voted for, some voted against, some abstained. There was nothing irrational or uncalculated about this. The one thing they did not calculate in advance was how seriously the Americans would take the whole thing.

When the Americans put their missiles in Turkey – just as close to the Soviet borders as Cuba was to theirs – no one in the Soviet Union panicked. There was no crisis. People were upset, because it was bold and disrespectful, so we put our missiles in Cuba. It was like a game of chess. Not a single person in the USSR ever though the Americans were going to *fire* those missiles. There were no shelters, no drills and no schoolchildren taught to duck under their desks, like turtles. I don't even know, why – the Americans, after all, had a record of being rather trigger happy with their nuclear weapons. But we had common sense – Americans were a bit paranoid, for sure, but they weren't crazy enough to end the world. At one point, McNamara reportedly sat and wondered whether the sun would rise the next day. Khrushchev beckoned the members of the Politburo to go out to the Bolshoi theater.

In the Soviet Union, we always thought this was funny. *The Caribbean Crisis* was an amusing episode, that showed how stupid, gullible and paranoid the Americans were. After all, the Americans' lack of a sense of humor was always legendary. We assumed that they would eventually realize that we were just messing with them. Boy, were we wrong! I learned that the hard way when, in 2012, I was ostracized and eventually forced to drop out of a PhD program in Public Affairs at Rutgers University, after earnestly trying to explain to faculty and fellow graduate students that they were never in any danger during the "thirteen days". That was one truth the Americans were still not ready to hear. Why was that? Why did they prefer, in their collective madness, to believe that the world was, and has always been, a scary place?

Today, I no longer think it was funny at all. The paranoid madness of Harry Truman, who was convinced that the Russians were *irrational,* did not just persevere and inform the Americans' outsized reaction to the placement of missiles in Cuba in 1962. As the Cold War raged on, untold riches have been made by the U.S. military industrial complex, all predicated on the same idea: the Russians were coming! Then the Soviet Union collapsed, and most of the Eastern

Bloc joined the EU and NATO. NATO still exists today, because the Russians are diabolical, everyone knows that! Just think of the Cuban Missile crisis.

The thing is, the Russians were never coming. Not for the United States, anyway. America was never a strategic geopolitical objective for Stalin; it wasn't for the Politburo; and it isn't for Putin. We did not start either of the World Wars, nor the Cold War, nor any of the "proxy wars" – and we most certainly did not start any of the currently ongoing wars. But the current American establishment is just as afraid of ideas as Harry Truman was. The scariest idea of all is the notion that Moscow is, and always was, *the capital of peace*. Its signage malfunction notwithstanding, it is dishonest to pretend that it ever wanted to be the *capital of the world*. Yet, we are continuously treated as if we were on a mission to conquer it.

Being a good Christian when you are atheist

"As I write, highly civilized human beings are flying overhead, trying to kill me."
George Orwell, The Lion and the Unicorn: Socialism and the English genius (1941)

The first thing I learned when I arrived in the United States in 1996, was that Christmas trees were always free. Impatient Americans discarded perfectly usable Christmas trees, for the most part, on the 26th of December. Shrewd Russian immigrants then had about 5 days to pick them up. To us, they were never *Christmas trees*. We decorate them all the same, and we put presents under them – but we do it on the night of the New Year, and so we call them *New Year trees* (more precisely, *New Year pine trees*).

The main reason the Americans were always so afraid of *the Soviets* was that, even after the death of Stalin, they considered us diabolical and irrational. I suspect that this was due to our ostensible atheism. Americans are God-fearing people – and if they think that you are not, they do not understand your *raison d'etre*, or that you have any. They are unable to parse your moral structure or ascertain that there are limits on how evil you are prepared to be. That is the ultimate reason we never feared their nuclear attack, but they, clearly, feared ours.

When you tell your American neighbor that you are taking their discarded Christmas tree because you celebrate New Year instead of Christmas, you are always followed by a steely gaze as you drag it away. Who knows what *else* you are up to, then? Americans are perfectly able (for the most part) to parse that someone might be Jewish, or Muslim. God-fearing, but, in their eyes, somewhat misguided. So long as you explain that, you get a pass – but you don't get a free *New Year pine tree*. It is us going out of our way to substitute a secular holiday for a religious one, that is the problem.

Meanwhile, that is precisely how the USSR's entire campaign to eradicate religion operated, at least in the post-war years. It did not prohibit religion or eradicate any remaining opportunities to practice it. It did preach atheism, but more so on common sense ground – we are not to believe in fairy tales, because we believe in science. *Cosmonauts went to space and didn't see God there* was a popular way to describe that approach. It was simplistic, because one's practice of spirituality, or decision to belong to a religious community, is not determined solely by whether they *really think* that there is a God.

55

Scientific anti-theology was not, however, the main focus of the Soviet government's approach to religion. It concentrated most of its efforts on creating more appealing alternatives to religious practice. New Year's Day was made into a religion of its own – celebrations were lush, special performances and once-a-year variety shows were put on by the TV channels (or the one channel, as the case once was).

The beauty of that approach was that it worked against all manner of religious belief – instead of what would be different religious holidays, one secular holiday was created for everyone. Soviet Jews and Muslims, as well as Catholics, all decorated *New Year pine trees* and gave their children gifts on January 1st (and many continue to confuse their American neighbors even further by doing this in emigration).

But the Soviet government did not stop there. It made sure to schedule the year's most coveted television event – a live performance by a top pop star, or something of sorts – for the late night of January 6th. For that, of course, was Christmas Eve – as marked by the Russian Orthodox Church, using the Julian calendar. The government's effort on that night was about simply keeping people at home. Observant Russians do not normally mark Christmas with parties and family gatherings, they mark it by going to church. The service leads up to midnight, at which time the parishioners light candles and march around the church three times, singing hymns. It is actually quite pretty, and it was always a culturally unifying experience. (At one point in my American life, I discovered that Presbyterians do a version of that, too). No one in Russia gets any presents on Christmas, because they had already had theirs for New Year. You were either in it for the faith, or you were not in it at all.

Every immigrant family's dilemma in the West was always what to do with the *December Christmas* itself. Children expected presents and had a hard time explaining to their peers why they hadn't got any *yet*. When I was young and susceptible to peer pressure, I just gave my kids two sets of presents. We had [the Protestant] Christmas, and we had New Year. Whatever. When I got older, I could no longer be bothered – I told them that Santa was too busy to get to everyone in one night, so we were going to get ours on New Year because it was the second shift.

When each of them turned 6 years old, I simply told them cynically, that there was no God, no Santa, no Easter Bunny and, by the way, no tooth fairy, and

56

they had to get over this and wait until New Year, for that was the Russian way. They didn't mind doing things *the Russian way*, as much as they were each traumatized to learn, specifically, that there was no Santa. "But who was buying all this stuff?" – each one of them asked, with a slight variation. When I told them that it was me, the answer usually was: "Why do you always say then, that we can't afford things?" My middle daughter, now in her twenties, still maintains that it was child abuse to traumatize her with this sensitive information at such a young age.

Religion was a very big part of the fabric that held the Russian Empire together. In its waning years at the start of the 20th century, the Empire was retrograde and shamelessly failing. Its peasant population was ignorant and barely liberated from serfdom. The country produced next to nothing and depended largely on agriculture, never mind that most of its land was covered by snow for half a year. Illiterate people without any means to better their circumstances, for the most part, believe everything that they are told. The idea that the Romanovs were entrusted to rule by God, and did so in His name, was the sole reason that the tsars lasted as long as they did[9].

Russian Orthodox Church, however, was always prone to accumulate excessive privilege. Its priests, starting with local parish priests, were usually not humble. They were not forbidden to marry and engaged heavily in alcoholism and other vices. Churches were treasure troves – expensive icons, clad in silver and gold, golden or gold-plated crosses, chalices. A local priest in his parish, by the sunset of *tsarist Russia,* was often the local ruler on Earth, and not always a very reasonable one. A lot of resentment against the Church, that spilled over into destruction of churches and plundering of their gold and silver at the time of the Revolution, was not necessarily resentment against the notion of religion, but rather against self-indulgence and tyranny of the clergy. By destroying churches, the Bolsheviks rebelled against the institution, rather than against faith.

---

9 In reality, of course, the Romanovs absolutely weren't entrusted to rule by God at all. In a process that can tell you a lot about the tradition of democracy and elections in Russia, the first Romanov was actually elected to rule in 1612, upon the extinction of the Rurik dynasty without an heir, by the *boyars* - the aristocracy of the time - who could not fathom ruling the peasants without a tsar. That is right - we used our first democratic election to elect ourselves a new monarchical dynasty.

Atheism was, of course, the cornerstone of the Bolshevik ideology. Karl Marx postulated – as we were all constantly reminded – that *religion was like opium for the population.* That meant that it was bad, and it was the means by which the Romanovs had hitherto held the population in thrall. But there was also no real way to control the population at all if you took that one structure – belief – away from them overnight, and Soviet leaders knew that it was always going to be a work in progress. After all, egalitarian ideas about the rule of the proletariat could not possibly work outside of Moscow and St.Petersburg, in the vast land where no proletariat could yet be found.

Both Vladimir Lenin and Joseph Stalin took a cautious approach toward religion. Stalin thought that direct and open repression of religious practice served only to drive it underground and entrench the least literate segments of the population in their supernatural beliefs. Religion was neither proscribed nor eradicated. All efforts focused on persuading people out of it on the basis of reason, or, failing that, distracting them with more attractive things to do.

If the government managed to distract you on the evening of January 6th for long enough, then you missed the Christmas midnight liturgy, and that was half the job done. Going twice a year, on Christmas and Easter, was considered observant enough in our lax version of Russian Orthodox culture. It so happens that January 6th was also my mother's birthday, so the struggle was real. In the years when it fell on a weekday, we usually went to church. For most of my childhood, we went on both Christmas and Easter. While some of the churches were plundered during the Revolution and stood, throughout the Soviet years, as empty shells (or have been re-purposed into libraries and warehouses), the church we went to, in our new model subdivision of Moscow, had clearly been a new build, or at least a complete renovation, glistering in all its gold.

The attempt to eradicate religious belief in the educated classes by means of reason did not work even on my grandparents. All of them received advanced degrees in sciences and humanities from the country's top universities, and all were devout members of the Communist Party, for which they were handsomely rewarded. Yet, both of my parents were baptized shortly after their births, while Stalin was still alive. Grandma Tonya even gave my father, whose name is Victor, a separate Christian name. I wonder how much trouble would she have gotten in for this at her Pravda job. "Just in case", – she explained to me years later. "Because, who really knows?"

58

My parents, both of whom were also superbly educated, were not particularly religious when I was growing up. I was only baptized when I was 2.5 years old, and it seems to be the earliest memory of my childhood. For fear of getting in trouble, it was done at someone's apartment – back then, several families who wished to baptize children, would get together and hire a priest to come to one of their homes and get it done.

My mother initially did not intend to baptize me. When I was 18 months old, I fell down a flight of stairs in our apartment building – a dog running downstairs for a walk, off the leash, knocked me over. I suffered a serious concussion and was reportedly near death. My parents were told to prepare for the worst. Then, my mother prayed: "Just in case, because who really knows?" She made a bargain with God. If I survived, she would have me baptized the following summer (presumably, to make sure I was definitely going to live – no cheating, God!). I do not have any memory of the fall, but I recall the baptism. It was all highly irregular and embarrassing, and, obviously, they were pouring cold water over me.

My understanding was that we went to church not because we had to, but because the Communist party did not want us to. It was a form of political dissent, which my parents could afford because my grandparents' position protected them. Walking up to the church on Christmas or Easter was my only explicit interaction with what must have been KGB people. They were posted on approaches and scanned the crowds for those who, they thought, were amenable to reason. My parents looked enlightened enough, so we were always stopped. "Why are you poisoning your child with this nonsense, you are a communist!" – the faceless people in suits would say. My parents shrugged and walked on, without engaging. Neither of them was, technically, a communist. They were not members of the Party, and so the Party could neither reprimand nor expel them.

To be sure, I was poisoned with all of "this nonsense". The whole nine yards. My mother had a tasteful silver cross made for me by her jeweler friend, and I wore it under my school uniform, which was adorned with the red "pioneer" tie and a Lenin pin. I was taught to cross myself when I passed a church or entered it, not to turn my back on the altar, and to cover my head while inside (to this day, I still cross myself on airplanes). I was taught to recite Our Father's prayer, and given the New Testament to read. Four versions of the gospel. My parents invited me to ponder the differences between them, too.

As I now understand, my religious education was a version of religious studies in a modern school, except it was the study of only one religion. My parents wanted me to understand the religious teaching and the foundations of Christian culture – not so that I could worship, but so that I could have a grasp on the basis of morality upon which our society stood. It was also a way to interpret literature and art, abound all around, that drew on religious references. Godless as it may have seemed to the outside world, there is no doubt that the Soviet society was a deeply Christian society, and its moral foundations, at its core, were exactly the same as any Western Christian society.

In our culture, we have a rather liberal relationship with sin – we think that pretty much any amount of it can be wiped out with penance (usually donations, but failing that, incessant praying). But our notion of what is or isn't sin is exactly the same as yours. Whether one went to church or not, we all shared the same moral values. (And they were not, in principle, that much different from stated communist values, anyway).

Vladimir Lenin, the founder of the Soviet state, was from an enlightened family and completed a full course of education – which, in the 19th century, was a deeply religious education. He erred on the side of atheism later in life, but accepted that it was *a debate* – and his moral foundation was absolutely laid by the Church. For what it was worth, Lenin had expressed dissatisfaction that common anti-religious propaganda of the early Soviet days was primitive, in bad taste, and failed to engage with the subject meaningfully.

Joseph Stalin – on whose lack of morality and perceived evil nature Harry Truman, who had never met him, built his justification for the betrayal of prior agreements reached by FDR, creation of NATO, the Marshall Plan and the Cold War – was from a peasant family in rural Georgia, in the Russian Empire, where his mother worked as a cook. Georgians are Orthodox Christians, and young Iosif Dzhugashvili, as he then was, was baptized shortly after birth. His relationship with God and sin must have been complex at best, but his view that persecution of religious practice only entrenches belief cannot really, upon close examination, be said to be a clearly anti-religious view. It is more of a demurrer.

Nikita Khrushchev, whose perceived diabolical unpredictability and lack of self-control forced Robert McNamara to fear for his life so much in October 1962, was born in tsarist Russia, in a peasant family. There is no doubt whatsoever, that he would have been baptized, and raised to fear God as a child. That may have been why he shrugged and hit the Bolshoi, instead of hitting the nuclear button, as the Americans expected him to do.

Khrushchev's successor Leonid Brezhnev was born in 1906 in present-day Ukraine. He was of the proletariat – his father worked in a factory – but the family was very religious, and their children were all baptized in a local church. Some evidence suggests that Brezhnev later took steps to destroy the records of his baptism as he ascended the Party leadership ladder because he perceived a conflict between his religious upbringing and stated political beliefs. One might surmise that he would not bother if there was not, really, a conflict in his heart – after all, there was nothing irregular about being baptized before the Revolution.

Mikhail Gorbachev, born in the 1930s in Soviet Russia, was also baptized as a child. A non-believer later in life, he fondly recalled the dichotomy between his family's religious faith and their communist ideals. "They had an icon on the wall and a lantern. Below, on the table, there were portraits of Lenin and Marx. In our family, ideology and faith were in absolute parity", – he once said in an interview.

Vladimir Putin, a late, miracle child of two survivors of the Siege of Leningrad who had lost their two older children, was baptized promptly after his birth in late 1952. He tells the story himself in a documentary commemorating the 70th jubilee of Patriarch Kirill, the current head of the Russian Orthodox Church. Maria Putina took her son to church to be baptized, in secret from Vladimir Sr., who was a member of the Party and feared repercussions. The priest in charge attempted to persuade her to name the boy Michael – it was St. Michael's day in the Russian Orthodox calendar. In the documentary, Putin can be heard saying that Orthodox Christianity played a crucial role in Russian culture throughout history, and Russia and Christianity are inseparable.

Most of the God-fearing Americans, inexplicably, never gave any benefit of the doubt to the moral foundations of all these people, even as Russians consistently failed to live up to the worst expectations about them. They fought – and won – two wars alongside the United States, failed to nuke the United States when provoked, and, when told to "bring down that wall", pretty much complied and ate the dreadful "Bush legs".

Today, some God-fearing Americans (including President Joe Biden) keep calling Vladimir Putin a "murderer" on TV. Perhaps, if their starting point on morally judging him – and all of the Soviet leaders – was different, pending evidence, a lot of recent history could be understood with much more nuance.

"Just in case, because who really knows", as uttered by my Grandma Tonya, is actually the perfect description of the true relationship between most Russians and God. I cannot truly say whether I ever *believed* – rather, like most of us, I was covering all my bases. As an adolescent, I even sang in a church choir for a while, although I wasn't sure why I was there. It was en vogue. Everyone went, and I went.

In the post-Soviet revival, religion became popular. Many church buildings that stood in ruins and disuse since the Revolution were returned to the Church – but it had no icons and gold to fill them, and no priests to serve the liturgy in them. Understandably, there had been no seminaries. An extraordinary call was made in the early 1990s, for anyone with a degree in philology (which included a component of ancient Slavic) to step forward and be ordained.

As it happened, a lot of people I knew were either studying for, or already had, degrees in philology, and all of them were unemployed. One of my buddies, who used to hang around Nikolina Gora and drank a lot at parties, became a priest and was given a nearby parish – at the ripe age of, I think, 23 years old. The church was four walls without a roof, the frescos had all faded, and there were no icons and no means of liturgy whatsoever. Plus, the newly ordained Father Alexey knew zilch about religion. Things worked out quickly though – a lot of the local residents were various notables of science and culture, or the offspring of such. They were relatively wealthy, and clearly had a lot of sins to catch up on. Some of them, it turned out, were mysteriously in possession of large numbers of icons plundered from churches circa 1917, and dutifully performed a penance of returning them.

One of the first holy acts in Father Alexey's Church was the baptism of my oldest daughter Darya, in 1994. The walls were still covered with graffiti, and the roof hadn't yet been laid. There was barely anything inside. By then, I was pretty sure I did not believe in God, but, as they say, *no one really knows*, right? The godmother, a once baptized but carefree friend of mine, declared "just so that you all know, there is no God", as her observant Jewish husband waived cheerfully from outside. I think it may have been Father Alexey's first baptism, but ultimately, it worked out.

Due to the high profile of some of his new parishioners, Father Alexey quickly became nationally known. Neighbors fawned over his success. My mother, at the height of her TV fame at the end of the decade, found God. In 1999, some time around the 25th anniversary of their civil marriage, my parents had a wedding. The Church was fully repaired and painted by then, the icons glistened with gold and the television cameras were on. The replica of Christ the Savior Cathedral, demolished in the 1930s, was completed in central Moscow the same year. Driven by the best of intentions, it was nonetheless an architectural abomination.

By the time I returned to Moscow from the United States in 2003, I was a convinced atheist – by far more so than I had ever been in the USSR. What I found, alarmed me. By that time, Putin was President, and religion was getting fused with the State at what seemed then like an alarming rate. Before long, I saw Father Alexey on TV, claiming that homosexuality was a cardinal sin. In 2004, the Moscow city government paid from its budget to plaster the ten commandments onto the advertising billboards all around the city. I had already managed a year of a US law school by then, and this did not sit well with me.

Freshly emerged from a leftist political project and flanked by communists, I decided to do something about it. My friend and I, having just co-founded an NGO we called *Ravenstvo (Equality)*, organized a picket on Pushkin Square in central Moscow. A whole two dozen of us, not counting the journalists who showed up to make fun of us, stood there with signs reading "separation of church and state" and "no preaching at the expense of the taxpayer".

My media rounds did not go any better – I was mostly made fun of. Ascendant democratic media icon Masha Gessen interviewed me live on a popular local radio station, and – even though I figured Masha, as an American, should know better – she seemed to lean toward sarcasm on my crusade. She then opened the line for calls, and God-fearing callers, who failed to grasp that my opposition was not to their belief, but rather to the use of public funds to preach it, phoned in *en masse* to insult me and hang up, until I walked out. If Lenin was around, he would surely lament that there was *no debate*.

I concluded that Russia was doomed, for there was no appetite for separation of church and state even among the ranks of its democratic opposition.

The march of religious doctrine and conservative values continued. Somehow, the opposition did not yet see that the rising tide of taxpayer-funded commandments also lifted the boat of Father Alexey's anti-gay propaganda on TV, leading to the well-known results that Masha Gessen herself would soon lament to the tune of fleeing the country, in fear that her adopted child would be taken away (of which she later wrote and publicly spoke).

Those billboards were a harbinger of things to come, but the opposition of the day did not see my fight against them as anything more than a quixotic fight against windmills, because my problem with the billboards was not political in nature. I did not protest them being installed, I just did not want my city's social advertising budget to be plundered for that purpose. My protest was not colorful enough.

When Pussy Riot punk band decided to make a similar – but more colorful, ear-bending and excessively loud – point 8 years later and mentioned Putin a lot in the course of their screaming, the Russian opposition finally awoke to the problem. Pussy Riot supporters did not care where was public land, or private, or whether any people were indeed upset at the desecration of a house of worship – distasteful as the replica of Christ The Savior Cathedral was. They simply made fun of religion this time around, in a crude way (their tactics involved getting into everyday people's faces and screaming "Do you really think there was a snake?" – to me, it seemed as if they'd watched Bill Maher's *Religulous* as part of their training.) The points made about corruption in the Church, or, for that matter, Putin, were entirely lost on domestic audience. To much of it, Pussy Riot were dumb and disrespectful bores.

In Lenin's terms, the anti-religion propaganda, in this case, was in bad taste, and it was also ineffective. Pussy Riot raised a lot of support – and, I am guessing, funds – in the West, but there was never any chance that they would change a single mind at home in the way they ostensibly wished to. Stalin would have probably suggested that their intervention entrenched religious beliefs. He would not be wrong.

Father Alexey performed the funeral rites for my mother in his church in 2005. He had reached the same levels of local influence that had been common among parish priests in the Imperial times. My mother wanted to be buried at the cemetery near his church, next to Nikolina Gora, but there was no legal basis for

64

it: cemeteries are municipal, and she had been a resident of the city of Moscow, which itself was legally a different region. It took one call from Father Alexey for my father to be invited over "to pick a plot". They picked one on a hill, with a view of the countryside below. Too bad my mother wasn't going to *see it*.

I stood by the casket through the whole service, defiantly refusing to cover my head, just as *babushkas* sneered around me – still, I told my daughters to cover theirs. It had turned out to be nearly impossible to buy a wholly black outfit for a 5-year old; clearly, no one expected preschoolers to be taken to funerals. Yet, I wanted my children to learn to deal with death. At the cemetery, my then-youngest threw earth on her grandmother's casket, while Father Alexey enthusiastically waived his *kadylo*. The procession of mourners stretched all the way down the hill.

When she was dying, my mother found solace in religion. My father, too, says that faith helped him deal with her death, and face his own eventual mortality. I, on the other hand, lost any shred of respect for religion, as a result of exactly the same experience. I have not entered any church, temple or any place of worship since the day of my mother's funeral.

Tucker Carlson, who is a deity in my substitute pantheon, often speaks eloquently about the increasing prevalence of atheism and society's inability to adequately deal with death. He is right, in that religion provides a way to deal with mortality and stay sane – but I still beg to differ. If my mother suffocating to death in front of me was really a part of some diabolical creature's *ineffable plan*, I wish to know nothing about it. That notion gives me much greater anxiety than the realization that my mother is truly no longer with us, or that my death will, too, be the end of *me*.

In the Russian culture, we deal with death a lot, and at close range. It's quite simple, really: it is only in the memories, and dreams, of the survivors that we live on, and it's up only to us what those will be. Yet, in the quest to shape those future memories of our time in existence, we, atheists, are bound by the same moral values upon which others might base their hope to earn salvation. We might have a different imperative for following them, but the rules are the same.

The rules are the same because all of us are still the product of the same system of moral truths, labeled famously by George Orwell as *the Judaeo-Christian scheme of morals [sic]*. It has become a norm in America during the

Cold War to postulate that defense of those morals necessitated a complete eradication of communism. The Soviet Union was always presented as the dark tower of antithesis to those morals – yet, no reasoning was ever given.

American sociologist R. Cherry pitted the notion of equality of all men against the idea of equal distribution of goods among them. Indeed, equality of opportunity versus equality of outcome is the focal point of the capitalism vs. communism debate; however, it is a discussion about means rather than an end, and it is dubious in every possible sense to argue that either side of it represents the complete failure of accepted morality.

Every self-described or perceived atheist in modern Western society today – be it Bill Maher, Michael Moore, the late Christopher Hitchens, or myself – was brought up an observant Christian. So was, also, every leader of the Soviet Union. There was simply no other world for us to grow up in, and no other system of values to adopt. Just because we all came to reject religious belief in the course of our lives, we did not lose sight of that morality. Our enduring knowledge that one shalt not kill nor desire their neighbor's wife, that sacrifice is noble and suicide is wrong, comes from the same place as yours.

I wondered a lot whether my mother would be less likely to have an abortion in the 1970s if she had been religious then, or whether she would be less likely to regret it in 2005 if she wasn't, but I think the answer to both questions is *no*. These are simply unrelated things. As an atheist, I abhor abortion and absolutely value human life – but it's not because it was created by God, but precisely because I believe that there is nothing beyond it: whosoever's life it is, their only chance is here and now. The reasoning is different, but the conclusion is the same. The same values that the conservative right struggles to continue to defend with religion in face of the increasing prevalence of atheism, can be defended with reason.

In the doctrine of moral-based anti-Sovietism, the flip side of the main false premise (that the USSR was principally Godless) and its companion assumption (that Godlessness is inherently immoral), was, of course, the very notion that religious foundation is an inoculation against evil. President Dwight Eisenhower, who fought in WWII and then made the decision to keep up with Harry Truman's Cold War after Stalin's death, said that "[The American] form of government has no sense unless it is founded in a deeply held religious faith". Faith was the secret ingredient.

66

Adolf Hitler was brought up as a practicing Catholic and went on to brutally murder tens of millions of civilians. Yet, it is not the German moral fabric that the Americans ever claimed to have an issue with. Hitler was seen as an aberrant individual whose faith could not have possibly been deep enough, and the millions that carried out his orders were absolved of responsibility, for the most part, as law-abiding patriots of their state, such as it were. Meanwhile, the Americans collectively impugned all communists (an ideology that is egalitarian, if nothing else), regardless of any individual's relationship with faith or his or her personal choices. They may have forgotten that George Orwell, when he coined the oft-quoted notion of Judaeo-Christian morals, was impugning Hitler, not communists, for deviating from them[10].

The point Orwell was making was that neither Christian faith, nor enlightenment, guaranteed that one was going to be benevolent in their actions. In response to the dichotomy of "highly civilized beings flying overhead trying to kill [him]", Orwell suggests that we should no longer view the societies on the whole as guilty or innocent based on what those societies ostensibly represent, but only individual people within them based on their personal actions. He was skeptical of the idea that soldiers should be excused for their war-time atrocities because they were "just following orders", even as he remarked that most of those same people would unlikely commit a murder in their private lives.

Orwell, reportedly a non-believer, did not distinguish equality of opportunity from equality of outcome. He made a case for socialism in *The Lion and the Unicorn*. Yet, he posits a view based on individual, not collective, responsibility, a view that should have been embraced by the adherents of American capitalism, but it wasn't. They took Orwell's notion of Judaeo-Christian morality out of context, and, for generations, used it to collectively impugn the Soviet society in principle and to collectively absolve the Germans.

---

10 *"The whole English-speaking world is haunted by the idea of human equality, and though it would be simply a lie to say that either we or the Americans have ever acted up to our professions, still, the IDEA is there, and it is capable of one day becoming a reality. From the English-speaking culture, if it does not perish, a society of free and equal human beings will ultimately arise. But it is precisely the idea of human equality, the Jewish or Judaeo-Christian idea of equality, that Hitler came into the world to destroy"*. George Orwell, The Lion and the Unicorn: Socialism and the English genius, 1941

A few years ago, Grandpa Georgiy started to dabble in faith. That's when, to be honest, I knew it was time for the retirement home. The last time we visited my mother's grave together, he insisted on lighting a candle at the cemetery chapel. "Shame on you, Grandpa Georgiy", – I said. "You are a communist! There is no God". "There probably is not", – he answered. "But there *is* a chapel, so why not? *Just in case*".

Two tales of one Russia

"I love my country, I do not want to do it any harm, and I will not".
Soviet movie star and underground songwriter Vladimir Vysotsky
on "60 minutes" with Dan Rather, taped in New York in 1976

The Iron Curtain guaranteed the success of domestic propaganda in the Soviet Union – it is easier, of course, to convince people that they have it good, if they don't know any better. But it was also the reason for the inevitable failure of the country's image abroad: no one out there knew any better, either. For years, the story of the USSR had been told in the West by ostensible refugees from it. No one ever questioned that some people had reasons to claim political asylum from the Soviet Union – yet, it was rather gullible of the Western society to continue to form its opinion of the place based only on their accounts. Would you want someone's bio to be written only by their ex-spouse after a bitter divorce? Exactly. But that is what's been happening for years.

Further, the notions of "good" and "better", even in Soviet times, were not as clearly defined as you might think. The majority of those who were permitted to travel abroad from the USSR were people who *really* had it good within it. (Owing to the Party-sponsored careers and *payok* parcels for some, but others, for example, popular artists, often enjoyed genuine privilege and relative wealth). They had apartments, cars and *dachas*, and often had no reasons to defect in the first place – or they could see that they would not have it any better on the other side. Diplomats, journalists, athletes, trade representatives and touring ballet stars all traveled and, for the most part, came back. In Moscow, they then walked among us, so it wasn't as if we were not aware of the greater world at all. Grandma Tonya, Grandpa Boris and Uncle Yuri spent huge chunks of their careers abroad. A son of an Italian diplomat was one of my best friends in primary school. Our world was not as insular as was commonly thought.

My father grew up in Prague, during the time when Uncle Yuri was the editor of the Soviet bloc flagship magazine there. While in Eastern Europe no doubt, Czechoslovakia was very much the West, compared to Moscow. Fortuitously, they shipped my father back to Moscow for high school just before *the Prague Spring* – the Embassy school did not have the upper grades. At 15, he was stuck in that giant apartment alone with the housekeepers and chauffeurs, wandering between the city, the elite English-language immersion school and the giant *dacha* on the leafy Nikolina Gora, where his mates were the offspring of families just as privileged. My father's closest friend was the stepson of Viktor Suhodrev, personal English interpreter to both Khrushchev and Brezhnev, who accompanied the leaders all over the world[11]. In many ways, these young men were the golden youth of the Soviet Union, its global citizens. The rest of the world was not a mystery to them, and yet, for them, it would have been silly to look elsewhere, or desire more than which they had.

Grandpa Georgiy never left the Soviet Union, other than with a military contingent on some covert mission. His work in the Navy was considered secret and he was banned from travel. For all of his ostensible patriotism, and his very comfortable life within, I could tell that it bothered him. His civilian research partner at the Institute of Physics, with whom they worked on neutralizing naval mines together, managed to emigrate to the United States in the late 1970s, and the tidings brought back made it sound like it turned out well for him. Grandpa Georgiy still suspects that the colleague sold their research in America, and appropriated his would-be share. I think that was the real reason we never raised the Soviet flag at our *dacha* on Navy Day. Come to think of it, Grandpa Georgiy never said anything, either way, whenever Grandma Clara took to praising Stalin. That was the extent of his silent dissent.

Many of those whose dissent had been less silent, still did not want to leave. Most of the Soviet Union's famous emigres were expelled from it forcibly. That includes Nobel Prize laureates Joseph Brodsky and Alexander Solzhenitsyn. By the time of their respective expulsions, both had been in open dissent, one way or another, for years, and neither had any intention of leaving (although I concede that it was may not have been a practically available option). Many others – for example, writer and poet Boris Pasternak, who was also awarded the

---

11   The boy, Alexander Lipnitsky, became well-known in Russia in adulthood, due to his involvement in the rock music culture as a musician and journalist. He and my father remained friends throughout their lives, and, as a child, I practically grew up in the Lipnitsky household, where stars of the age gathered. This later launched my own early career in music journalism. On March 25, 2021, when this chapter had already been written, Alexander Lipnitsky, aged 68, drowned in the Moskva river near Nikolina Gora, trapped under breaking ice. His body was recovered two days later on *dip* beach. His beloved dog, T.Rex, died with him.

Nobel Prize – opted to stay in the Soviet Union, even though he had an opportunity to emigrate. For the literary minds, I think, Russia was their natural environment, one inseparable from the language and culture that defined them. Of the famous dissidents, only Vladimir Bukowski was in prison in the Soviet Union immediately prior to his expulsion.

I do not deny, of course, that many people did leave voluntarily, and had their reasons for it. Most of that emigration was Jewish – Jews were a frequent target for discrimination since the Stalin era, and, in the 1970s and 1980s, still were limited in their education and careers by humiliating numerical quotas. Jewish emigration was the only sort that the Soviet Union allowed. The 1970s saw its biggest wave, including not just Grandpa Georgiy's research partner, but also the family of Sergey Brin, the future founder of Google. Brin's father, a mathematics professor, decided to emigrate after attending an international conference in Poland. He secured a teaching position at the University of Maryland prior to arriving in the United States. It is easy to see how, from that family's perspective, they made a good choice.

Little did anyone know, that their infant son's entrenched anti-Sovietism and, later, anti-Russian fervor, will play such a huge role in Russiagate in the 21st century. Sergey Brin's comments about Russia, which he visited with his father in 1992, after the USSR's collapse, are particularly bitter and vicious. There is no trace, in his thinking, of any acknowledgment that it was the Soviet Union that gave his father the free credentials with which he was later able to go straight to the University of Maryland teaching job, an opportunity that was hardly the experience of most immigrants in America. The depth of Brin's unprovoked personal hatred for post-Soviet Russia is something that can only be examined by a psychologist. For my part, I consider Sergey Brin a traitor to the diaspora.

A number of artists, of course, also defected during overseas tours, most notably Mikhail Baryshnikov during the Bolshoi theater tour in Canada in 1974. Baryshnikov was celebrated in the USSR and had various state awards, but he was also in a rare position to know that he would be equally as celebrated in emigration. An offer of a place in the American Ballet Theater, apparently, contributed to the spontaneous decision. The Soviet-era most high-profile defection – that of ballet dancer Rudolph Nureyev in 1961 – was precipitated not by political disagreement, but rather the fact that Nureyev was gay. One can see how the outing of him in the West created tensions with the KGB and made him fear repercussions upon return to the Soviet Union, but that is a different sort of problem. After all, the United Kingdom had chemically castrated war hero code breaker Alan Turing, as punishment for homosexuality, not long before that.

At the end of the day, defectors and expelled dissidents defined the narrative of everything that was ever known about the Soviet Union in the West – and the most vocal ones were the people whose experience in the USSR was the most awful. Bukowski was a professional dissident. He dedicated his entire life to annoying the Soviet state, and nothing much else – his mistreatment in the psychiatric system and eventual imprisonment were appalling, but he was, as a result of all that, uniquely positioned to be aggrieved and to air those grievances. Solzhenitsyn, who fought valiantly in WWII and was promoted in rank all the way to captain, ended up in the GULAG for criticizing Stalin, in writing to his friend, in the final months of World War II. While his were, in all likelihood, valid criticisms, this was certainly a very foolish time, place, and means to express them. His imprisonment in the GULAG was destined to follow – but his term in the labor camps ended in March 1953, the same year that Stalin died.

After his post-imprisonment exile was commuted by the Khrushchev government, Solzhenitsyn returned to Moscow. He was able to join the official Union of Writers and publish some of his literary work. The point of friction between him and the regime was, of course, the existence of yet more work that the USSR would not publish, which he successfully smuggled to be published in the West. Yet, he remained free and not particularly constrained. The movement against Solzhenitsyn gained traction toward the late 1960s, mainly, because of his accounts of alleged atrocities committed by the Red Army against German civilians on its march to Berlin. He reasoned that the army had come to Germany for retribution and acted no better there than the Germans have done in the Soviet Union. Understandably, many in the Soviet Union, and not just the KGB, found his pronouncements deeply offensive. These, and his other comments targeting Stalin's conduct of the War, were viewed in the USSR as apologism for Hitler.

Like a hot potato, Politburo could not decide what to do with Solzhenitsyn, and their only desire was to be as far away from this toxic madman as possible. They started shopping around for countries that would take him. Understandably, since his pronouncements appeared to partly absolve German soldiers by similarly vilifying the Soviet army, FRG stepped forward. The KGB grabbed Solzhenitsyn, took away his Soviet passport, put him on a plane and flew him to West Germany, where they simply dropped him off and breathed a sigh of relief. It was February 1974.

At the time Solzhenitsyn was on the plane to FRG, my mother was working hard on her thesis on Dutch Renaissance, due to graduate from Moscow State University in June that year. A month later, she would find out that she was pregnant, and my parents would marry in August 1974. In December that year, on his 50th birthday, Grandpa Georgiy would retire from the Navy and dedicate himself solely to the Institute of Physics.

At the time *The Gulag Archipelago* was published in the West in the early 1970s, it was 20 years after the death of Stalin himself, and almost 30 years since Solzhenitsyn's own brush with the GULAG. Yet, his account of those events became the standard of how people viewed and understood the Soviet Union in the West. The Soviet Union of the stagnation era, in which I was born in January 1975, was a completely different place. It was the place from which Nureyev and Baryshnikov had already defected; Brodsky and Solzhenitsyn had already been expelled, and Bukowski was about to follow in 1976. In 1977, Mikhail Brin returned from Poland and started to fight for the right to emigrate from the USSR with his wife and then-3-year-old son. In 1978, my parents and I took our first vacation in Crimea. By that time, I could read, write, recite and compose poetry, and type on a typewriter. They didn't let me bring the typewriter with me to Crimea.

The prevailing narrative of life in the Soviet Union, in the years that followed, continued to be shaped in the West by the emigres that left it by the late 1970s. Extraordinary, but inapplicable accounts of Stalin-era repressions were mixed with experiences of people who, like Bukowski, intentionally and persistently brought a lot of what befell them upon themselves. After their collective torturous exodus, the USSR descended into the era of stagnation, and, at the time of my childhood, was mostly confused and benign.

Alexander Solzhenitsyn was in the GULAG in the late 1940s, at the same time as George Orwell was writing *1984*. In 1985, when the eponymous film came out on VHS, we gathered to watch it in the apartment of my father's childhood friend, whose stepfather continued to translate for Soviet leaders and brought VHS tapes back from his foreign trips. The film provoked no recognition. Its dystopian world was as far from mine, as it was from yours.

The world of dissident defectors and Soviet loyalists was not black and white, either. The late Vladimir Vysotsky, arguably the Soviet Union's biggest star, straddled the world of official stardom brought on by his career in film and theater, in which he was reportedly one of only three Mercedes owners in late 1970s Moscow (alongside Leonid Brezhnev and Anatoly Karpov, then the world chess champion), and underground fame, in which hundreds of his songs, most of them not published officially, were recorded on tape, copied person-to-person, and ultimately known by heart to everyone in the country.

Vysotsky married actress Marina Vladi, a French citizen who had a home in Paris. Vysotsky traveled repeatedly to the United States, where he performed in front of emigres, mingled with dissidents and defectors, such as Joseph Brodsky and Mikhail Baryshnikov, and hung around Hollywood for weeks, drinking, taking drugs and making buddies with some of its famous, and soon to be famous, residents, including director Milos Forman. He was completely unsupervised by the KGB, to the bafflement of American pundits (my personal guess is, the government, who could not touch him in the USSR due to his enormous popularity, probably hoped that he would defect).

In 1976, Vysotsky appeared alone for a taped interview with Dan Rather for 60 Minutes (it aired on February 20, 1977). On Dan Rather's official website, it is currently captioned as an interview with a Soviet "dissident", except that Vysotsky wasn't one[12]. In the interview, the Soviet bard famously refuses to discuss any qualms that he had with the Soviet regime. "I love my country and I do not wish to do it any harm", – he says. In more depth, one can listen to the interview to hear Vysotsky explain, non-specifically, that songs of protest are those that strive for things to merely get better, as distinct from songs of revolution, that call for radical change.

42-year-old Vladimir Vysotsky died in his home in Moscow in July of 1980 of a drug overdose, and the city was paralyzed by tens of thousands of

---

12 Hilariously, in his intro to viewers Rather, clearly under a recent impression of a 60 Minutes appearance by Vladimir Bukowski, who referred to the entire USSR as "one huge prison camp", repeats a frequent false rumor that Vysotsky had been to prison in the USSR, which he most certainly had not. Vysotsky led a privileged childhood, most of which he spent in East Germany while his father was in the military, and then went on to a drama school and work in theater and cinema. Vysotsky was only 38 at the time he met Rather.

mourners lining the streets to view his body lying in state at a local theater. It was the summer of the Moscow Olympics, boycotted by the United States. My father was drafted into the public "peace corps", civilians brought in to keep public order because police numbers were insufficient, and he had to wear a silly blue shirt and red patch on his sleeve. My mother mourned the emigration of dissident writer Vasily Aksenov (the author, among others, of *The Island of Crimea*, he settled in Washington, DC and became a George Mason University professor).

In a later interview for a Vysotsky-related documentary, Aksenov says that Vysotsky and Vladi visited him on his *dacha* in 1979, asking for his advice on whether they should emigrate. Aksenov says that he talked them out of it, persuading Vysotsky that his success and fame in the West will never match those he enjoys at home. Himself, Aksenov made a different choice, coincidentally departing the USSR the same month as Vysotsky were to die.

I remember the summer of 1980 very well because we got a puppy, an English cocker spaniel. I had been deathly afraid of dogs until then, ever since one had nearly killed me in infancy – even though I did not remember the event itself. But my parents were firm in their own way: Aksenov, her beloved author, was gone from the country, my mother explained to the 5-year old me, so the dog was here to fill the void. It rhymed, but I cannot reproduce the rhyme in English.

To many globe-trotting Russians, Vladimir Vysotsky alone remains an epitome, in the Soviet times, of a principle that one should not besmirch his or her country's reputation abroad, whatever problems he or she may privately have with its government. If Vysotsky thought there was something wrong with the USSR, he would not tell Dan Rather when he was abroad – even though he would, and did, tell his fellow Soviet citizens when he was back home. Most Americans, to their credit, hold this principle dear – Republican, Democrat, or God knows what, they almost never – at least, not until very recently – talk trash about the United States while overseas. This is Geopolitics 101; the narrative of modern Russia abroad is still a duopoly of those of us who got that memo, and those who skipped the class.

The dichotomy of the narrative of a country being shaped entirely by the people who were aggrieved by it and excluded from it, should have ended when the Iron Curtain fell. But it didn't. There are two tales of Russia in the world today, two narratives that diverge from one another almost as much as my childhood was different from *The Gulag Archipelago*. But this divergence is not due to a gap in time: they both relate to the present.

The narrative that wins in the hearts and minds of the Russia-hating Western politicians, remains the narrative of the emigres. There are two main groups among them. The first one consists of political or quasi-political figures who, after years of participation in mainstream politics and some involvement with "the regime", found themselves spent and irrelevant, and viewed their move to the West and participation in the "Russia in exile" project as their only remaining currency. Art gallerist turned political consultant Marat Guelman (whose protege I was once considered to be), is one of such people nowadays; chess champion Gary Kasparov is another. Vladimir Kara-Murza Jr., the son of my mother's ex-colleague, the late TV anchor Vladimir Kara-Murza, is another flake, along with the slain Boris Nemtsov's daughter Zhanna (I admit that I take issue with the Nemtsovs based on adverse personal history with them).

The second group is comprised of businessmen fleeing prosecution for embezzlement or tax evasion, rather than political persecution. Every time a new one pops up and says "I am persecuted for my views", you can always trace their bona fides directly to a pending embezzlement or tax fraud case. The West must be thinking that no actual embezzlement ever takes place in Russia, seeing as all of its anti-Russia darlings have successfully managed to convince the society that the allegations of such against them were politically motivated.

In some cases, I grant you, the "oppositional" views pre-date the embezzlement charges, and you can even make the case that the prosecution was selective in nature – but, in many, the views are quickly adopted at the time of flight. Sergey Pugachev, Evgeny Chichvarkin, Vladimir Ashurkov and his girlfriend Alexandrina Markvo (Alexey Navalny's associates), and former YUKOS owner Mikhail Khodorkovsky are all in the second group, although, in the case of the latter, he did not flee in time and went to prison first.

The members of the former group are unrequited in Russia, and the latter are wanted by the authorities but unwelcome by the public. For the most part, they join forces and weave the web of fear surrounding Russia and Russians abroad. They parade around, in front of gullible Americans and Brits, their temporary exports, the likes of Alexey Navalny and Pussy Riot – presumably, for fundraising purposes. Revolutions aren't cheap. They are not integrated into the societies in which they live and have no stake in their future, nor in the future of

76

tens of thousands of their fellow Russians who comprise most of the diasporas within these societies. In some cases, their complete lack of understanding of Western society and geopolitical forces at work is astounding.

"Russians in exile" all have a higher mission, which they ostensibly represent as regime change in Russia. In their version of the story, they are the exiled elites, some day triumphantly to return, like the remnants of the Romanov clan post-1917. When their propaganda is directed inward at the Russians, God bless and good luck with that. But when they start airing their personal animosities toward other Russians out in front of the gullible, Russian-hating Western politicians and their Russophobic press and call for more sanctions; or when they turn up Western-produced and English-subtitled anti-corruption fundraising videos, passing the hat around for money with which to destabilize Russia, the rest of us take issue[13].

It is also of note that the United States, even today, still accepts swaths of ostensible non-political "asylum seekers" from Russia, even though the UK and other European countries have long declared it a safe country. Those asylum claims are elaborately constructed and almost uniformly fake, produced by a cottage industry of fraudsters making use of the U.S. system's prejudice against Russia, about which an average U.S. government official is prepared to believe almost anything. Even though all of those "asylum seekers" openly flaunt the system that they benefit from, and most of them take trips back to Russia immediately after gaining asylum (and use third countries to disguise the trips), their collective tall tales feed back into government agency country guidance, and public perception, to the overall effect of painting a grim enough picture of Russia that more can follow in their wake.

Not all poisoners of the well are Russian; Bill Browder, the British-American investor who fell out with the Russian state rather spectacularly in

---

13 The late Boris Berezovsky, the original Russian oligarch who lived in London from 2000 to his death in 2013, was in both categories, and particularly grumpy for that. He managed to do more damage to the image of Russia and Russians abroad than anyone had ever single-handedly managed before, then promptly wrote a letter of apology to Putin, and then hanged himself. The genie of his madness, however, could not be put back in the bottle. In Russia and in the diaspora, to this day, we are all involuntarily defined by the fallout from the Age of Berezovsky. The next chapter of this book is about that.

2007 and who is the former employer of the late Sergey Magnitsky, the namesake for one of the "Russian sanctions" laws in the United States, is always *running ahead of the train.* Although they stem largely from a failure to act like the Romans while in Rome, I acknowledge that Browder's grievances, particularly as they relate to the fate of Magnitsky himself, are legitimate. I even grant him that he has every right to be very cross still. His experience, however, is unique in nature and frozen in time. It is neither scalable to a greater context nor transferable to any other issue or situation. His attempts to continue projecting it, all these years later, onto everything to do with today's Russia and Russians, would be pathetic if they were not so harmful. Browder has been excluded from Russia since 2007. In the faster-moving global world of today, his understanding of it is hardly more relevant to the present, than *The Gulag Archipelago* was to my childhood.

Yet, Bill Browder was one of the key witnesses to the infamous 2019 report on Russia by the Intelligence and Security Committee of Parliament in the UK (what exactly is his expertise on the diaspora, to which he does not belong, of a country from which he had been expelled many years prior, is not explained – presumably, being the best known Russia-hater makes Browder the best possible independent expert on all things Russian).

Most of the report is too ludicrous to comment on – that would be akin to arguing with a person next to you on the train about whether or not they have really been abducted by aliens. It has a couple of somewhat salient thoughts in it – an accident, perhaps. For example, it notes, presciently, under the heading "What does Russia want?", that *"Russia's substantive aims (...) are relatively limited: it wishes to be seen as a resurgent power, in particular, dominating the countries of the former USSR".* I wish some American legislators, still obsessed with the idea that the Russians are coming for them, heeded this part of the report. For our purposes, the most harmful assertion of the report, by implication, is in paragraph 57, under the subheading "Russians at risk", in the sub chapter "Russian expatriates":

"Whilst the oligarchs and their money have been the most obviously visible part of the Russian diaspora, recent events have highlighted the number of Russians in the UK who are on the opposing side. Since Putin came to power in 1999, a number of critics of Putin and the Russian government have sought sanctuary in the UK, fearing politically motivated criminal charges and

78

harassment. They are of interest to the Russian Intelligence Services (RIS), which may seek to target them in a number of ways".

The assertions themselves, clearly fed to the Committee by Vladimir Ashurkov, who is wanted for campaign finance violations in Russia (and his girlfriend, Markvo – for embezzlement of millions of roubles from the Moscow city government), are unremarkable. "The number" of Russians to whom it applies is limited to the people previously personally mentioned in this chapter. It's a non-issue.

The real issue is that the report completely fails to acknowledge the existence of more than 100,000 Russians who live permanently in the United Kingdom. Many of us are now British citizens, but, image-wise, that does not make any of us any less Russian, where Russophobia is concerned. According to the report, there are mysterious oligarchs, their enablers, and brave Russians that oppose the Putin regime. The rest of us – the people who are neither oligarchs nor "enablers", but would, nonetheless, consider it beneath them to shake hands with the likes of Vladimir Ashurkov – do not exist, as far as the members of our Parliament are concerned. The whole tens of thousands of us. Did anyone ask us, how we feel about all this?

In the five years of legal practice in England between 2014 and 2019, I represented hundreds of families, most of whom were Russian-speaking expats. Among all of them, there was only one family the members of which were, one could say, in any sort of opposition to the Putin government. Even so, they certainly have not fled Russia and had not been charged with crimes. In fact, they derived all of their money and means of existence from the family's business that was continuing in Russia. As I was writing this book, during the COVID-19 pandemic, I found them living back in Moscow, to which many Russians, myself including, fled to obtain early vaccinations, and to get away from the ludicrous lockdown policies in England.

The rest of anyone I ever met in the diaspora does not consider their interests, as Russians, to be distinct from those of Vladimir Putin – or, for that matter, from the nameless "oligarchs". The prevailing understanding in this group has always been that we are all in this together, reputation-wise. When Russophobia went on the rise in 2018, many of us looked around in panic: will anyone remember us?

They did. According to the media, the report by a think tank called the Henry Jackson Society, published in 2018, asserts that out of an estimated population of 150,000 Russians living in London, up to half are informants of the Russian intelligence services. That's only 75,000 of us then? Nice. It says they may be "using false identities to pose as Russians living openly in the UK". (How is that supposed to be any more advantageous than being an actual Russian living openly in the UK?) Granted, the author, one Dr. Foxall, was quick to point out that most of us were not "engaged in assassinations". Cheers, mate! Boy, is he going to consider my book "an active measure"? I do not even wonder.

I have not read the report, but I think I know how this "Dr." arrived at his findings. He broadly estimated that at least half of Russians in the UK, having arrived here in the last 20 years, failed to deny Putin three times, like Peter denied Jesus, and continue to visit Russia. Of those who are arrivals from Putin's Russia, that category includes everyone whose surname is not Ashurkov, Markvo, Chichvarkin or Khodorkovsky. Everyone else belongs to a new breed of immigrants, that the West is still failing to understand, to the peril of everyone involved – the *Global Russians*.

It doesn't look like the Western countries, who continue to fancy themselves *shining cities on the hill*, took notice – but, in the last 20 years, people no longer leave Russia. No one is keeping them: Russians travel internationally more than they ever have and more than citizens of many other nations. But they no longer *leave Russia behind*. Unlike the emigrants of the Soviet era, whose journeys were one way, no one in the Putin era had looked back at the Sheremetyevo airport, as it was getting smaller and smaller, and said to themselves: I am never coming back. (No one Russian, anyway: I don't want Bill Browder complaining, in case if he did).

The reasons for that are manifold. They include not only the relative stability and prosperity in Russia itself, but also globalization, proliferation of the Internet, universal availability of consumer goods and many others. Life in Russia is good enough that it makes no sense for the poor and the unskilled to emigrate: they will universally be better off where they are, and now, thanks to the Internet and access to Western films and media, they know it. Most Russians who can afford to travel around the world and set themselves up for study or business in foreign countries, owe their ability to do so to the current Russian economy, and acquired it under the Putin government.

I am not talking about the super rich, I am talking about everyone: internationally mobile professionals, owners of sports stores and shoe stores, real estate brokers, doctors. For a successful mid-range businessman, who is affluent but not in possession of such cash reserves that they can be reinvested for interest on Wall Street and provide a comparable lifestyle, their life is virtually not exportable to the West. They can relocate with their families, but their business will remain in Russia. Professionals – teachers, accountants, lawyers, doctors – find that even if their skills are somewhat transferable, their practice in other countries would require re-licensing, and their experience and qualifications are most likely moot there. Going to get some experience in a junior role, or going in for some training, is one thing – but it is often a question of going to a third country afterward, or coming home to a higher salary.

If you are wealthy, however, chances are you will find that return on investment in Russia, for many reasons (the main ones having to do with higher perceived risk, due to volatile local currency and potential for political instability) is much, much higher than you can possibly receive in the West. And, yes, the Faustian bargain in getting those returns often involves staying on the good side of "the regime". Defensive against foreign influence and wary of foreigners and their incessant nagging (our friend Browder being the case in point), the country affords its opportunities more readily to Russians – and, being one, I imagine, it is rather difficult to resist.

Whatever of your capital you could manage to export from Russia, you will, at worst, spend, and, at best, preserve – but it can also be expropriated or frozen in some new iteration of some dumb politician's anti-Russian crusade. (It may sound like those crusades hit some mythical "oligarchs" the hardest, but the people hit hardest are actually those who only had $100,000 to their name, and are separated from it forever by a frozen bank account. I have seen that happen to many.) In Russia, you can still lose it all, perhaps – but, if not, it can grow exponentially. Russian businessmen today, for the most part, are all ex-Soviet citizens: they started with nothing, and always, it seems, viewed their wealth with some incredulity, as if it were ephemeral. In the big scheme of things, if you came in with nothing, you lose nothing – even if, notionally, you lose *everything*.

Thus meet the Global Russians. For many of you, they will be people on your block who own or rent a constantly empty property. I know dozens of people for whom it's been years since they have spent 183 days in any one country in that country's tax year, because they live simultaneously in 3 or 4 countries. Most of them have several citizenships, too, but they are all originally from Russia. That phenomenon is not limited to the super rich and, with the advent of telecommuting, includes most of the middle class. Only large corporate employees stay put in one place.

The latter, however, may be in your city or country only for a year or a couple of years. They will move to a third and fourth country next year, depending on where the pay is higher. When I ran an immigration advice practice in England, I had numerous clients who had prison-style calendars on their walls, on which they crossed out the days left until they could leave the country and still comply with minimum residence requirements for naturalization. (Yes, Home Secretary, they were all advised of the "future intentions requirement").

This phenomenon permanently changed the fabric of Russian immigrant diasporas in Western Europe and the United States. Today, they are no longer comprised of people who arrived because they had somewhere they had to leave; their journeys are of exploration, experience, wonder – but not of despair. They compare the opportunities that exist in emigration and take them only if they are better than those at home. They speak languages, study local societies in which they end up, participate in social and political life, and look around critically, trying to assess whether the stress of living in a country that treats you with unfriendly suspicion is worth it. To many, the global community of Russians, united notionally only by what we understand as *the Putin doctrine* – a belief, basically, that Russia is neither a bad place, nor evil – has become the only community to which they permanently belong.

It is a mistake – promptly made by those folks at the Henry Jackson Society – to divide Russians into "pro" and "anti" regime, such as to make all of those who refuse to speak ill of their country abroad into Russian spies. The reality is more complex, because it is not black and white. Most of the modern exports are, perhaps, just like Vladimir Vysotsky, who was the original *Global Russian*: whatever questions they have for the Russian government – and most do – they are not going to discuss them with institutions and governments in the countries openly hostile to it. This is because they know that, as Russia's reputation or power is weakened, so will be their own, wherever they are[14].

---

14 See RBTH.com "Russia no longer exports emigrants, but a new cohort of Global Russians". Feb. 5, 2020

Those of us who are 1990s emigrants from Russia are not, technically, *Global Russians*. We left at the time when there was not yet much to leave behind to later come back to, and when it was not yet possible to maintain a 24/7 connection with the place when you were across the globe. That lack of constant connection in pre-globalization era enabled our integration in the receiving societies at much greater rates than are seen today. The *Global Russians* remain Russian – most of us, culturally, are not. Many of us ended up marooned overseas permanently by children who were born and grew up there, and often do not speak Russian. Meanwhile, the community of Global Russians is infused with former emigrants who returned to Russia in the Putin years and reintegrated there, while maintaining connections with the West – often, they are connections with grown children who remain there.

Life in Moscow today is so much like life in London or New York – and in many ways more convenient – that it is easy for someone who spent years overseas, and even for their children, to come back and live comfortably. Many high-profile figures in the Russian sphere of domestic influence have spent years abroad. The wife of Putin's press-secretary Dmitry Peskov, renowned figure skater Tatiana Navka, lived in the United States for many years and appears on the IRS list of expatriates. Her children, reportedly, barely speak any Russian. Sergey Brilev, a longtime anchor on Russian state TV and its best foreign policy expert – haters would say that he is one of the most recognizable faces of state propaganda – is reportedly a British citizen. (My mother worked as a reporter for Vesti Nedeli in 2003, which Brilev anchored at the time). Vladimir Solovyev, perhaps most-noted today as the face of Russian state TV, lived in the United States for several years; so did Margarita Simonyan, head of RT. The list goes on.

The knowledge and understanding of the West that informs the Russian elites, as brought back by Global Russians and returnee emigrants, is much greater than the knowledge and understanding vice versa. That difference was laid bare, on one hand, by the very possibility of the allegations of 2016 U.S. election interference – which, in order to be true, required the actors behind it to understand America better than many Americans do. On the other hand, however, the idea that this alleged sophistication was the work of some "intelligence services", ordered by Putin himself, is the epitome of simplistic, close-minded Cold War-era stupidity of the people behind Russiagate, as I will discuss later in this book.

The morale of this fable is simple: whatever you think you know about Russia or its inner workings, is likely not the case. If you dropped in on any social or cultural event in Moscow in the past ten years, the narrative of Russia as a quasi-totalitarian state, intolerant of dissent, would immediately fall apart. The same people who you would perceive as those in, or very near, power, freely mingle with, and sometimes date and marry, those who are supposed to be in fervent opposition to them. People who are supposed to be "Putin's stooges" in the Western narrative, sponsor and finance artistic endeavors of those who claim to be "persecuted by the regime". "Leaders of the opposition" sit on corporate boards of state-owned companies[15]. Life goes on.

Just like in the society in Washington, DC pre-recent polarization, there are no lines drawn at "Putin's associates" and "the persecuted". Where there is court, there is favor, which can be ephemeral for some but not others; there is no one who doesn't seek it, and those who have it, generally, are envied and not impugned. There is also much more freedom to dissent, change your allegiances and associate, than you can possibly imagine. Like the Sneetches on Beaches, there is no reliable way to tell the loyalists and the opposition apart.

If you charted the course of the lives of only the Russians well-known or oft-mentioned in the West as either pro- or anti-Putin, and their close associates, you will find that they have all been constantly socially connected in a simultaneous myriad of ways that will not chime with what you think you know about their beliefs, loyalties or affiliations. At the same time, their connectedness is near-random. Attempting to find a pattern in all of their permutations would mean to become one of those paranoid schizophrenics in Hollywood movies, who connect newspaper clippings with red pieces of string in their basements, looking for causal connections between coincidences. There is no pattern.

There is only one Russia. In it, there is only one Moscow, everyone in it knows each other but acts, most of the time, based on an immediate imperative or preference, rather than as part of some greater cause, affiliation, or plan. There is no *us and them* in Russia. Some of us, out of vanity or in hope of raising funds, try to convince those in the West that there is *a them*, but that is not, strictly speaking, true.

---

15 Alexey Navalny, lately fashioned into a persecuted dissident by the Western press, in recent years sat on a board of directors of *Aeroflot*, Russian flagship airline, 51% of which is state-owned.

The Age of Berezovsky

"Poor people are crazy; rich people are eccentric"
a piece of proverbial wisdom

Whether or not it is true that all Russians know each other, everyone, in Moscow and in emigration, knew the late Boris Berezovsky. My mother knew and liked Berezovsky, which baffled me. Nothing about his rise, his reign, or his fall, suggested that she should.

Instead of an opportunistic gifted mathematician turned the country's largest car salesman, a hustler entangled with hooligans, the one original oligarch who propped up the ailing Yeltsin regime and allegedly, albeit according only to himself, personally recruited Vladimir Putin as Boris Yeltsin's successor, a madman who made light of moral principles, whom many, my mother including, blamed for a host of severe atrocities – instead of all that she saw in Berezovsky, ultimately, only that he was from Moscow, a fellow Moscow State University alumnus, and Jewish. Those three characteristics were enough for my mother to like anyone. It helped that Berezovsky could also be gallant, if he wanted to.

In the years following his 2000 self-exile, Berezovsky took to bankrolling the Russian opposition to the emerging Putin regime, and dissent appealed to my mother. All of her dissident friends were then instantly in love with Berezovsky, whom they had previously thought a villain. After a brief sojourn at the Berezovsky-owned TV6 channel, my mother marked the Putin era by joining the *VGTRK Rossiya* TV holding, the infamous "state TV" – thereby, in opposition terms, "selling out". Nonetheless, she retained sympathy for Berezovsky. In the end, my mother died before the great *BAB* (common acronym for the man's name, patronymic and last name) lost all of his remaining marbles.

It was after my mother died, in the summer of 2005, that I decided to give Boris Berezovsky a call, leading to my only ever conversation with him. "Conversation", perhaps, is too strong a word for that experience. I dialed his number, introduced myself, and then held the receiver in my stretched hand, far away from my ear, for about twenty minutes, as the ex-oligarch's endless sentence, comprising a multitude of non-sequiturs, came spitting out of it. All I could make out was to do with "revolution" and that, despite him knowing nothing of who I was, I likely wasn't doing enough to bring one about.

I faintly attempted to struggle my way back into the conversation (such as it was), confirming, for the avoidance of doubt, that I definitely wasn't going to take part in any revolution. Without inquiring why I had called, Berezovsky then declared that he could not help me, and hung up. This was the only conversation in my life with anyone, except my mother, in which I wasn't the one doing most of the talking; I decided that my mother must have liked BAB because he was the only person in the world who talked more than her.

When I learned of Boris Berezovsky's death in England in 2013, I did not know what to make of it. I was in America when I heard, and resolved to visit his grave upon return. Mad as he undoubtedly was in his last years, I thought, at the time, that Berezovsky represented something in all of our collective past, the passing of which we must contemplate. In the end, I never bothered.

Berezovsky was certainly suicidal, a man for whom there no longer was a place in the world of his own creation, and he knew it. Whether or not to believe that he actually committed the rather strange ostensible suicide in which he died is a dilemma that I took a long time to ponder. The BAB we all thought that we knew, perhaps, would have done it differently, if he were to do it at all. But the BAB of his final days, by all accounts, was not the man we all once knew. Not to believe would mean to clear the way for the implication that he was killed by the Russian state. That narrative is damaging and false, for the state was long done with Berezovsky[16]. He was over, miserable, and a threat to no one.

Berezovsky had enemies in many strange places, beyond the knowledge and imagination of most in the West – and, even if one were not to believe that he ended his own life, one nonetheless would not want to follow down the path where that belief would lead. I choose to believe in his suicide, as the Surrey police does, because it reflects the ultimate truth about Boris Berezovsky – the man was his own worst enemy. And, his passing left me standing alone as the person who talks the most in any conversation.

The quaint demise of Boris Berezovsky, lost beyond the end of his era, and the sentimental memories of many of those who lived through the *age of Berezovsky*, somewhat obscured the true nature of his deeds in life. "About the dead, speak fondly or not at all", goes a Russian proverb – once an apt

---

16 Formally, he was still wanted for prosecution on criminal charges in Russia, but in reality, the world back home had moved on.

propagandist, BAB thereby re-wrote his narrative by the genius last stroke of his suicide. Vladimir Putin, whom Berezovsky spent the preceding 13 years trying to discredit, spoke publicly on Russian TV about Berezovsky's death with sadness.

Putin told the mesmerized audience that he had received two personal letters from BAB in the months leading up to his death, in which the exiled oligarch expressed contrition for the damage that he had done to Russia, and asked for permission to return (as a Russian citizen, Berezovsky, of course, did not require permission to return, so what he probably sought was a dismissal of criminal charges pending in Russia against him). The President said that he had not responded to the letters, and now thanked God that he hadn't[17]. Putin must have aimed for pity, but came across as almost sentimental. One got the impression that Putin ultimately made peace with Berezovsky. About the dead, he would speak *fondly, or not at all*. As for me, all these years later, I no longer feel sentimental, and I am not quite at peace with Boris Berezovsky.

Like most Russians, I have made peace with the 1990s – the strange and tumultuous era that elevated Boris Berezovsky to an unprecedented position of power. Books have been written about that time, and about this man, and assessment of his contribution to Russian history varies, depending on who you ask. The 90s were dark and fun at the same time: many Russians, myself included, would not recognize, and do not wish to face, ourselves from back then. We chose to move on, and it worked for all of us. Even if I were to offer my own assessment of those years, it would require a separate book to do so.

Boris Berezovsky fled Russia in 2000, under threat of arrest for embezzlement and corruption. Ultimately, he spent more active years stirring up trouble abroad than he had done on the inside[18]. As the era of Berezovsky in Russia ended, the *age of Berezovsky* in the diaspora had only just begun. My concern is, principally, with Russia's image in the world, and so I take issue with Boris Berezovsky, above all, for his shenanigans in emigration.

---

17 Presumably because his answer would have been harsh, and, once the suicide followed, he'd be forced to blame himself.

18 If you count his ascent there from the 1989 founding of LogoVAZ, which elevated him to eventual wealth.

The Godfather

Boris Berezovsky was a benevolent genius to his many fans, but, as an individual, he was certainly capable of evil. Whether or not he has committed any, is not settled – and probably never will be. He rose to the top at the turn of the 1990s, in a time and a place that was, by any measure, unforgiving – and, he dealt in cars, which was a particularly brutal, gang-infested sort of business, a far cry from exploits that were typical of enterprising intelligentsia of the day. By the time of an attempt to assassinate him in 1994, Berezovsky was no longer a mathematics professor, but a hardened, ruthless man. BAB walked away, with minor injuries, from a mangled Mercedes and a decapitated driver – paving way to rumors that he himself was behind the attempt. It was in the wake of the tragedy that he became a confidant of Boris Yeltsin and a shareholder of the country's main TV channel (ORT), which he privatized for his own benefit.

In his London years, Berezovsky struck me as a man gone mad, without much more to it. It is instructive to note, however, that the most scathing judgments on Berezovsky always came from Westerners who encountered him in Russia in the 1990s. George Soros, in his 2000 essay "Who lost Russia?", expands a lot on his mistrust of Berezovsky. According to Soros, BAB was "incapable of making a transition to legitimacy", such as was necessary on the verge of the Putin presidency. Soros writes that Berezovsky "gave him the chills" and that he, Soros, was certain that BAB could kill him. I do not put it down simply to a cultural misunderstanding: Soros, himself Hungarian, had spent a lot of time in Russia. Given his interactions with multiple Russians of that era, that BAB is the only one of whom he ever spoke in such terms is quite telling.

Just like George Soros, and some other observers with a Western slant, my mother suspected Berezovsky's hand in the September 1999 bombings of apartment buildings in Moscow. This was her initial reaction: surely, one could not put it past Berezovsky? She was in the United States at the time of the events, and would have gotten tidings from her colleagues. Those tidings could be biased, because my mother worked for the NTV channel, controlled by Vladimir Gusinsky, a principal political rival to Berezovsky and his ORT channel[19].

---

19 It might also be relevant that my mother was, clearly, no expert in terrorism: two years later, her initial assessment of 9/11 would be to blame it on "the Palestinians".

The apartment building bombings, and related allegations advanced by various parties, are difficult to understand in retrospect, because the allegiances of the players involved changed rapidly between September 1999 and September 2000. At the time of the bombings, Berezovsky was at the height of his political power, and, as is commonly believed, had just tapped the then-FSB director Vladimir Putin as Yeltsin's successor[20]. In August 1999, Putin became acting Prime Minister of Russia, amidst a worrisome escalation of the Chechen separatist insurgency in the South.

At the time of the September bombings in Moscow, the succession had not yet been announced – but it was clear to everyone that Yeltsin was faltering, and the elections were just a few months away. A political block rival to Yeltsin's, one comprising the former Prime Minister Evgeny Primakov and Moscow Mayor Yuri Luzhkov, was gaining power, with support of Gusinsky's NTV. The bombings appeared to be a useful pretext for escalation of a renewed hard line against Chechnya – which, if nothing else, would be a last-ditch attempt to strengthen the Yeltsin administration and rally public support around him. It was on that theory that my mother, and many around her, initially decided that such a PR intervention would be right up Berezovsky's alley. Having just lived through the 1990s, most Russians were not prepared to take anything at face value. Some sort of a multi-leg scheme, a *многоходовка*, must have been afoot. Boris Berezovsky was the grand master of schemes.

In the following months, things moved fast. Yeltsin resigned on New Year's Eve, making Putin acting President and prompting Primakov to give up his ambitions for the upcoming presidential election. Putin was elected in March 2000, without serious opposition. Berezovsky found himself shut off from power, quickly losing influence – and, as Soros noted, *incapable of making a transition to legitimacy*. It was then that he latched onto the apartment bombings with vigor. Clearly aware of the rumors that he himself was to blame, he threw his media assets behind claiming that the FSB was behind the bombings, ostensibly in an attempt to strengthen the then-Prime Minister, Putin (one of the service's own).

---

20 Most of the literature that describes BAB as the one who picked the successor, does so based on BAB's own assertions, including Masha Gessen's biography of Putin, for which Berezovsky was also a source. While this is an accepted version of the events, it might be wise to view it with caution, given Berezovsky's well-known propensity for self-aggrandizement.

Berezovsky had stuck to this crusade for a while, even as he fled Russia in late 2000. The sad irony, of course, is that the two sets of accusations, to the public, are essentially the same theory. After all, no one thought that Berezovsky did it *literally himself*. Whether it was carried out by the special forces, or some Chechens that had been contracted, and who exactly gave the order, was almost of no import. The toxic notion was the very idea that it was an act planned to a political end, rather than a genuine act of Islamic terrorism.

The casual implications of such a thought were horrendous: most Russians tend to believe, just as Vladimir Putin said at the time, that no fellow Russian would murder hundreds of their compatriots in cold blood for political gain. For all the innuendo and conspiracy theories that surrounded the explosions (pinned officially on the Chechens), no one was ever personally accused of being behind them. No one, it seemed to largely religious Russians, would have personally taken such a sin upon themselves. Except one man. Many of the people who knew Berezovsky said: *him – maybe.* I do not believe that Berezovsky would have taken such a sin upon himself. But it is still telling that he would be many people's first idea of *whodunit*. After all, accusing someone of blowing up a multi-story residential building is not quite the same as accusing them of a contract murder of a business associate.

The matter of unexpectedly dying interlocutors was also there, of course. Once we move into middle age, people around us start to die. That's a fact of life. Most of them die of cancer, and some of heart attacks. Most of us have known someone, perhaps one or two people, who killed themselves. We all probably knew someone who died in a car crash. Yet, looking back, Boris Berezovsky was a troubling common denominator in a long line of sudden and usually unexplained deaths. How many people did you personally know who were a victim of a murder – let alone, an unsolved murder? Most of us don't know any. Murders are statistically rare, and murders by strangers outside of the victim's family – even more so. Being acquainted with Boris Berezovsky seems to have been a significant risk factor – he knew a whole bunch. Perhaps he was just living so close to danger. Perhaps there was more to it.

The three most notorious unsolved murders from the Russian universe – of ORT director Vladislav Listyev in 1995, of Forbes Russia editor Paul Khlebnikov in 2004, and of Alexander Litvinenko, the former lieutenant colonel of the FSB, in London in 2006 – all had *something* to do with BAB. He was either the main witness, or the vocal adversary of the deceased, or, as in case of the latter, took on a profound role of the No.1 grieving relative, even though there was scarcely any evidence that the two had been close. I do not wish to be like one of those conspiracy theorists, connecting newspaper clippings in the basement with red strings; I don't have any reasons to believe that Boris Berezovsky ordered any murders at all. But no one ever claimed that I murdered anyone – it is not a usual claim to make about any person. Yet, a lot of people thought that about Berezovsky.

Paul Khlebnikov, an American with vaguely Russian roots, was obsessed with Berezovsky. Writing for Forbes magazine in December 1996, he aired the theory that BAB was behind the Listyev murder, as well as a host of other grim allegations. A lot of Khlebnikov's reporting was inaccurate and bizarre, but the West assumed that there was smoke where there was fire. Berezovsky sued Forbes for libel in London, and eventually settled for a partial retraction (to wit, of the specific claim that he had Listyev killed). That early litigation success gave Berezovsky the idea that British people were easy to manipulate, and launched him as a prolific vexatious litigant for the rest of his life.

Meanwhile, Paul Khlebnikov doubled down. He turned his Berezovsky-related conspiracy theories into a book, "Godfather of the Kremlin". It came out in 2000, just as BAB was on the way out of the Kremlin. Once Khlebnikov was gunned down in front of his office in Moscow in 2004, his murder was pinned on a Chechen warlord, about whom Khlebnikov had written a later book. Khlebnikov initially survived the drive-by shooting, and was taken by ambulance to a nearby hospital, where he died on the way to the operating room, as his gurney was stuck in a stalled elevator – a frustrating and bizarre end. In a further twist, a Moscow jury subsequently acquitted three Chechen men accused of carrying out the murder.

The emigre

When Boris Berezovsky, freshly glorified by Paul Khlebnikov's magnum opus, arrived in London in the end of 2000, the British authorities could not figure out what to do with him. At that time, Russia was not yet evil, and newly elected President Putin was, at worst, an enigma. In fact, much more was publicly known about Berezovsky himself – and that knowledge did not endear

91

their newest house guest to the Blair government one bit. BAB was keen to claim asylum, but no one could quite see a theory on which his life was in danger in Russia. According to his public profile, it was rather those around him that feared for theirs. He was, of course, wanted for financial crimes – but the United Kingdom, at the time, did not yet see itself as a safe haven for Russian fugitives from justice; Berezovsky and Co. pioneered that trend.

As is now obvious in hindsight, it was at that juncture that one Alexander Litvinenko, previously vaguely acquainted with Berezovsky, stepped forward to play a crucial role in his life. Litvinenko first met Berezovsky when he was assigned by the FSB, for which he then worked, to investigate the infamous 1994 Moscow assassination attempt. Somehow, as a result of that investigation – which may or may not have come upon, and concealed, any evidence that BAB may have staged the crime at the cost of his driver's life – they established a rapport and afterward maintained an acquaintance. In 1998, Litvinenko was behind a host of publicly aired allegations of corruption within the ranks of the FSB, central to which was a claim that FSB wanted to have Berezovsky killed. The scandal ultimately led to the departure of the FSB director of the day, and the installation in his place of one Vladimir Putin, yet unknown to the public.

Whether or not Berezovsky's claims to have had a hand in the pick of Putin as the new FSB director were true, Putin, although he was friendly with Berezovsky, certainly did not share BAB's enthusiasm for Litvinenko or his crusade. Litvinenko was promptly ejected from the FSB and eventually charged with a host of crimes, leading to a brief stint in jail. After that, Berezovsky ostensibly employed him, presumably to prevent his destitution, and, in the autumn of 2000, BAB provided some high level assistance to Litvinenko's escape from Russia and subsequent passage to London with a view to seeking asylum. This was a pivotal point that indebted Litvinenko to Berezovsky, and apparently made him, now penniless in England, dependent on a stipend provided by BAB.

At the turn of 2001, Berezovsky and Litvinenko were two men in one geographic location with the same legal problem: need for asylum. Litvinenko's own asylum claim in the UK went smoothly – he was a vocal traitor expelled from the Russian security services, and the said services did not camouflage the disdain they had for him. Litvinenko was embraced by the Western intelligence community – after all, no Americans had written books accusing *him* of any murders[21]. Litvinenko swiftly received asylum and later wrote books himself, to the tune of Russia being a mafia state, and Putin – the source of all evil. In London, Litvinenko almost made the proverbial *transition to legitimacy,* but one problem remained – he was in Berezovsky's debt.

Litvinenko's 1998 claims of a planned FSB assassination of Berezovsky defy belief – if nothing else, for the reasons of how he chose to publicly present them. The whole mess, with the publicity that accompanied it, and the crucial part that ORT took in promoting it, certainly smelled like a Berezovsky idea. Whether there was any truth to the claims, or why Berezovsky promoted them publicly, is hard to say – but BAB was certainly obsessed with making it known that everyone wanted to kill him. (Projection, anyone?) The 1994 assassination attempt started off the chain of events that ingratiated him to Boris Yeltsin, and it is possible that he was attempting a remake of that movie. Either way, in London in the early 2000s those claims finally found their use, as Berezovsky sought to found his asylum claim on the idea that he fled Russia for his life, and Alexander Litvinenko was to become his star witness.

That plan, of course, missed one very important point: all of those alleged attempts on Berezovsky's life occurred when he was, as far as anyone could tell, the Russian state himself. Moreover, all of that trouble took place before Putin was FSB director, let alone President. Asylum exists to provide protection from a state. The state, such as it had been, underwent a massive

---

21 In hindsight, the enthusiasm with which the emigre intelligentsia dissidents and cheerful British pundits anointed the FSB lt.colonel, while at the same time impugning the raison d'etre and core values of the organization he chose to join and faithfully served, is striking. Most of the former Soviet citizens – and particularly those who fancied themselves dissidents – in whose collective memory disdain for the KGB was still fresh, would not break bread with anyone who made a career of a service in the security forces of secret police of any kind, and falling out with the said services hardly bought one a retrospective indulgence. After all, this was the sole focal point of the intelligentsia's claimed problem with Putin: that he was ex-KGB. Berezovsky had long abandoned all intelligentsia footing by mid-1990s, but even he appeared to have kept Litvinenko at arms' length. Meanwhile, that someone like dissident Alex Goldfarb, who has written a book about Litvinenko's death – and, according to the inquest into it, most of the latter's famous deathbed letter accusing Putin of his murder – would treat someone like Litvinenko as almost a friend, stuns me. Apparently, it also stunned George Soros, who reportedly fired Goldfarb from his employ for assisting Litvinenko, on the grounds that befriending FSB agents was antithetical to the values of the Soros Foundation.

change from 1998 to 2001 – and, coincidentally, the state discovered that Berezovsky may have been himself corrupt. What danger, other than being exposed for the alleged crimes that had been laboriously described by Western journalists, was there *now*? BAB presented a lot of other elaborate evidence of attacks on his commercial interests, but his right to physically reside in the UK in no way cured those issues. His asylum claim ran into difficulty.

Moreover, the Russians vigorously pursued Berezovsky's extradition (something that I found surprising – one would think that his arrival back and airing of whatever he wished to say would not be conducive to the public good in Russia). This was made a big deal of in the Russian media; brigades of patriotic youth movement were dispatched to London to stand in front of Berezovsky's residence in Surrey and chant *chemodan-vokzal-Rossiya* ("suitcase – train station – Russia"). By the time 2003 rolled around, Berezovsky's unresolved asylum claim and his extradition case were fused into one. Litvinenko's definitive expertise in one narrow field – uncovering the threats on the life of Boris Berezovsky – became the critical skill. And boy, did he uncover a few.

Writing for The Independent years later on 18 March 2015, Mary Dejevsky provides a somber analysis: *"Berezovsky's sojourn in Britain always posed questions, but the inquiry into Litvinenko's death has raised more. One concerns the extent to which Berezovsky's life was really in danger in Russia [...] The inquiry has heard from several witnesses that Litvinenko and Berezovsky fell out in the summer before he died, though it is not entirely clear why. [...] The quarrel, most agreed, was patched up well before Litvinenko's death. But a recurrent theme of some testimony was that Litvinenko held a crucial secret: at least some of the death threats against Berezovsky, it was said, had been concocted for the sole purpose of obtaining UK asylum. It is not necessary to "buy" this theory's extension – that Litvinenko was preparing to blackmail Berezovsky – to feel that such knowledge could have given him a hold, and provided a less noble motive for his patronage."*

Following a flurry of freshly uncovered threats on his life made, ostensibly, by all sorts of FSB-related actors, Berezovsky's asylum was granted in 2003, and his extradition to Russia was blocked. He was wanted by the Interpol though, and so legally changed his name – well, not legally, because that would require a change of name *for all purposes* – to have a travel document issued to him by the British government as *Platon Elenin*. The name *Platon* was that of a title character of a blockbuster Russian film *Oligarch (2002)*, that was rumored to be based on Berezovsky. Perhaps he found the film, where Platon is portrayed by the famous Russian actor Vladimir Mashkov, flattering – and did not mind that the film's narrative was based around an investigation into *Platon's* mysterious death. *Elenin* in Russian means *one that belongs to Elena* – BAB chose it after the first name of Elena Gorbunova, his long-time domestic partner and the mother of his two youngest children. Even as Berezovsky, as we will soon learn, swindled this woman out of all means of existence the last years of his life, this assumed name would serve at least one other purpose – it now appears on his grave.[22]

One of the people ostensibly involved in the making-up of death threats against Berezovsky in order to enable him to seek asylum was Vladimir Terlyuk. My assessment is that he was simply a Russian in London by 2001, wandering without purpose and money, and that he hung around at some public events that he knew would be attended by Berezovsky in order to meet him (and, presumably, ask for money). He must have made chit-chat with someone in the oligarch's posse at some point, and then started to just follow them around, hoping to be useful. It happens. Later, his story became that he was carrying around a poisoned pen with intent to strike down BAB with it. He may, or may not, have served in the Soviet KGB once, but it is doubtful that he had any relationship with the FSB. After Litvinenko died, Terlyuk claimed on Russian TV that he was forced to make up that threat under duress, by Litvinenko – and was, of course, sued by Berezovsky, for whom a lawsuit was the answer to everything.

I did not follow any of these legal events at the time (nor any of the other Berezovsky-related litigation contemporaneously). I first learned of the existence of Vladimir Terlyuk when, one chilly late evening in February of 2017, he unexpectedly appeared in my office, along with his wife. My office was then in Watford, and they took Overground from London. Terlyuk was wearing slippers and looked as if he had just woken up. The purpose of his unannounced arrival was to seek immigration advice, for which he never paid. He expected me to have heard of him, but I had not – so he gave me a brief recap of it all in a tale

---

22 It is also plausible, knowing Berezovsky's revolutionary state of mind at the time, that he fashioned the name as word play on *Lenin*, which itself was a pseudonym of the man known by it.

that, there and then, seemed even more bizarre than Grandpa Georgiy's newly claimed attendance at the Tehran Conference. After Terlyuk finished telling me his story, he walked out as abruptly as he appeared, and left no contact details. I never heard from him again – if anyone does, he owes me 50 quid[23].

I did not believe any of it – but even less so, could I believe that Boris Berezovsky, or anyone in his posse, would, for any length of time, entertain entangling themselves with this man. Terlyuk's madness meant nothing to me – but the new window into Berezovsky's own madness, potentially as early as 2002, was a revelation.

Somewhat entangle themselves with Terlyuk they clearly did. I do not wish to undermine the English court decision in *Berezovsky v. Terlyuk* that judged false Terlyuk's principal claim that he was an ex-KGB officer who had made up an assassination attempt at the urging of Litvinenko, in order to support BAB's asylum claim. But it was a libel suit, in which Berezovsky was suing *VGTRK Rossiya* – Rossiya TV holding, Russian state TV and my mother's last employer before her death – for the 2007 broadcast of a program that pinned the Litvinenko murder on him. The program featured a disguised interviewee, voice distorted, under a false name. Berezovsky promptly named Vladimir Terlyuk as the second defendant, because he *recognized* him in that disguise. Clearly, he wasn't a complete stranger. And, yes, it was not the first time Berezovsky sued for libel to quash a media allegation that he had someone specific murdered – surely a once-in-a-lifetime, at most, necessity for the rest of us.

In my experience as an immigration lawyer, concocted tales wither. That this mad man in slippers in the middle of winter stuck to his as late as 2017, by which time everyone else involved in it was dead, tells me something. Maybe he wasn't this mad 15 years prior? Maybe entering BAB's world *made* him mad? Terlyuk notwithstanding, it is now clear to most in the UK – and it was always clear to Russians – that Berezovsky took the British asylum system for a ride with his 2003 case (and, by the way, most of the Russians that claim asylum do). The man who pioneered the new era of the fugitive emigre embezzler in London did it under the same false pretenses as those who keep coming in his wake. While the British government was initially confused by all of this and did not

---

23 I suppose I stand no chance of collecting any sooner than the estate of Boris Berezovsky, to which Terlyuk owes something to the tune of £150,000 pursuant to a court order.

know what do to with him, by 2005, as we will see shortly, his welcome wore off, and soon the new Russian extradition request gained strength.

Like Mary Dejevsky of The Independent, I do not necessarily believe that in 2006 Litvinenko, by then fully beholden to the idea of Putin-bashing, was on the verge of turning BAB in for concocted asylum claims – especially since he'd have to admit to concocting them himself. But if one thinks like Berezovsky, one can't help notice that the timing of Litvinenko's *political martyrdom* in 2006 served BAB very well. The demise of Alexander Litvinenko provided retroactive justification for BAB's claims of FSB ruthlessness, and fueled the fear of Putin in London for years to come. No one was extraditing anyone anymore.

As a traitor to security services and a Russian citizen turned foreign spy, Litvinenko may have had only one end waiting for him – but it's hard to think that the state would be as foolish as to bring about that end at the very moment when it would undermine the country's last hope for a possible extradition of Russia's public enemy No 1. If BAB had nothing to do with his death, it is pretty clear that Putin didn't either: that murder was a huge inconvenience to Russia, and the best thing that happened to Boris Berezovsky in exile.

I am ambivalent about the fact that Berezovsky gained asylum in the UK. As a former lawyer, I cannot endorse concoction of evidence, if such took place, but this is more of a question of who should, or should not, be granted the status more generally. A whole host of people followed, and also received asylum, shortly thereafter, including those who were wanted in Russia in the same criminal cases at BAB: Nikolay Glushkov (the only one of BAB's circle to mysteriously die in London *after* BAB's own death), wanted in connection with charges related to *Aeroflot – Russian Airlines*, and Yuli Dubov, wanted in connection with charges related to LogoVAZ. Without delving too deep into 1990s revisionism, many of them probably did commit the claimed crimes (just as their previously noted modern era successors in political emigration). Yet, there is something to be said for statutes of limitations and giving Russia a clean break from the 1990s. It was, in that context, desirable that they all left Russia rather than stayed. The problem with BAB, rather, was that he never really *left*.

The agitator

I am watching a grainy 1990s video of Berezovsky speaking in some government setting in Russia to other officials. He is upbeat and tells a well-worn joke. "What is the difference between an Englishman and a Jew?" – he asks. "An Englishman leaves without saying goodbye, and a Jew says goodbye but never leaves". BAB means himself, of course. The people in the video laugh politely. In a greater sense, that is what Berezovsky would later do to Russia: he would say a very loud goodbye, but his presence would linger.

When Berezovsky moved to London, he sold his shares in ORT, but still had significant media assets in Russia: namely, *Kommersant* publishing house, home of a reputable broadsheet newspaper (for which I once worked, but that had been prior to BAB becoming the owner), and an obscure television channel, TV-6, which he now revamped into a massive opposition media machine. Just as Gazprom, a state-owned entity, took over Gusinsky's NTV in 2001 (BAB's rival ex-oligarch promptly moving to Israel and later Spain), most of its dissident-minded employees, my mother included, floated over to Berezovsky's TV-6. Until 2002, it continued to spew BAB's FSB-related conspiracy tales and anti-Putin propaganda of all sorts.

Berezovsky's closest friend and associate, Arkady Patarkatsishvili, was at the helm of TV-6 until 2001, at which time he was accused by the Russian authorities of organizing Nikolai Glushkov's escape, and later co-accused, with Berezovsky and Dubov, in the LogoVAZ case. Afterward Patarkatsishvili lived in his native Georgia, of which he was the wealthiest resident. He ran unsuccessfully for President in January of 2008; he had a home in London as well, where he would meet an unexplained death in February of 2008.

Between the two of them, Berezovsky and Patarkatsishvili developed a persistent record of installing state leaders who later wished to have nothing to do with them. Patarkatsishvili provided considerable support for the 2003 *Rose Revolution* in Georgia, which deposed the country's Soviet-era leader Edward Shevarnadze, and installed Mikhail Saakashvili as President. Patarkatsishvili then promptly and bitterly fell out with Saakashvilli, leading to the happenings much similar to those that befell himself, and BAB, in Russia. When Patarkatsishvili tried to sell his TV channel, Imedi, to Rupert Murdoch's News Corporation, the Saakashvili government sent in the SWAT team to nationalize it instead.

Berezovsky, using his new British travel document in the name of Platon Elenin, traveled to Ukraine, where he spent, according to Forbes, close to 70 million dollars on bankrolling the 2004 *Orange Revolution*. It deposed the pro-Russian president Viktor Yanukovich, and installed Viktor Yushchenko in his stead, ultimately setting Ukraine on the course of anti-Russian nationalism on which it sadly remains today. Yushchenko later claimed to have barely known Berezovsky and, according to Forbes, reneged on his promises to BAB – but the damage to Russia was already done, and that, without a doubt, was what Berezovsky really wanted.

Boris and Arkady later also bankrolled the *Tulip Revolution* in Kyrgyzstan to a similar end, although spending – again, according to Forbes – much less money. All of the above were the same "color revolutions" that, as is considered common knowledge among the U.S. conservatives, were substantially financed and organized by the U.S. Department of State – but Forbes reports that the Americans provided mostly talk and promises, whereas Berezovsky brought in the cash.

All of these shenanigans have done more damage to Russia that Berezovsky could ever have hoped to do on the inside. Ultimately, the destabilization of the ex-Soviet region, directly liked to BAB, paved way to what we now understand to be part of *the Putin doctrine* – consolidation of Russians that perceive themselves as persecuted and entrenched and see the need for influence and control in the country's immediate environs as the only possible guarantee of their collective security.

The extent to which Russia could be threatened with the same scenario in 2005 is unclear, but Berezovsky, fresh from the three "color revolutions" that succeeded so marvelously in destabilizing their respective countries and undermining Russia's geopolitical interests, certainly set his sights on a new Russian Revolution. He started to handsomely give out money to the Russian opposition, backing any idea, and every charlatan, who would promise to him that they were up for it. (This was the time when my own aforementioned phone call with BAB took place). According to the New York Times, BAB spoke openly about planning a violent overthrow of the Putin government in an interview in early 2006. The BBC reported that Berezovsky admitted on air to a radio station, that he was "planning a coup" in Russia.

"Overthrowing", "violently" and "coup" were, finally, too much for British Foreign Secretary Jack Straw. In February 2006, Straw took the rare step of issuing a written statement as a warning to Berezovsky, in which he pointed out that "advocating the violent overthrow of a sovereign state is unacceptable". The Foreign Secretary, in the statement, went to great lengths to assure the

Russians that the UK enjoyed a close working relationship between the two countries, and had utmost respect for Russia's constitution and territorial integrity. The statement brashly noted that no one "invited" Berezovsky to England. Straw – who was also Home Secretary at the time of BAB's asylum case – reminded the ex-tycoon that he would be kicked out of the UK if his presence was no longer conducive to the public good.

To the Russians, Jack Straw's statement signaled a chill toward BAB, and they promptly filed a new extradition request. Berezovsky shut up about a coup and re-focused his efforts on staying in the UK – at which point, some time in summer of 2006, he mysteriously fell out with Litvinenko, according to The Independent. In Moscow, Arkady Patarkatsishvili sold his and Berezovsky's remaining substantial media interest – *Kommersant* publishing house – and it was also at that time that the two made public claims of an impending business "divorce", sale of all jointly held assets and division of all proceeds between them. If one did not know any better, it would seem as if Patarkatsishvili, who mulled over a possible run for office in Georgia, wanted to distance himself from Berezovsky. BAB's world was collapsing around him all throughout the 2006: until, that is, Alexander Litvinenko met his mysterious end in November.

Litvinenko's theatrical demise of polonium poisoning in central London paved the way for a new wave of Russophobia and Putinophobia, which continues to this day. Berezovsky was allowed to stay and eventually granted permanent residence (known in the UK as *indefinite leave to remain*). However, as of 2007, he was out of friends, and out of money.

Exactly how and why Berezovsky ended up being *out of money,* all the while the media estimated his assets to be at about $1 billion, is a great mystery, if you consider the matter as a Westerner. It was common ground in later legal action, and is now public knowledge, that Boris Berezovsky received a total of around $1.6 billion from Roman Abramovich after he left Russia. Further to that, according to Forbes, the proceeds from the sale of ORT in 2000 were estimated at $150 million, and the sale of *Kommersant* in 2006 circa $250 million. This is a total of $2 billion of receipts in the space of 6 years, and everyone in the capitalist world knows: you cannot possibly run out of $2 billion.

In fact, you would be hard pressed to run out of even $1 billion, because any such amount of money would endlessly replenish itself, if invested conservatively with at least the minimal prudence. Most people could even make a couple of million work nicely, to enable themselves to live carefree for the rest of their lives. Most unassuming British retirees, without any training in business and finance, could arrange that easily. So how did the supposed certified genius manage to blow $2 billion in a few years?

The answer is, of course, that Boris Berezovsky was no businessman. He was a genius in schemes, PR and attainment of political influence. Of business and investment, just like most older Soviet people – products of a virtually cash-free society – he knew and understood next to nothing. On all available evidence, money was an abstract concept to Berezovsky – he had no instinctive understanding of its worth, and seemed to understand poorly how much it was prudent to spend on what. Outside of Russia, he had zero knack for distinguishing legitimate opportunities from scams.

Berezovsky's inability to *make a transition to legitimacy* was also reflected in his inability to *benefit* from legitimacy, and total lack of willingness to store, or invest, money in legitimate ways. To his last day, he was a walking anachronism of a bygone era. He had, according to reports from his London-based interlocutors, zero interest in conservative investment strategies employed in the West, because he saw the returns they offered as insufficient. As a result, he preferred to spend it all instead – seemingly without asking himself what would happen when the money ran out. He certainly spent most of it on destabilizing Russia and causing anti-Russian unrest in other ex-Soviet countries, but he was also, according to Forbes, constantly duped out of millions by various charlatans and con artists who presented him with outlandish ostensible investment plans and business proposals that no British or American schoolchild would be stupid enough to take seriously.

It transpired later that Berezovsky did not actually trust himself to keep and manage money that he received, or was supposed to receive. According to numerous statements by BAB himself, his funds were all held and managed on his behalf by Arkady Patarkatsishvili – and, of course, nothing of the sort was ever recorded anywhere in writing. This sounded like a pretty bizarre asset management strategy for a wealthy individual living in England in the 21st century. When pressed for details, Berezovsky later claimed that he let Patarkatsishvili put everything in the latter's name, because his, Berezovsky's, assets were being hunted for by the Russians who accused him of embezzlement.

This is a wonderful theory, but it fails to account for the fact that Patarkatsishvili was BAB's co-accused in the Russian embezzlement case, so one cannot claim that assets in his possession would be any safer from arrest, than those in Berezovsky's own. The idea that some of BAB's funds were given to Patarkatsishvili for safekeeping is even more bizarre, since, unlike Berezovsky, Patarkatsishvili did not live in England, and had no permanent legal relationship with it. Most of his interests were in Georgia, a country BAB had nothing to do with, and did not understand.

One could spend some time entertaining the theory that Berezovsky had reasons to put assets in other people's names, and not have any record of it, in Russia – after all, who could have possibly known what went on in scary Russia! However, the tale that a man in today's' England gave upwards of $1 billion – money that had been already received in Western banks and legitimized as to its source (in other words, did not require laundering) – to a foreign resident "to keep", without there being any record whatsoever of it, does not hold water.

One cannot help but think that something else entirely was going on between the two – such as, perhaps, the money was already owed by Berezovsky to Patarkatsishvili and went directly to him, and, as sums were given by Patarkatsishvili to Berezovsky to spend, the latter was borrowing them back. Maybe BAB had not really given that much, or anything at all, for Patarkatsishvili to keep – instead, all of it was spent on his political subversion ventures, or given away to fraudsters. Unable to properly calculate, BAB could have convinced himself that the money should still be somewhere. On that, Patarkatsishvili could have indulged him out of pity, and simply gave BAB funds when he needed them. Depending on the depth of Berezovsky's latter-day madness, all of these are viable possibilities.

Either way, the ostensible "business divorce" between the two, that Berezovsky expected to take place in 2006-2007, did not bear fruit neither as quickly, nor as efficiently, as he had hoped. He later claimed not to have received the funds due him, and even that he was betrayed. Whether or not Patarkatsishvili really intended to split his wealth with BAB, something clearly prevented him from doing so in the course of 2007. He died in London in February 2008. On the eve of his death, Patarkatsishvili left a panicked message for businessman Roman

Abramovich, requesting an urgent meeting[24]. Upon Patarkatsishvili's demise, Berezovsky turned his attention to the only way in which he thought he knew how to make money: he started suing.

The litigant

The majority of mentally secure individuals abhor litigation. On account of my legal training, I abhor litigation more than most. Most lawyers abhor litigation. When I took Evidence – its core subject – in law school in the United States, the professor, on the first day, asked the class of future attorneys to raise their hand if they hoped to never see the inside of a courtroom. An overwhelming majority – probably, 90 percent – of those present, raised their hand.

Boris Berezovsky was, in no respect, like the majority of mentally secure individuals. He liked litigation a lot. His first brush with litigation in England came when he sued Forbes in libel (for claiming that he had Vladislav Listyev killed). Berezovsky did not win any monetary awards in the case, and the partial retraction was agreed in a settlement – but the process clearly empowered BAB. He projected that early success onto a lifelong belief that he could sue anyone in the English courts for just about anything, and win – because the English, as he already knew from his asylum and extradition cases, could be told anything, and they would believe it.

In 2007-2008, Berezovsky filed a prolific number of lawsuits, speculative to a various degree, and sought to maintain them all in parallel, at the same time. He sued Russian TV and Vladimir Terlyuk for claiming that he killed Litvinenko; 18 different relatives and descendants of Arkady Patarkatsishvili for a half of his estate (which was already subject to intense litigation among all of those parties); Russian businessman Vasily Anisimov for $500 million that he allegedly owed BAB; and Roman Abramovich, the owner of Chelsea FC, of whom Berezovsky modestly demanded over £5 billion.

As this went on, Berezovsky also became a Respondent in a few cases himself, including a demand for divorce by his second ex-wife, Galina Besharova, and demands by *Aeroflot – Russian Airlines* (from whom, as per Russian court findings, Berezovsky embezzled money). Later, BAB also tried to sue his former

---

24 As claimed by Abramovich in a witness statement in Berezovsky v. Abramovich.

manager Eugene Ioffe and Ioffe's firm, Salford Capital Partners, for various proceeds from alleged business interests. BAB's common law wife, Elena Gorbunova, joined the litigation scene in 2012. Overall, there was *a lot* of litigation.

BAB achieved courtroom victory only once in all this flurry – he was awarded £150,000 in his suit against Russian TV and Terlyuk, because Russian TV withdrew from the case and refused to defend itself, and Terlyuk, understandably, could not prove that BAB killed Litvinenko.

After making a protracted media spectacle of his case against Abramovich, in which Berezovsky would lose the last shreds of his credibility and be labeled a liar (not in so many words) by the judge, BAB would eventually obtain nominal settlements from Anisimov, Salford Capital Partners and the Patarkatsishvili family, in exchange for dropping the cases against them. Meanwhile, *VGTRK Rossiya* went AWOL, Terlyuk was judgment-proof, the ex-wife settled for £200 million which BAB did not have, *Aeroflot* obtained an enforceable judgment against him, Abramovich was awarded tens of millions of pounds in court costs to be paid by BAB, and HMRC realized, at that point, that BAB underpaid it tens of millions of pounds as well. Boris Berezovsky's last crusade failed more spectacularly than anything else he had previously failed at: his outgoings from all this litigation greatly exceeded his incomings.

Berezovsky v. Abramovich went on for years, culminating in several weeks of hearings from October 2011 to January 2012 and, in August of 2012, a 500+ page judgment in favor of Abramovich. The case attracted unprecedented media attention, partly by its virtue of being the highest value legal claim in history of English jurisprudence, partly because its particulars gave rise to mountains of evidence, and hours of testimony, about business dealings in 1990s Russia. Much of it came across as spectacularly bizarre, and the overall effect was, without a doubt, enormous damage to the image of Russia, and the Russian-speaking community in England. Having made so much effort to appear relatively modern and enlightened, we were now suddenly relegated, in the minds of our British interlocutors, back to the age of vodka and bears.

The world in which millions of dollars were moved in cash, nothing was ever written down, disputes settled based on "understanding", Presidents and Prime Ministers were picked at random, unthinkable sums were paid for

104

"protection", Chechen warlords settled disputes which *understanding* did not resolve, and everyone around was dearly afraid for their lives, was laid bare. The differences between *understanding,* oral contracts, and the honor system were debated by academics. Multiple billionaires testified as witnesses.

All of this was interlaced with matters related to glossy investment prospectuses issued by Western banks, and, at one point, the judge was very involved in a dispute as to which airport closest to Cap d'Antibes had a runway long enough to land a jet in the year 2000. On another day, she delved deep into different instances of Berezovsky's purported hostage rescues during the war in Chechnya (the judge found, coincidentally, that Berezovsky lied in his 2003 asylum claim about rescuing specific British hostages, who were, in fact, rescued by Patarkatsishvili, pursuant to a ransom paid by Abramovich).

One could not write a soap opera like this, if they tried. I am sure it was all very interesting – unless, of course, it was written about you. Berezovsky reportedly enjoyed *Oligarch – the movie*, but the rest of us didn't enjoy his fan fiction sequel to it. All of the Russians who had been active in business or politics in the 1990s, felt like we were escaped animals from the zoo, who had managed to live for years in disguise among humans, but were just found out. Any progress as to acceptance of Russians in polite society was set back, broadly, by about 10 years. Many asked: could it all have been avoided?

Berezovsky's main claim was, by its own logic, self-defeating. He claimed that, upon fleeing Russia under threat of prosecution, he accepted the aforementioned sum of $1.6 billion from Abramovich as settlement for his, Berezovsky's, alleged interests in companies that Abramovich owned. Now, with the passage of time and upon running out of those funds, he realized that his purported interests must have been worth more, so he now wanted more money. You should all try this with the last person to whom you sold a used car, and see how well that goes.

The claim sounds familiar to you now, because it is, essentially, the same claim that Berezovsky advanced against the estate of Patarkatsishvili. In both cases BAB claimed that he was the beneficial owner, broadly, of half of whatever the respondents owned. He did not advance any proof, and constantly changed his story. In the Abramovich case, Berezovsky claimed that he had previously accepted $1.6 billion under duress; however, at the relevant time he was already in England, and it is not clear what sort of duress he could have been under.

Abramovich defended the case valiantly, including a week of daily grueling testimony in person. His position was that Berezovsky had not had any interests in any of the businesses as claimed, and the $1.6 billion was protection money, paid as a settlement to sever the relationship between the two. The judge accepted the defense in full.

Would it have been more reasonable for Abramovich, once again, to settle with Berezovsky in this case, rather than to subject himself, and the Russian community, to all this humiliation? I heard that question asked many times, but I understand why Abramovich did not settle. Firstly, Berezovsky, by virtue of his very claim on its face, proved himself to not be a reliable party to any settlement – that he would not be back for even more, could not be taken for granted. Secondly, and most importantly, Berezovsky could no longer be trusted with money.

Whatever money Abramovich had previously paid him, Berezovsky used to permanently destabilize several ex-Soviet states with anti-Russian revolutions, start a years-long anti-Russian nationalist movement in Ukraine, and fund everyone in Russia who committed to violent overthrow of its government. What would he do, if he had more funds? At the time the case moved toward trial, Berezovsky had already had the opportunity to notice the phantom menace of the ascendant Alexey Navalny and declare him a genius. We all know where that money would have gone.

It is admirable, in the end, that Abramovich did not seek to buy himself out of the embarrassment of this trial – he must have understood, that by doing so, he would be inadvertently funding the very same Russian Revolution, the prospect of which once unnerved Jack Straw. Berezovsky's ambitions to violently destabilize Russia could only have been put to an end by defeating him. For that, we are all indebted to Roman Abramovich. Essentially, he took one for the team.

In the end, this was the case not of Berezovsky v. Abramovich, but of old v. new, of past v. future – for all of us, collectively, as Russians. Do we dwell in the 1990s, or do we finally move on? We thought we had already moved on: but then Berezovsky, like the ghost of Rasputin in one old Disney cartoon, gained his last strength and tried to drag us into the abyss with him.

For those of us who remember the past, there is sad irony in BAB's last crusade. Boris Berezovsky sought redress, according to his own case, on the

106

basis of an unspoken "understanding" – but by doing it in the first place, in the manner in which he did, he violated the basic core principles of any such "understanding" to the point that, at a minimum, undermined his ability to seek redress based on it.

As to the British legal system, from its standpoint his story was merely bizarre, even if fascinating. There was never anything to gain for BAB. He most certainly knew that – for even as he descended into madness, Boris Berezovsky was still a relatively smart man (and one that must have been so advised by others as well). The only possible explanation for his actions, therefore, was that he aimed precisely for the result that they achieved: to discredit Russia and bring the Russian-speaking community in the UK into disrepute. That is what Russians do not forgive.

The psychopath
Berezovsky is usually labeled "weird", "frenetic", "mad", "eccentric" by the Western media. All of those things, he was. My own ultimate conclusion, however, is that Berezovsky was a classic sociopath. The Judaeo-Christian moral principles that ultimately guide all of us – be it Vladimir Putin, me, or all of you – were imperceptible to this man. Boris Berezovsky lived and died only by his ego. Despite considerable wealth, he was never benevolent – not any more than was necessary to manipulate people whose complacency he required. There is no evidence that Berezovsky was capable of empathy – I would be shocked if he has ever so much as rescued a kitten, and he certainly did not house the homeless, feed the hungry, or build hospitals.

Boris Berezovsky was obsessed with neverending disruption of a status quo, whatever it was. He strove on strife, chaos and destruction. Once we accept that this man was a classic psychopath, it is easy to also accept that he was capable of all manner of unspeakable evil that seemed to occur around him. Your conspiratorial basement then becomes a citadel of sanity. You notice that, even as Boris Berezovsky said "goodbye" to – but never really left – Russia, it was mostly people connected to him in some way, that continued to be notoriously murdered there. For example, when politician Sergey Yushenkov was shot in Moscow in 2003, the official theory of the crime amounted, broadly, to a disagreement with a colleague over control of the funds provided to their party by its donor – Boris Berezovsky.

107

Anna Politkovskaya, a U.S.-born journalist crusader against the war in Chechnya, who was shot in her apartment building in Moscow in 2006, openly detested Berezovsky, and once blamed him for starting, and fanning the flames of, that war, face-to-face during a live broadcast on NTV. She also called him a con man and a liar. Politkovskaya held Berezovsky responsible for the Chechen war, which started in the 1990s, at least as much, if not more, than she blamed Putin for any of it. Politkovskaya somewhat warmed up to BAB when he was in London and funding the opposition, but there was no love lost between them. The list goes on.

The point is not to claim that Berezovsky killed everyone Russian in the span of 20 years, whose murder is unsolved. I don't claim that – I think, in all likelihood, that all of these people died for different reasons, and those reasons often would have been more mundane than we think. My point is, every death which the Western Russophobia traditionally pins on Vladimir Putin, or "the Russian state", may just as well have been ordered by Boris Berezovsky, and it fits. In many of them, he would have had the motive, the means, and the opportunity, and actually benefited from the outcome. If you are inclined to see a conspiracy behind it all, and are looking for a single villain to suit it, Boris Berezovsky is as likely your villain, as anyone. Many Russians believe it.

One could – and many of Berezovsky's zombified adepts still do – claim that it was the faceless Russian state that killed everyone in Berezovsky's life. They point out that the victims were, at the time of their deaths, in league with him, or on his side, *ish*. It would seem that, in many cases, he stood to gain nothing, but had everything to lose, from their demise. But that, of course, would be exactly the point.

The day he either did, or did not, decide to blow up the residential buildings in Moscow in September of 1999, Boris Berezovsky invented *political martyrdom* in Russia. People had to die so that their death could be blamed on someone else, and that someone can be vilified for it. The earlier of his alleged questionable deeds were penned on the Chechens, who, conceivably, could have been simply contracted to execute them, given Berezovsky's extensive and well publicized connections in the Chechen community [25]. When that became

---

25 BAB was friendly with several separatist leaders and had been rumored to have financed them, in order to prolong the Chechen war. This was, in part, the point Politkovskaya advanced against

inconvenient – and, certainly, once the war in Chechnya was principally over – a new narrative of blame took hold, in which the nameless *Russian intelligence services*, or FSB, were blamed for executions that continued to occur. Either way, people who died, whether in Moscow or in London, became martyrs for Berezovsky's crusade of the day.

Since he was himself disloyal to a fault, Berezovsky did not understand, nor value, the loyalty of others. I am inclined to think that Alexander Litvinenko died because he was a security services agent who signed up with a foreign intelligence service: a crime punishable, by any state's standards, in only one way. Yet, retribution curiously caught up with him, just as The Independent points out, at the precise moment when the UK government started to look into revoking Berezovsky's asylum, of which Litvinenko held potentially damaging details. I have seen how immigration matters turn even non-psychopaths into animals; to BAB, his refugee status was central to his *raison d'etre* of a decade. A decade of Litvinenko's loyalty would mean absolutely nothing by comparison. In the end, the 2015 inquest into the 2006 Litvinenko murder made one thing perfectly clear: his eventual death warrant was pre-ordained on the day Litvinenko, as an FSB officer in Moscow, arrived to investigate the 1994 assassination attempt on Berezovsky, and thus entered the latter's web of lies.

As many psychopaths, Boris Berezovsky was a brilliant man. He was smarter than most, and could, in his prime, see endless combinations and possibilities across the event horizon from any single point in time. This bred limitless arrogance. He clearly thought that, by the strength of his intellect alone, he could fool, manipulate and subjugate everyone in his path – low level car-selling mafia, gang leaders on the outskirts of the early 1990s Moscow, Chechen tribe leaders and warlords, a string of enablers and business associates, a succession of elected presidents of one of the largest countries on Earth, 21st century British judges, or women that loved him and bore his children. In many of these entanglements, Berezovsky was in way over his head. His raw intelligence did not translate into emotional intelligence: while he always

---

him. He also made a point of swooping in to effortlessly rescue Russian and Western hostages taken in Chechnya, on more than one occasion, in the late 1990s - although an English judge, as we know, found that he exaggerated his role in some of those rescues.

overestimated himself, he was very bad at reading people, misunderstood their motives and underestimated their convictions. In his wake, lay a trail of destruction in which we all still dwell.

The philanderer

Before Berezovsky's posthumous cheerleaders condemn me, I would like to suggest another measure of the man. I am prone to read BAILII (the British court decision database) in my spare time. As a mother of three young women, I think that the British press, mesmerized with the drama of *Berezovsky v. Abramovich* and *Berezovsky v. VGTRK Rossiya*, had been reading the wrong cases. They should read *Gorbunova v Berezovsky et al*, or *Gorbunova v. the Estate of Berezovsky*, instead. Russian tabloid press is misogynistic, and the ex-oligarch's treatment of his women and children never caused outrage back home, but emigre defenders of Berezovsky's sainthood, such as American dissident Alex Goldfarb, better have a good explanation for the horrid tale that these cases tell.

I do not wish to pass moral judgment on other people's relationships, but the way Elena Gorbunova, and the two minor children she had with Berezovsky, were treated in a legal, financial and fiduciary sense is appalling. Having been by his side for 20 years, Gorbunova had been repeatedly duped by Berezovsky into believing all sorts of falsehoods, including his staging a marriage to her in 1999 that had later turned out to be a fake, because he was still (and remained until 2011) married to his second wife. Can a man – especially a rich and powerful man, as he was in 1999 – be so genuinely mistaken as to whether or not he is still married? I do not think so.

In the last years of his life, Gorbunova – a mother to his two then-teenage children – was duped into signing away all of the rights to the family home that was worth circa £40 million and which she, technically, owned. BAB, who, as we remember, was involved in numerous major court cases simultaneously, promised her proceeds from the litigation, which, he assured her, he would win. He eventually sold the estate altogether to fund his legal costs, and, again, persuaded her to sign off on that. He executed – with the complacency of his lawyers, who, at no point, suggested that she get any legal advice about any of it – clearly meaningless promises and unenforceable agreements in order to do so, which, on their face, had no prospect of ever holding up in court (and the evidence is on record that he had been so advised, and she was not).

In other words, Berezovsky knowingly swindled Gorbunova out of everything she had as means of security for herself and the children, and essentially held her hostage in order to elicit her ostensible support, and testimony on his behalf, in his litigation against Roman Abramovich. It transpired later in *Gorbunova v. Berezovsky*, that the relationship between the two had been over by mid-2011, and she only showed up in court and testified for him in *Berezovsky v. Abramovich*, because she was duped into believing not only that the litigation had a glorious prospect of success – which it clearly did not – but that she was to make money from it[26].

It was only when the estate was sold in 2012 and she did not see any proceeds at all that Gorbunova realized things were worse than she had thought; when the verdict in Berezovsky v. Abramovich came down, she saw that she was deceived, and, probably, that Berezovsky was mad. Having been called by the judge in the verdict, essentially, an unreliable liar, BAB had been forced to hastily settle his ongoing case against the descendants of Arkady Patarkatsishvili, and accept a much lower sum that he had previously hoped for. He told Gorbunova that he was agreeing to a lesser sum because it was somehow going to enable him to return to Russia, and chart his way back to prosperity. Again, she believed him.

By the time Berezovsky managed to settle another concurrent case against Vasily Anisimov in October, Gorbunova filed a lawsuit seeking to recover what BAB had pilfered from her, as well as a share of litigation settlement proceeds under the agreements, which no one had told her were unenforceable. Gorbunova succeeded in freezing some of his remaining assets, but did not otherwise progress far enough before Berezovsky died the next spring. Upon his death, it came to light that he had also secured the divorce settlement with his second wife on the future proceeds from the same (as of then not yet reached) litigation settlements.

---

26 A number of Berezovsky's witnesses were forced to admit in open court that he had promised them proceeds from winnings. This was as unthinkable to the judge as it was, apparently, normal to Berezovsky. It remained unclear whether he understood that it was wrong to bribe witnesses, yet the finding itself, most certainly, doomed the prospects of all his other then-pending cases, to any extent that those prospects hadn't yet been doomed by the finding that Berezovsky was a liar himself.

He had been disgraced and defeated. But it was when he was finally abandoned by the woman to whom he had lied for 20 years, and from whom, along with their minor children, he stole, that Berezovsky contemplated suicide. I doubt that he felt empathy or remorse. Perhaps his intellect had finally forced him to see the depth of his madness, and madness that clouded judgment was one thing that he could not bear.

In contemplation of suicide, Boris Berezovsky remained true only to his vanity. He made peace not with his women and children, but with Forbes magazine. In a stunning publication that appeared online on the day of Berezovsky's death, the magazine's Russian edition contributor Ilya Zhegulev recounts his "off the record" meeting with BAB in a London hotel the day before. In it, the disgraced tycoon confided in the astounded reporter that he had overestimated the West, and realized that his ideas about the future of Russia were impractical. He opined that Mikhail Khodorkovsky, who stayed in Russia and served time in jail, remained true to himself – implying, but not quite saying, that he, Berezovsky, had not. He wanted nothing more, he said, than to return to Russia – but did not elaborate as to what (except, perhaps, lack of travel money) kept him from getting on the plane. "I am 67 years old", – he said. "And I have no idea what to do next". Next morning, he hanged himself.

Just days before he voluntarily joined the line of political martyrs into which he, conceivably, may have forced countless others, BAB, according to the Court in *Gorbunova v. the Estate of Berezovsky*, amended his will. Trying to adjust the way history would see him, Berezovsky attempted to leave whatever he still owned to Gorbunova and the children (it is rather telling that, until March 2013, the will apparently did not provide for them, even though Gorbunova's children with Berezovsky turned 16 and 17 that year). It was too late – there was nothing left but debt. Out of several people that were named in Berezovsky's will as executors, only his daughter by first marriage, Ekaterina, stepped forward for the role. The court refused her request, except as to care for the decedent's gravesite and personal effects. The judge ruled that professional receivership was preferable, because the estate was insolvent.

The assets that had been previously frozen pursuant to Gorbunova's suit seeking redress from the still living Berezovsky, were eventually allowed to be sold in an attempt to satisfy his debts, which, according to the receivers-executors, ran into hundreds of millions of British pounds. Berezovsky's second wife Galina, who separated from Berezovsky in 1993 but obtained a divorce settlement from him only in 2011 (when her own daughter with Berezovsky was 19 years old), was among the creditors.

BAB had been effectively homeless after being asked by Gorbunova, in 2012, to move out of their family home (the one that he mortgaged twice to raise money for litigation costs and later sold). Berezovsky had been staying in Galina's house as a guest, and killed himself there. She was the one who identified the body. Elena Gorbunova had not obtained any judgments in her favor while Berezovsky lived. She and the children were left with nothing. The estate remains insolvent even as to obligations to creditors, and there was never going to be anything left in it to distribute under the will.

The England from which Boris Berezovsky took the easy way out in March 2013 was not the same England where he arrived some 12 years earlier. Vladimir Putin, who oversaw the resurgence of Russia as an economic and geopolitical power, had already been demonized by those who, once again, feared it. The Russians were no longer amusing, we were scary. The vicious and unfounded persecution of parliamentary aide Ekaterina Zatuliveter – the first disturbing sign that the only immigrant the West was now willing to accept was a taxi driver and a home care worker, but not someone who would take interest in public life and politics – already had taken place. The tormented ex-tycoon had only to wait months for the Ukrainian *euromaidan,* and the extraordinary resurgence of Russophobia to Cold War levels that followed it.

Yet, both the current war in Ukraine (including the Crimea conundrum) and the resurgent Russophobia in British politics, are the fruits of Berezovsky's labor. Without the *Orange Revolution* of 2004 in Ukraine, which he substantially funded and actively helped organize, Ukraine would not have set out on the path of nationalist *revanche*, and there would ultimately be no *euromaidan* in 2013, no annexation of Crimea by Russia in 2014, no war in Eastern Ukraine, and no sanctions. In all likelihood, Russians and Ukrainians would have remained, as they always have been, one people. Imagine!

The Russophobia resurgence itself was precipitated by the success of modern Russia to a larger extent than by the efforts of its detractors. Berezovsky's very public madness, vexatious litigation incessantly covered by the media, lack of discipline in private life and endless lying, with which he

113

substantially undermined British institutions (including the immigration system and the courts, on which he simultaneously sought to rely), did not help. All of this, at its baseline, did not paint a very sympathetic picture of Russians, just as everyone was already back to being afraid of us. Once again, all of this made us look *immoral*, and our intrinsic value as human beings easy to dismiss.

Berezovsky's departure ended the 1990s in Russia, but he had brought them with him to London, replete with unexplained deaths, irresponsible personal behavior and shady dealings. He continued to tell tall tales of olden times, like your crazy grandpa at Christmas dinner – except that he told them to courts and reporters, most of whom knew better, but still considered his claims and wrote the stories. He publicly aired the antics and grievances of the era that everyone else had otherwise happily managed to move on from. For every step forward that the Russian-speaking community took in the UK, Berezovsky pulled it two steps back.

Just as George Soros predicted, BAB never made *the transition to legitimacy,* and made every effort to drag the collective perception of Russians back into the 1990s with him. Berezovsky, although Jewish, was an Orthodox Christian. I do not believe in hell; but *just in case,* if he is in it, I am not sorry.

114

Ode to Moscow

It was the summer of 2013, and American whistleblower fugitive Edward Snowden had been camping out in the transit zone at Moscow Sheremetyevo airport for days on end. The U.S. authorities canceled his passport. He made it known that he wanted a passage to Ecuador – which, at the time, was providing shelter to Wikileaks founder Julian Assange in their Embassy in London. The plane belonging to Bolivian President Evo Morales, on his way from Moscow, had been forced to land by the European authorities so that they could search for the suspected stowaway on board. It was clear that Snowden was in Moscow to stay – to everyone except himself. He applied, unsuccessfully, for asylum in almost every country on Earth, but not the one that he was already in.

Scores of journalists and high-profile Russian attorneys bought tickets for flights they had no intention of taking, in order to make it into the airside zone of the terminal and offer Snowden their services connected to applying for asylum in Russia, or ask him why won't he. Yet, days went by before Snowden emerged, with what seemed like the most reluctance that anyone ever had about entering Russia. "What's so wrong with Russia, that the man needs time to pick it over Guantanamo Bay?" – fumed millions of Snowden's future new compatriots, most of whom, it goes without saying, would rather die than go live in Ecuador[27].

Snowden is lucky that the U.S. canceled his passport while he was en route from Hong Kong to Sheremetyevo. He probably *would* die if he went to Ecuador at that time, or, at least, he would definitely be somewhere much like Guantanamo Bay by now. The politics in Ecuador changed a lot since 2013; Assange was thrown out of the Embassy in London, and barely survived an extradition attempt to the U.S. Thankfully though, Edward Snowden ended up staying in Moscow, and in 2020 he shared the joyful news on Twitter: a son had been born to him and his wife, Lindsay Mills. In the tweet that followed, Snowden announced their decision to apply for Russian citizenship[28].

---

27 In his book, Permanent Record, Snowden makes light of the big question, explaining that he had only managed to determine the course of action once one of the attorney-suitors, Anatoly Kucherena, had the common sense to buy a second useless plane ticket, for an interpreter.

28 In legal terms, this is a sound decision: while Russia enjoyed notorious continuity of government in recent years, things could change there. Asylum decisions are subject to revocation; yet, the cherished Article 61 of the Russian Constitution, by now an almost unique provision of its kind anywhere in the world, forbids extradition of its citizens, in any circumstances.

In 2018, on the fifth anniversary of his asylum, Snowden discussed his life in Russia with The Guardian, and finally shed light on the big question: why did it take him so long to make a decision to stay there? The answer stunned me. Snowden explained that he simply had no idea what Russia was like. In The Guardian, he speaks with almost childish excitement on how surprised he was to discover that the infrastructure in Moscow was the same as in major Western cities, and that the same fast-food chains and stores were available, as there are in the United States[29].

Apparently, until the day he finally left *the terminal*, Edward Snowden had genuinely thought that Ecuador would be a more comfortable, Western-like and convenient, place to live for an American. Honestly, he did. And that man was an analyst at the CIA. What hope is there for average Americans, then?! What do they know about Russia? This is not a rhetoric question.

It was May 2003 in California, and I had just told my 9-year-old daughter that we will be going back to Russia to spend some time there. Darya was born in Moscow but grew up in the United States since she was 2 years old. She spoke not a word of Russian and had no idea what the place was like. Well, she had some idea, and that is why the news made her cry. My daughter was scared. Her only idea of Russia came entirely from news reports on American TV, and the only footage in those reports was of the war in Chechnya. Although technically Chechnya was part of Russia (its attempts to gain independence having been the subject of the said war) it was, of course, thousands of kilometers from Moscow, and even today, along with most Muscovites, I am not 100% sure, to be honest, where exactly is it.

When my scared child related to me that she was afraid to go back to our hometown because there was a war, I realized that, indeed, nothing except rubble and tanks was ever shown on American television, that was labeled "Russia". It took me a while to convince her that there was definitely not going to be a war in Moscow. I did not have a lot of credibility – the child knew full well that I hadn't

---

29 Snowden noted the exception of Taco Bell, and I am with him there: it's a known problem, and I think it is owing generally to low popularity of Mexican food in Russia. So it is, that this is now the man's sole enduring punishment for his whistleblowing crusade against the most powerful state on Earth: no more *tex mex*.

been to Russia myself since 1996. I had to get Grandma – my mother, who was about to take up a post at the Russian State TV after years of languishing in opposition – on the line to confirm.

My then-boyfriend and future ex-husband, who was traveling with us, was born and raised in New Zealand and had lived most of his adult life, up to that point, in the United States. He knew that the war in Chechnya wasn't happening in Moscow, but the variety of sources by which he was informed about Russia were also haphazard and partly Soviet-era: his expectations were of a somewhat third world country. The reality struck all three of us in a way we did not expect: the Moscow in which we arrived in the summer of 2003 was a much more comfortable, livable place than the America that we left behind. Not because it was the place I grew up in, but because it wasn't.

Having left behind a grim, derelict and unsafe post-Soviet city in 1996, just seven years later I arrived in a sparkling, clean and safe modern metropolis, with large shopping malls containing all of the familiar Western store and cafe chains, and violent crime rates similar to those of both London and New York City. Having taken a flight from John F. Kennedy airport in New York to Sheremetyevo in Moscow, we did not descend into the dusty grind of the third world – instead, we took a leap into stunning relative modernity.

Supermarkets and cafes were open 24 hours, public transport was clean and bright and ran on time, use of mobile networks, and sophistication of such use, considering the sort of devices widely available and the range of technology used by residents, was way ahead of that seen in the U.S.; low cost private medicine was ubiquitously accessible, and all bank ATMs accepted cash deposits in real time and performed numerous other functions, which was unheard of in the U.S. at that same time.

I had trouble finding the building in which I had lived for the first 21 years of my life. Surrounded by numerous new 20+ story high-rises and a re-planned neighborhood, its weathered 1968-construction 9-story frame stood as a sad-looking anachronism. Old municipally-owned buildings had been covered by colorful new decorative panels or repainted, to make them blend in with newness around them; residents in ours, it being a co-op run by grumpy pensioners, could not agree on anything among themselves, so it was left as it were.

That was 18 years ago; now, in 2021, that city is gone, too. Today's Queens, New York, into which you are thrust once you deplane at JFK airport, is

117

exactly the same as it had been 10 years ago, or 20 years ago. New York City overall, in which I spent 7 years of my life living or working (at different times over the years), looks and feels the same as it ever was in my memory since I first arrived there in 1996[30]. London, which I had first visited in 1991, is somewhat modernized from 30 years ago, but remained exactly the same in the last 13 years since our family moved to England. The pace of change in Moscow, meanwhile, has been tremendous. It is not only a completely different city from that which I left in the mid-1990s; it is also completely different from its 2003 self, and, to be frank, from itself even 10 years ago, when its most recent (at the time of writing) mayor took office.

Overall, crime rates in these three cities remained relatively at par throughout the naughts. As it had been before the Rudolph Giuliani mayoralty once, and as it stands once again in 2021, New York City is now much more dangerous than Moscow; London, even though its population has no guns, had slipped behind both, according to data on numbeo.com. As of May 2021, its listed crime index in Moscow is 38.77 and safety index 61.23; in New York, it is 46.96 and 53.04 respectively, followed by London with 52 and 47[31]. Things in Moscow have got much better in recent years, just as things in London have got much worse, and in New York, somewhat worse.

Russia is a safe country in which residents enjoy stability and relative prosperity. It is increasingly more and more so, compared to the United Kingdom, large swaths of which have become bleak, run down and unruly only in the last ten years, and the United States, which is, of course, experiencing unprecedented levels of crime, the downtowns of its large cities having been boarded-up for a while, and shootings of civilians by other civilians up manifold.

The 2021 world crime index for cities features only one Russian city in the top 100, at number 98 – Rostov-on-Don, near the border with Eastern Ukraine. The top 100, meanwhile, features 18 large American cities, including Washington, DC and San Francisco. Of those 18 cities, five are more dangerous

---

30 Not taking into account chaos and dereliction that ensued there in the wake of COVID-19 pandemic and BLM riots.

31 According to numbeo, which calculates its indices itself, "*Crime Index* is an estimation of overall level of crime in a given city or a country. We consider crime levels lower than 20 as very low, crime levels between 20 and 40 as being low, crime levels between 40 and 60 as being moderate, crime levels between 60 and 80 as being high and finally crime levels higher than 80 as being very high."

than Baghdad, Iraq. Memphis, TN, in 17th place out of 100, is only very marginally safer than Kabul, Afghanistan in 12th (and, of course, American soldiers, at the time of writing, are still dying in an ostensible effort to improve conditions in the latter, while residents are shot every day on the streets of the former[32]). British cities of Bradford, Coventry and Manchester all have the dubious honor of being more dangerous than the least safe Russian city (in the case of Bradford, it is also, apparently, less safe than Tripoli, Libya). Moscow today is the safest large city of comparable size in the world, on par with Beijing, and just slightly behind Sydney – a former prison colony of the British Empire.

The important point is that, overall, most Westerners, including politicians – and, as it turns out, even CIA employees – have no idea whatsoever, what Russia is like. All of their ideas, from simple assessments of standards of living to some sort of strategic projections of what Russians will think or do, are based on a complete lack of knowledge and understanding of real Russia. Many have visited at one point in the 1990s and assume that they have seen it (sadly, it includes the hate-spewing founder of Google, Sergey Brin, who still shares the horrors of a 1992 visit, seemingly unaware that this was not today's Russia). The fact is, Russia changes so fast, that you have no idea what it's like unless you visited in the last 10 years[33].

It is well-known around the world, that most Americans and Brits delude themselves into thinking that they reside in what we once admiringly called "shining cities on the hill". The rest of us – citizens of the world – now use the phrase only derisively, but sometimes it seems as if most Americans and Brits are unaware of the change in tone. It is not that those countries never *were the shining cities on the hill* – in some sense, of course, they were, perhaps as late as the mid-1990s.

When I moved to the United States from Russia in 1996, the former was the leader of the world, while the latter lay in ruins. Things have changed very,

---

32 At the time of writing, the Biden administration announced the planned withdrawal of troops by September 2021, but we will believe it when it happens

33 This is true of a number of countries, including, I am told, Venezuela, Cuba and North Korea. Having most recently been to each of them in 2007, 2006 and 2008 respectively, I never undertake judgment on what they are like now, even North Korea, because I know how fast the pace of change can be. At the same time, residents of inert, never changing places such as London or New York, make this mistake every day.

very much – not as much because of the fall of the Soviet Union, but rather because of the Internet and globalization. The same movies, consumer products, shiny cars, fast-food chains, shopping malls, and a global public square, which once were seen as unique features of coveted America, are now ubiquitous not just in Russia, but even in small, obscure places all over the world, such as, for example, Montenegro.

Yet Russia, in many ways, is way ahead of the curve of that change. When I left in 1996, Moscow had one supermarket. Of course, things had to change – so, now they are on every corner, they are all new – having been recently built – modern, with automatic checkouts and such like, and many are open 24 hours. Soviet Union had no banking as such, no plastic cards, and no ATM machines – so when it was time to bring those things to the Russian consumer, the offerings came with the newest available technology, including those video playing 24-hour real-time cash taking ATMs. When change is an urgent imperative, it comes with a vengeance – by stark contrast with "if it ain't broke, don't fix it" attitude in America.

Most of us make fun of American massive gas-powered household dryers that look and run as if they are from the 1970s, but this is a tendency in everything, really. America was once ahead of the curve in technology, and many appliances and innovative pieces of tech first appeared there in the 1960s and 1970s, years before they were available anywhere else. Many of those still *work* since the 1970s, so replacing them with newer innovations has not been an imperative for anyone. Russia, by contrast, is like a country built in the last 30 years from scratch, where the newest tech was used at every point in the process: it was replacing what had been a lack of any consumer tech, instead of slightly older tech that "still worked".

Over the last ten years, a trip to America for most of us had been like a journey in a time machine into the past – even if it was a quaint, beloved past. A rare Russian – or any European – does not have a sad tale of being stuck in the United States without money as late as 2013, when only a handful of places there had the first chip-and-pin reading ATM machines. By then, it's been years since anyone in Europe, or Russia, had used a magnetic strip on their bank card. All Russian and European bank cards had been chip-and-pin, and many had demagnetized or unencoded magnetic strips, a deficiency which their holders had been unaware of until they arrived in the one country where all payment

120

processing was still 100% reliant on them. Even today, in 2021, my UK bank gives me an automatic warning to enable my card to be used with a magnetic strip when it learns that I am in the United States.

A Muscovite's first standard reaction to emerging in midtown Manhattan is to throw up – so strongly it smells of urine. If Moscow smelled like that anywhere at all, ever, I think most of its citizens would immediately emigrate. Moscow never smelled of urine, and certainly doesn't now – firstly, we have restrooms, but second, we don't have homeless people. San Francisco-style homeless encampments, being chased through the boarded-up streets in downtown Sacramento by crazy homeless drug addicts – those scenes, now ubiquitous, belong in an apocalypse movie, and an average Muscovite immediately assumes they have stumbled onto a staging area when they see them.

You can say many things about Moscow's current mayor – and I do – but there are no potholes in Moscow today. Not really. Certainly not the massive tank-size ones, into which half of your car can fall – which are ubiquitous in many U.S. cities. At the time of writing this book, I have driven a lot up and down El Camino Real, the principal thoroughfare in San Mateo county, California, in the heart of Silicon Valley. The roadway, up and down which some of the country's wealthiest residents stumble along in their Teslas, was in such a poor state, that my entire front wheel periodically plunged into massive craters, or the whole car jumped on the dislodged patches. I ended up trying to remember the location of particularly bad ones, so as to get into a habit of driving around them – as I would have done in the early 1990s Russia, during the chaos of post-Soviet transition.

If we had a single pothole like that in Moscow today, let alone at least a couple of San Francisco-style homeless tents somewhere, our mayor would be lynched in the streets; Californians, by contrast, saw the roads in San Francisco and elected its mayor, Gavin Newsom, governor of the state. No wonder the whole state turned into a pothole-ridden homeless camp. But one cannot expect residents of Moscow to fly there for a vacation and take in the sights with a straight face.

In most American cities – and a great many British cities – a Muscovite's first thought is that there must have been a landfill explosion, because of how much trash is in sight. There is no trash in Moscow. I admit that some Muscovites

121

– or, at least, definitely visitors from out of town! – do throw trash on the ground. But we have people in bright orange uniform (mostly illegal migrants from Middle Asia) diligently picking it up, everywhere throughout the city, all the time. Whatever is thrown, is picked up – and where it is clean, people are less likely to throw more (U.S. college students will recognize this as a famous "broken windows theory", which liberals now deride because it was once successfully employed in New York by mayor Rudy Giuliani. Since the theory has been abandoned there, the post-apocalyptic wasteland landscape is taking over again).

The much-maligned current mayor of Moscow had done a lot for the city's beautification, albeit in his own provincial taste. One of his most notorious achievements had been the tiling of all of the sidewalks in the city's central part. The tiles turned out to be slippery when wet. Such is the climate, of course, that they are wet most of the time – and, so, they are not too popular with largely walking and public transport-taking Muscovites. But the tiles look very pretty, and so do public spaces full of decorations, quaint swings and hammocks and lit-up bonsai trees, with thousands of coffee shops, including all of Starbucks, Costa Coffee, Dunkin Donuts and Krispy Creme competing for market share with hundreds of independent and local chain shops.

What strikes a Muscovite most in the West, is that the London Underground is a joke, because of how slow and overburdened it is, and how few trains there are. The New York City subway is disgusting, dirty, dangerous and very, very slow. I swear, I literally have experience outrunning a No. 1 subway train on foot between stations in midtown Manhattan – they recently made the trains slow to a crawl because crazy people keep pushing fellow passengers onto the tracks in front of them.

Moscow, of course, is known for the best subway in the world, since Soviet leaders, and particularly Stalin, considered the architecture of the stations and the artwork in them to be the subject of national pride. The Moscow subway – which is called *the metro* – is bright and spotlessly clean, and trains run as close together as every minute in rush hour. Four minutes was the longest ever I had to wait for any train, and it was late at night. It takes approximately 20 minutes from a terminal point to the center of the city – a distance of about 20 kilometers, on average. You would spend hours traveling the equivalent – 13 miles – on the NYC subway. In fact, it is much faster to drive from the Bronx to Brooklyn, even accounting for traffic, than it is to go by subway.

122

In the last ten years, *the metro* in Moscow has been expanded tremendously, with not just the revamp of payment terminals and turnstiles (you can pay for all city transport by a bank contactless card now, and biometric lanes are now appearing as well) but dozens of new stations, and hundreds of kilometers of new lines dug. Many now go so far into the suburbs, especially in the Southwest of the city, that I have joked that we are planning to invade Ukraine by subway. The express train to Sheremetyevo airport now runs from almost as far West as Minsk.

Suburban overground train stations have all been revamped and included into the Moscow transportation network, with the same payment system. Trains run on average once in 6-8 minutes in all of the suburban overground lines, more frequently than on the infamous District Line on the London Underground. The buses are mostly electric, there are USB chargers, and cheerful videos are played to all passengers on public transport.

Nota bene: I praise progress, but not necessarily the idea of *Greater Moscow* itself. In recent years, the government expanded the administrative boundaries of the city to encompass hundreds of square miles of what was once suburbs, and the reasons behind that were pragmatic. The city of Moscow itself and its surrounding region, *Moskovskaya oblast*, are different administrative regions with different governments. Wages in Moscow proper are much higher than in the rest of the country, and so are the social security and retirement benefits paid to its residents. While the contrast is not nearly as great as it has been in Soviet years, it certainly remains: without doubt, Moscow skews the nationwide statistics on wages and living standards. Moving millions more people into Moscow administratively increases that effect, by allowing millions more to benefit from increased pensions and larger social security payments. Yet it is, of course, a poor substitute for measures that would bring even the adjacent regions up to anywhere near par with the capital. The last, but not least, motive behind the expansion was malicious: it allowed the Moscow city government to move the residents from certain older apartment buildings, that were subject to demolition, as well as those on waiting lists for municipal housing, into the great plains many kilometers outside the *MKAD*.

Moscow is a 24-hour city. At 2 am, you can not only get a coffee, or dinner, in its thousands of cafes, but you can do grocery shopping, or go get an MRI at one of its ubiquitous private medical clinics. That is right, you can have

123

an MRI or a CT scan at 2 am, and, in fact, you can usually get a slot the same day, and there is a discount of up to 30% to do it at night. It means that instead of $100-200, you will be paying $70-$130 for your MRI or CT scan. You don't need a referral.

Russia has free medicine for residents, and the quality of it, at least in Moscow, has gone up significantly in recent years. Private clinics do MRIs and CT scans, as well as ultrasounds, specialist doctor consults, and outpatient procedures, and they are cheap and widely available – you will walk away with a CD of your MRI that you can show to other doctors if you want, something that it is almost impossible to get in most places the U.S., and completely impossible in the UK. State hospitals have private wards that provide the same elective surgery procedures faster and in better environment, and the cost is astonishingly low. I once needed a cholecystectomy, which would take ages to get approved and wait for in the UK – the polyp growing in my gallbladder would have probably malignated, metastasized and killed me in the process, as happens often. In Russia, it was done in a private ward of a public hospital on a 2-week notice, the total cost was less than $1500 and I had my own room.

Immigrants in the United Kingdom, for the most part, are so terrified at the ineptitude of the NHS – its National Health Service, which so many British people seem to be irrationally fond of – that they have gone to enormous lengths only to avoid being treated by the NHS, even though many of them had been forced to pay money for the right to use the NHS during their immigration process[34]. Most of the women immigrants that I know have flown back to Russia, Ukraine or Ends of Earth in order to give birth to their children there, because the state of maternity care on the NHS is so awful.

When a dental bridge, installed in my mouth almost 30 years prior, fell out when I was in California, my reaction was instant: we got to get on the plane. The cost of the best orthodontist in Russia would be at least five times cheaper than the most hapless village dentist in Sacramento, who will treat me like dirt, where I'd have to wait months for each appointment, and to whom, frankly, I do not trust my teeth. It is true: I changed all my plans, and gave up an apartment in California, and spent the following year traveling all the time between England

34 The incredibly poor quality of the services ostensibly provided by the NHS is really the insult added to the injury of the government requiring payments for the right to use it.

and Russia, in order to get my teeth re-done in Moscow, and a few other elective surgeries on the side. Putting up with the awful state of Western medicine and dentistry is something I never learned to do. Most immigrants don't. While the hapless Brits clap on their front lawns for the awful, life-threatening NHS, seeking medical or dental care is the primary reason for most trips back home from the UK, in any diaspora.

This, of course, has limitations. I understand that the highest level of medical knowledge available in the United States and the United Kingdom is superb, and some facilities in large cities are unparalleled. If I had to have a heart transplant or a surgery for aortic dissection, and I could have it done by a top surgeon in Guys and St. Thomas in London, I'd probably prefer that. But in terms of routine procedures or diagnostics available and affordable to an average person in such a time frame that is not endangering their health, Western medicine does not work. If I am a nobody with a sudden-onset appendicitis in the middle of the night far away from the country's best hospital, I'd certainly prefer that to happen in Moscow. At least I'd be taken to a hospital where I would be seen by actual doctors immediately, and they know what appendicitis is (not usually the case in NHS emergency room triage).

The recent COVID pandemic is one more example of Moscow's efficiency. I must preface this by saying that I was, in fact, stuck in Moscow at the start of the COVID pandemic in March 2020, and some of the measures initially implemented by the Russian government irked me. Yet, by the standards of what unfolded in the West later, they were mild and efficient measures – such as, in order to force the pensioners to stay home, the city simply invalidated their (otherwise free) travel passes. At the peak of the scare, police cars drove around the suburban sleeping neighborhoods, yelling at people to go back home through loudspeakers. By the summer of 2020, Moscow was done with the restrictions. The government realized that not too many people were dying from COVID. Except for the rather stupid international travel restrictions, which are a topic for a separate book, the measures were off.

Throughout the fall of 2020 and into spring 2021, when Europe and England went into numerous "lockdowns", everything in Moscow was open – restaurants, bars, shopping malls, skating rinks, cinemas. Life was almost normal. COVID vaccinations were available to everyone without an appointment, and to market them the city opened drop-in vaccination centers in shopping malls. You

125

could get a COVID vaccination while you were walking from the food court to the cinema. In fact, vaccination propaganda went a bit over the top. More than half of all newscasts were devoted to it. Yet, unlike in the U.S., no one was forced to obtain vaccinations – and people who have had COVID itself were strongly advised to check antibody levels before having a vaccination. Instead of reminding you to mind your luggage, public announcements on *Moscow metro* called upon recovered COVID sufferers to donate plasma for treatment of active disease and research. The government paid 5000 roubles – circa USD 66 – for such donations.

By March 2021, all willing adults have had two doses of the vaccine, and up to estimated half of Muscovites have had the disease: COVID rates were falling, but even to the extent that it was still prevalent, everyone simply stopped paying attention to it. When I fled the continuing senseless UK lockdown in February 2021, I arrived in Moscow to a life that had fully returned to normal, and many of my former clients and other expat Russians normally living overseas now congregated on this unlikely island of sanity. I was able to visit Grandpa Georgiy in his retirement home. Residents there had been confined to their rooms – in his case, a mini-apartment – since the start of the pandemic, and visitation was now taking place outside, seeing as COVID was not very transmissible outdoors. In Grandpa Georgiy's retirement home, there had been no extra deaths during the COVID pandemic, as compared to a number of residents that routinely die.

Life in Moscow has moved on. In order to bring municipal services to the people, the city administration started to open its flagship "My Documents" centers in the same shopping malls. In those, a citizen can perform almost all imaginable bureaucratic functions provided by either the city or the state. You can get a new passport, sort out your social security number and state medical coverage, transact with property and do many other things, all in one office. In the one I have been to recently, a creepy human-size robot with facial recognition technology was bugging me to check my temperature, blood pressure and oxygen saturation.

I must admit, at this point, that this is an ode to my hometown of Moscow, specifically. Just like 40 years ago, I still do not have any perspective on life outside the *MKAD*. At the time of writing, I have been to 50 different

126

countries around the world, and only 10 Russian cities outside Moscow (not counting suburban satellites). On both of those criteria I might be slightly ahead and behind, respectively, of an average Muscovite – but the trend would be the same. Russians are very aware of the world and travel around it a lot – more so than around Russia itself. They know a lot about the United States – not some hackers in some secret building somewhere, but all of them.

Headlines from the United States are often at the top of nightly news shows, and voiced over segments of American cable news are often featured[35]. Russia's political talk shows – which it has a lot of – are geopolitical talk shows. At least 50% of the time is usually devoted to affairs in Europe and the United States, and the level of understanding of those affairs is relatively high. It is not only the countries' foreign policy as related to Russia that is discussed, but quite a lot of their domestic issues are covered. Overseas-based analysts and expats are usually featured in those debates. I look on, every time, with enormous envy: after all, I live in countries where even spies do not know that Russia has Starbucks. What can we expect in geopolitics then, except misunderstanding? Russians talk to everyone like adults, and everyone talks to Russians like they are children or savages.

Once you are more than a couple of miles outside of Moscow, you are often a few years into the past, and public transport becomes an irony almost instantly. I am told there are other differences as well. But so there are differences between London and most of rural England – and most Londoners have not the slightest idea of how derelict and destitute much of it is. In fact, most non-Brits do not have that idea, either. In the United States, life in New

---

35 In line with prevailing conservative views, they are mainly Fox News segments, Tucker Carlson being, by far, the most popular host. Carlson segments are sometimes allowed to run for minutes, with mere translation, instead of Russian news hosts bothering to frame the stories themselves. Hannity and other Fox News segments are also occasionally shown. I once saw MSNBC's Ari Melber, but when I unmuted the TV, I realized he was being made fun of in the report. In general, Russian news media understand different political factions and social and political debate in the United States, and attempt to explain to viewers how it unfolds, in great detail. The recent banning of Dr. Seuss books, for example, was widely covered in Russia, even though Russians, unless they lived in the U.S., will have been generally unaware of who Dr. Seuss was, his books (unlike, for example, Shell Silverstein), having never been translated into Russian.

York is not at all like in middle America, and the contrast between excesses and desolation is even starker, because they often exist in close geographic proximity.

In their 2019 book *The Club*, authors Joshua Robinson and Jonathan Clegg reportedly claim that Roman Abramovich remarked in 2003 on Tottenham, in North London, being "worse than Omsk", in Siberia. I have no idea whether the anecdote is true, but if Abramovich did say so, he was certainly right – there are, in fact, many parts of London that are still worse than Omsk today, and even more so, given that large Russian cities were since gentrified much more than London. Many places in the UK are much worse than anywhere in Russia.

I had broadly the same observation to make in 2000 when I decided to go with the children on a touristy boat ride around the island of Manhattan. The poverty and desperation of South Bronx, as could be seen from the boat, was astounding. Tall apartment buildings missing windows, trash piled outside to second-floor level – it was like an abandoned movie set, a part of the city that the government had left to the zombies. There has certainly never been poverty like that anywhere in Russia. Of course, there were, and are, people who are very poor, but, at least, they manage to retain some dignity in their poverty.

When I moved to pre-Katrina New Orleans that same year and was required, by my law school, to ride along with police officers, I not surprised that there were neighborhoods into which they refused to go, even after receiving 911 calls. There certainly wasn't, and isn't, anywhere in Russia where local police would refuse to go. (Chechnya, during the war there, would be an exception).

While most Americans, probably, guess that American cities aren't the most modern in the world, I bet none of them thinks Moscow is doing any better. If asked, most Americans would probably name somewhere in Japan (which, in my view, mostly resembles Indianapolis, Tokyo being the 1990s Manhattan). There is a reason for that: how *would* Americans know what Moscow is like, if no one ever tells them? I realized recently that, in my 25 years in the West, I have almost never – and certainly never since Putin took office – seen an actual street panorama of Moscow on American TV to accompany a news story that involves Russia. Such street panorama that would show ordinary people, stores, Starbucks, shopping malls, the infamous sidewalk tiles, the parks and the squares, the public skating rinks... Most Britons and Americans genuinely do not know what life in Moscow is like because they never see it[36].

---

36 The surprise and delight at not being eaten by bears of the few football fans, who visited for the FIFA 2018 World Cup was a case in point

No one tells them, either. No one even tells the CIA analysts, apparently. No one ever comes out and counters any Russia-bashing nonsense with arguments like – "hold on, this is a modern country with comparable living standards in large cities". When emigre reporter Anna Nemtsov (no relation to the late Boris Nemtsov) wrote in a column in The Daily Beast that "26% of Russians do not have indoor plumbing", no one even bothered to fact check that. This was, of course, a ridiculous and utterly untrue claim, but The Beast never apologized.

That number – 26% – refers to people whose country homes are built on a septic tank, as opposed to being connected to the central sewage pipes. Some of them, needless to say, are very expensive homes with better indoor plumbing than any which Anna Nemtsov has ever seen, or can imagine. The percentage of such homes – around a quarter overall in the country – is broadly the same in Russia and in the United States. The real percentage of people that live without indoor plumbing – which is around 2% – is also similar in both countries. But when someone suggested that Russia was a place where tens of millions of residents relieve themselves in an outhouse, The Daily Beast said – yeah, sure, why not? That figures.

The Daily Beast did not bother to call Anna Nemtsov out on this nonsense because, as far as it was concerned, it chimed with everyone's understanding of what Russia was like: vodka and bears. We, Russians, use this as a joke, but I am starting to think, as of late, that some Americans use it seriously, or at least semi-seriously. When Tucker Carlson – who is enormously popular among Russians – became the only public figure in the United States to suggest, early into *Russiagate*, that the United States was not a part of Russia's strategic interests, he did so by referring to it as a *"cold, vodka-soaked place"*.

Many Russians, although grateful for the intervention, remained sour about the *"cold, vodka-soaked place"* for a while. We think Tucker was joking when he said that, in order to simplify the point; but then, we cannot be absolutely sure. What can we really expect, if even the CIA doesn't know that we have Starbucks and Dunkin Donuts? To suggest that we were too feeble and weak to interfere in the U.S. election was still to suggest that we didn't do it, so – cheers, mate, I guess. But this came down sort of the same as escaping a murder charge with an insanity defense: do not worry, your honor, the defendant was too crazy to know what was going on. A bittersweet victory for those who hadn't actually killed anyone. And, although the United States most certainly is not a part of Russia's strategic interests, and has never been, it is not because we are feeble – it is because we aren't. We will talk about it later in the book.

On a more serious note, you often hear Americans referring to Russia's GDP per capita and its "economic weakness". A leap is then made from GDP to assumptions about standards of living, plumbing, and people's level of satisfaction with their lives – but it is absolutely a wrong leap to make. GDP per capita is not a valid measure of standard of living in Russia in a way as it is in the Western countries, nor is any data about people's salaries or incomes. Western journalists and expats that arrive in Moscow and see $5 lattes being sold, and pay top dollar for a large apartment somewhere in the center, go back and write stories about Moscow being a very expensive city. Those are misleading stories.

One of the huge factors that never figures into any of the Western analysis of the Russian standard of living is, of course, that the overwhelming majority of Russians have zero housing costs. The main reason for this is the post-Soviet privatization, which simply turned people's once-municipal homes into their private property. When prices went up subsequently, in Moscow it was like a housing market in which everyone is given $250,000 free money to start playing with. Many still live in those privatized apartments, and they do not have to pay anything for them. Municipal housing program still continues, and quite a lot of people live in non-privatized municipal apartments, also nearly for free.

There are communal services and utility payments, but they are negligibly small in relation to the median income in Moscow. Those over 65, children under 7, parents of 3 or more children of any age, or parents of a disabled child, enjoy free public transport. But even for those that don't, transport is also quite cheap, the cost per ride being less than a U.S. dollar (42 British pence at the time of writing, 23 for a transfer). Over 90% of the average Muscovite's income is disposable, which, in practice, makes for a standard of living greater than anywhere else in the world. An average Muscovite will not lose their home, or have their lights turned off if they lost their job. They simply won't be able to go buy a latte.

In a recent survey conducted by a private Otkrytie bank, 38% of Russians selected 50,000 to 80,000 RUB a month as a "decent living wage", with 11% selecting amounts under 50,000 RUB, and 28% requiring 80,000 to 120,000 RUR. At the time of the survey, 1 USD was equal to approximately 75 RUB. Less than 10% of Russians nationwide were of opinion that over 200,000

RUB – in other words, more than $2670 a month – was necessary for success. In the United States, of course, this will be what pundits call a "poverty wage" , but applying the U.S. understanding to Russian reality is misleading, even if you had to pay more for a latte in Moscow than in New York.

In a recent publicly aired debate about the true poverty levels in Russia and whether or not the numbers that measure it are being fudged in official statistics, one very wealthy Russian weighed in on the side of skepticism: wages of as much as 80% of the country's population, he said, are below 27,000 RUB a month. Surely this sounds like an obscenely small amount to someone worth billions of dollars, but the reality on the ground is that, in Russia, it is not necessarily a poverty wage. If I had zero housing costs, I could very well live on 27,000 RUB a month, even in Moscow, if I lived alone, and many people live no less than that. Even two people can live comfortably on 27,000 RUB without housing costs. In the regions, prices are lower and the number sounds even less dramatic. At the time of writing 27,000 RUB is about 360 U.S. dollars, but their buying power is times more than the buying power of that same sum in the U.S.

In economics, there is a number referred to as *purchasing power parity (PPP)* – an adjustment in the price of goods and services in U.S. dollar equivalent, that has to be made in order to adequately compare economic data from countries with different local currencies. In 2021, despite one U.S. dollar being worth around 75 Russian roubles, the real purchasing power in Russia is considered to be around 25 roubles per dollar. In simple terms, it means that overall prices for goods and services there are broadly three times lower than prices of the same goods and services in the United States. In other words, I could trade in $100 and buy the same things that it would require $300 to buy in America. This will not apply across the board to everything you could try to buy, for example, imported goods – but it does ring accurate when applied to a minimum set of goods and services that is used to determine poverty levels.

The official poverty line in Russia is around 12,000 roubles a month per person, but it should be viewed by Americans not as $160, but as $480. That is $5760 per year. In the United States in 2021, $12,000 is poverty level for one person living alone, but it is only $26,500 for a family of four, and then $4500 is added for each extra family member. In other words, these numbers are comparable – and they fall favorably on the side of Russia once you consider that the majority of Russians, even those classified as poor, own their homes free and clear, and most of the poor in the United States spend at least half of their income on housing. I could certainly feed myself in Russia on 12,000 roubles a month, if housing, medical care and public transport were free. In reality, most people do not actually live alone, so there is a synergy of wages in two-income and vertical families, where expenses are shared among multiple wage earners. Even a poverty wage is not yet poverty, because, in Russia, you are never quite as alone.

Traditional communitarianism of the Russian culture and multi-generational families play a part. In the new era, many young families no longer want to share homes with the in-laws, and have taken out loans for their own apartments, thereby forming the emerging class of mortgagors – but the mutual multi-generational support is still there. Members of vertical families, even if they do not share the same residence, are much closer and would do much more for each other, than in the West. So would friends and relatives, and, at the end of the day, strangers in the community.

If I did not have money for food in Moscow, I could turn up at the home of any relative or friend, and they would feed me. If I did not have anywhere to sleep, they would house me. The idea that adult children become estranged from parents in the West, and that young mothers in Britain sometimes rely on homelessness support while their parents live in a house somewhere, is alien to Russians. It is us, on this point, who think that something is really wrong with the understanding of our shared Judaeo-Christian values in the West.

The more telling surveys, perhaps, are not those that ask people how much money they make and what they spend it on, but those that ask whether or not people perceive themselves as poor. It is an important political measure – after all, content societies are stable societies. It is also true that people who do not perceive themselves as poor – even if a billionaire thinks that they are – are less motivated to act out of a need to better their circumstances when they do not perceive such a need. At that point, their circumstances might not be defined only by externally perceived lack of economic measures taken for their support, but by lack of action on their own part. According to recent surveys, only around 25% of Russians consider their financial situation to be very difficult.

It is not only the number of homes without plumbing that are similar in the United States and Russia. In fact, most of the criteria designed to compare living standards are similar in Russia and the United States today. In 2017, official numbers in the United States placed some 12.3% of its population into poverty, by American guidelines. In 2021, the Russian statistical office declared – in those very findings that provoked debate – that 12.3 % of Russians live below Russia's declared poverty line. The Gini coefficient of wealth inequality, which measures the size of the gap between the country's richest and its poorest, is almost the same in Russia and the United States (in contrast with Western European countries, where wealth distribution is much more even). The percentage of the country's GDP help by each country's top 1% wealthiest residents is also similar in America and in Russia. The only starkly perceptible differences are the rates of violent crime and incarceration – both of which are much higher in the United States.

I am not calling on all Americans to move to Russia immediately – no one wants them there; I am merely asking them to allow, in their mind, for an understanding that most Russians do not have any incentive to move to America, either. Russia has got problems, no doubt – but it is comfortable enough for most Russians. Russia cannot be properly understood, or engaged with, without a realization that it is not, in fact, a c*old, vodka-soaked place*. It is a country with a decent living standard, which it takes locals much less effort to achieve than a comparably decent living standard in a Western country. Russia has functioning education and free medicine. It has a booming consumer economy and, at least in Moscow, a huge segment of the population with large disposable incomes. Its people are worldly, educated, adventurous – and, as I write this in Moscow, many of them zip back and forth on weird futuristic single-wheel self-propelled devices, the likes of which I have never seen anywhere else. I have no idea what's up with that, but boy, do those things go fast.

Many Brits are open to the idea that life might be at least as good somewhere else – most Americans, by contrast, react defensively to the suggestion that they have something to learn from, instead of to teach, the rest of the world, including Russia. "Why are all these Russians here, then?" – they ask. This is an extension of erroneous thinking. Firstly, not that many Russians are *there*. Not relative to the number of Russians that are fully content in Russia. Secondly, most of us left Russia in the years before it became all of those things that I describe. In my case, in the 1990s, it *was* for the perceived standard of living – I had a 2-year old in a country that had no functioning playgrounds, let alone a Toys'R'Us.

Today, that 2-year old is 27. She is getting married this year, to a fellow Brit. As I was writing this, I stood and watched toddlers play at a gigantic playground in an ordinary "sleeping" neighborhood in Moscow. The play structure was a ship – much like The Princess of Wales playground in London's Hyde Park, except all shiny, new and with fall-resistant mats instead of dirt and sand. I caught myself thinking that I lament, this time around, that my future grandchild will not live in the new, shiny Moscow with its parks, playgrounds, skating rinks and cafes. Nor, of course, will they ever set foot in a Toys 'R'US, which had gone bankrupt.

Emigration is a trap – once you cut ties with a country, once you acquire a different worldview early in life – as happened to me in the United States – you lose touch with your country of origin. You no longer belong. You can see things and judge things, but your place is no longer there. You no longer share your country's aspirations and no longer see your future there. In recent years, the new generation of Global Russians managed to overcome that, but our ship, as the earlier, pre-globalization migrants, has sailed in one direction. So much so, that my newly acquired worldview, for what it was worth – not very much, I now think – destroyed my marriage. The only disagreement between me and my first husband was that he begged me to return to Russia with him, but I wouldn't. How brainwashed must have I been?

Leaving Russia made sense as a young single mother, but I look at my fellow Gen X-ers who haven't, and I know that we would be better off now – and for all these years – if we hadn't, either[37]. Things that it took us years of struggle to achieve in the West, could be taken for granted in Moscow without effort. Today's Russians of my generation and social stratum play leading roles in society and have more opportunities to influence and travel the world. They are all *Global Russians* now, while I am the ghost of ages past. I am of the last generation of emigrants whose exit from Russia was ultimately one-way, but it is a tragedy for my family, not a blessing. There are millions of Russians like me in the United States and the United Kingdom, and we all share this burden.

---

[37] As an immigration lawyer in England, I saw families who would absolutely be better off if they stayed put. In the States, I see them every day, as well. The cruel truth behind emigration is that it almost never makes ultimate sense for majority of the people who undertake it.

On the balance, I came to regret leaving Russia – and I made that conclusion a long time ago. I pondered – and attempted – different plans for a return, but later abandoned them. Could I live in Moscow? I absolutely could, and I do not rule out that, some day, I might. I am forever a Muscovite at heart, even though Russia is not my home anymore. As a foreigner, I am irked by as many things as I like there, and I do not harbor illusions that I fully know or understand this country now, 25 years after leaving it.

Which is not to say that I, as a member of the Russian diaspora abroad, do not share the fate of Russia in terms of rising Russophobia and anti-Russian paranoia. Every day in my British and American life – the life I have lived for 25 years – it is directed at me as well, and lately more and more so. When I gather thoughts to confront it, I find myself thinking more and more like Putin – thinking like Russians think. Like never before, Russia and I are in it together. So, what do Russians think about major issues, trends and events? You are about to find out.

PART TWO. WHAT WE THINK

Democracy

"I'm perplexed: are they going to keep on replacing whoever's in charge?"
King George IV, in Hamilton: the Musical

"We elected a leader today, and also a God of Sun and Rain; a man really needs a God, for, without one, the man is a loser", – goes a recent song by the Russian ska band *Nogu Svelo*[38]. The song, arguably, is a protest against what its authors perceive to be President Putin's personality cult, but it highlights a prominent feature of the Russian psyche – a tendency to want to submit to a sovereign.

When 13 colonies in North America declared Independence from Britain in 1776, it was referred to as "the American experiment", because this is what a representative democracy without a monarch was, at the time. The novelty of it was too much for some of the Founding Fathers. The American Revolution was fought against the idea of being subjugated to the British monarch on another continent, but to say that it was fought for representative democracy would be a leap. At the time, self-governance was understood to be a local government with local priorities in mind, such as - a government *for the people*, but it did not yet mean a government *by the people*.

In his speech at the U.S. Constitutional Convention in 1787, Alexander Hamilton acknowledged that both monarchy and democracy were equally flawed in principle: "Give power to the many and they will oppress the few, give power to the few and they will oppress the many". Hamilton was an unashamed monarchist: "the British government is the best in the world, and we need something like this in America", – he declared. The elitist nature of The House of Lords, Hamilton said, was the guarantee of stability, a "permanent barrier" against both a peasant revolt, such as expressed in the actions of directly elected House of Commons, and the King's extravagant ideas. He reasoned that U.S. Senators should also have lifetime appointments, in order to protect them from popular whim.

---

38 In the original, "Мы сегодня выбрали вождя, и по ходу Бога Солнца и Дождя. Человеку очень нужен Бог, потому что он без Бога – лох".

Hamilton thought that the wealth and power inherited by the King of England, by definition, made him not corruptible, and made sure his own interests in security and stability were indistinguishable from those of the state. The United States needed such a sovereign, too – that was Hamilton's plan. "When naive and weak get to be in charge, it is easy to flatter and manipulate them", – he said. A strong chief executive of the United States, Hamilton insisted, should be also appointed for life.

Needless to say, the soon-to-be Treasury Secretary did not get his way at the Convention. A more populist idea ultimately won, and the U.S. Constitution was written as we know it today. Yet, the rest of the Founding Fathers accepted that checks were necessary on the novel idea of a popular election – that is how we ended up with Electoral College, whose delegates, as late as in the year 2000, were apparently not bound at all by the popular vote in their states when casting their own. The Founding Fathers of the United States did not trust the people very much at all.

The Russians already knew that, of course. 175 years before the U.S. Constitution was written, the last of the Rurik dynasty of Russian tsars died without issue, sparking what Russians call *smytnoe vremya - the murky times.*[39] Russian nobility decided that chaos could only be ended by installing a new monarchical dynasty. Back in those days, mere *lifelong* did not cut it, especially seeing as life expectancy was low. Society, exhausted from 15 years of lawlessness, needed certainty.

The *boyars* – the aristocrats of the time – held an election, in order to select a new monarch from among themselves. It was won by one by one Mikhail Romanov, whose authority to rule on that basis was accepted, more or less, without question. A generation later, peasants just as likely believed that the Romanovs were appointed by God himself to the task. The descendants of *boyarin* Mikhail Romanov would found the city of St. Petersburg, defeat Napoleon, survive the Decembrist uprising, quash the failed Revolution of 1905 and almost win the First World War alongside the Allies, before being deposed by the 1917 Bolshevik Revolution.

Almost 250 years later, representative democracies with a full separation of powers remain rare, Britain not truly being one. Those who follow the

---

39 Usually translated into English as "The Troubles", not to be confused with The Troubles in Ireland.

progress of the American Experiment closely would agree that its results are, so far, inconclusive. Boy, are *naive and the weak* susceptible to flattery and manipulation! Perhaps, even Alexander Hamilton was too charitable to the idea of democracy.

With the world more sophisticated and complex today than it was 250 years ago, enlightenment is even more crucial for governance now, than it was then. You do want wars to only be started by people who have ideally been to one, and to do so on the advice of those who know where foreign countries are. You want central banks run by people who are up to date on macroeconomics, decisions in the system of education made by people who have been to a classroom, and immigration policy made by people who have been to another country. All of this makes sense.

Years ago, when all private real estate transactions in Russia were still conducted in cash U.S. dollars, we sold the house that my mother had built in Nikolina Gora. I called my oldest daughter, 16 at the time, into a room to watch the cash, to the tune of a few hundred thousand dollars, being counted. In her adult life in the UK, she would be constantly getting ostensible financial advice from people who have never had or seen actual cash. Money is a notion to them, not a reality. I wanted her to get a feel for real money. Ultimately, a government by the people is all like that, legislature upon legislature stuffed by eccentrics and lunatics making life and death decisions on subjects they do not understand the scale of, and executives who have never seen a map sending people to die in places the names of which they can't pronounce.

The wisdom of giving power to the people is, so far, unclear. The dilemma is highlighted best by Michael Cane's character in The Quiet American. "You give people the vote, and they will elect Ho Chi Minh", – he says to Brandon Fraser. Holding the popular choice as the highest sacred value in itself, as Americans purport to do, leads to the election of Ho Chi Minh, and Kim Jong Un would most certainly get elected, too. *The people* keep electing Vladimir Putin, and, of course, *the people* also elected Donald Trump. Any member of the British Royal Family, including the embattled Duke of Sussex, would likely be easily elected to rule any day, instead of *any of those useless wankers in Parliament*. I posit that, if elections were held in 2001 in Iraq, Saddam Hussein would have been elected. In 1937, at the height of political repressions to which we refer by his name, Joseph Stalin was elected with 99% of the votes.

You will say – *oh, but surely that would not have been an honest election, and wasn't it Stalin who said that elections were decided by those who count the votes, rather than those who vote?* Trust me, if Stalin did say this, it was a joke. As he well knew, very few would dare vote against him, and manipulation of results would absolutely not be required. Nor was manipulation or results ever required in any of Vladimir Putin's elections – admittedly, some manipulation, usually by local officials eager to distinguish themselves, did occur, but even Putin's most fervent opponents do not dispute that the overwhelming majority of *the people* voted for him each time.

So what is an *honest election* then? Does ballot harvesting count? Mail-in ballots? Brainwashing? Or is it only the one in which plausible results are achieved? The degree of hypocrisy that the Americans exhibited the moment half of them refused to accept the results of the 2016 Presidential election, ostensibly because those who voted in it may have read the wrong sort of Facebook posts, ended any authority they hitherto had in the world as a nation entitled to teach anyone a lesson in democracy.

Yet, the elephant in the room is rarely mentioned: isn't it the main premise of democracy, that voters are capable and competent? Do we not then ascribe to them an ability to take into account all available information and use their own heads when casting votes? Who cares if Putin himself made all those Facebook posts in 2016 – why should they have mattered to anyone with half a sense? And, if your actions as a voter are ultimately determined by exposure to Internet memes written in non-grammatical English, then what is your franchise worth, really?

It just might not be worth very much. In addition to, as Hamilton put it, *naive and weak* proving to be *easy to flatter and manipulate,* relative freedom or enlightenment of the voters does not necessarily produce more palatable results. People who voted for Adolf Hitler were neither oppressed nor enslaved. George Orwell defined them as *perfectly civilized beings:* the presumably informed, Christian voters in a developed, and hitherto democratic, European state. Either those were all dishonest elections too, or we must accept that *the will of the people* is not all that it is ramped up to be.

If we insist that the will of the people, expressed through a vote, is sacrosanct, then why do we not universally abide by it? What, then, of the will of the people of Catalonia, Crimea or Eastern Ukraine? Why is the will of the people equally effective when they vote for Hitler and Biden, and when they choose to form an independent state in Montenegro, but less so when they elect Putin and Trump and choose Brexit? Whether any of these are bad choices or good choices is equally a matter of perspective. That understanding is a logically necessary postulate in democracy-worshipping. If the people, by definition, are always right, then so they are – and if the people are *naive and weak*, then so they also, always, are, and shouldn't then govern.

The idea of representative government by the people, of course, drove the Russian Revolution of 1917. "We will teach every cook how to run the state", Vladimir Lenin famously uttered. The quote was somewhat deliberately misinterpreted over the years. The proverbial cook was believed to think that they were supposedly running the state through electing the lower-level decision-making bodies, *the soviets (soviet* in Russian means *advice or council)*. This interpretation of self-governance was, in fact, exactly the same as the idea behind *the American experiment*. That same proverbial cook runs America today. Lenin, himself being of the elites, just as likely may have meant otherwise: his emphasis was, it seems, on the word *teach*. We were supposed to *teach* the cook about governance first, not just let them run the state directly.

Vladimir Lenin, a son of a school superintendent who himself went to law school, without doubt, would have been familiar with Alexander Hamilton's scholarship, just as he was with that of Karl Marx. The Revolution purported to pitch *the people* against the anachronism of the Romanovs, but there was something to Alexander Hamilton's vision of the learned classes being in charge. In an apparent hope that *the learned* that should rise to the highest level of the *system of the soviets*, Lenin theorized *democratic centralism*, which ultimately enabled what was later seen by Soviet detractors as totalitarianism. Citizens within joked dryly, that democratic centralism was defined as "everyone individually – against, but all collectively – in favor".

It was not before long at all, that the proverbial cook, himself a high school dropout, ascended to the top of the *system of the soviets* instead of *the learned.* Joseph Stalin's power over minds – not just those of the weak and the naive, mind you, but also those like Grandma Clara, with her Masters in History from Moscow State University – came with disastrous incompetence. Enabled by the nonsensical theory of democratic centralism, the cook was running the state now, and *the learned* were running for cover.

Joseph Stalin ran the Soviet Union for 29 years; it had been 17 years by the start of the Second World War. "For Motherland, For Stalin", – was the battle cry of the Soviet people. Had he not been in power for that long, would millions have sacrificed themselves with Stalin's name on their lips? Likely not.[40] Leonid Brezhnev was in power for 18 years, and his time in office had been decried as an artificially prolonged stagnation – but when his successors started dropping like flies, the people became disoriented and confused.

The quick succession of Soviet leaders between 1982 and 1985 was derisively dubbed "the catafalque race", and, without doubt, precipitated the collapse of the USSR. Gorbachev was elected by his peers in the Politburo, in part, because he was young enough to not die any time soon, but the flip side of that turned out to be his itch for reform. At the same time, the country's reality in the years leading up to Gorbachev's reforms was already subject to change too often for comfort. Through our failure to elect a sustainable sovereign, we have become unstable as a society.

How long is too long to be in power, then? At the turn of the 17th century, when *the boyars* elected Mikhail Romanov to govern, people were dying so young that only a pre-determined dynasty would provide any sort of stability. At the time Alexander Hamilton proposed at the U.S. Constitutional convention that the executive be elected *for life*, life expectancy in the developed world, such as it was, was broadly half of what it is today; effectively, it meant that the *executives for life* would serve shorter terms than the Soviet *executives for life* later did in the 20th century. Four-year-long presidential terms, ultimately written into the U.S. Constitution, may have seemed like a long time when life expectancy was 40, but they seem like a maddening kaleidoscope of unnecessarily frequent change of direction now, when near-octogenarians inhabit the White House, and 40 is seen as too young to run for office.

Even if you are uneducated, incompetent, and unprepared for office, you might learn to govern in time. Once foreign countries and their leaders become your reality, you will eventually get a hang of dealing with geopolitics. Once you

---

40 Speaking of names, of course, almost none of the early Soviet leaders used his actual name. Vladimir Lenin's real surname was Ulyanov; Leon Trotsky was actually Lev Bronstein; Joseph, or Iosif, Stalin, who was from Georgia, was actually Iosif Dzhugashvili.

live through one financial crash, you will get better in economics. Once you wage one war, you will learn the value of human life. Upon a certain level of aptitude, knowledge and experience will accrue. But it does not happen if you spend the first half of your four-year term proving that you have really been elected, and the second half - running for re-election.

This reminds me of a conversation I once had with a well-known political consultant in Russia, in whom I confided that all my campaign staff were incompetent idiots and that I wanted to fire them. "The new ones will also be idiots, but without experience", – he replied. Indeed, what is the point of bringing in *new idiots without experience* just as the previous ones started to learn anything at all about their job? Hamilton looked at the British royals, educated directly for governance from childhood, and sought to at least give the sovereign a chance with a lifelong appointment. The more weak and naive *the people* are, the less equipped they are to deal with change.

FDR was President for 12 years before he died. In all likelihood, with Victory in World War II achieved, he would have been re-elected again. It was rather his ill health and death in office from natural causes that prompted the amendment limiting the number of presidential terms. In other ostensibly democratic countries, such limitations do not exist. Tony Blair was Prime Minister for 10 years; at the time of writing, Angela Merkel is in her 17th year as Chancellor of Germany. Vladimir Putin, whose 20th anniversary in office was widely celebrated at the turn of 2020, had actually only been *in office* for 16 of them, making it also his 17th in 2021.

By and large, Russians abhor the 1990s and think of them as another coming of *the murky times,* once seen at the turn of the 17th century. I disagree. Although they brought a lot of trauma to a lot of people, to the country as a whole and its elites the 1990s were not all that bad, really – and, in any event, they were necessary. On this, mine is not a popular opinion. All the while *the learned* thought that the 1990s were a transition to a fully functioning capitalist democracy to come, *the people* saw them as *the troubles*, and, consequently, were ready to crown the next sober guy as the sovereign. For the rest of us, it was just as well that, at least, he was a law school graduate, rather than a cook.

Initially a reluctant ruler, Vladimir Putin today is a hostage of his own personality cult, damned if he stays, and damned if he goes. If the new 1990s were to ensue, he would be blamed for eternity for abandoning the people to experience *the murky times* again. And yet, the longer he lingers, the more his popularity wanes on one hand, and the harder it is to envision an alternative for the masses, among which there are now people who were born and came fully of age during *the Putin era*. With every day now, the orderly transition of power in Russia is simultaneously more of an imperative and less of a realistic possibility. If a referendum was held today to install Putin as a sovereign for life, it would probably be successful – of which the 2020 Constitutional amendments, enabling him to run for further presidential terms yet, were a harbinger, if not a proxy.

Governance *by consent of the people*, as it happens, is not the same as governance *by the people*. Yes, it is likely that we do not have a government by the people in Russia today, and, watching the scenes of devastation all across America – boarded-up downtowns, looted stores, burned down police stations and fast-food restaurants – the Russians think: thank God for that! If that is government by the people, no thank you. They watch the perpetual decadence of "democracy" that the Americans have forced on Ukraine, and they think – oh my God, anything but this! The countries that have avoided a total collapse so far, are the ones that are governed by consent, rather than by the people. Only a few, as it happens, desire power – *bread and circuses* tend to do for the rest.

The United Kingdom is one example, and let Russia be another. A Russian citizen until recently, I never voted for Vladimir Putin (for me, the KGB thing would be a no-go). But Putin always had my *consent* to govern, and, to the extent that my opinion is relevant, continues to have it so far. Stability and continuity were of absolute importance to Russia in the last 20 years, and Putin provided it. He also provided the necessary sense of a sovereign, without which the Russian people seemed to be culturally unable to function. Lack of constant change allowed Russia to grow, modernize and get stronger. The majority of the elites today are not "Putin's people", but those who continue, if only provisionally, to give that consent, for broadly the same reasons. They may choose to one day withdraw their consent – but, with the sanctions and Russiagate, that day is now farther away, rather than closer.

When the West paraded around campaigner Alexey Navalny's video of an expensive piece of real estate in Gelenjik, near Sochi, that had been ostensibly built for Putin, I watched in disbelief. So what?! Not a single person in Russia would be against Putin having that "palace". It isn't even clear that Navalny himself is against that. It's an unfinished estate worth a couple of hundred million

143

U.S. dollars, nothing out of the ordinary for Bell Air and Beverly Hills, and a far cry from any amounts of money involved in the alleged corruption of the Russian state, that the West loves so much to go on about. Where is a longtime leader, revered by millions, supposed to live, once he is out of office? In a hut? Gelenjik is our Martha's Vineyard now. Give him a pardon, all the money, the palace, make the grounds its own country if need be – the location is perfect for that. What's the problem? In viewing the stupid palace video millions of times, the West seems to have missed the original tagline: "the palace" was, ostensibly, intended by the elites for when Putin *leaves office*. The idea being, presumably, that he was on the cusp of doing so. What gave, then?

I do not personally know Putin, but if I were him, I'd have had enough of it all by now, and I must assume that so has he. I can also now, for the first time in a long time, think of people who could run for office and possibly govern without crashing the economy of the whole country, and the world markets in the industries that its capitalists control. But petty agitators in the style of Alexey Navalny, financed by the U.S. Department of State and Western European elites, are not among them. Russia will not be governed by the mob, be it, or not, any part of *the people* – which, at the present, they aren't. But that is a scenario for which neither the majority of the population nor the elites would give their consent. The intensified attempts to destabilize Russia from outside make its elites hold on to any resource of stability that exists within. In such times, a change of the guard, which would be destabilizing by itself, is not an option.

As long as external attempts to instill chaos in Russia, which are viewed domestically as attacks on the Russian sovereignty, continue; as long as we are vilified around the world for everything that goes wrong in the farthest reaches of it; as long as poisonous morons, such as Bill Browder, feed gullible misinformed politicians the false paradigm in which everyone who is not ready to betray Russia is a *Putin's person*, the Russians will rally around the leader they have, such as he is. The attacks on Russia in the West today are not attacks against Putin for the benefit of the people, as they are falsely represented to the Western public to be. They are a new type of war against the Russian people, and Putin has nowhere to go now, for he is their wartime leader. Unlike the USSR before her, Russia is strong enough to insist that it makes a change on its own terms. The attempts to weaken it are not anywhere near bringing that change about, but are rather postponing it indefinitely.

144

Wealth

Before *Russiagate*, Russians haven't really been much discriminated against in the United States. Partly it was because the U.S. society did tend to target, identify, and form groups based on racial characteristics. Russians, being very white, were never really distinguished from other *Caucasians* there. But Russians were also afforded respect because they were thought to have money. And nuclear weapons. But mostly, money. Americans are conditioned to respect money as a measure of achievement and worthiness.

The relationship between Russians and money is peculiar. Both the untold riches of the few, once quickly and unexpectedly gained, and the uniform virginity of the masses on even the most basic aspects of consumer finance and household economics, are products of the same awkwardness that persists in our collective relationship with money. All of us – both the *haves*, and the *nave nots* – grew up all the way into adulthood without a firm concept of money at all. Well, some of us had *a concept* of money. But that was all it was. A notion. One's degree of exposure to money in the Soviet Union varied, but, most certainly, no one was conditioned to love it, respect it, or strive to accumulate it.

An alien who arrives on Earth in today's Russia may decide that Russians detest wealth and those who accumulated it. That would be simplistic. Former Soviet citizens detest *money*, and consider wealth, by extension, to be a curse. When coalesced around a person, wealth marks that person as cursed, with all the implications that it entails: that it cannot have been accumulated by normal people leading ordinary lives prudently; that it is a burden to carry; and that the natural way in which an unfortunate person in such a position should seek to save themselves, should be an immediate distribution of the said wealth for the benefit of everyone around. How did we get here? It's a long story.

The leaders of the Soviet revolution of 1917 needed to equip the masses with a simple test of *us vs. them*. Wealth was such a test – on a very basic level, it was possible to see if someone was wealthy. Redistribution was a huge point of the process. The idea was not to kill the wealthy but to expropriate their property for the benefit of the people. Who, when and how comprised, and represented, *the people*, and then, who decided what exactly constituted *the benefit of the people*, was admittedly in flux – and Orwell captured it aptly in The Animal Farm.

But this is where the idea of toxicity of wealth came from. It would literally be toxic to be wealthy if it made you a target of an angry mob. Much has changed since – but then, not really that much.

It was neat for Orwell to posit that the idea of *some [being] more equal than others* was snuck up on the triumphant Soviet populace as an afterthought, but it seems to me that it was always baked into the cake. Contrary to what many in the United States or England seem to believe, Soviet Russia never claimed to have built communism, and therefore full equality – where everyone contributes based on their ability and receives according to their need – was not the operative principle. The idea of socialism, ostensibly as a stepping stone on the ladder to communism, was that everyone contributes according to their ability, but receives *according to their labor* – i.e. contribution to society.

It only followed then, that revolutionary leaders were more equal than anyone; union leaders were more equal than union members, union members were more equal than non-members, and, eventually, people who made unique, life-sized contributions – wrote the national anthem, became world-famous musicians, made scientific discoveries or became ballet stars – were more equal than others. Privilege variation existed on 100s of different levels, and every new level afforded at least a little more privilege than the lower one.

Due to Uncle Yuri's position in the Communist Party and the Academy of Sciences, and Grandpa Georgiy's rank in the Navy, I experienced that system of privilege close to its upper crust. Yet, the same system distributed privilege of all different kinds in many different ways, to all sorts of people who had managed to maneuver themselves into positions of more importance than others. Soon you found that you simply had to belong to some system of privilege distribution to have any life at all. A proverbial sign that read *"Beer is only for union members"* became a Soviet shorthand for this understanding.

One could argue that it was a false distinction, but the supposed difference between the Soviet system of privilege, and what was seen as filthy riches of the bourgeoisie, was that privilege in the Soviet Union was not transmitted through money. Money was the toxic element that was taken out of the equation. There was, as a result, almost no effective market for the most desirable goods and services – the more desirable something was, the less of a market there was for it.

146

Real property was not bought and sold, it was provided for you to use by the state. The same state that housed millions of people in communal flats, a whole family to a room, housed Grandma Tonya and Uncle Yuri in a two-level apartment in a tower overlooking a river, because the state decided that Uncle Yuri was *more equal than others*. If the state wanted you to have a car, it would either provide you with a car or give you an opportunity to purchase one – but that itself was a privilege; you could not simply walk up with a bag of money and buy a car. There were waiting lists and all sorts of quotas for everything, from housing to cars to furniture. Money was an element in some of these exchanges, once you maneuvered yourself close enough to acquiring the items sought. But there was not a consumer economy, as such – outside of the system of privilege, money by itself was useless, and supply of the more desirable goods and services had absolutely nothing to do with funded demand for them.

This paradigm is described best in two well-known Soviet novels by satirical writers Ilya Ilf and Evgeny Petrov. Theirs was mass-market literature, read by, and familiar to, everyone in the Soviet Union. The novels undertake to popularly explain the brave new world of the economy ostensibly designed for the benefit of the people, as seen through the eyes of one Ostap Bender, admitted swindler and adventurist. Bender sets out to amass wealth in the wake of the Revolution. In the first book, *12 chairs*, he teams up with a former aristocrat, who is now flat broke. The ex-aristocrat's hastily expropriated property, as he had come to realize, included a dining furniture set where diamonds had been hidden in one of the 12 chairs. The chairs had been given away one by one, and the protagonists have to find each chair individually, suffering disappointment in the first 11 cases. The 12th lead takes them to a newly built Palace of Culture, which, they are told, was built with funds from diamonds found in an old chair.

But it is the sequel – *Golden Calf* (a more apt title in English would be "Golden Goose") that epitomizes the world in which Ostap Bender finds himself. The protagonist tracks down an "underground" Soviet millionaire, who is understandably afraid that someone would find out that he is rich, and does his best to masquerade as an ordinary Soviet citizen. Bender takes to successfully blackmailing the poor soul into handing over the coffers, only to find out that the money he thus acquired could not be put to any use at all. With all the cash, he is unable to obtain lodging and even food, to say nothing of status. Bender converts

147

his cash into gold, silver and furs on the "black market", and successfully flees Soviet Russia over the ice of the frozen Finnish Bay, near St. Petersburg – only to be robbed of all of his possessions by border guards on the Finnish side.

The writings of Ilf and Petrov make me think about an elaborate and complicated children's cartoon, such as The Lego Movie or Schreck, where the most sophisticated jokes could only be understood by the parents, but the films are nonetheless wholesomely entertaining from a child's perspective. However many of the layers of irony embedded in *12 chairs* and *Golden Calf* you could absorb, you were bound to respond to their universal appeal on the nominal, censor-proof level, and the message of toxicity of money was hammered into mass consciousness. Money made you miserable, and only hapless swindlers would ever strive to acquire it. Normal people were to obtain happiness through self-fulfillment, by taking up useful positions in society.

My upbringing may sound posh. I ate caviar and filet mignon. I was taught to speak English and Latin, to play violin and guitar, to skate, ski, sail, play tennis and volleyball, to paint and to tell a Manet from a Monet. Yet, I emerged from this bizarre childhood without any concept of money. I wrote earlier in this book, that on my 12th birthday Grandpa Boris gave me a 100-rouble bill "for sweets", and that he didn't seem to realize how much that was. Neither did I. People who grew up posh in the Anglo-Saxon world also grew up without a concept of money, but that was because they did not have to worry about it. Their families simply had enough. I grew up in much the same way, but without any understanding of how goods, services, housing, entertainment or knowledge were gained through or paid for by money – in my case, all of that privilege arrived by entirely different means. We didn't even have any money.

I realize that in the more humble margins of Soviet existence people did have to budget their salaries, use money to buy food, and so forth. Perhaps they understood nothing of capital, economy, the real value of money, business imperatives – all of those things the Soviet economy did not feature. But at least they had an idea of a budget. In Western societies, it is the more enlightened that have more expertise with money, because their enlightenment is a product of wealth. In the USSR, the higher up the ladder of privilege you went, the less connection there was between the lifestyles you encounter and the real value of money. Of course, the *payok* food parcels that my father had to go pick up at

148

certain times in a certain place, had to be paid for – but the price had nothing to do with the value of the items included in them. And while there may have been a real way to measure at least something in society by how much a peasant or a bus driver had to pay for a loaf of bread, a liter of milk, a kilo of *kielbasa*, or a trip on a *metro*, the nominal charge paid for caviar-containing *payok* by members of the Academy of Sciences conveyed no useful information.

Nothing in the Soviet Union was priced based on what we are used to calling *market value*, of course – but things that would be normally more expensive were disconnected from any real-life value much more than cheap, commonly consumed products and services. Often, they did not require payment at all. Privilege disconnected from money by design was not a factor of corruption, but ostensibly a system that rewarded achievement. Unlike the wealth you accumulate as a result of hard work in a capitalist society, much of Soviet privilege was arbitrary by nature, it could be bestowed disproportionally or easily taken away. You were not in control of the things you did or did not get. The fruits of that privilege were partly heritable, with a bit of nepotism thrown in to launch the offspring into lucrative careers. By the third generation, it produced lifestyles nearly as parasitic as the lifestyles of the third generation wealthy in America. Not the entirety of those parasitic lifestyles was *distributed privilege* though; some of it was social capital, and some was simply chutzpah combined with a sense of entitlement.

We had a cocker spaniel (the one my mother acquired in the summer of 1980 in order to replace the void left in her soul by the emigration of writer Vasily Aksenov). My father obtained a gun license and took the dog to special training sessions that teach hunting dogs to raise ducks. It was thought to be good for the dog's emotional balance, because hunting was, supposedly, the call of his nature. The time and opportunity to worry about the emotional balance of a dog on such a profound level was definitely not afforded to my father by money. He was employed at a societally useless job as a junior editor at some social science digest and made less than half of what a bus driver made. Yet, there were no bus drivers in the hunting club – and the proverbial bus driver, who definitely did not eat any caviar for breakfast, probably lived with his parents, along with his own wife and children. I cannot imagine that the hunting club was socially stratified by some rules – it was more so that the idea of belonging to one would only occur to certain people. It is not clear how much bothered about your dog's emotional well-being you are going to be if you sleep in the living room and drive a bus for a living.

Growing up in Nikolina Gora all summers and holidays, I was forced to spent weekends listening to classical music concerts performed for the benefit of the neighbors by fellow residents, such as Russia's most famous musicians of the time, Mikhail Rostropovich and Sviatoslav Richter. It wasn't something you paid for, it was something you did because you had to. Sitting on a lawn chair in front of our perennially dilapidated village club and listening to Rostropovich play was as much of a chore in my childhood, as being forced to attend lectures for young art historians at the cursed Museum of Fine Art. The chore of classical music became even worse when young, up-and-coming musicians took to the dacha stage. The then virtually unknown Yuri Bashmet was particularly persistent, because he didn't have a dacha and was very keen to acquire one. At least Richter and Rostropovich performed classical music, whereas Bashmet in those years was fond of *avant guarde* works by Alfred Schnittke[41].

It only followed that people who spent time in this manner would also torture their children by teaching them to dance the polonaise and forcing them to perform the said dances, all dressed up, in yearly end-of-summer recitals. In Nikolina Gora, we also had our own tennis tournament and volleyball tournament, with former Olympians serving as coaches. Perhaps, some nominal payment was required for all this, but it wasn't the point – in order to participate, you had to had been a local resident, and the privilege of that stemmed from *dachas* themselves being initially distributed by the state to those who made substantial contributions to art and science. You could not buy one back then, nor could you simply show up and take a place, payment or not. It was like a country club membership, in modern understanding – except money could not get you in. By the time my generation came along, you were *born into it – it* being the membership, sans money.

There was the rest of the year, too. My mother did not work, but everyone she knew from school or college did, and they all worked in either a museum or a theater. My mother's best friend from high school married a guy

41 Evidently, there was only so much experimental music anyone in our dacha co-op could take and still pretend to understand it, and so Bashmet eventually got his way. Years later, by the time my mother built her own home in Nikolina Gora at the peak of her television fame, Yuri Bashmet had become the chair of the dacha co-op.

who became the choirmaster of the Bolshoi theater. His name was on the posters. I had no idea how anyone else got into the Bolshoi in the USSR, seeing as Grandpa Georgiy retired from the Navy by then, and could no longer use the assigned seats – but we could always go see operas. There was some kind of quota for participants, or a system of passes, or something, but I remember going to see a few operas at the Bolshoi.[42]

On weekends, I had to go to one of my mother's high school friends' house to take private Latin lessons. Latin was not something taught in the Soviet Union routinely, and the only textbook she could find for me was a tsarist era one, with the extra Russian letters, pre-orthographic reform. If we paid that woman, it could not have been very much. Mainly, she must have just been amused to be passing the knowledge on to someone.

Cross-country skiing was a popular pastime of the masses, and also a compulsory school PE subject. The music school, skating school and sailing school that I attended at various times, were all merit-based programs open to the population. Of course, we lived in Moscow, where all of them existed and were reasonably high quality, I had a stay-at-home mother and a stay-at-home grandmother, both of whom could afford to spend time taking me to these places. But ultimately, those required purely nominal fees and were designed to select and train future talent in music and sports for the benefit of the whole Soviet Union, which the most successful alumni were to, one day, represent. This is probably why I duly flanked out of all of them by the age of 12[43].

Uncle Yuri and Grandma Tonya actually had money – but, like Ostap Bender, they did not know what to do with it. When all of the Soviet citizens' savings were lost in the collapse of its economy, much of us shrugged – who had so much money that it would be kept in a bank?! It then transpired that Grandma Tonya lost upwards of 10,000 Soviet roubles held in Sberbank, an enormous amount by Soviet standards. In post-1961 Soviet money, it was an equivalent of a lifetime of salary for my father's job at the social science digest, or more than the

---

42 Mercifully, we didn't know any dancers, so I hadn't been to ballet as a child at all. Here was the limitation of social capital in the USSR! To this day, I love opera but can't suffer ballet.

43 In a 5-grade system, where 5 is "excellent" and 2 is "fail", my last grade in violin was a 3, with "minus" so long that it continued on to the next page. My parents got the message, sort of - they hired a guitar teacher instead. I had just used money given to me "for sweets" by Grandpa Boris to buy a guitar.

combined cash price of ours and my maternal grandparents' co-operative apartments in Moscow[44]. In a modern day foreign currency equivalent, Grandma Tonya had been a millionaire, and the money was, most likely, simply *her* lifetime salary, to the extent that she worked. It probably piled up there, because she didn't use money for anything.

I entered adulthood at the moment of the total Soviet collapse, a granddaughter of privilege and a child of a stay-at-home mother with expertise in Dutch Renaissance. At the same time, I had the economic skill set of a child who grew up in an orphanage and had never witnessed their parents balance a checkbook. I was a typical, if only a bit extreme, example of a child of *intelligentsia.* My principal skill was to be *entitled* in the worst possible sense – but, unlike my counterparts in the West, I had no actual entitlement to show for it. Communist leaders in the USSR failed to emerge from the ranks of Muscovites, who lacked the requisite propensity for upward mobility, having not had to experience geographic mobility first; so did the rich fail to emerge from the ranks of its Latin-speaking, tennis-playing and polonaise-dancing *intelligentsia* at the moment of USSR's collapse. Just like privilege in the Soviet times was just given to us, so, too, we now expected money to be. Having lived the lifestyle that, in a market economy, is normally a result of wealth, we did not possess the skill set that could lead to primary wealth accumulation.

I rant a lot about the 1990s, in a sense that no one in Russia wants to go back to that time. This is what most Russians think. The 1990s were wild and out of control, crime was rampant, etc. – but the truth is, I did well in 1990s Russia, so did my mother, and so did everyone else I knew. Most of us didn't become rich, but it was an unforgettable adventure. I gained early fame in 1992, when my first book came out. Soviet-era distribution systems were still in place, and more copies of it were quickly sold, than of all my successive books combined (in all likelihood, including this one). The book was a biography of a rock band, *Aquarium,* which had quickly gained super celebrity status in the late 1980s and early 1990s.

---

44 But that did not, of course, mean that a person who found a suitcase with this much money could go and buy even one apartment. You had to live in Moscow – which was not open for relocation to – and you had to have been awarded the co-op membership based on some criteria of privilege, waiting list, profession, et cetera.

I remember an episode from the mid-1980s when a fan handed Boris Grebenschikov, the band's front man and lyricist, a rouble bill to sign. Boris wrote "money is dirt" on it, reflecting popular opinion. Fans cheered. It is lucky that he had this attitude – because, by 1992, there were screaming crowds of fans, multiple LPs and movie soundtracks, books and sequels featuring lyrics and prose, but none of it made Grebenschikov, easily the top living rock star in the new Russia, rich.

In the summer of 1992, there wasn't any cash in Russia. People and companies had money on their bank accounts, but it was impossible to cash the money out – we did not have plastic cards yet, so money in the bank was just a notion for consumers. I contracted with Grebenschikov for rights to a book of his novels and short stories. The publisher had money in the bank, but no ability to get the cash out, either – and the rock star was strapped for cash.

Eventually, I realized that a girl from my *externat* (a night school where I took exams after dropping out of my posh high school) worked as a teller in Sberbank, where her mother was a branch manager. I took Grebenschikov to that specific branch, had him open an account, had the publisher transfer money to it, and, under the shroud of secrecy, my classmate's branch manager mother somehow procured the coveted cash for him to withdraw. I learned afterward that the meager sum, thus obtained via a corruption scheme involving two 17-year olds, was the only cash the superstar has had in all that summer.

In summary, we had fun in the 1990s. Journalism and politics of the 1990s Russia were a once-in-a-lifetime adventure. Business must have been even more so. Around me, in Moscow, everyone's lives were exciting – although it was, in hindsight, a rather dangerous excitement. There was no effective government in the early 1990s, no rules or laws, and no enforcement thereof. The city was not safe, and people did die quite a lot. To Generation X, this was our rite of passage – our collective consciousness started with Perestroika, and, by 1991, all bets had been off for a long time. The way you perceive reality is a factor of your expectations, and we no longer had any. The reality was whatever we were to make it, every day. Anything was possible. You could absolutely get shot any minute, or you could find yourself on a front page of a national newspaper, or in Parliament, or you could get rich, or all four at the same time. We were all a little bit like Neo in The Matrix. *There was no spoon.*

Opportunity was everywhere – and, to the extent that the super-rich emerged during that time, most of them also Gen X-ers, it was simply a way of taking that opportunity, as interpreted by people with a more technocratic way of thinking. While those of us who were in humanities viewed the opportunity around us as one for fame, manipulation of the minds or peddling of ideas, the nerds among us saw a diabolical, life-sized game of chess, albeit in which rules were subject to change all the time. Just like in Wizard Chess in Harry Potter, you could die if you made a wrong move, but untold rewards beckoned if you won.

In that environment, many of the people whom you now derisively call *oligarchs,* were *technari,* as we called them – STEM graduates, who viewed the potential for privatization-based enrichment as an intellectual challenge with high stakes. While the popular view is that the value was there and some unsavory characters took it before others could get to it, the reality was diametrically opposite. The value was not yet there at the start – this was *the big bang.* The puzzles, comprised of conflicting interests, non-existent legal framework, political influence, lack of adequate credit system, and pressure from organized crime, that needed to be solved in order to turn the ruins of a dysfunctional economy into monetizable assets, were of such difficulty that no MBA student can comprehend. The fortunes of the time were born out of excess intellectual capacity, not greed: success at any step was not guaranteed, exposure to physical risk was high, and the whole country could very well go to the dogs at any moment, just like our previous country had done only a few years prior. If you succeeded, your life was to be forever tumultuous, because Russians were still conditioned to abhor wealth[45].

Getting rich in the 1990s required brains and stamina, and sustaining that wealth afterward required self-discipline and professional management. None of these fortunes is an accident – yet, they were a result of a gamble and a lot of luck. Instinctively, every gambler knows that luck can run out. The bravado of the outsized outward displays of wealth, for which the Russian rich are often made fun of in the West, is a tacit acknowledgment of its ephemeral nature. Those who possess generational wealth in the West may think that theirs is a constant world, but the Russian rich know for a fact that theirs is not.

---

45 When Forbes published its first ever ranking of the Russian rich, all of them, reportedly, were distressed at being included.

On the back of every Russian's mind is a nagging feeling that what was born of chaos can, once again, be consumed by it. It may not come to pass, but it is rational for us to allow for that possibility, given how much chaos we already lived through. It's like seeing the entire event horizon simultaneously. Plague, climate catastrophe, coup d'etat, revolution, nationalization, currency devaluation, complete failure of energy sources, sanctions, assassination, nuclear war, persecution – all of those go into our consideration daily, along with the obvious risks of getting cancer or being struck by lightning. Our wealthy are still taking part in that life-sized chess game – more like a computer game now – that they entered in the 1990s and haven't quite managed to get out of. No one knows what calamity awaits at the next level. With that in mind, why not build a superyacht? I recently realized that some of them are intended to be arks.

The 1990s seemed to work for the Soviet Generation X, the members of which managed, usually through extensive self-education, to breach the gaps in their upbringing when it came to economics, finance and technology. People often ask me why I did an MBA, having no interest in management. The answer is simple – I was trying to fill knowledge gaps. While an MBA is not normally necessary for an average college-educated American to understand, in general terms, how economic and business forces operate in society, for me it was an efficient way to make up for the complete lack of such understanding.

My MBA was in IT management – that way, I was trying to also make up for not having grown up around computers. Most Americans of my generation had at least the primitive DOS PCs with Tetris, and some even had Macs, growing up. I did not have use of a computer until about 16, when one was finally brought for us by someone from the United States. I have not been exposed to consumer Internet at all, until arriving in the United States in 1996, aged 21, and hadn't acquired my first cellphone until 1997. What everyone my age knew about tech, I did not – and I felt that I had to aggressively learn not just word processing, but networking, HTML and even programming, to get to par.

For the Russian wealthy of my generation, not just taking control of, but managing and growing the country's finance, energy and industry, required skills they had to learn, and deference to Western-imported knowledge that did not exist in Russia. While turning ex-Soviet resources into assets, or creating banking

155

from scratch in a place where none existed before, was a unique process, once these assets became large businesses of a universally recognizable type, expertise was needed to operate them. You could not run an oil company, a bank, or a factory by a combination of common sense and chutzpah alone. You needed to learn a lot of new things yourself, delegate and embrace teamwork.

By contrast with Gen X-ers, baby boomers did not do so well in this whole process. The older the age to which one lived in the Soviet Union, the harder it was for them to adapt to change. Many possessed the intellect necessary for short-term enrichment but proved unable to sustain a systematic approach to it, or unwilling to envision their operations as anything other than the outsized versions of their selves. Boris Berezovsky was a stark example of this phenomenon, but there were others in his time. Learning was not for everyone.

At one point in 1995, I discovered that my parents, typical baby boomers, hadn't paid for electricity since 1986. It's not that they didn't have the money, it was just not something on their radar (that, and there were *proles* in Sberbank, just like the bakery). Their world was full of exciting, important and profound, and paying bills was none of those things. We had an old-style electricity meter, on which 4 digits rotated in a loop, 9999 thus being the maximum possible reading. I took down the reading it displayed and went to the local office of Moscow Energy to turn myself in. Employees there weren't fazed at all. They took my reading, cheerfully subtracted from it the previous reading from 1986, gave me a payment slip for a meager sum equivalent to a monthly bill, and sent me on my way. "Don't fret", – they said. "We have no way of knowing how many times had this thing gone around in all these years. It's everyone".

It *was* everyone. A substantial portion of the population in their mid-thirties to mid-fortiess, as the baby boomers were then, could not run their affairs sustainably, even if they were able to embrace the opportunities of the time. Most of them were not business-minded at all. By the time of my insightful foray into that Moscow Energy office to deal with 9 years of unpaid bills, my mother was a high-profile reporter on a trendy TV channel. She constantly perceived herself to be strapped for cash, despite being paid well, and, an art critic who never visited stores in the Soviet Union for fear of mixing with *the proles*, could not calculate even on a basic level. She was never aware of how much change she was supposed to get, and often walked off forgetting to take it. When my father got into considerable debt trying to trade in the Forex market on a margin (a typical

156

boomer folly, come to think of it), she asked me to explain how it was possible to lose money one did not have in the first place. My mother may have authored a Master's thesis on Dutch Renaissance, but I got nowhere trying to explain margin trading to her.

Just as in the Soviet years she was just given things, my mother's success in post-Soviet Russia ultimately translated into people just giving her money for things. Vladimir Gusinsky, the owner of NTV, gave her money for a new apartment. *VGTRK Rossiya*, which she joined shortly before she died, gave her money to buy land on which she built her own dacha in Nikolina Gora. My parents were a good example of boomers who, despite being in the right place at the right time, never quite left the Soviet economy. When my mother died, people gave me envelopes stuffed with money, without explanation. Being an apple that fell only as far as one MBA from the tree, I took it. For granted, too.

Technology also left many Soviet baby boomers behind. During Berezovsky v. Abramovich trial in London in 2011, one witness, a Gen X-er, drew laughter by pointing out that Berezovsky unlikely knew how to use email. I am certain that he did not. Nor did his pal – my mother. Even in the early 2000s, she scribbled her *voiceovers* across several ripped pieces of paper, which she then piled up in front of a frustrated typist. Given that the TV channels that my mother worked for (one of which Berezovsky owned) still employed typists in the 21st century, I assume it wasn't just her. She has never sent a text message, and physically wrote down mobile numbers in a phone book.

An old colleague of my ex-husband's, activist Marina Litvinovich, recalled in a documentary on the history of the Russian Internet how she was, at the tender age of 24 in 2000, assigned to explain the Internet to then-candidate Vladimir Putin. A baby boomer as well, Putin is rumored to be skeptical of the Internet, and not a personal user. Perhaps it is better that way from a security perspective. To give Putin credit, in the last 20 years he certainly engaged in extensive self-education that statesmanship required. But let's just say, it is not an accident that most of Russia today is not run by other 70-year olds.

With Gen X-ers emerging mostly in one piece and baby boomers experiencing mixed results, it was the older generations that were totally and completely devastated by the 1990s. Most of my grandparents' generation – the war generation – permanently lost all grip on reality at the moment of the collapse of the Soviet Union. Loss of life savings, stress at constantly being told conflicting information which they lacked a useful paradigm to independently evaluate, disastrous voucher-based privatization, the mechanism of which the masses completely failed to understand, loss of social guarantees previously relied on, coupled with a sudden wall of crime that besieged the country, were a deadly blow to that generation. Aged in their sixties at the time, they, together with the less fortunate part of unprivileged baby boomers, to whom no one wanted to *just give* money, were the framers of the main post-Soviet narrative.

Simplistically, the narrative held that Mikhail Gorbachev was a war criminal for destroying the Soviet Union to suit the Americans, that the untold riches of Soviet industry and its natural resources were then stolen from the people by unscrupulous grifters who manipulated heavily drinking and senile Boris Yeltsin, and the population was duped into going along by being promised a piece of the action through the so-called "voucher privatization", which turned out to be a scam. That is what many Russians still think.

For the latter – specifically, not getting a piece – the population was to blame Anatoly Chubais, the unfortunate civil servant considered the father of voucher privatization in Russia. The idea behind it was that each Russian citizen would get a voucher, which he or she could either sell or exchange for shares of a previously state-owned enterprise. The scheme arguably had some merit behind it, and acquisition of shares of viable companies was possible, subject to prudence and good luck. Chubais and other advocates of the scheme carelessly proclaimed that each voucher would be worth "two Volgas" (Soviet luxury passenger cars) before long, but the masses at large were unable to appreciate, in the moment, what vouchers were, and were quickly dispossessed of them by opportunists in exchange for nominal sums of money. "It's all Chubais' fault", - proclaimed a 1990s TV cartoon doll depicting popular politician Alexander Lebed, and everyone had a laugh. Except, I assume, Chubais himself. In the end, people considered themselves duped by him personally, because no one had gotten *two Volgas*.

Studies show that an investment into shares, prudently made with one voucher valued around $20 in 1994, can be worth thousands of dollars today, and in some cases enough to buy more than two Russian-made passenger sedans (they no longer make *Volgas*). Those who recognized the value of a voucher as an

158

investment instrument, and had the audacity to imagine that long-term future was real, bought up vouchers and used them to make their own investments in sizable shareholdings of former state enterprise[46]. One of the people often reported by the media to have done so, businessman Oleg Deripaska, now owns, among other things, the GAZ automotive concern, which used to manufacture *Volgas*.

By the standards of capitalism, there was nothing unethical about either the voucher privatization or the loans-for-shares program in the mid-1990s that ultimately disposed of the shareholdings initially retained by the government. It was natural selection: some people were smarter than most, and not quite as lazy as the rest. Popular anger was directed at politicians – Gorbachev, Yeltsin, Chubais, ex-prime minister Yegor Gaidar – who enabled the perceived injustice, rather than those who had the wits to take the opportunity thereby laid bare. Much as there was politically motivated talk about *a review of privatization* at the turn of the century, the idea of challenging it never gained legal traction, and the statute of limitations on privatization deals expired a long time ago. The 1990s revisionism died as a domestic issue, and even the most ardent populists are no longer calling for it.

The country moved on from what was a challenging – even if thrilling – time, and many of us who were young and adrenaline-filled then, are middle-aged and conservative now. This is not about privatization, as much as it is about anything anyone has done 30 years ago. I have certainly made plenty of flawed decisions in my twenties, that I'd like to finally move on from – and I think that other 50-year-olds should be able to, as well. The reason we all get so angry when we are being forced, again and again, to go through the history of business in the 1990s, is that the overall state of Russia at that time was not a source of national pride. Forcing us to re-live the 90s is like forcing a victim of child abuse to recount their ordeal, again and again, 30 years later. No one wants to be continuously defined by victimhood that they worked so hard to get over.

A new generation had been born and grew up in the interim. In mid-2000s, the Russian state, strengthened financially during the unprecedented rally in oil prices early in the Putin presidency, bought back quite a bit of the assets that had been privatized in the 1990s, once again consolidating a large part of

---

46 Such foresight was rare: I, for one, haven't got the slightest clue what happened to my own voucher.

natural resources and financial enterprise in its hands. Some, including certain beneficiaries of the first privatization, are already calling for a new one.

While it sounds absurd at first, the idea might not be entirely mad. Whether or not any sizable portion of Russians today can truly be turned into active and informed business investors with any more success than 30 years ago, is a big question – but the attempt itself can be politically expedient. Millennials and Generation Z have grown up with the capitalist mindset, and attitudes toward wealth improved. To those new generations, money is no longer toxic – so, perhaps, it can be trusted into their hands with better results.

In the older generations, the idea that the people missed out on "their share" because someone had beaten them to it, persists. A belief that someone out there has *their share*, targets, at this point, anyone who is rich, especially considering that original privatized assets have been restructured, merged and re-sold many times, often back to the state. People think that all Russian wealth has, within it, an element that is held *for the benefit of its people*. While this belief is a fancy, Putin has played into it. In 2010, when Russia was awarded the right to host the 2018 FIFA world cup, Putin took the stage to famously call on Roman Abramovich in the audience, suggesting that it was he, Abramovich, who should *open up his purse* to shoulder the expense. Watching from the West, this came across as rude and inappropriate – but this sort of talk still won points with Russians ten years ago.

It is ultimately the same idea – the idea that wealth, coalesced around a person, is a burden to them, which can and should be lightened by sharing – that forms, on a lower level, a rather unique culture of money circulation in the Russian society, where many people of much more modest means routinely give each other money, simply because the other person needs it more, or just asked. Money is viewed in a much more communitarian sense than anywhere else in the world – the ephemeral nature of wealth and the random possibility of reversal of fortunes are both reasons for that, so is our deep-seated Soviet-era belief that "money is dirt". There are many more. Many Russians no longer borrow money, they simply ask others for it. Western pundits that have recently taken to proclaiming one Russian person, or the other, bagmen or custodians for Putin's, Yeltsin's, or anyone else's money, miss the point of the hidden collectivism here. All Russian people ultimately view every fortunate Russian person as a custodian of all of our money.

160

A new privatization could arguably fix that attitude. The older money-detesting generations are being phased out of the public debate due to demographic change, and the bravado of 2010 would, probably, no longer fly today. The process by which new generations aspire to accumulate wealth and become *like* Roman Abramovich on the strength of their own effort, rather than having him pay their bills, is a healthy process, and giving all of them shares in large, dividend-paying enterprises, such as Gazprom, would encourage a portion of them onto the right path. Businesses that are no longer majority-owned by the State would also be protected from U.S. sectoral sanctions, which seems like a long-term concern now.

But that process, of course, would also be a slow-moving revolution, one that could assure the eventual demise of what the West views as the authoritarian, or let's say *centralized*, Russia. The substantially reduced reliance on the state that such privatization would portend, would be a hallmark of American-style "small government" conservatism, of the Ayn Rand kind. It could certainly "bring Russia into the Western family of nations", so much so that protection against sanctions would no longer be a concern – but I fear that this isn't the vector of current trends. After all, as we all remember from Soviet times, centralized distribution of privilege is effective means of population control. And the population that needs to be controlled right now, is one that has been substantially alienated from all Western ideology by U.S. sanctions currently in place, including those imposed on certain fans of Ayn Rand and proponents of the new privatization.

Last but not least, Robbie Williams. Are we mad at him for "Party Like a Russian?" No, we are not. We play it at our parties. First of all, we are capable of self-irony, but consider also this: no one had ever built a superyacht in order to show it off in Russia, where money has long been considered dirt, and wealth – a curse. There is no sea in Moscow, and St. Petersburg is quite cold. Outsized displays of wealth are designed for consumption by the West, which is so childishly in awe of them. When he sings, "it takes half the Western world to keep this ship afloat", Williams makes fun of the Western world itself, as it continues to duly oblige. Us – we care about success and power, but we still don't measure those things in money.

This is the ultimate folly of those Westerners who keep looking everywhere in the world for Putin's imaginary wealth. Money may be means to an end, such as achieving power – but, for Russians, it is never the end itself. Why would a man want to accumulate any money at all, having already achieved ultimate power? Winning is never about owning the trophy.

Gender and sex

The conventional view of Russia is one of a socially conservative, patriarchal society. A patriarchy it certainly is, and remains. Whether or not it can be described as conservative, within the commonly understood meaning of this word in the West, I am not sure. Russian culture is traditionalist on issues that stem from the patriarchy itself – our ideas of gender roles and courtship are, perhaps, slightly dated by Western standards. We expect men to take on leading roles in relationships with women, to be heads of households and primary breadwinners. Most Russian women, whatever their desires or intentions are, would not directly proposition a man.

Gender roles in Russia are merely similar to what traditional gender roles in Western countries were some years ago. Russian society is not fundamentalist. One cannot say that men enjoy more respect, as would be the case in Muslim countries. Russia is a secular country, loosely based on Christian values, and, to the extent that the men rule Russian society, they do so by consent of the women – who, in turn, rule the men. Chivalry is an expected behavioral norm in all settings, including between strangers. We expect men to not only provide and protect in relationships, but to pick up the tab in restaurants, give up their seats to female strangers in public settings[47], get doors and coats.

All the while, men do not expect anything in return. The same culture still seems to view sex as a favor that women may extend to men out of earned benevolence, rather than a mutually desirable collaboration, let alone an entitlement. Traditional Russian humor would widely feature men desperate to stay on the good side of their wives in spite of misbehavior (usually excessive

47 In my case, it may also be because, by Russian standards, I am old now - even young *women* give me their seats nowadays! At first, I was alarmed, thinking myself quite young in my late forties, but then I realized that these young women are my daughters' age. Being Russian, they all have parents in their forties, for whom they would probably also give up their seats.

drinking, rather than promiscuity), or "bringing the cash home" and giving it to their wife, who would deal with household spending decisions.

I do not know to what extent all of this is changing in the younger generations – and I have certainly tried to take a lead in relationships with men when I was younger! But I can see now that this was why those relationships, ultimately, failed. It was against my nature. Those of us who are above the age of 40 now, are forever in the 1980s on sex and relationships. And our 1980s were very different from your 1980s.

In our 1980s, of course, we did not have Western television and cable channels, and very little of Western contemporary literature. Apart from a rare glimpse of *The Blues Brothers* or *1984* on someone's VCR, we did not have Western movies, either. There was a lot of education related to manners and gender behavior, but none about sex. As an adolescent, you were left to guess what it was, and a lot of initial sex experiences, routinely gained at a later age than they were in the West, were engaged in by people who have never seen not just any porn, but any erotic films, nor anyone doing any part of it, at all. They have read neither Kama Sutra nor the Cosmopolitan, let alone Playboy. It was, mildly put, a disaster.

When a talk show guest by the name of Nina Andreeva posited, at the cusp of *perestroika*, that there was *no sex in the USSR*, she was widely mocked. Yet, Nina Andreeva was onto something. Of course, Soviet people had very little idea of sex, and it was partly because they had much less opportunity to engage in it, let alone to do so in any way that could possibly give them a better idea. In the 1980s, quite a lot of Soviet people still lived in multi-generational families, where married couples occupied walk-through living rooms or shared rooms with their children. The idea of sex as a covert activity undertaken silently under the covers in the dark did not take hold because they were all predisposed to be prudes – quite a lot of them were simply never alone.

In a society where information about sex and relationships could only be passed down to children from parents, you can imagine the outcome. Often times the parents did not even bother or were too shy or embarrassed to do so. My mother, supposedly a progressive woman, certainly did not. She had barely managed to mention to me that girls can get menstruations – too bad I was 9 at the time, so it did nothing to preempt the shock I later experienced at 12. Between 8 and 12, I remember girls getting together and whispering, trying to

163

desperately figure out what sex was, but no one had any idea. It was sort of like talking about *dust* in Philip Pullman's literary universe. When I let go my virginity at 16, a tender age to do so by Soviet standards, it was mainly out of curiosity to discover what exactly was, in fact, meant by it. Let's just say, this was not the experience of American Gen X-ers.

There are, of course, exceptions to every rule, and I do not want this to be a book about the affairs of the bedroom, a subject on which I am still hardly an expert. But I have lived, for most of my adult life, with a foot in both worlds, and consider myself to be embedded in both cultures, so I have a few further observations to offer.

In Russia, gender-based self-expression is unusually liberal by modern Western standards, but people's actual sexual behaviors are not. If you are a Western woman, you would be initially stumped by what feels like a hurricane of innuendo that you are subjected to – but, before long, you will realize that it is all just talk. This is how they talk.

It doesn't matter that you might be at a corporate board meeting. To the extent that you somehow – unlikely for Russia – ended up in one, casual conversation between you and the men present would be revolving around the fact that you are a woman. Even if that conversation is about accounting, it will probably be flirtatious in nature. Russian men and women flirt as they talk, but it does not signal any intentions whatsoever. You would also find that pop culture and show business are quite sexualized, and a lot of ads center on the sexual objectification of women, even if they are selling breakfast cereal. Eat your cereal if you want your mom to be hot and sexy!

Jokes and comments based on gender role assumptions will be made, and your appearance will be complimented. Men will probably venture to see you out to your car and get your coat, and they will invariably pick up the bill for a lunch, even in a business setting, and even if you have never seen them before and will never see them again. It would take quite an adjustment for you to realize that none of this means anything, nor are they aware that any of this may be perceived as disrespectful. In 99% of the cases, none of them has even the slightest interest in getting to know you intimately – and if they did, they would probably proposition you verbally and unambiguously. Otherwise, this is just chivalry, and chivalry is a societal norm in Russia. It is not to be taken personally. It's not you, it's your gender.

At the same time, all of this is talk and no action. As a bunch, Russians are still constrained by cultural norms in private behavior, and are, for the most part, shy and sexually repressed. They may make a lot of inappropriate jokes and talk about sex all the time in the abstract, but they are having much less of it than you might think – if not in terms of quantity, then definitely in terms of variety. Not in a sense that they are not philandering enough – although that too – but in a sense that many standard bedroom practices in the West are still sacrosanct taboo here, and there is only scarcely more of a public conversation about sex than there was in the USSR.

It is almost the opposite in the West – where men are quite restrained in what they would say and how they would act, and there would be no gender jokes or sex talk in the presence of women, other than the women the speaker is already intimate with. Western men will routinely plow through the door ahead of you, and forget that you had a coat. The age of chivalry is dead, we are told. Even if they remember, they might fear that getting your coat would be taken as a sexual proposition. They will probably expect you to split the restaurant bill, unless, perhaps, they are *buying dinner*, which is a big deal, or unless they are already sleeping with you. In the Western popular culture, when men hope to have sex, they ask women over for a cup of coffee, or Netflix. They are repressed in their conversation and manner, partly because all words and gestures could be interpreted *the wrong way*. Nowadays, if you believe television, women just have to tell men if they want anything to happen (meanwhile, if you proposition a Russian man, he would probably assume that you are a fallen woman).

Yet, even as they talk – and, probably, obsess – less about it, Western men, overall, have much more sex, and certainly a greater variety of it, with a huge part of the written culture devoted to various strategies of achieving satisfaction and happiness in the bedroom. Western men genuinely concern themselves with satisfying female desires, and, even if misguidedly, think that they bring joy. Meanwhile, Russian culture tells men that, no matter how hard they try, they are, and will remain, an imposition on women.

I recently read, with amusement, my own memoirs of an election campaign in Russia in 2003. The events took place quite some years ago, but are still instructive. I had just arrived from the United States, after many years away. In my late twenties at the time, I ended up the only woman on senior campaign staff, and could not understand what to make of the behavior of men around me. For the most part, I had not been subjected to anything untoward or offensive, such as could be taken as harassment in the West. Yet, I was constantly a target of love letters, poetry, chivalrous competitions between men desirous of taking my bag to the car, and particularly late-night calls from men complaining, for hours on end, about the futility of being.

There was also a universal manner of conversation, which I could not even call flirtatious per se, in which men were eager to outdo each other in impressing me with their oratory, knowledge of literature and history, or wit. It was funny and sad at the same time, but it was clearly not sexual. Not even the confessions of love, of which there were a couple. It was simply the society of men that had no idea how to deal with a young woman in their professional midst and were trying their best, in confusion. It was disorienting, but not distressing.

The only truly distressing comment in that campaign, in fact, came from a female junior staffer. She asked me whether there was a particular reason why I never ironed my clothes. "What's an iron?", – I asked, earning a look that made me immediately thankful for all the men around. It also made me switch to "dry clean only" suits. So, it ended up being an expensive comment.

Younger Russian women would dress up, do their hair and, if applicable, make-up, and probably wear heels, to go shopping – but it is not the frivolous in them that determines this behavior, it is the conservative. It is not because they are planning to pick up a date at the mall, it is because their upbringing suggests that appearing in public disheveled or badly dressed is disrespectful. In fact, married women will care more about their appearance than single women, because married women would not want to embarrass their husband and children by looking ungroomed or under-dressed. In the West, there is an opinion that Russian women, who take care to look good and who flirt in conversation, are *easy* – but, on the contrary, all they are trying to do most of the time is be respectful and polite.

I may be a product of the Western culture in this respect – and, perhaps, that is also why I am single! – but I certainly would, occasionally, dare to walk my dog in gym clothes without any jewelry on. I have worn make-up only once in my life, and that was a photo shoot for Cosmopolitan[48]. In Moscow, I get

---

48 And, that was also in 2006! But my youngest daughter is trying to get me into that now, so watch this space.

looks of pity from other women. I went in for a pedicure, for the first time in my life, when I was already in my forties. The pedicurist looked at me and asked immediately how long I've lived in England. She explained – realizing halfway, in embarrassment, that this must be insensitive – that *looking after one's appearance is not part of female culture in England*. Clearly, this was the only way to explain my pathetically ungroomed state. God save the Queen!

Yet, just as Western men have more sex, and the sex they have is *more fun*, empirically, they do most of it with those same Western women who *do not have looking after their appearance as part of their culture*, apparently. In other words, sexualization of their own appearance by Russian women, and all the sex jokes and overbearing chivalry of Russian men, ultimately, fill the empty space from which a more evolved sexual culture is still missing. But it is missing not for reasons for prudishness, or religion, or morality, or fundamentalism – it is missing because, by and large, they are children of the Soviet Union, in which, as we have all been told, *there was no sex*. One can easily learn to deal with new things that were not a part of their upbringing at all: for example, Internet, Camembert or mortgages. It is much harder to go against nature on cultural norms, such as they were, that you did observe and absorb growing up.

As for any gender imbalance, I do not get a sense that the Russian patriarchy is an imposed practice, as far as women are concerned. Any lack of participation in politics or business is, for the most part, due to the lack of women willing to enter those fields. I do not think that Russian society has anything against a female president – there just isn't anyone willing and electable. While, admittedly, there are some women on the political margins, in the mainstream, which is where the bulk of society is, this is not something they want. Some, of course, do. At the time of writing, there are three women in the Russian cabinet, the chair of the Central Bank is a woman (and the press pool has taken to predicting impending monetary policy moves by her choice of brooches), and so is the speaker of the upper house of the legislature.

It is not talked much about in the West, but one of the historic reasons behind the lack of sex culture in the Soviet Union – apart from housing problems – was the forcible attempt to equate sexes, undertaken by the Soviet government at the time when it was way ahead of the curve of societal expectations. While American women happily stayed at home and raised children, Soviet women worked at factories, drove trains, painted and plastered at construction sites. We even sent one to space. Some were elevated to positions of power of various sorts, their image intentionally de-gendered in the process. Even in the highest echelons of Soviet society, all women worked, although they did not need to. Preschools were free, and there were nurseries for infants, and boarding preschools in case your job demanded that.

The infamous laws that criminalized unemployment exempted women with children under a certain age, but my mother had been the only stay-at-home mother I ever heard of because raising a child at home was unfashionable – and even then, she felt the need to fight the stigma by hanging out at her old job at the Museum of Fine Arts for days on end. Femininity itself, for a long time, was a form of protest, and so it came to be cherished in Russia. More women than, perhaps, would admit to it in the West at the current conjuncture, are fine with the role of the *weaker sex*, and happy to leave the *hunting and gathering* to the men.

Gay rights

There is one man that I blame for the escalation of anti-gay sentiment in Russia, which eventually led to an unhelpful law banning "gay propaganda among minors", prohibitions related to adoptions by single individuals from countries that allow gay marriage, and all such infamous like. That man is Peter Tatchell, a well-known British campaigner and gay icon. You read it right. It was Tatchell's incessant drive to force his rules onto societies whose culture and customs he did not understand, and the hysteria in the West that followed the beating he, predictably, received from members of the public while trying to conduct a Pride march in Moscow in 2007, that led to a confrontation of values, backlash, and, as a consequence, the impugned laws[49].

Male gay sex was technically illegal in the Soviet Union, but the provision, at least by the time of my childhood, was not more meaningful than similar legacy provisions in many U.S. states. I wrote earlier in this book that American writer Andrew Sullivan was the first openly gay person I met when he arrived in Moscow in 1986, but that requires qualification.

There were certainly gay people in Soviet Moscow, and my parents knew a few. I knew who they were, and that they were gay. Best as I can tell, no one

---

49 At least one homegrown idiot, not worthy of being mentioned by name, set up public provocations in Tatchell's style in order to enable himself to pursue asylum in the West. That did not help matters, either.

cared, and they had same-sex relationships, such as were known to family and friends, with relative openness. At the same time, it is also true that I am aware of at least two instances where heterosexual marriages have been entered into by people whom "everyone knew" to be gay, and my parents thought that it was a *cover*, meaning that the women involved participated knowingly. So, in terms of what was meant by being *openly gay* by Western standards, they were not.

At the same time, depending on where one was in the United States, surely, a similar level of reticence could be found in those same years. Quite a few American women, as late as in the 1990s, made a big deal out of their discovery that their husbands were gay all along: for example, the wife of the former New Jersey governor Jim McGreevey. I still remember the solemn shock with which she presented a book about her terrifying lived experience, titled *Silent Partner*. From that title, one could have thought that McGreevey turned out to have been a serial killer.

In 1980s Moscow, hushed tones and *cover* marriages were intended to ward off societal prejudice, rather than state persecution. In a more liberal Sochi, a seaside resort – ungentrified as it was, but also *niche* – gay clubs, veiled thinly as variety shows, operated semi-openly even in those years. The Soviet law banning homosexuality ceased to have effect in 1993. For the next 20 years, it was perfectly legal to be gay in Russia.

Arguably, the Putin years brought a resurgence of fundamental religion – and, as I wrote previously in this book, by the mid-2000s I caught my old pal Alexey, now Father Alexey, arguing on a TV talk show that homosexuality was a cardinal sin. But even then, gay bashing was still a marginal phenomenon. You would have probably not been aware of it if you did not watch daytime TV talk shows with priests on guest panels.

A lot of prominent Russians were now openly gay, including cohabitation in same-sex relationships, at least in Moscow. They included popular musicians and actors, whose popularity it did not seem to adversely affect. They also included the aforementioned emigre journalist Masha Gessen, who grew up in the United States. In those years, Masha lived in Moscow with her female partner and adopted a boy from a Moscow orphanage. They raised the child openly as a couple.

My late mother, a few years before she died, made a TV documentary on adoption, featuring Masha, with whom she was friendly. Mother was ostensibly

169

very progressive and liberal, but privately a bit of a prude. She was weirdly obsessed with Masha being gay and made an elaborate effort to cut any mention of a second mom from the adoption documentary. When I returned from the U.S. in 2003, my mother unexpectedly insisted that I attend a birthday party for Masha's newly adopted kid (who is the same age as my middle daughter). When I suggested that it was awkward for me to crash a party of someone I barely knew, mother posited that Masha needed "support" because she was gay. I am pretty sure Masha did not need *support*, she seemed to be doing just fine. But my mother's misguided attitude is a good example of how gay rights in Russia became an obsession of heterosexual liberals, whose involvement could be counterproductive.

Because she is originally from Russia, Masha Gessen, I think, always understood a few things that Peter Tatchell never could. Firstly, Russians were not, by and large, homophobic. Instead, several other things were in play. Russians are private people, and they are not particularly sexually liberated. Any talk of sex or forced knowledge of someone's private life is frowned upon and makes them uncomfortable. They don't care that someone is gay, or that someone has a mistress, or whatever else is going on behind someone's closed doors. It is all awkward. They do not want to know, and least of all they want to be forced to deal with it, be it by proactively condoning it, or in any other way. Russians do not like to be made to feel awkward.

If two hot men sharing an apartment simply tell neighbors that they are army buddies, the neighbors will be content. Not because they believe it, but because they are not being put on the spot. You may have read a lot of complaints from tourists that Russians do not smile at strangers on the street. If they don't even smile at you, how much do you think they care about your sex life? The beauty of it was that people who were gay in Russia were, mostly, also Russian. They were the same people who did not smile at strangers. They were also private people, for whom the idea of sharing details of their sex lives with strangers would be awkward. Most were fine with keeping it to themselves.

Secondly, the same lack of cultural awareness that may have led some Russians to be, indeed, overtly or latently homophobic, also usually prevents them from recognizing that someone *is* gay. Western gay stereotypes related to appearance, style, grooming and behavior traits are, of course, a product of Western culture; gay people who choose to conform to them, do so consciously.

Without that, you cannot *tell* that someone is gay unless they told you themselves. Where those stereotypes are not present in the local culture, they are also absent as a set of personality traits that can help identify someone as gay. Some in the gay community in Russia may adhere to the traits that they know from, or acquired in, the Western culture, or they are foreigners themselves. Most Russians, still, would not *read* those signs.

Unless they were told about it directly and put on the spot to react, the mind of most Russians will instinctively seek any other possible explanation in the world for any close affectionate same-sex friendship or co-habitation that they witness. For example, two women cohabiting would be assumed to be sisters, out of town relatives, co-workers sharing the room on the cheap, best friends from high school who have nowhere else to go, or whatever possible explanation, especially given that extended families and strangers sharing accommodation for financial reasons is historically common in Russia. Until all the recent escalation came about, Russians were not looking for anyone to be gay, and, in fact, often stubbornly refused to see it. That way, they did not have to react to it. Problem solved.

All of the above laid a perfect foundation for an equilibrium that can only be described as a sort of "don't ask, don't tell" policy that operated in the U.S. military during the Clinton years. It later took Obama a lot of effort to dismantle, but as recently as the 1990s was seen as super progressive and accommodating of gay people: they were free to serve in the military all they wanted if they did not tell anyone they were gay, and no one was allowed to ask them. The permanent fog of innuendo actually prevented things from otherwise coming to a head. So it was in Russia, too. No one was against anyone being gay. All you had to do – or, as the case was, not do – was to refrain from coming up to strangers and saying: "Hi, I am gay, doesn't it make you happy?" It was safe to say that no one who had spent a day of their lives in Russia, gay or straight, was ever going to think doing that was a good idea.

Enter the man who had never set foot in Russia before: Peter Tatchell. By the time of his foray in Moscow in 2007, Tatchell already had an impressive record of cultural insensitivity. The most famous stop on his world tour, the motto of which may as well have been "when in Rome, make the Romans do like you do", was his 1999 attempt to re-educate the President of Zimbabwe Robert Mugabe, a task to which he took in person, and was promptly beaten up for that

171

by Mugabe's bodyguards. And then, in 2007, he heard of an abomination: Russia, a large, socially conservative and Orthodox Christian 1000-year-old country of which he knew absolutely nothing, had no Pride parade held in it. None whatsoever. Peter Tatchell decided that he would be dispatching himself to Moscow personally in order to hold one.

The reason why we never had Pride parades in Russia is manifold. Sure, the certainty of being beaten up by members of the public was a huge deterrent; moreover, acting in that way was sure to upset the delicate social contract around being gay that existed in the country for years – the local version of *don't ask, don't tell* policy. But the aforementioned trait of Russians being private people with somewhat puritan attitudes to sex was probably the main reason. No one in Russia would want to march in Pride or engage in any sort of weird explicit shenanigans that do go on in Pride parades in the West nowadays. As we all know perfectly well, 99.9% of gay people in Western countries lead normal everyday lives, do not go to Pride, and would want nothing to do with it, either. Nor did the Russians.

Upon his attempt to march in Pride in Moscow, not only was Tatchell promptly beaten up again, but they hit him on the head really hard this time. It was no joke; the beating caused permanent brain damage. Tatchell was forced to resign his seat in the European Parliament. It gave the incident widespread headlines, that it would not have otherwise received. For months to come, Russia's ostensible hatred of gay people was front and center of the anti-Russian agenda. Russophobia was resurgent in the West. Worst of all, it all prompted a renewed, public discussion in the Russian society about whether or not being gay was, after all, a cardinal sin.

Even the least bigoted were on the fence about that, having seen Internet videos of what Pride parades were like in San Francisco. The majority verdict, while it was still short of prohibition or persecution, was motivated, I think, by the public's desire to do whatever they can to make sure they never have to see a Pride parade in real life. They realized that gay couples, from countries where gay marriage was legal, adopted Russian orphans while posing as single straight people; the government then banned single parent adoptions from all countries where gay marriage was legal. By then, it included the United States.

This sounded really bad, but the disruption was only short-term. Russia was, by then, running out of adoptable orphans. Improved economic conditions and huge government incentives, designed to promote large families, drew adoptive parents in troves. Coupled with the age-old law that gave Russian citizens the first shot at adopting every eligible child, it meant that very soon virtually no babies were left for any foreigners to adopt. Today, orphanages in Moscow, including one from which I adopted my youngest daughter in 2006 and from which Masha Gessen adopted her son a few years earlier, stand empty.

It was precisely because Russia was running out of babies, that real concerns appeared in the Russian gay community – members of which, of course, also adopted babies posing as single people – that the government will use social services to remove previously adopted children from parents known to be gay so that it can re-adopt them into traditional families. It was then, and because of that concern, that Masha Gessen left Russia with her family, a decision on which she later elaborated in the New Yorker and other public comments.

For a period of time, things only got worse. What Western idiots had failed to take into account, was that Vladimir Putin was a centrist, a socially moderate, worldly man. The elites in Moscow and St. Petersburg may have been to his left on social issues, but the rest of the country was way, way to his right. Russia has its share of dim, uneducated and unenlightened people, whose bigotry defies imagination. Putin always understood, for his part, that anti-gay sentiment had to be contained and managed at any cost, in the face of the then-upcoming Sochi 2014 Olympics and the later 2018 football (soccer) World Cup, both of which expected to draw a lot of Western spectators and foreign press. With dug-in orthodox hillbilly politicians out for blood to make sure we never have to see a Pride parade, he was stuck between a rock and a hard place – one of the very few times I can think of, that he was in this uncomfortable position domestically.

The much-maligned law, one that ostensibly bans "gay lifestyle" propaganda among minors, was the Great Compromise of 2013. Oh, those lovely years before Russiagate, when this was the world's biggest problem with Russia! I look back at those years almost fondly. At least 20% of foreign journalists that arrived ostensibly to cover the Sochi Olympics in February 2014, clearly did so in search of evidence of anti-gay persecution. I know a TV crew from a major European TV channel that did not go to a single Olympic event. They just ended up being shuffled by local fixers to a local gay club. The club has been there since the 1980s, but I am sure 2014 became its most profitable year.

173

In the wake of Western bashing of Russian "gay persecution", a number of public figures in Russia came out as gay, including RT journalist Anton Krasovsky and former NTV journalist Pavel Lobkov. A number of other prominent Russians are widely believed to be gay, including several ostensibly single men who are raising children born of surrogate mothers.

The chain of events that were set off by Peter Tatchell's misguided intervention gave Russia a bad name in Western propaganda; a name that stuck, and, from then on, just the reason had to be adjusted. First, it was gay rights, then it was Crimea, then it was Trump, then it was *novichok* poison, now it is Navalny. Reasons given were never the real cause, of course. Either way, Peter Tatchell's Moscow Pride project ushered in the renewal of Russophobia, and it has not let up since. It also prompted a resurgence of traditional orthodoxy in Russia, that spilled from priest-featuring talk shows into legislative chambers big and small. In the end, no one's – or, according to some reports, almost no one's – children were taken away, but things would never be the same.

It is good that Tatchell did not come back to Russia again, because Russian gay people would have beaten him up this time.

Race

There was a ludicrous outburst of wokeness last year, when a well-known African-American ballerina condemned the Bolshoi Theater in a tweet for using blackface in ballets. They should have simply cast black dancers, she said. "There aren't any black dancers, or, for that matter, black people, in Russia", – numerous Twitter users duly observed. She responded by calling them all ridiculous racists.

There are, of course, no black ballerinas in Russia. Nor are there any black people. Well, to be precise, we do have four or five, perhaps. An odd American diplomat, a famous TV personality (she is also American), and a couple of international students from Rwanda. Maybe even an illegitimate child or two from liaisons with Olympic athletes in 1980. But it is fair to say that the absolute majority of the Russian people, and even many Muscovites (Moscow being the only city in which the above mentioned four or five people are to be found), have never seen a black person in real life.

A lot of Russians who arrive to live in the West, come across there as racist. But they are just confused and, perhaps, uncomfortable, because they have zero experience of racial diversity. None. All of them encounter non-white people for the first time, let alone in any significant numbers. Appreciation of diversity is a learned skill, and it is not possessed by those not exposed to it.

I do not think that Russians are racist whatsoever toward black people. Racism, or any other ethnic hatred, is not a position by default, and you will not hate people you never met or lived alongside. Racism in the United States is a protracted result of slavery and segregation, generations-long animosity born out of two groups living alongside each other. If you have never seen a black person, you will not hate them, but you might initially be wary, or curious, once you do.

Russia has its own race relations problems. There was a degree of ethnic diversity in the Soviet Union, of course – there were several middle Asian republics, the *stans*, and many Russians ended up living in them. Some of the Tajiks and Kyrgyzs, of course, lived in Russia as well – but the limitations on geographic mobility in the USSR meant that there was not that much day-to-day mixing and no mass migration.

In that sense, there is more of what you might call racism today, now that half of Tajikistan had made their way to Moscow to do menial jobs. I myself will be first to admit that I am confused at the now ubiquitous signs, brochures and announcements in languages I cannot understand, presumably Tajik, which seem gratuitous anyway, because they all speak Russian, at least somewhat. The numbers of low-skilled Asians flooding Moscow and occupying all those endless small apartments built in the vast expanse of Greater Moscow (which Russians do not want), are staggering. You can hardly recognize the city. Let alone that half of them, I am sorry to say, insist on standing on the left side of an escalator in the Moscow metro. If only they all stood on the right side, and left the left side for civilized people to pass, there would be less racism.

This calamity helped me understand the desperate need for Brexit in the United Kingdom in an entirely new way. Just as I am frustrated to see Moscow fall to what feels like an invading army, be it or not because Russians are unwilling to sweep streets and deliver food, so are the English people in a panic over totally losing any sense of their cities, on the high streets of which, nowadays, there would be store after store without any signage in English whatsoever. Are they racist for not wanting so many perfectly white Lithuanians and Poles around? Would the English have as much problem with the Eastern Europeans if the latter learned English and posted signage in English in their "international food stores"? If all those people from Tajikistan in Moscow consumed brochures in Russian and stood on the right side of escalators, would we have so much problem with them? Outside of the painful historic paradigm of racism in America, what comes across as racism as applied to all other people and cultures, is often just cultural confusion.

Middle East

Russia has always had an odd relationship with the Middle East. The USSR backed Middle Eastern countries politically, in order to oppose the growing power of Israel, which it considered a hostile state. Yet, there was no cultural connection, nor particular empathy, between the Russians and these predominantly Muslim countries. There is no other issue on which the sympathy of the Russian elites, which has always been with Israel, diverged so strongly from the general line. Whether or not the government acknowledged it, quite a lot of people in those elites have always been Jewish, of course – or, at least, they were big city Russians who knew a lot of Jews, but have never met a Muslim. Huge numbers among all of our friends and neighbors have left for Israel and comprise a very large chunk of the population of that country. Why should we ever militarily support its enemies, was always a little beyond most of us.

Soviet policies of friendship with Middle Eastern secular governments – and make no mistake, Lebanon, Iraq, Libya, Syria, Egypt were all secular countries – led to a considerable amount of travel to those countries by Russians, and Iran joined the list during more recent years, due to nuclear collaboration. I know people who spent time living in Lebanon and laud it as a modern and progressive state. I also know people who have visited Iran, and Iraq under Saddam Hussein, and they all report that it was a peaceful and modern society, not unlike the Soviet Union of our childhoods. Saddam was no gift to humanity, for sure – but otherwise, people had weddings and children went to music lessons. That the United States presumed the right to mass murder them and turn their country into a wasteland, was a calamity the Russians could not stand for.

176

The rather brutal treatment of Hussein should have been a lesson, and yet it was not learned. Colonel Muammar Gaddafi was a friend of Russia. A bit eccentric, for sure, but he was loyal to us – and to the Brits, I must say[50]. That we failed to rescue Gaddafi – who met his grim fate during the Dmitry Medvedev presidency – was a huge blow to all Russians. Not a single person in Russia does not think it was a mistake, one Medvedev made consciously and defended by saying that Gaddafi "had become irrelevant". This monumental failure sealed the dislike of Medvedev within the elites.

It was not only that we allowed the unthinkable inhumanity of the ultimate treatment of Gaddafi to happen. More importantly, he was our ally. Once he was abandoned, what message did it send to our other allies or those who might be thinking of becoming one? Excuses were made, including that Gaddafi himself refused rescue when it was offered to him – but this was a conflation. Yes, he may have refused rescue before all was lost. But when one looks at the timeline of the events closely, it is clear that the window of opportunity for Russian forces to go in and extract Gaddafi existed very close to the end, at the time when he would have, undoubtedly, come along. The particularly brutal way in which he was treated, and the thought that every future ally of Russia might envision themselves ending up this way now, legitimized Putin's return to the presidency in 2012. At least *that* would no longer happen, Russians assumed.

And here comes Syria. Whatever he is or not, Assad is a secular leader in the region where the fall of secular governments portends chaos and brings terrorism to our own cities and towns. While America cares nothing about the world, but only about its geopolitics, Russians care about not making the same mistake – putting it mildly – that we made with Gaddafi. If it kills us, we will make sure that Assad is nowhere near ending up the same way – and since we do not particularly want him in Russia, we rather he stay in power, as the last barrier of sanity against fundamentalism, all other countries around him having fallen.

I am making a *patriotic* case now, but this is not necessarily a popular case. Russian people do not care a bit about Syria or Syrians. It is far away, it is

---

50 Much as Russians are devastated at Russia's abandonment of Colonel Gaddafi, I, as an alumna of the University of London, have always been disgusted with the London School of Economics' severance of ties with its alumnus Saif Gaddafi, who had donated considerable sums to the school and whose academic work in it had never been called into any doubt.

Muslim, and no one in Russia today would suggest that it is a part of our strategic interests anymore. This is all just our rebuttal of America's madness, and us not wanting to let down any more people who trust us. But Russians' hearts are not in it. In December 2016, when a plane of civilians, including a military song and dance ensemble and Russia's most famous charity activist, Lisa Glinka, died in a crash of a military jet heading to Syria for a holiday concert for the troops, there was backlash in the elites. Why did they have to go? Why were we there, anyway? Syria is a crazy place. If the Americans miraculously disappeared from the Middle East, I fully believe that so would the Russians. We do not want it any more than anyone in the U.S. wants it.

China

As I write this, former President Donald Trump is speaking on *Hannity*, his first Fox News interview since leaving office. Trump is making an argument that the "Russia, Russia, Russia" scandal pushed Russia out of the alliance with Western nations and into the arms of China. "The worst thing you can do," – Trump says, "is put China and Russia together. And [now], they are together".

In that, Trump is right, but it is more than that. Many Americans fail to see that China is an inevitability for the Russians. Most, probably, do not even realize that China borders Russia, let alone that Russia's land border with China is longer than the U.S. border with Mexico. While it is certainly better guarded on both sides than the U.S.-Mexico border, there is a lot of movement across it, and a lot of cultural blending and intermarriage in the areas surrounding it on both sides. This phenomenon is almost imperceptible from as far away as Moscow and virtually unknown in the rest of the world, where any alliance between Russia and China is seen only as a factor of geopolitics. For the Russia's Far East, it is a reality.

Chinese regions near the Russian border have a strong presence of Russian language and culture in them, and many Russians live and work in China or attend Chinese universities. I still recall the awe and horror of an ominous TV report showing thousands of Russian citizens in China, pets and suitcases in their arms, running on foot toward the Sino-Russian border in the last few hours before it was to be sealed at the dawn of the COVID-19 pandemic. It reminded me vaguely of the exodus of Germans from East Berlin in the hours before the Wall went up. But my main question was – what were they all doing there?!

178

I asked myself that question because I had just returned to Russia – serendipitously – after more than a year's absence. I found out quickly that things have changed, and not in the least in terms of the proliferation of all things Chinese. In Moscow, all city notices and direction signs had been supplanted with their versions in Mandarin, underneath the previously ubiquitous Russian and English versions.[51] Vastly increased numbers of Chinese visitors and tourists were visible on the streets with a naked eye. The Country's fanciest department store, *GUM*[52] on Red Square, had splashed out on translating all signage and notices into Mandarin. It felt as if the announcements in Mandarin in the Moscow metro, where English had only been added to Russian in anticipation of the FIFA World Cup in 2018, were imminent.

Things are now worse – if you consider it all bad – in the Far East, on the Russian side of the Sino-Russian border. An old late-night comedy sketch about a Russian policeman in a Far East border town, who greets incomers from China every day with a cheerful "Learn Russian!" until he, one day, inadvertently starts saying it in Mandarin, is reportedly coming true. Let's face it, there are *a lot* of Chinese, more than a billion. In fact, there are roughly ten times more Chinese than there are Russians, and yet, we have much more *space*. Empty space. It's almost physics.

It is difficult to compare Russian and Chinese living standards. In both countries, they vary vastly by region and social strata. But you can bet they are broadly similar in provincial China and provincial Russia, places like Harbin and Khabarovsk, in the regions where the countries come together along their long common land border, culturally equidistant from either Moscow or Beijing.

Some other factors are in play, that draw the Chinese over the border. Years of "one child" policy in China (recently abandoned), and the resulting prevalence of men in the generation of current adults, are in sharp contrast with Russia, which mirrors the declining birth rate of all Europeans. In Russia, there are more women than men. Unprecedented incentives were introduced in recent years in order to encourage families to have more children, in an attempt to avert what is perceived as an upcoming demographic crisis. Chinese men, who are

---

51 Muscovites often joke that knowledge of English is necessary to get around the city, because English translation on direction signs deciphers obscure Russian acronyms. Those acronyms make the original signs about as intelligible to most of us, as their Mandarin translation.
52 *Glavnyi Universalnyi magazin* - the Main Department Store.

disciplined workers, not nearly as susceptible to alcoholism as ethnic Russians, and desperate to mate, have become popular marriage material for Russian women in border regions. Those marriages confer immigration and naturalization benefits, and produce, as offspring, increasing numbers of Russian citizens who are ethnically mixed.

This presents Russia with an uncomfortable truth. For all of its professions of multi-culturalism, Russia today is, for the most part, a nation state of people who are pale white, culturally European and Orthodox Christian. Just like in the rest of Europe – and possibly even more so, owing to harsh climate, alcoholism and lower life expectancy – its population decline is catastrophic, and all of the economic measures designed to boost the birth rate are not enough to avert the worst to come. By the year 2100, the world's largest country by land mass, which is already scarcely populated today at just under 150 million, could see its numbers fall to barely over 80 million. On top of that – and I may say so, being an ethnic Russian myself – we are an incredibly lazy bunch. We hate toil. Our defining cultural proverb goes, *work is not a wolf, it won't run off into the woods*. So much for global competitiveness.

Everywhere through the Western Christian world, the same knowledge persists: white Europeans do not procreate enough to be statistically sustainable. The demographics of all our countries will change by 2100. Whether it bothers us or not, depends, by and large, on the way of life we envision for our grandchildren going forward: a scaled down lifestyle of living local in harmony with nature, or global hegemony on the world stage. Culture and tradition vs. economics. Most countries that are already bent on domination seem to be geared to choose economics.

Certain factions in the United States persistently attempt to answer the demographic crisis by opening its doors to unlimited immigration – reasoning, perhaps, that most of the influx comes from the predominantly Christian population of Latin America (yet Catholic, and, therefore, procreating at a much higher rate than the locals). The fusion, the theory goes, will not bring offense to *Judaeo-Christian values*. When Western Europe did the same, and hundreds of thousands of Muslim men came, things did not go nearly as smooth (even if you consider that they are going smooth in the United States, which they are not quite, mainly because the execution of its immigration process is inherently mismanaged).

180

Russia was watching, harboring its own demographic secret. For our competitiveness on the world stage just two or three generations from now, it is either go Chinese or bust. In the last 30 years, Russia enjoyed substantial immigration, mainly due to ethnic Slavs relocating from other parts of the former USSR and returnees from Soviet-era emigration to Israel. But these waves have already been absorbed and did not affect the dire demographic projections very much. Low-skilled migration of workers from Middle Asia, mainly Tajikistan, appears to be temporal in nature – and, as their numbers increase, so does the resentment among the local population.

Despite being unwilling to sweep the streets themselves, Russians argue that population replenishment needs to bring with it like for like skilled workers, scientists and entrepreneurs. There are only so many street sweepers and menial workers Russia can absorb, and their further influx will not address our economic competitiveness problem. It doesn't help matters that people from Middle Asia are Muslim. Russians, who have long happily shared the country with moderate Tatars, are already struggling to coexist with fundamentalist Chechens. A further influx of Muslims is not on anyone's agenda – and, in any event, there aren't enough Tajiks in the whole world to fill the demographic void.

The overpopulated country with which Russia shares more than 4000 km of land border, whose current childbearing generations are struggling with the effects of population control, can be barely contained from spilling into our scarcely inhabited land, where they are, by contrast, met instantly with vigorous, and race-blind, government incentives to procreate[53]. White and Christian they are not, but Russia, after years of official atheism, has a low rate of religious observance, and no one really cares. The only real way to preserve Russia's population levels is to concede that its Europeans will be slowly replaced with hardworking and sober Chinese, who are a mixture of atheists, produced by years of Communist rule in a lived experience not dissimilar to our own, and Buddhists,

---

53 I used to joke that frequent changes in British immigration policy seem to be guided by the government's attempts to draft it in such a way that it will bring in anyone other than predominantly Indians and Pakistanis; yet, each time they redesign it, the result is always the new influx of the Indians and the Pakistanis. In some way, Russian demographic policy is similar. Its unprecedented procreation incentives were, it seems initially designed to boost ethnic Russian population growth in order not to be "overrun" by the Chinese, but it is clear now that, if these policies are to have any significant effect on the population decline, it will be through the increase in the numbers of Asians.

who, at least, definitely aren't going to take anyone hostage or blow anything up. At the same time, Russians are well aware that the Chinese, unlike the Tajiks, come from a society of comparable spoils, a competitive economy and high-quality education. They are our only demographic hope.

All of these factors are independent of Sino-Russian geopolitical relations. We can neither ignore China nor simply turn Westward and pretend that it is not there. China is already here, and it is here to stay. Geographic proximity, in turn, leads to more mutual awareness. Many Russians, even those who live thousands of miles from the border, have been to China for a vacation, and China is largely "normalized" in their eyes.

To a Muscovite, Beijing is a version of our Soviet past, while Shanghai, in many respects, is a more densely populated version of modern Moscow, with taller residential buildings and better trains. In terms of the physical appearance of its built environment, much of China feels familiar and comforting to a former Soviet citizen. It still runs Soviet trains between cities, and its smaller villages, nameless on a map (still, with multi-million populations) look like provincial Russian cities, having been built with Soviet assistance. If aliens abducted a non-worldly Russian from the middle of the country and deposited them in the middle of China, they would probably feel comfortable enough, and quickly figure out what to do. More so, than they would be in the United States.

The strange and uneven transition from a planned economy to semi-capitalism, that the Chinese are going through, is not very different to what Russians went through in the late 1980s and early 1990s. China's glaring gap between the super rich and the very poor is also familiar to us. The language barrier is the last one to stand, but it is receding – Russians are prone to engage in seemingly pointless intellectual exercise, much more so than they are to do meaningful work, and the uptake for Mandarin instruction is increasing. More and more public schools offer it in place of previously ubiquitous English and German. For their part, the Chinese are quick learners, as everyone in the education system in the United States already knows. They tend to have terrible accents, but they are able to learn Russian as easily as English (or mathematics).

Not all Russians are happy about the march of Chinese culture in their land. In fact, Russians are a pretty guarded people, who grew up in a mono cultural, mono racial society, and, apart from Muscovites, most have trouble coping with any sort of diversity of ethnicity or language. The Asian culture is

182

alien to them. The elites in large cities are perennially engaged in "East vs. West" debate, and exploration of an identity we, as Russians, must – the theory goes – find on either of the two continents that we straddle. This has been going on for many years, and the search is still on – but it seems like most of us will not have a say. Russia does also share a small section of its land border with Norway, but hoards of Norwegians are as unlikely to move to Russia and breed like rabbits, as they are to move to the United States[54].

For the West, it is important to understand that the much-feared idea of "Russia and China together" is more than a geopolitical or economic idea, but rather a process of cultural fusion that is a result of geography. Love it or hate it, that fusion cannot be entirely avoided. It is absolutely true that Russiagate in the West in recent years pushed us into China's arms, but only blame yourselves partly, because we were always going to end up there anyway. It's not personal, it's economics and human nature.

England!
England is the most boring place on Earth. I am not sure it's a bad thing – in fact, I sense that the singular unifying national idea that keeps England together, is that it is boring, and its people like it that way. Not much happens, and thank God for that.

Russia is the exact opposite. Conditioned by their lived experience, Russians are all about what we call *dvizhuha*. It is slang for "movement", but the more apt translation would be *the happening*, such as, when *shit happens*. Any stability in Russia is fragile because Russians tolerate high levels of personal and financial risk, and are internally prepared to accept status quo disruption.

I first visited England in the summer of 1991, aged 16, and noticed its quaint antiquity, and lack of *dvizhuha*, right away. At that time, there had been plenty of *shit happening* in Russia, of course. I remember telling people, in my teenage wisdom, that I was definitely going to come back and live in England "when I am old, in my forties". In the event, it did not take that long.

---

54 For those who did not follow the Trump presidency closely, he once caused laughter by suggesting that cultural cohesion in the country can be aided by inviting Norwegians to immigrate.

In early October 1993, I got out of my office on the back of the rock-music accessories store in central Moscow, which I owned at the time, and realized that I cannot leave. The store was adjacent to a trolley bus park, and my car, parked outside, was blocked by the stalled trolley buses. Sounds of gunfire were coming from the nearby Garden Ring. Distraught people were running away from it. I had just learned that I was pregnant, and was even more terrified than most. Later, we all watched our military fire tank cannons into our own Parliament building, setting portions of it on fire. Ostankino television center, at which my mother was miraculously not present at the time of the events, was stormed by armed formations, and several dozen people died.

I do not want to say it was business as usual – in fact, it was the first and last armed disruption in Moscow in my memory (by contrast, the events in the wake of coupe d'etat in 1991 were relatively peaceful, other than a couple of people who were accidentally run over by a rolling tank not far from the American Embassy). But it was followed soon afterward by the presidential election of 1996, in which those of us who were variously involved in the campaign to re-elect President Yeltsin were in fear for our lives – or so we thought – in the plausibly likely case of a communist *revanche*. My oldest daughter, Darya, was 2 years old at that time. After the first round of the election, there was panic in Moscow – it was like the days before the fall of Saigon. The American Embassy was besieged by crowds. *Kommersant* publishing house, where I worked at the time, produced the election-themed newspaper titled *Ne Dai Bog – God Forbid.* Our real names were in the paper – the wisdom of which I question in hindsight, although I keep a copy as a souvenir – and we were told that we were all on a hit list of one sort or another.

Kommersant's relationship with the U.S. Embassy was not great at the time. Some of its staff had received visitor visas, went to America and failed to return. Serendipitously, yours truly turned out to had been behind our only positive collaboration with the Embassy. A few months prior, I had been dispatched to interview U.S. Ambassador Thomas Pickering on the subject of emission of new $100 bills. Russia, at the time, was the one place on Earth where the absolute majority of cash $100 bills were in circulation. I had never contemplated traveling to the United States, but a framed photo of myself shaking Pickering's hand sat in my office. That photo earned me a place on a secret list, the rest of which included the then-owner of Kommersant, Vladimir

Yakovlev, and some of his close associates. We all managed to secure U.S. visas, literally, on July 2, 1996 – the day before the run-off election. Yeltsin won, but I decided that it was all too much *dvizhuha* for me, after all. So I used mine.

Even though the 1990s ultimately worked out for most of the elites in Russia, the experience of living through those years also exhausted us. Most of the Russian Gen X-ers, who had children born in the 1990s and early 2000s, ultimately reasoned that we'd rather they never had to go through the same experience. Most Russians have warmer feelings for America than for England, but that is because Americans are more like us, and, therefore, America is also quite screwed up. *Shit happens* there too, and, for young people, it is difficult to navigate. Meanwhile, England was homogeneous, relatively safe and dull. It was also not quite as far from Moscow – essentially, it was a slightly remote safe neighborhood. All you had to do was send a kid there, and you could be reasonably certain that they would never have to deal with *dvizhuha*. They would grow up not wanting to ever see any.

We, who watched our shelves empty first, then our state fall, then our Parliament burn, and were then threatened with physical elimination, wanted our children to grow up in the most boring place on Earth, one where they still can't get over Guy Fawkes, who didn't even manage to blow anything up. Were we ever, or are we now, reasonably certain that Russia will become such a boring place? I am not. Nor are ordinary Russians, it seems. At the start of the COVID lockdown in the spring of 2020, most of them reasoned that COVID was a cover for something bigger. *Don't you think it's a coup d'etat?* – an Uber driver asked me. He was my age, and there was a sparkle of excitement in his voice. Clearly, he thought life had got too boring.

It is important to understand, however, that England never was anything more than a safe neighborhood to us. America was exciting, and, love it or hate it, it provided a teachable lesson in economics, politics, democracy, capitalism. England provided none of that. I never heard anyone say – *England is so cool, its economy is great, and there is democracy and freedom that we should all aspire to!* Not that anyone disputes that there is a safe level of democracy and freedom in England – how much, I suppose, is a matter of debate and subject to fluctuation – but it is taken for granted, rather than aspired to. People go to America to experience democracy or participate in the economy, and to England, if they want to do nothing at all.

185

Not that you could do business in England. I assume that you could, and some do, but if you were considering it alongside Russia or the United States, England loses to both. Things are slow, inefficient, both the elites and consumers are wary of foreigners and newcomers, there is a regulatory burden and bureaucratic ineptitude. I practiced immigration law in London for 5 years and know a huge chunk of our diaspora there. A total of one person who actually started a mid-size business in the UK from scratch saw it through to profitability. It is a retail business with a turnover circa £5 million a year – but it took 5 years to achieve profitability, and that same person already had that same turnover in their Russian business when they started. They were set back by 5 years, with a noble motive of permanently raising their children away from *dvizhuha*.

It is great to be poor in England, because the social safety net is generous. It is better to be poor in England than in either Russia or the United States, assuming that you are a British citizen. But if you are anything else but poor, England loses. It is not a place for investment, for which Russia offers better returns, and America – less risk. It is not a place for business: in America, just like in Russia, five years to breaking even would be a joke. No one even has an attention span this long! If you are a professional, England is a joke to start with. While it has a booming job market for janitors, baristas and care workers, it has no professional job market to speak of, compared to the United States, and the salaries are simply incomparable. Since it would make no economic sense whatsoever for a low-skilled person to leave Russia, where they would be better off in terms of economic security and job opportunities, most Russians in the UK are at least professionals, who perceive themselves in a constant process of choice between England, OAE, United States, Canada and anywhere else. The gap between how they see themselves, and how England sees them, is stunning.

As a destination, England provides an economic advantage to only one group of people: private school and undergraduate students. British education is awful. If we want to fix it, we have to acknowledge that British secondary schools are a joke, compared to almost any other country, and most of its universities are a joke compared to their U.S. counterparts. But British private schools and universities are much easier to get into, and a large number of them cater to international families seeking to get their young away from *dvizhuha* more than to educate them; and they are much cheaper. Even without government finance, it is much cheaper to put a kid through school and university in England,

186

than in the United States. It is also cheaper to come and live in England yourself, leading a middle-class lifestyle while having your kids attend a decent government-maintained school, than to pay tuition at an international school in Moscow. The latter is true for even just one child. The education advantage disappears sharply after the Bachelor's degree level. Postgraduate education in England is a cruel joke, compared to the United States, where almost anyone with half a brain gets generous stipends, and research funding is easy to come by.

Needless to say, England is not a vacation destination. I am a fan of the Suffolk coast and Isle of Wight myself, but let's just say that no one who is choosing a seaside holiday from Moscow is heading for the Norfolk Broads. The only marketable seaside that we have would be on the Channel coast, but Brighton caters to backpackers and hippies and has only rocky beaches, while nearby Hastings is, for want of a better word, run down. Popular domestic destinations on the Irish sea coast have no infrastructure for international holidaymakers. While there are things you can buy in London if you are already there, it hardly offers a shopping experience that one can travel for, either.

In other words, England is safe and average, which is exactly what most of us are looking for when it comes to our children. England is good for the British, and our children *are* British. Most of us, the older generation – only nominally so. In America, you can get off the plane and be American immediately, whether or not you speak any English. In Britain, I feel no more British after 13 years, than I did on day one. Having been a British citizen for most of those years did not change that. The high society treats foreigners as a mere curiosity, and ordinary British people have a tendency to be racist in ways they are not aware of. They think that they are being cheerfully accommodating when they ask every person with a foreign accent *"how long are you here for?"*, but from our perspective it is a daunting daily reminder of non-acceptance. My daughters, although they speak the internationalized version of American English with me, can *do the accent* when speaking with others, so as to avoid having strangers cheerfully ask them, in a gist, when are they going back to wherever they came from. For my part, I know I will always be beyond hope.

Judging by my immigration clients over the years, most of the Russian Gen X-ers, as well as its older Millennials – the Global Russians – consider their residence in England, and sometimes naturalization, only as a necessary step to assuring the continuity of such residence for their children. Where the

187

immigration status of the children is not connected to the parents, the parents usually skip the permanent residence or leave altogether, when the kids are old enough to stay. Those of us who ate *the Bush legs* at the fall of the USSR will forever require the levels of adrenaline that the United Kingdom alone cannot provide. It is a curse, and we do not wish it on our kids; but personally, we all find the boredom and pretentiousness of England unbearable.

It is not that we all want to live out the rest of our lives in Russia. Israel, the United States, Canada, many European countries – these are all valid destinations. Older Millennials, those too old to be the children of Gen X-ers but too young to have internalized the trauma of the 1990s, might raise their kids in England but take jobs in the Emirates, or anywhere else in the world. America is a sustainable destination for Russian entrepreneurs: it has a huge diaspora, is conducive to the production of adrenaline, and receptive to chutzpah.

Many Russians, whether they are British citizens or not, have bought and maintain homes in England. England has marketed itself, fairly or not, as a benchmark of stability and desirability – so it is rather amusing when it responds to the influx of affluent foreigners with purported indignation. Just as most of its secondary schools and universities cater directly to international students, so do its courts and most of its legal industry – boy, we wouldn't need half as many solicitors and barristers, if half of them weren't dedicating themselves full time to fleecing the Russian rich! While a considerable percentage of the population of England is functionally homeless, it has a massive luxury property market that there aren't enough affluent British citizens to sustain. Harrods would be out of business tomorrow if Russians did not shop there.

It is a perpetual mistake for Russia-haters to claim, however, that Russians have some sort of agenda toward England, let alone that they have purchased homes and made investments there as an "influence operation". Influence on whom? Most Russians would not give a rat's rear end if *the Island of Doom*, as we call it, were to sink – if only their children weren't on it at the moment when it happens. England is like a trendy gated community or a new neighborhood. It was advertised, amenities were offered, so residents came. If it becomes run down, or residents feel that they are being harassed, they will leave. England has no intrinsic value, it offers nothing. Being there is not an end of itself. It is just a place to be, and increasingly, to visit one's adult children.

The most frequent cliche used in Parliament in the afternoons, by haters raging on about Evil Russians on the empty floor when no one is listening, is that Russians came to England to "park their money". Park their money? Boy, this sure sounds like the money should still be there when you come back. Who would *park* money by investing it into tuition at substandard universities and finishing schools, or overpriced real estate in a place with bad weather where everyone hates you? Trust me, money spent in England is money you might never see again, and that is everyone's starting premise. No one in our generation made any amount of money in England, but we have all brought and spent at least tens of thousands, if not hundreds of thousands, as in my case, or millions and hundreds of millions, as in other cases, pounds. In the experience of my own family and countless others, England has not been a money *laundromat*, but rather, a shredder. If you want a place to permanently dump all the money you have in exchange for a fleeting and uncertain promise of safety and stability for your children, come to England.

The same goes for the extraordinary claim of "reputation laundering", which is so stupid that it must have been conjured up by Bill Browder himself. Why would private persons, about whom no one had previously heard, suddenly care what anyone in a place called England thinks about them? And even if they decide to perform good deeds in order to be known for them, why is it not a noble quest? At what point did "reputations" of people who had been unknown to the public before they did something wholesome, started to require laundering with that same public in the first place? Seeing as Browder himself is a single source of smearing of most of the "reputations" he alludes to, a rather cheaper way of solving the problem would have come to the mind of any person who was as evil as Browder makes Russians out to be. Browder is lucky that he is crazy.

The Russian diaspora in London presently finds itself at a crossroads. Do we continue to invest money and effort in *the Island of Doom*, as it becomes increasingly disrespectful and ungrateful for it, or do we let it sink into decadence of its own madness? The only problem with the latter plan is to somehow coax our kids off it – for now, most of us linger aimlessly, our children being the only people in the face of whose rage we falter. Admittedly, England is not yet as far gone down the road of Russophobia as America. I feel there is still hope.

The reason it is not too far gone is that Russians are much more present in England – and England knows us better, so *it* knows better. After all, Russians

189

and Brits are the two top nations in the world, when it comes to propensity for dry sarcasm. According to a recent study, a Brit is far more likely to laugh at a joke made by a Russian, than a person from anywhere else in the world. (But we also know, of course, that they are simply being polite). In the Soviet Union, Jerome K. Jerome's *Three Men in a Boat to Say Nothing of a Dog* was considered the funniest book ever written. Enough said.

As a diaspora of skilled middle-class professionals and wealthy people, we would like to stop being called "spies" by newspapers that our children read, we want Britain to stop parading our fugitives from justice around as arbiters of morality, we want to stop being told that the country we still love, that does not care about Britain one way or another one tiniest bit, is the "number one threat" to it. I do not think we are asking for much, in view of our collective contribution to Britain's GDP.

Jen Psaki

When Jennifer Psaki was appointed President Biden's press-secretary, she was virtually unknown in the United States; many American journalists barely knew or remembered who she was. Perhaps, the Biden administration thought that they were appointing a fresh face, starting from a clean slate.

But it was not so, of course. Most Americans either did not know or forgot, that Jen Psaki was previously a spokesperson for the U.S. State Department under the Obama administration (later, she was briefly Obama's spokesperson). Domestically, this didn't mean much, perhaps, except that she had relevant experience. Internationally, however, Psaki's appointment as Biden press-secretary was a PR disaster: the Biden administration, already faltering from the start, is now publicly represented by a woman who has long been a laughingstock of the whole world.

Russians could not have been more amused if Biden appointed Bart Simpson as communications director. Jubilation at the *Return of Jen Psaki* in the Russian media and blogosphere was endless. "She is back!", "NOW America is finally going to be fun again", were only the tip of the iceberg of the sentiment it produced. The meme collections, and the endless hours-long "Jen Psaki's funniest blunders" videos, were top of the viewing charts once again. Russians have always gone to town on the subject Jen Psaki – and now, the unthinkable was happening; the gift, literally, was going to keep on giving!

Psaki's hiring as the White House press-secretary was an enormous gift to the Russians. Even if she somehow didn't make any more blunders, it would not matter, since hours of Psaki stand-up comedy were already on tape, and thousands of memes memorializing her pre-existed online. Russians were thus given a huge head start in making fun of all things Biden, courtesy of his own ignorance. Their favorite tape, where Psaki famously describes the flow of natural gas "from Western Europe, through Ukraine and into Russia", was playing everywhere on a loop.

Jen Psaki's initial rise to infamy in Russia coincided with the events in Crimea and the first wave of sanctions in 2014. Her ignorance and inexperience in foreign affairs did not help. There are tapes of Psaki confusing Iran and Iraq, accusing Russia of "provocation" for holding military exercises in its Astrakhan region, which she referred to as being "on the Ukrainian border" (Astrakhan, on the shores of the Caspian Sea at the Volga river delta, is many hundreds of miles away from Ukraine), or suggesting, to the amusement of her arch-interrogator, AP correspondent Mike Lee, that images on social media show people operating in Ukraine who "look like they are from Russia" (Russians and Ukrainians belong to broadly the same ethnic group, and cannot be visually distinguished from each other – let alone that the entire premise of the conflict was that ethnic and cultural Russians populate most of Eastern Ukraine). Jen Psaki's tendency to demur instead of answering questions also got the attention of the Russians. *Jen Psaki gets into a taxi,* -- a joke went. *"Where to?",* -- *the driver asks. "I will tell you when we get there",* -- *she responds.*

The apotheosis of Psaki's infamy in Russia came with her assertion that a referendum in Donetsk, in Eastern Ukraine, was flawed because of "carousel voting". When asked by reporters to clarify what that term meant, she responded that she did not know, having just read it off the prepared notes. After Psaki was appointed Biden spokesperson, that old video was edited together with a bit from Biden's own first press appearance, where he scrambles for his "notes", and later looks around, in a confused way, asking "where is my staff". The two, it seemed to the Russian people, have truly found each other.

My favorite Russian Internet meme about Psaki is based only in part on her actual assertion. It's a lively child's drawing titled "World Atlas according to Jen Psaki", showing lush mountains on the shore of a blue sea, labeled, respectively, "Rostov mountains" and "Belorussian sea".

191

Psaki claimed, at one point, that a flood of refugees from Eastern Ukraine into Russia's neighboring Rostov-on-Don region were simply tourists seeking to "enjoy mountain air". Hopelessly flat, boring and dusty, the Greater Rostov area has, in recent years, surpassed Chechnya and Dagestan as the country's most unsafe region. All major countries advise their citizens to stay away. The tandem assertion that Psaki threatened to bring the U.S. Navy "to the shores of Belarus" (which is landlocked), may as well be Psaki-inspired fiction, as I found no evidence that she actually said that. She did not have to – that ship has sailed a long time ago. To Belarus, no doubt.

Back in 2014, *VGTRK Rossiya's* flagship evening news program coined the term *psaking,* which they used, broadly, for buffoonery – being not very well informed, and yet righteous. Russia's NTV channel (my mother's old alma mater) established a mock nightly news-based comedy show, titled *Psaki at Night*. Nowhere else in the world, I am sure, had Jen Psaki been the butt of so many jokes and memes as in Russia. Every Russian knew, way before Joe Biden even had a shot at the Presidency, who Jen Psaki was. She was a household name in Russia way before Joe Biden became one. She was the living, breathing caricature of all that was ludicrous about America, and now she was back. How was the United States expecting anyone, let alone Russians, to take seriously any White House pronouncements now?

I do not argue that the United States should guide themselves with *what Russians think* when making staffing decisions. I would also agree that the targeting of Psaki in Russia was somewhat misogynistic. But it was also evidence-based: she is poorly informed on subjects of geography and geopolitics, and not at all quick-witted. Was it truly wise to appoint, as the American messenger-in-chief, a person in whose namesake units – *the psakis* – the citizenry of that country's chief competitor state habitually measures everyday stupidity, in an adopted term so widely recognized that it is akin to calling a photocopy machine *a xerox*?

For rather mysterious reasons, Bill Maher was never much known or quoted in Russia, but Psaki's appointment to the Biden administration gave literal meaning to Maher's recent quip: Americans, indeed, were just *a silly people* now.

Ukraine

You would think this is a big deal – but the truth is, it is not. Russians, for the most part, view "the Ukrainian problem" as a non-issue. At least, not an international issue. Russians are still struggling with a rather bizarre idea that Ukraine is now a separate country. Imagine that you have a somewhat grown-up child who left home and broke off all contact with you. They are now screaming that they are being kidnapped each time you approach them on the street, and the incident makes national news every time. That's Russia and Ukraine for you, as far as most Russians are concerned. It's embarrassing, but we'd rather keep it in the family.

The Western thinking behind this goes something along the lines of – well, Ukraine was one of the 15 former Soviet Republics, they all gained independence in 1991, and if Russians claim that Ukraine is not *really* a separate country, then, surely, Latvia is next. But that is not what it is, at all. Latvia is not next, neither is Georgia or Tajikistan, nor anyone else, for that matter. Reasons for that have nothing to do with the fact that Latvia is now a NATO and EU member, or that half of the population of Tajikistan already lives in Russia, sweeping our streets, toiling on construction sites and bagging our groceries. No one else is next, because no one else is Ukraine. Allow me to explain.

No one in Russia (and, I suspect, in most of Ukraine, despite their recent geopolitically motivated pronouncements) had ever thought that Russians and Ukrainians were different people. There are no racial, ethnic or cultural differences between these two peoples, who always had the same language, religion and cuisine. In the Soviet Union, we had a saying – *elderberry in the garden, uncle in Kiev*. It meant to not make any sense, speak in non-sequiturs. But it did actually make sense – everyone, at the end of the day, had a metaphorical *uncle in Kiev* or had some part of their family originate there, or reside there at one time in the past[55]. Russians are convinced that we do not need to *take Kiev* because we have already done it once – in 882. Prince Oleg of Novgorod, then regent for young Igor Rurik, took Kiev, according to legend, by trickery – and established in it the capital of what became known as *Kievan Rus*.

Rurik became known as Prince Igor of Kiev. After his macabre death, his widow, Princess Olga, ruled *Kievan Rus* in his stead, as a regent for their son. At

---

55 In our family, rumor had it that Grandpa Boris hailed from Kharkiv.

the time, *Kievan Rus* was still pagan. Wrath of Olga's retribution against those whom she held responsible for Igor's death was legendary; if you read up on her, you will, hopefully, be convinced to stay on a good side of any Olga. Later, Princess Olga became the first Russian ruler to be baptized into Christianity, which paved way for the eventual establishment of *Kievan Rus* as a powerful Christian state. Modern-day Russia, Ukraine and Belarus all derive their cultural and religious heritage, and write their history, from Kievan Rus. To Russians, Kiev is the former capital of their country.

Most people in Soviet Russia and Ukraine had difficulty sorting out whether to call themselves *Russian* or *Ukrainian* on state ethnicity rosters. For some reason, Jews – who were forced to disguise their ethnicity, if at all they could, in order to avoid being subjected to discriminatory policies and quotas – tended to put themselves down as *Ukrainian* more often; it was a sort of an inside joke. No one discriminated against Ukrainians, as they were not otherwise distinguishable from us. Soviet leaders Nikita Khrushchev and Leonid Brezhnev were both from Ukraine.

Alexey Navalny, the newly found and lately imprisoned darling of the anti-Russian zealots, is obsessed with ethnicity and, famously, thinks that being a *Russian citizen* is meaningless. In a recent interview with economist Sergei Guriev, he expressed a view that people should identify by their ethnic group instead. When asked how he himself identified, he replied: *Russian-Ukrainian*. Even Navalny, the great divider of people by ethnicity and an EU stooge, could not find it in himself to distinguish between Russians and Ukrainians.

Vladimir Putin agrees. He explains the same in Oliver Stone-produced documentary, "Revealing Ukraine". "In reality, this is one nation", – he says of Russians and Ukrainians. He goes on to point out that, historically, no one in *Kievan Rus'* ever thought of themselves as anything other than Russians, and Orthodox Christianity, which originated in those years, always united the relevant population, as opposed to the Catholic world to the West of it.

Since the Soviet years, the principal derogatory term for a person from Russia in Ukraine was *moskal'* – one from Moscow. That's because distinction on the basis of someone being *Russian*, strictly speaking, was not valid. Everyone was, to a degree, Russian. If a person got a job in Kiev, there they went. Then they would get a job back in Moscow, so that was where they went. You did not cross any borders or enter any sort of a different world as you did so.

194

Parts of Western Ukraine are, of course, predominantly Catholic today – and Romania and Hungary made claims to those regions as historically theirs. Both of them started handing out their passports to residents of those parts of Ukraine, indiscriminately, since the expansion of the European Union in 2004, and way before Russia ever issued one to an Eastern Ukrainian or a Crimean.

There is also now a Ukrainian language. In the Soviet years, it was a regional dialect of Russian, which we could all easily understand. Within my lifetime, especially since newly independent Ukraine mandated the use of Ukrainian in all official settings, it somehow developed into a language a spoken variant of which I no longer understood at all. To add insult to injury, many of the people I have known for years, who spoke absolutely pure Russian since childhood, have been forced to switch to Ukrainian, which I never knew that they possessed any knowledge of. Imagine if your best friend, or your uncle, suddenly starts speaking a non-intelligible language all the time and insists that they have always done so. It's stressful. Nowadays though, not having a common language no longer matters, because none of us has spoken to each other since 2014.

In recent months, we watched in amusement as nationalist Ukrainian politicians attempted to reconcile their ban on the use of the Russian language with the fact that large chunks of their populations do not speak the prescribed Ukrainian at all. In the end, they got around their own rules by declaring that the Russian spoken by half of their so-called country was merely an *Eastern dialect* of Ukrainian.

This is not to say, of course, that Russia is not prone to what was, in the Soviet years, euphemistically called *isolated excesses*. I am partly thankful that most of its airwaves nowadays are taken up by resentful coverage of the United States; before Russiagate, it was all Ukraine-bashing wall to wall, and creative temperature ran high. One story on cable news posited that Adolf Hitler was the architect of Ukrainian statehood. Surely, anyone who saw it thought that the divorce was getting out of hand.

A divorce like this can only be a result of a long marriage, one that was once filled with love, and in which children were jointly raised. Ukraine is much less of a separate country, as far as anyone is really, truly concerned, than the Baltic states, annexed by the Soviet Union in the 11th hour, or the culturally distinct and predominantly Muslim former republics in Middle Asia, or even the hapless Georgia and Armenia, which are both Christian but, nonetheless, have

195

somewhat of an Eastern culture, their own cuisine and languages with indecipherable scripts. Russia and Ukraine were one, and, much like a couple breaking up after a lifelong marriage, neither really knows how to live apart. Our cuisine is Ukrainian cuisine. *Borscht* is a Ukrainian soup, and now they are trying to take it away from us. No wonder that for the last 17 years, since the first *Orange Revolution*, courtesy of the U.S. Department of State and Boris Berezovsky, we have all been deeply, profoundly confused.

Imagine, if one day Florida decides to secede from the Union. Not Puerto Rico or Guam, which aren't really in it. Not Hawaii or Alaska, to which most of you have never been. Not California, which has always been only trouble, or Vermont, which is sort of its own place anyway. It's Florida: no more Disneyland for you! If you are British, imagine that it is not Northern Ireland that wants to leave the United Kingdom, and not even Scotland, but it's Wales. Or even, Devon and Cornwall. It's not a somewhere. It's where you always went to the seaside, and where your Grandma retired to. One day you are told that you can no longer visit, and then you learn that Americans are on their way to prop up Devon and Cornwall in their war against England. Salisbury and Taunton, overrun with refugees from Exeter, become Britain's most dangerous cities. Stonehenge lies in... well, ruins. Imagined? Would you not also be confused – that is, more so than an average British person is already confused on any given day?

Make no mistake about it, we are aware that Ukraine, technically, is now a separate country. One certified genius, acting in our name, signed up for that in December of 1991. But, for most of the time since, nothing changed that much. Not like it did with other ex-Soviet states. There was, eventually, somewhat of a border with Ukraine, but it was a formality. You did not need a passport. Russian railroad on the stretch from Moscow to Rostov continued to cut through what was now sovereign Ukraine for 37 kilometers, without any border controls, and it was difficult to tell, around those parts, whether you were in one country or another. It was pretty much the same empty field, and so it remained until 2014.

From 2015, after the war broke out in those parts, no one could really take the train to Rostov, or on to Sochi, anymore – a rather massive inconvenience in an otherwise modern country. It took us until 2017 to lay the new stretch of railway around Ukraine, 140 kilometers long. To most Russians and Russia itself, the realization that there needs to be a railroad around Ukraine is recent. Ukrainian independence, to us, did not really register in 1991. It did not register fully until 2014. In 2018, my middle daughter was on the plane from Moscow to Varna, in Bulgaria, to connect on to a further flight to the UK, after running a legal errand in Russia. I remember watching her flight path traced on Flightradar24, as her plane flew hundreds of extra miles, unnecessarily, just to get around the territory of Ukraine. "This is really, truly nuts", – I thought.

The biggest untruth, on which the Western hysteria about "Russian meddling in Ukraine" is predicated, is a notion that these are just two random independent countries – as if Ukraine to Russia is just the same as, say, Finland. If they admitted that it was a place that was integrally one with Russia for hundreds of years until very recently – not just legally, but culturally and politically – then we could at least have a productive conversation about Ukraine. So far, no one admits that.

I must admit that we always took a sarcastic attitude toward Ukraine and its statehood, all through the *Orange Revolution, maidan* and such like. To us, it was like the autonomous zone that the BLM activists set up in downtown Seattle in 2020 was to the U.S. conservative media. For the most part, we rolled our eyes and sighed. Spain can get obsessed with Catalonia's attempted secession, but if Benidorm set up their own government, I am sure Madrid would simply shrug. *Vaya con Dios!* Whatever. No one is actually trying to kidnap their petulant child who moved out, let alone kill them, for doing that, no matter how much embarrassment they caused. If you are shouting "I am going to kill you!" at your child, you are simply reminding them who is boss. It is not a threat.

Much like, I must say, President Putin's now infamous remark: *"if we invaded Ukraine, we would have taken Kiev by now"*. Sarcasm was lost in translation, as always. Of course, we could have taken Kiev any day, before lunch. How do we know Russian forces are not fighting in Eastern Ukraine? Because, if they did, they would have won a long time ago. If Russia went to war with Ukraine, there would not be a Ukraine by now. Does anyone really doubt that? The point is moot because we won't. No one was ever going to fight Ukraine, not any more than the British Army would fight Devon, or Spain would fight Benidorm. Just like, I might add, no one was going to nuke the United States in 1962 – but actually, even much, much less so.

The events in Ukraine since late 2013 were no laughing matter. Initially it was a domestic matter, but one that pitted its Russian-speaking, Ukrainian-Russian cohort against those who sided with a vicious resurgence of nationalism in the country. People died, and needlessly so – it was as if the runaway child turned out to have been schizophrenic, after all. Dozens of civilians from the Ukrainian Russian-speaking community were burned alive in the Palace of Unions building in Odessa on May 2, 2014, as they were blocked from exiting – the event on which U.S. media hardly reported at all, but Russians watched unfold live on their TV screens. Seeing Russian-speaking Eastern Ukrainians with signs "Russia, help us!" provoked a lot of emotions across the border.

Some people answered the call by joining the breakaway regiments. They were Russian, but they were not *Russia*. During the Clinton-Yeltsin years, many Russians traveled to Serbia to assist the *Orthodox brotherhood,* as they saw it, against a perceived U.S. aggression – just as their more cowardly supporters, as I recall, pelted the U.S. Embassy in Moscow with projectiles, mainly canned food[56]. This sort of thing was always a thing. Not everyone who is Russian consults either the alien mother ship, Vladimir Putin or *the KGB* on their actions. Russians are pretty big on taking initiative. Using one's own head is their thing.

The rag tag assortment of characters that joined the fight in Eastern Ukraine and muddled in its affairs was not, necessarily, a selection of our best or brightest. They were just random people. Some of them were military people, and I fully allow for the possibility that their decisions to go and join were, on some level, condoned by sympathetic superiors. But they were not *the army.* Russian army today is modernized, well equipped and high tech, its main potential for dominance being with its weaponry, not people. No individual with a rifle, whether or not enlisted, adequately represents it. The war in Eastern Ukraine is both a tragedy and an inconvenience to the Russians, but it is not, in any shape or form, our victorious war. We could win it if we joined it, but we rather that it did not take place. We rather none of *it,* starting with the late Boris Berezovsky's *Orange Revolution*, took place. No one is happy, no one is proud, and no one doesn't wish to wake up and learn that it was a bad dream.

There is, however, a silver lining. Its name is Crimea.

---

56 To my astonishment, the Embassy permanently ceased to fly a U.S. flag after that, presumably in a hope that fewer resentful Russians will be able to identify it.

Crimea

I have a special relationship with Crimea. All middle-class ex-Soviet families do. Crimea was a source of treasured memories of our summer vacations, much like Florida to Americans, or Cornwall and Brighton to Brits. Crimea was our seaside. Technically, the nearest big water to Moscow was in Leningrad, followed by Jurmala in Latvia. But the Baltic Sea was too cold to swim in, and the weather in those parts was frequently overcast. It was Crimea, not Jurmala, that was Soviet Union's primary seaside destination[57].

Having left Russia on the brink of adulthood, I do not really have a post-Soviet era relationship with Crimea. I went once in 2008, with my youngest two daughters, and recall being mildly annoyed at how run down and dilapidated it seemed. My clearest memory of that vacation is getting back to Moscow late at night and falling asleep, instead of going to the airport to pick up 14-year old Darya, who flew in from London. This ultimate parental failure is more vivid in my memory than the reunion with the magic memories of my childhood. Its magic gone, the once beloved peninsula did not have much to offer a modern era globe trotter. To most Russians, however, Crimea still had a place in their hearts.

Russian adults, especially those who did not have children in school, usually went to Crimea in September, when, I was always told, it was beautiful. I have close friends, a childless couple, to whom Septembers in Crimea – Russians call this time *velvet season* – were always absolutely integral. This was who they were. It was all that they were. They loved each other, and they loved their autumns in Crimea. There were thousands, tens of thousands of Russians who could say the same about themselves.[58]

Grandpa Georgiy's relationship with Crimea was even more profound. Upon graduating from the Naval Academy in 1948, and marrying Grandma Clara,

---

57 Soviet Union always had Sochi, of course, but it was farther away from Moscow, not as developed in those years, and never nearly as popular with the masses. The redevelopment of Sochi into the destination that exists today, took place mainly in the Putin era, in response to the desolation and mismanagement of Crimea by independent Ukraine. As a child, we went to Crimea twice, and others went more frequently. By contrast, I have never been to Sochi until 2006, when the 2014 Winter Olympics were awarded to it, prompting a building boom and considerable gentrification.

58 In 2014, during my short stint as a replacement producer for Sky News, I put the couple forward for a vox pop interview about Crimea, in which they expressed faith in the then upcoming independence referendum. The resulting report promptly made fun of them.

he was unexpectedly posted to Vladivostok, in the Far East. Having reluctantly made the two-week long journey, the couple – both ardent Muscovites in their mid-twenties – were devastated at the provinciality and desolation of the place. At first, they were reluctant to protest – in the waning years of Stalin's paranoia, arguing was never a good idea. Then, Grandma Clara learned that she was pregnant. She was not going to bring a child into this world in Vladivostok.

In desperation, Grandpa Georgiy devised an unprecedented gambit: he applied for admission to the Institute of Energy in Moscow, where a new track for the study of mines and torpedoes had just been announced, and petitioned the high command, over the heads of his immediate superiors. Rather than expressing dissatisfaction with his current assignment, Grandpa Georgiy shared his patriotic dreams of naval mine neutralization and pleaded for leave to attend graduate school in order to develop his skills and bring those ideas to fruition. Most of his fellow officers thought he was simply going to be executed – but, by miracle, some sympathetic official took pity on him.

In those years, passenger travel across the Trans-Siberian railway was intermittent, depending on the weather. By the time the permission to leave came through, it was winter. Grandpa Georgiy was being transferred on military orders, but tickets were impossible to come by for civilians. Grandma Clara, literally nine months pregnant, got one with the help of a local maternity clinic. Perhaps they simply wanted her out of their care. Our family lore is filled with tales of courage and perseverance on the journey back to civilization that Grandpa Georgiy and Grandma Clara made in December 1949, as the falling snow constantly threatened their progress. They arrived barely in time to ring in 1950. My mother was born just a week later and became the most entrenched Muscovite to have ever lived.

Now on the radar of high command for his chutzpah, and stuck in the landlocked Moscow, ostensibly, due to his study of physics, Grandpa Georgiy took a day job at the Navy headquarters[59]. His home port was now the flagship installation of the Soviet Navy: nearby, in Crimea. For the next 40 years, Crimea would become Grandpa Georgiy's second home, where he will forever leave his

---

[59] Prosaically, my grandfather himself puts his luck down to nepotism. One of his many cousins had, by then, married a man who was serving in the personnel department at the said Navy headquarters, and had apparently put in a word about Grandpa Georgiy's aspirations with the Torpedoes and Mines department – which, yes, was a thing.

heart. Grandma Clara, who tended to think that Stalin personally made all decisions in the Soviet Union, credited the Great Leader with her miraculous salvation from savagery, as she took her assigned seat at the Bolshoi.

Back when Grandpa Georgiy first set foot in Crimea in 1950, it was part of *RSFSR* – the Russian Socialist Federated Republic. Crimea was regarded as a special territory, separate from Ukraine, due to its strategic location and status as the home of the Navy, among other things. The shocking decision to convey the Crimean peninsula to the Ukrainian Socialist Republic came in February 1954. There weren't, at the time, a lot of practical implications for common folks, since both Russia and Ukraine were in the USSR, there was a single economy and there were no borders. But there were some administrative implications for the military, which many considered a headache.

An attempt had been made previously, in 1948, to convey special status within the then-RSFSR to the city of Sevastopol, where the Soviet Navy was based. That ostensibly made Sevastopol into a separate entity, administratively unmoored from the rest of RSFSR, and from Crimea as a region within it. Precedent for that existed – Russia already had two *Republic-level* cities with status of their own region, the cities of Moscow and Leningrad (now St. Petersburg). Due to its strategic importance, Sevastopol was supposed to become the third.

Since 1954, confusion reigned whether the law that transferred Crimea from RSFSR to Ukraine, as it was written, took account of Sevastopol's special status. You would guess, perhaps, that the RSFSR and present-day Russia's position on that always was that the transfer of Crimea to Ukraine in 1954 did not include Sevastopol, on a theory that it had not been in the administrative region of Crimea since 1948. Aside from convoluted admin, there weren't many real implications – until, of course, Ukrainian sovereignty in 1991. At first glance, it seemed to place the flagship base of the now-Russian Navy in a foreign country.

Relations between newly independent Ukraine and Russia were, for the most part, amicable during those years, but the status of Sevastopol remained an issue. The two countries entered into an agreement to use the bases in Sevastopol alongside each other, so that both Russian and Ukrainian Navy fleets would be based in the city. They also agreed to divide the assets of the Soviet Navy Black Sea fleet between them, which was eventually done. Russians, nonetheless, continued to lay claim to the city of Sevastopol.

Russian parliament took a vote in 1993, proclaiming Sevastopol a Russian city – much to the chagrin of not only Ukraine, but also of Russia's own President Yeltsin, who happened to be at odds with Parliament at that time. Ukrainians appeared at the specially called meeting of the UN Security Council, arguing that Sevastopol was Ukrainian, with the enthusiastic support of the Russians (the Yeltsin administration, of course, had exclusive power over foreign affairs). The back and forth continued for years afterward, and the exact details are not important. The point is, Crimea's status as a disputed territory is not new.

Sevastopol was not the only base the Navy had in Crimea. Grandpa Georgiy retired from the military at his 50th birthday in 1974, a month before I was born, but continued to be based in Crimea for his military physics research and de-mining exercises. His base was in Feodosia, which, unlike Sevastopol, was indisputably well within Crimea and, consequently, Ukraine. The disintegration of the USSR in 1991 brought to the fore realization that Grandpa Georgiy reached civilian retirement age – and, 45 years after Victory Day, there were no longer any naval mines left in the Black Sea for him to practice neutralizing. His research was de-funded. Since 1991, Grandpa Georgiy had only been to Crimea as a holidaymaker. He went every year and despaired more and more at the state of dilapidation and disrepair of the former naval bases and the surrounding environment[60].

Separatist movements in Sevastopol, as well as Crimea more generally, continued to flourish. Like in Scotland or Catalonia, where talk of secession is a daily reality, Crimeans were used to the notion of the peninsula becoming a part of Russia again, some day. The 1990s were chaotic in both of the newly independent states, but at the turn of the century things in Russia started to look up. The Russian economy was growing along with the price of oil, unemployment in Russia was low, and wages and social security payments were much higher than in Ukraine. More importantly, they were on time. The Russian state was solvent, and considerably more prosperous than Ukraine.

Joining Russia, for the residents of Crimea, meant an opportunity to move anywhere within Russia, even to Moscow, if they so wished. Muscovites

---

60 An agreement, signed by President Yeltsin in 1997, fixed the permission for Russia to have its fleet in Ukraine, and assigned bases in Sevastopol and Feodosia for its use. The Russian Navy maintained, and still continues to this day to maintain, the fleet in Sevastopol, but has abandoned Feodosia.

loved Crimea and always went there for a vacation in droves, bringing with them tales of prosperity, as well as cash. To the struggling Ukraine, Crimea was not a priority. Ukraine had a lot of coastline, and not a lot of funds to spread around. Residents of the peninsula were left to fend for themselves, relying on income from Russian tourism. Be it Stockholm syndrome or not, but it is no surprise that they started to identify with Russia – after all, they depended on vacationing Russians for survival.

By the end of President Putin's second term in 2008, when I last visited Crimea, Russia offered a markedly higher standard of living. A trip to Crimea from Moscow was like a journey 20 years into the past – and even worse, due to 20 years of dilapidation. It was clear that there had been no investment or development in Crimea since the disastrous dawn of Perestroika. It was the peninsula that time forgot.

What is entirely missing from the Western narrative on Crimea, is that the 2014 annexation enjoys almost universal support both in Russia and in Crimea. The few ardent Western-pandering liberal opposition figureheads that have fumed about it, for some years, demanding that we "return Crimea", based their demands on the notion of international decorum, the harm from sanctions and pariah status that ensued, rather than dared to argue that this was not what the Crimean people wanted.

They complained about alleged falsifications during the Independence referendum in Crimea. Knowing how close the issue is to many people's hearts, it may even be true. There would have been some falsifications, for sure. But it is of no import – no one, including those who complain about the 2014 referendum or think that we should "return" Crimea, seriously suggests that the referendum results would have been any different, had it been beyond reproach. The majority support for the annexation, among the population of Crimea, is agreed common ground. Majority support may not be universal support, but it is as damn near universal as support for anything ever is. Tales of "ballot box stuffing", which usually plague Russian elections, as well as Jen Psaki's famous "carousel voting", are red herrings, because a God honest personal vote taken from each eligible individual one by one for the whole world to see, would have still resulted in the same outcome every time.

We can argue about the validity of self-determination as a basis for secession or annexation, for sure – looking at you, Spain! But let us not dispute that the current status quo is consistent with that self-determination, just like the current status quo of numerous other regions is consistent with self-determination, or lack thereof, of their residents. Lied as they may have been to – and they were – but Scots did not vote for secession in the last Independence referendum, and residents of Montenegro did in theirs. If a referendum were to be held in Northern Ireland today, unionists might, once again, win (and in expressing a preference for the UK, as opposed to Ireland, to be a part of, many there also take account of the higher standard of living in the former).

It baffles the Russians that the so-called "international community" suddenly devalues self-determination in this case, while respects it in others. At the end of the day, the reasons why most Crimeans want to be in Russia, as opposed to Ukraine, are not geopolitical: just like Northern Irish unionists, they want to live in a more prosperous country, have their children move to Moscow and start careers there, and be paid higher pensions, on time[61]. The flurry of investment, development, infrastructure projects and superyachts that came in the wake of 2014 was also easy to predict for the Crimean voters. The expectation that Russia will defend its actions with its pocketbook was a no brainer, and it came true.

The one problem that was not easy for Russia to solve quickly, was to provide Crimea with drinking water. Following the annexation, Ukraine simply cut off the canal which brought most of the drinking water to Crimea. The peninsula had no commercially usable wells and no desalination plants. Crimean activist Natalya Poklonskaya, who now represents Crimea in the Russian State Duma, had attempted to bring in a delegation from the UN, to look for ways to address the water shortage. Instead, the United States imposed sanctions on Poklonskaya, and the UN visit failed when their people refused to obtain Russian visas and submit to Russian border control.

To Russia, Crimea is not just a source of our childhood memories. Its location is strategic, and vital to defense interests. The Black Sea fleet in Sevastopol was always viewed as absolutely paramount. We did not have any problem with the fleet being in Ukraine, subject to the agreement on leasing the Sevastopol base, which we dutifully extended in 2010, to run until 2042. The

---

61 I lived in Belfast, and am well aware that the factional conflict in Northern Ireland has been historically disguised as a religious conflict, but, in my observation, it is anything but.

euromaidan – which was, simply put, a coup d'etat – in Ukraine in December 2013 terrified the Russian defense ministry. It immediately ordered all of the Sevastopol-based fleet of the Russian Navy off shore, ostensibly to be reassembled in the Mediterranean for the support of operations in Syria. At that moment, the annexation became the only rational way for those ships to eventually come back to port.

The annexation of Crimea, I am sure of it, was spontaneous. The status of Crimea was a long-brewing problem, sort of like the decades-long truce in the Korean War; there was no imperative to solve the problem of Crimea until there suddenly was. It was neither a plan nor a strategy (if it were either, one should think it would have been better thought through). It was driven by a combination of threat and opportunity brought on by the events in Ukraine in December 2013. At the onset of those events, Ukraine was governed by a pro-Russian administration, and those events took everyone, including, most certainly, Russia (which had just gone to great lengths to sign a new 25+5 year lease for the port of Sevastopol with the Yanukovich administration in Ukraine), by surprise.

By the time of *euromaidan* in 2013, Boris Berezovsky was dead, but his ideas of subversion and unrest in Ukraine lived on. Without BAB's psychopathic genius this time around, the unrest and strife that lead to the ousting of the Yanukovich government, the separatist war in Eastern Ukraine and, eventually, the annexation of Crimea by Russia, were left entirely to the Obama-Biden State Department to finance. The same Obama-Biden administration then blamed the outcome on "Russian aggression". Projection, Russians think.

The annexation of Crimea was even more popular in Russia than it was in Crimea. So much so that in 2021, seven years later, you would struggle to find anyone who was still against *keeping* Crimea, even if they had initially been against acquiring it. The Russian public, elated at the prospect of bringing gentrification and superyachts to the dilapidated and abandoned peninsula that once held key to their childhood happiness, turned its wrath on anyone who publicly opposed *the reunification*, and it was a genuine, widespread sentiment.

Soon, *#Крымнаш*, or #Crimeaisours, became a hashtag, literally and figuratively, that denoted general agreement with the Putin doctrine, among Russians both at home and abroad. If a client in London asked me what I thought about Russia, Putin, Ukraine or whatnot, I would say "I think Crimea is ours", and this would give them all the information they needed – even though, in my heart of hearts, I do not give a rat's rear end about Crimea.

The United States and the EU (which, at the time, the UK was still part of) adopted, it seems, a reverse approach to the application of sanctions. They put everyone Russian who had made even the vaguest public remarks in support of *the reunification* on a personal sanctions list, as an anti-Ukraine aggressor. Several people that I know and have worked with are on the "Crimean" sanctions list. Overall, the list seems to have been adopted with all the seriousness and precaution of social media *cancellation* campaigns. Some of the people on it, like the former presidential candidate Sergey Glazyev, are *from* Ukraine. Glazyev was born and grew up there. *Russians think* that it would entitle at least him to express opinions about Ukraine and its affairs. Clearly, the Americans did not think so, and the British, who adopted EU sanctions in a "blanket" approach after Brexit, were not thinking at all.

Today, the U.S. sanctions are a self-fulfilling prophecy in Crimea. As their less-known effect, they impede the Crimean residents' ability to travel internationally, and local businesses suffer due to inability to import and export. Russian banks that were prime to enter Crimean markets halted those plans in fear of being sanctioned. There is no Apple Pay or Google Pay. Would be franchisees of international fast-food chains were forced to rename their businesses into something less conspicuous. Starbucks became *Starducks*.

It is notable that neither the Americans, nor the EU, sought to sanction my once-friend-turned-foe Alexey Navalny, whom they have taken to calling "Putin's main rival" and "opposition leader", and whose own calls on more Russian sanctions they appear nearly willing to heed. I am guessing Angela Merkel, during her famed 2020 meeting with the allegedly poisoned Navalny in Germany, forgot to ask him what he thought about *the reunification*. For his part, Navalny wasn't in much of an opposition to Putin on Crimea at all. Like many, he expressed reservations about the conduct of the independence referendum, but accepted that the result of a perfect poll would have likely been the same.

Speaking on the liberal opposition *Dozhd (Rain)* TV channel, Navalny was challenged by Ksenia Sobchak, herself a former presidential candidate and daughter of Anatoly Sobchak, former mayor of Leningrad and Putin's once-employer, on whether Crimea should be returned to Ukraine. "Are we going to return it, or not? Are we?" – Sobchak asked, impatiently. "I think, for the time being, we will have to accept that Crimea is a part of the Russian Federation", – Navalny said, finally, and then tried to change the subject.

In the spring of 2014, Grandpa Georgiy was going on 90, and still had most of his wits about him. The annexation of Crimea made his decade. He took to composing poetry, most of which expressed sarcasm toward Ukraine's nationalist new President, *Petro Poroshenko*. Grandpa Georgiy changed *sh* to *s*, and referred to the politician as *Porosenko*, which sounded like a deliberately ukrainianized *porosenok* (piglet).

Later that year, Grandpa Georgiy took his last trip to a sanatorium in Feodosia. Ukraine having closed the land border with Crimea, and the bridge across the Kerch Strait from Russia having not yet been completed, the journey involved: taking a train that still ran through the increasingly problematic stretch of Eastern Ukraine, disembarking from a train and onto a ferry, and then getting back onto a train. Doctors feared that it could kill Grandpa Georgiy. I remember participating in a concilium designed to decide whether it was all of the above, or flying, that was more likely to kill my grandfather. Not going was not an option. Flying was a feat at his age, in his state of frailty, and with a pacemaker. Special arrangements with *Aeroflot* were needed to ensure they would agree to take him on board. It was not clear whether he had never been on a plane before.

In the end, he flew. Far from killing him, the journey reinvigorated Grandpa Georgiy, adding years to his life. He declared upon return, that he could now die peacefully, having seen with his own eyes that things in Crimea were looking up. As I write, seven years on, he is still with us, too frail to ever make the trip again, but a patriot once more.

America

"Vladimir Putin does not hate America nearly as much as they do", – quipped Tucker Carlson famously, speaking about the liberals behind Russiagate. He was right, in that Vladimir Putin, most certainly, does not hate America at all. It is true – as we will discuss further – that America is doing everything to make the new, Millennial and post-Millennial generations of Russians, hate it. But no former Soviet citizen hates America, even as we resent it for destroying our country in the 1980s. By that time, our collective emotional attachment to America had been too deep to be convertible to hatred. We were confused, but we still loved America.

For the Soviet Union, America was a Voldemort to our Harry Potter (or, depending on your point of view, the other way around). It was the ultimate *antipode* entity. It was not only our geopolitical counterbalance, but a world that was a distorted reflection of our own, and one the existence of which was absolutely necessary for our world to exist as well. I am a huge fan of Roger Zelazny and his *Chronicles of Amber* series, and, to me, the bipolar world hinged on the balance between the Labyrinth of Amber (representing Order), and the Labyrinth of Chaos, provides the best metaphor for this interdependence.

American movies were not widely shown in the Soviet Union, but its people were reasonably informed about the American culture. Not all of that information was contemporary. Mark Twain's *Adventures of Tom Sawyer and Huckleberry Finn* were required children's reading, and most would have also read *Prince and Pauper* and *Connecticut Yankee at King Arthur's Court*. Mark Twain was huge in the USSR, perhaps, on the account of him being occasionally censored in the United States. His short essay, *How I edited an agricultural newspaper (once)*, achieved cult status. To this day, Russians of my generation widely use the recommendation to "not pull turnips off with your hands" and instead "send a boy to shake the tree", as a universal bit of humorous advice.

Other American books of choice were even less obvious. One of the most popular children's books in the USSR was *The Headless Horseman* by Mayne Reid. At the age of seven, I was afraid to remain in my bedroom after dark, because the silhouette of a chair, with clothes thrown over it, looked like the Headless Horseman in the moonlight. James Fenimore Cooper's *The Last Of The Mohicans* was universally read, although I personally found it insufferable.

Quite a bit of contemporary U.S. literature was published in Russian as well, and *samizdat*, at least for Muscovites, did the rest. Hemingway was very popular, and so was F. Scott Fitzgerald. John Steinbeck was not only published in the Soviet Union but visited it in person. J.D. Salinger was huge with the bohemians – a baby boomer to the core, my mother's favorite book was *Catcher in the Rye*. We had a *samizdat* bound copy, even though the book hadn't been banned, there was a translation serialized in *Foreign Literature* magazine. I don't think Ken Kisi was published in the USSR, but most Muscovites will have read *One Flew Over Cooko's Nest* in *samizdat* as well.

In the mainstream, I know quite a few Russians who swear by *To Kill a Mockingbird* as the inspiration of their youth. Yet for others, Richard Bach with

Illusions, Jonathan Livingston Seagull and *Bridge Across Forever* determined their worldview. I even once heard a certain well-known Russian industrialist exalt *Atlas Shrugged* as a defining influence in a speech to students, apparently unaware of the stigmatic association that exists in the United States today between Ayn Rand fandom and a certain set of views (conversely, I think, many of her fans in America do not know that Ayn Rand's real name was Alisa Rosenbaum, she was born and grew up in St. Petersburg, and moved from the Soviet Union to the United States as an adult).

To me, Ray Bradbury was a defining childhood influence, for sure – although, weirdly, *Love Story* by Erich Segal also made a huge impression. In my teens, I was also influenced by Bach's *One* when it was serialized in translation in 1988, at the same time as I became a fan of Roger Zelazny.

We did not have the benefit of American television – any television programming, as such, was very limited in pre-Perestroika USSR. The lucky few, most of whom were among my parents' friends, had VCRs, and access to VHS tapes of American films brought over from the West by diplomat relatives, or obtained clandestinely from the cottage industry that copied and even dubbed many of those films into Russian (famously, one underground voice over translator, in order to avoid detection by the authorities, wore a laundry clamp on his nose to disguise his voice).

Several families would gather together to watch. Between the ages of seven and ten, I remember being brought along to watch not just *1984*, but *The Blues Brothers* and *The Thing*, all broadly around the same time as they came out on VHS in America. I was, admittedly, too young to make sense of much of it all, but it was all there. It is only now that I realize, with great irony, that my parents were only in their early thirties at the time, and, having had zero exposure to the wider world themselves (my father's childhood in the Soviet Embassy in Prague notwithstanding), were also hardly able to make sense of it all. American culture was partly forbidden, but it was exciting for that reason, and seemed familiar. Where information is limited, imagination fills in the blanks.

Imagination, overall, turned out to be a powerful tool. Soviet propaganda, which spared no effort in highlighting the negative about America, seemed to be constantly shooting itself in the foot. The skeptical masses had gotten used to processing anything officially published through a built-in assumption that most of it were lies, distortions or deliberately incomplete facts. It was with great shock that we all discovered, upon eventually visiting America, that anti-American propaganda in the USSR, at its worst, was merely one-sided.

Most of what we have been told was true. America did have a huge underclass of the poor, who subsided on the margins of existence. It had the homeless and the drug addicts, and it was certainly prone to racism, war mongering, and controlling the population by threatening it constantly with the menace of *the red scare*. Even though this was only one small part of the truth about America – we were never told the good things, of course – it was true. But no one in the Soviet Union had believed any of it.

Briefly famous Soviet bard Alexander Bashlachev, who tragically ended his own life by stepping out of a window in February 1988, aged 27, had put Soviet anti-American propaganda succinctly in a satirical ballad about an impressionable patriotic alcoholic, who aspires to espionage: "Washington is clouded in heavy smog. No fun being unemployed in the glorified jungle of stone-walled liberty, ruled over by the CIA and Pentagon. The capitalists of those countries are deluded with the arms race psychosis, as they keep tricking the gullible workers and peasants into falling for "the red scare".[62] Other than in satirical retelling, the Soviet public was so tuned off the propaganda wavelength, that America, in its collective imagination, could do no wrong. Soviet citizens were left to imagine America from the bits and pieces of information, and they secretly loved the version of America that existed in their imagination.

It was the rather deluded belief that America could do no wrong, fueled in large part by the slightly excessive Soviet anti-American propaganda, that precipitated the fall of the Soviet Union and ended our way of life. It was more complicated than Reagan calling upon Gorbachev to "tear down that wall", and Gorbachev deciding "why not?" – but not much more. All that the *intelligentsia* and politicians knew about America, came together with all that the diplomats knew and, importantly, the economists thought that they knew. When we stood by and watched the destruction of the Soviet Union unfold, it was our idea of American capitalism, as well as American-style democracy and separation of

---

62 In the original, it rhymes: "Тяжелый смог окутал Вашингтон. Невесело живется без работы в хваленых джунглях каменной свободы, где правят ЦРУ и Пентагон. Среди капиталистов этих стран растет угар военного психоза. Они пугают "красною угрозой" обманутых рабочих и крестьян".

powers, that filled our hearts with joy. America succeeded in its own propaganda, instilling in the Soviet citizens a belief that it was the ultimate template of perfection to be modeled upon.

As it happens, the American propaganda was also one-sided. At no point did it mention the crime, the poverty, the drugs, the homelessness, the lack of access to medical care, the inequality in education, the racism – all of those things the Soviet government pointed out as obvious downsides to the American model of capitalism. When the Soviet people, allegorically, signed on the dotted line some time in 1989, they loved America unconditionally, and were oblivious, in part intentionally, to the hidden darkness within it.

When the first post-Soviet wave of immigrants arrived in the United States, from the late 1980s to the early 1990s, we met people who were very much like us. There was *dvizhuha* there, too. America was vibrant, adrenaline-filled, exciting. It seemed like everyone was high on something, most of the time. In England, no one ever tells you what they really think – Americans, like Russians, are to the point and direct, but, unlike Russians, are naturally outgoing. An American would walk up to a complete stranger and tell them exactly what they think, no problem. Unlike the Brits, who – let's be honest – do nothing but complain all day long, Americans were perpetually filled with optimism. No matter how awful their private lives were when viewed objectively, they always managed to look on the bright side of things, and all believed they were in the best place on the planet, at the best possible time, and on a train to a better future. Their enthusiasm was contagious.

We did not know it then, of course, but the mid-1990s were also a peak of America's leadership in the world. Buoyed by its perceived victory in the Cold War, and enabled by the onset of worldwide proliferation of consumer Internet, the United States were in the eye of the hurricane. That hurricane, the last swirl of the century-long storm of globalization, within a decade, replicated the American consumer economy, business practices, goods and services offerings, culture and lexicon worldwide. The assumption in America was that, having made the whole world look like America, it can exert perpetual influence over it; that it was, so to speak, the ultimate and undisputed arbiter of all things that originated in America, because it was – well, America.

That was, of course, a grave miscalculation. Once everywhere in the world started to look and feel like America, America itself became redundant.

211

Today, you can watch American movies and shop in American chain stores not just in world capitals and large cities, but in all sorts of small places (like Montenegro) that no American can find on the map. Countries model their business practices, banking systems and monetary policy upon America's (proponents of American monetary policy in Russia will chuckle here, because Russia does not). Disneylands are open in Japan, France and Hong Kong. The internet allows you to teleconference into court hearings and business meetings in the United States without actually being there, and American politics has been so universally exported and so widely discussed, that in many countries people know more about it now than they do about their countries' own affairs.

In Russia, official announcements are so infused with business and consumer terms borrowed from American English, that older generations often struggle to understand them. I walk around Moscow, point at advertisements, and suggest *actually Russian* ways to say what they are trying to convey. The active vocabulary of *actual Russian* words, as known to an average Millennial, must be half of what ours was at their age. Everyone, from Venezuela – yes, so it certainly was in 2006-2007 when I lived there – to Vladivostok, is acting, dressing, thinking and talking like Americans.

All of the reasons that made us all once move to America no longer apply, because America is everywhere now. America itself is now like a model home on a housing development, frozen in time. Its exported consumer economy and culture were customized for different environments. No one wants to actually buy the model home – we have all seen *Arrested Development*, we know what they are like.

In the 1990s America perceived itself as the world leader, but it was rather the world's teacher. It taught everyone else to be American, and everyone knows how to do it better now – meanwhile, America itself, it seems, started to forget. The ridiculous election of 2000 tainted the idea of "American democracy" as the whole world mocked *hanging chads* and the electoral college. It all went downhill from there when, after 9/11, America decided to forcibly export the same discredited democracy to parts of the world that were entirely unwilling to adopt it. I lived in America at the time of 9/11, and I stood on the smoldering ruins of the World Trade Center. It changed my life, just as it changed many others. But whatever moral authority in the worldwide fight against terrorism America could have claimed as a result of it, it squandered.

212

For 20 years, Americans have been fighting and dying, for no reason whatsoever, in far-away places their families could not find on the map, its neocons claiming that the whole world was within its strategic interests – just as its own cities became at least as dangerous as Kabul. Except that, this day and age, all of it unfolds on the computer screens and TV screens around the world, making everyone ask: does America no longer have a strategic interest in Michigan? Baltimore? Chicago? Or, in the words of Hillary Clinton, *what happened*? It is not world leadership when you are sending your people to die in places no one in your country cares about, just as your own boarded-up cities burn. World leadership is being the model country at home – and we all long for the times when America remembered that.

The astounding fall from grace that America experienced in the 20 years since 9/11, makes for a grim consideration. Is this not, at least in part, what the terrorists had set out to achieve? May they have won, after all? The redundancy of the model as a result of replication of Americanism worldwide, due to the proliferation of the Internet, technology and travel, certainly played its part in America's loss of leadership in the world. But its paranoid schizophrenia, its disgraced lies about weapons of mass destruction, its actual destruction of the way of life in a growing number of hitherto peaceful countries, its cultivation of a breeding ground for a new, evolved form of terrorism in the Middle East, to say nothing of the murder of thousands of innocent civilians overseas, just as tens of thousands of its own citizens perish from dereliction and rising crime rates at home, has to have something to do with it.

Just as *Americanism* spread worldwide, Americans remained more oblivious to the outside world than any other nation in it. An average American appears to believe today, that they still have it better than most – which may have been true 25 years ago, but is empirically false now. If your cities are boarded up, there are homeless living on the sidewalk outside, if you have to hear gunfire and be harassed by crazy people on drugs while you are trying to eat out, if you have to drive through a wildfire on a way to work and your skies have turned red, if the landscape you see out of the train window on the way home from work looks like a post-industrial wasteland from a zombie movie, or if you have been arrested for swimming in the ocean without a mask – then, I have news for you. No one else in the developed or, in fact, most of the developing world, lives like

213

this. Not only does everywhere else have Starbucks, Gap and mortgages now. *Everywhere else* does not have the homeless crisis, gunfire and dereliction. The rest of the civilized inhabited world has been gentrified, just as America fell apart.

Worse than that, Americans now identify as victims, and there is no greater sin on any playground. American mainstream narrative denies its people any agency or responsibility whatsoever, blaming everyone and anyone in the world for everything that happens in their own country. The people voted for Trump – it must have been the Russians and Iranians that told them so, because, of course, the Americans are supposedly too dumb to think for themselves. They are also, we are told, too dumb to obtain government-issued ID in order to vote, and too fragile to read Dr. Seuss. Anything that happens is a fault of some malign conspiracy or other. There is a humorous saying in Russian – in the original, it rhymes: "Are you a drunk, a smoker and single? Blame Putin[63]. Well, Americans do – but, instead of their own government, they *also* blame Putin.

In my Soviet childhood, there was a popular joke around. It went like this: *A Russian and an American are talking. "We have freedom of speech", – says the American. – "I could go out in front of the White House and shout, "Reagan is an idiot!" And I won't be arrested". To which the Russian replies: "No problem. I can go out on Red Square, too, and shout "Reagan is an idiot" – trust me, I am not going to be arrested, either!"*

America is still our mirror, except the roles reversed completely, and, unlike the Brits, they still do not get our jokes. The joke is on them.

America, the once-feared world bully, is now the fragile loser of the class, the one whose parents sue everyone and the school district. The so-called Capital Riot is, of course, an apotheosis of that madness. So what, a few hundred people broke one window and took a walk, all the while smiling and posing for photos? Wasn't there once public access to The Capitol building anyway? Weren't they all carrying American flags, and supporting a guy who was still President at that time? OMG! Have you guys seen Verkhovnaya Rada in Ukraine? They punch each other in the face every day! Are your elected representatives really this cowardly and meek, and so terrified of their own electorate? What happened to letting the people in and holding a town hall, or posing for pictures with their

---

63 In the original: "Куришь, пьешь и не женат? Это Путин виноват".

214

American flags? No one will take America seriously now. It is even the same country that persevered through 9/11? We do not recognize it.

Having recently returned to live in the United States, I do not recognize it, either. Where is *my America*, the one I once fell in love with and allowed it to shape my worldview in the 1990s? I've looked in the fridge, behind the door, in the glove compartment of the car, and outside in the trash bin, but I can't find it anywhere. It's as if my America no longer exists.

Do Russians still *respect* America? Maybe not, but they may still have feelings for it. It is possible to still love a *debaucheur* relative who brought themselves into disrepute, or an ex-spouse. While our relationship with England was always one of convenience, our relationship with America was one of love. Like all love, it was blind to America's many failings. When love fades, it can turn to torture, but its once object is still not a stranger to you. Just like former spouses, you remain connected and, perhaps, even understand each other better than others understand each of you.

For the Russian elites, America is a lost cause. No one expects it to regain sanity anymore, nor counts on Russia's relationship with America to get better. There was no difference, as far as Russians were concerned, between Trump and Biden. To some extent, Trump was worse – despite his declared intentions, the Trump administration lacked the courage of any convictions, or any convictions as such. It was poorly informed and unable to appreciate the consequences of its actions.

Shortly before the 2020 election, just as Russian TV channels cheerfully aired blocks upon blocks of Fox News coverage of Hunter Biden's laptop, President Putin recorded an interview. Exhibiting the best of dry sarcasm that any Russian can master, he expanded on how much in common Russians have with the purported Biden ideology: after all, his proponents appear to be Marxists, and, further, the Soviet Union always cared deeply about racism toward African-Americans in the United States. "Angela Davis", – Putin said, – "Was a hero to the Soviet people". It was a hilarious bit of trolling – too bad Fox News did not pick it up! – but there was truth to it, too. After all, professional enemies are sometimes easier to deal with, than dumb friends.

There is a dichotomy today between the way Russian baby boomers and Gen X-ers see America and the way our Millennials do. Millennials dislike America, to put it bluntly. As far as they are concerned, it is a dangerous country

215

with nuclear weapons and an exaggerated opinion of oneself and its role in the world, that keeps biting and growling at Russia for no reason at all. If you are turning 30 now, you've lived under U.S. sanctions for most of your adult life, and, to the limited extent that you care, they did not endear America to you one bit.

Those Russians who grew up in the Soviet Union, whether they are *patriots* or in opposition, still live under the spell of nostalgia for the role once-distant America played in our lives, and the lessons it taught us when we were younger. It is the Gen X-ers that comprise most of today's elites, and many of them lived and were educated in America. They are prone to try and consider a relationship with America, after all – for its own sake, and the sake of civility, even though they may be at their last straw of sanity while trying to do so. We see America as a distant relative who is losing their mind. *Kakoi ni est, a vse rodnya*, – we say, quoting Vladimir Vysotsky, the dissident bard who refused to disparage the USSR overseas. *Whatever he is like, he's family*, says Vysotsky's character about his brother-in-law. Having once taken down the statues of Lenin at America's behest, we must have one more drink before we get America off the metaphorical pedestal in our minds.

Meanwhile, America is making it harder and harder for Russians to still love it. It claims that we are stalking it, and it took out the restraining order. It calls it "sanctions". We thought it was just acting out and will calm down, but it's been 9 years, and no one is laughing anymore. Going on a decade soon, what have the sanctions accomplished?

Sanctions

1.

For the past 9 years, any Muscovite who has ever been employed in media, big business, politics or government, shuffled anxiously through each new announcement of international sanctions, to see if there was anyone on the list of sanctioned individuals that they were personally connected to. At first, it was dangerously exciting. In more recent years, that process, in which we all had to engage over and over again, brought a lot of anxiety. Tensions now run quite high. It has become impossible to keep track of all the various sanctions programs, new and old, and variations between U.S., EU and UK sanctions.

Generally, there are three main sets of sanction "regimes" (an interesting name for programs intended to bring about regime change). They are, broadly:

216

the Magnitsky sanctions, the Ukraine sanctions, and the Election Interference sanctions. The Magnitsky sanctions are the oldest: they were adopted in 2012, under the law known colloquially in the United States as the Magnitsky Act. It was a slight of hand, effected under the guise of repealing the so-called Jackson-Vanik amendment, a Cold War-era sanction, that had been adopted in 1978 ostensibly to pressure the USSR to increase the allowance for Jewish emigration to Israel. As late as 2012, the Jackson-Vanik amendment effectively barred Russia from full membership in the WTO. The repeal was swapped for sanctions named after our old friend Bill Browder's lawyer, one who died in a Russian prison awaiting trial. The Act was much lobbied for by Browder himself.

The Magnitsky Act brought the first set of individual sanctions, initially for people and entities that Browder held responsible for Magnitsky's death. These were the first new era sanctions against Russians, and they upset the Russian public greatly. No one thinks that it's OK for people awaiting trial to die in prison, but this was a domestic Russian matter. Magnitsky was a Russian citizen. The degree of influence that Bill Browder, in his derangement, managed to gain over American policy toward Russia, was mind-boggling even then. After all, it's not as if people do not die while awaiting trial in U.S. prisons. Should we pass a *Jeffrey Epstein law*, banning Americans from drinking vodka?

And don't tell me that the difference is that Epstein was guilty of his alleged crimes – I have no reason to believe that Magnitsky wasn't, especially seeing as he was, although admittedly in response to the Act, convicted post mortem. In law, they were both just as innocent. But it's OK, it doesn't have to be Epstein. There are thousands more to choose from. On October 16, 2020 Reuters published a chilling report, according to which 4,998 people died in U.S. prisons before their trials from 2008 to 2019. You guys are super lucky that Bill Browder didn't secretly feel responsible for *their* imprisonment and death, like he clearly does for Magnitsky's – in my own personal humble opinion only. If he did, you would all now be clamoring to take the scenic walks in the *mountains of Rostov* (in case you forgot, this is what Jen Psaki calls a refugee crisis), because Russia is the only country where Browder can't get you. [64]

Whataboutism, you say? Nah, this is a new one. I am going to call it *noneofyourbusinessism*. No vodka for you! And, if you are in the EU – no natural

64 If you want to know more about the fate of Sergey Magnitsky, you will find a Norwegian documentary called *The Magnitsky Act – behind the scenes*, by Andrei Nekrasov, quite illuminating.

gas. According to the Council of Europe, fewer people die in Russian jails than in Portugal, an EU state. In Russia it's 41 per 10,000 inmates, in Portugal 50 per 10,000. You can probably see where this is going. Overall mortality death in prisons in the United States in 2018 was 344 deaths per 10,000 inmates.

Russian dissidents believe that the so-called *Dima Yakovlev law* in Russia, named after a Russian orphan killed by his American adoptive family, which prohibits adoptions of Russian orphans by U.S. citizens, was a response to the Magnitsky Act. That was what Natalia Veselnitskaya meant, when she was talking to Donald Trump Jr. about *Russian adoptions* (and that is why, as I also explain later, I believe she could not have possibly been a Russian loyalist - only the opposition, for reasons unknown, think that all Russian orphans need to be expeditiously shipped to the United States; no one with even slight patriotic inclinations would have gone for that approach).

Most people who are sanctioned under the Magnitsky Act have nothing to do with Magnitsky. They include the acquitted alleged killers of Berezovsky nemesis Paul Khlebnikov and the daughter of the former president of Uzbekistan. Nowadays, the U.S. Government continues to use the Magnitsky Act to ban people, most of them not Russian, for an entirely random variety of reasons. When Jamal Khasshoggi was killed by the Saudis, they banned a bunch of accused Saudis under the Magnitsky Act. The U.S. Magnitsky sanctions, however, are not to be confused with the British Magnitsky sanctions. Having successfully lobbied for the passage of the Magnitsky Act in the U.S., Browder moved his Russophobic circus to London and started to give "evidence" to various anti-Russian inquiries there, and so, Magnitsky's name lives, even 12 years after he died. As recently as in April 2021, Browder managed to get the British to pass a new set of Magnitsky sanctions. Mostly, as far as I can tell, they were against people who never had anything to do with the UK, and are unlikely to have assets or travel there.

The so-called Election Interference sanctions are a set of measures passed, reluctantly, during the Trump administration, in 2017-2018. They are connected to the allegations made in the Mueller report, and principally relate to people and entities indicted by Mueller. Most of them are outside of U.S. jurisdiction. Sanctions, of course, make sure they will never be within the U.S. jurisdiction and can't dispute the charges. The widely cited entities, such as Concord or "St. Petersburg troll farm", and the man by the name of Evgeny

Prigozhin, are sanctioned under this program. The other subset of the Trump era sanctions was adopted on March 15, 2018, as a result of a report under the so-called CAATSA law. CAATSA called on the government to produce a report on sanctionable entities in different countries, including Russia and North Korea. CAATSA was passed by a legislature hostile to Trump, and the administration tried to drop the ball on it. Reluctantly, it eventually produced the CAATSA report. Its authors admit that it simply contained a list of all Russians who were worth more than $1 billion, taken from public sources. It wasn't a sanctions list, but some sanctions were consequently adopted based on it.

Nowadays, there are various inchoate sanction initiatives, dead on arrival to a various degree, brewing in the U.S., the EU and the UK separately. The U.S. is trying to ban the Nord Stream 2 pipeline in Europe, an effort that isn't going anywhere, because the pipeline is in Europe, and Europeans do not want to ban it. They want the gas that is due to come down the pipeline. Then, the EU and the UK are constantly trying to ban an undetermined list of people, specifically, for their alleged role in the alleged poisoning of Alexey Navalny. Navalny himself, and his deranged associates, are trying to get everyone to ban everyone Russian for no reason at all. It's gotten a bit out of hand, and no one knows what exactly is going on anymore. But the overall goal – to make it toxic to be Russian – is being slowly achieved.

I had to take to watching BBC Parliament in Britain in the afternoons, when the most unhappy of the MPs crawl out from under their tin foil blankets and rant to an empty floor about evil Russia. I watch those rants in order to make a list of the most rabid Russian-hating MPs, so as to study their political background and try and understand what, apart from madness, moves them to this level of hatred against me and my community.

Still, the largest in terms of number of people and size of companies affected, and in terms of the domino effect on the economy, are the Ukraine-Crimea sanctions, first adopted in 2014. In this chapter, I rant mainly about the Ukraine sanctions, and all of the cases hereinafter described are of people sanctioned by the United States, specifically, under the *Ukraine regime*. It is generally the trend that the EU has adopted all U.S. sanctions on Ukraine-Crimea, minus those that applied to people with EU citizenship or their immediate family members; and then the UK adopted all EU sanctions in blanket form upon Brexit, and re-adopted them formally on an individual basis on December 31, 2020.

I am sour for having lost a bet on this one: at the initial point of Brexit in January 2020, I was certain that our government would simply forget to make any provision for re-adoption of sanctions, and encouraged people to act on assumption that there will be a period of time in the clear, until someone points that out. I was wrong. But even so, today, not everyone sanctioned by the U.S. is sanctioned by the EU, and vice versa, and the UK sanctions most, but not all, of both sets, and then some of their own.

It is easy to conclude from the media that sanctions affect only high-profile Russian politicians and people on the Forbes list of the rich, but that is not so. In summary, it is now the reality that hundreds of people, both citizens of Russia and Russian-speaking people from other countries, are sanctioned under a dichotomy of several different regimes – and, even to the extent that a lot of them duplicate and triplicate (EU having adopted U.S. lists and UK having adopted EU lists), the restrictions that they impose are different, in terms of what exactly the sanctions proscribe.

The EU sanctions, in general, are less draconian, in the sense that they tend to regulate mostly commercial, but not private, activities (likely owing to the constraints of the ECHR[65]). A situation could arise when I, as a U.S. person, cannot not do the same things with a certain sanctioned person that I could still do with them as a British citizen, even if the UK adopted EU sanctions against them, and the EU had sanctioned them because the U.S. had done so.

It is not particularly helpful that a lot of random, seemingly ordinary people, mid-level operatives whom no one ever heard of, who have no financial resources and have never been to the United States or the United Kingdom, are now sanctioned. I think some don't even know. But just as hundreds of people may not even know that they are under sanctions, there are thousands, and even tens of thousands, of people who aren't under any sanctions at all, but lost jobs and livelihoods due to the near-collapse of sanctioned companies. Due to political imperatives both in Russia and in the West, this has not been widely reported – neither here, nor there.

In Moscow, sanctions have spread like COVID: at first, there were only a few cases, and we all knew who, and where, they were at all times. Nowadays,

---

65 European Convention on Human Rights

they are everywhere, and no one knows who they are anymore, because many cases are asymptomatic. Cue in herd immunity – and, as you will learn in this chapter, it unfortunately looks like total quarantine, complete with border closures, is coming as well.

Recently, I realized that I had been introduced to a random unknown person at a business lunch a year ago, who had turned out to have been be on the sanctions list. No one told me. Perhaps people should wear a badge, or something? In the case of this specific guy, I doubt that he even knows. He was too broke to pay for his own lunch, and the friend who introduced us paid for everyone. The person who paid for that lunch had previously given up his greencard. Otherwise, he would, technically, be providing a material benefit to a sanctioned person.

Every meeting in Moscow has to now be analyzed in the style of the old riddle that calls for you to find a way to safely transport a fox, a rabbit and a cabbage across a river: who here is sanctioned, for what and by whom? Who here has US citizenship, greencards, EU citizenship, UK citizenship? In a random selection of people in Moscow, many do have one or more of those. Who can and cannot pay for whom? What can they each do to each other, or not? It's like a real-life strategy game.

I felt sort of legally violated, if you will, having realized that I had dealt with someone, not knowing that they were under sanctions. I do not think any sanction-related restrictions were violated in this case, but that still unnerved me. I had only found out at random, killing time on the Moscow *metro* by searching the UK brand new searchable PDF sanction list for everyone in my phone book (yes, this is how we kill time now). I am not one to discriminate, folks, but I feel like I have the right to give informed consent. If people on dating sites have to give out their STD status and their HIV status and their COVID vaccination status, why don't we force people in restaurants and offices to give out their sanctions status, before they shake someone's hand? It's only fair.

I am writing this book because I am deeply upset. Not just at the sanctions already in place, but at the constant talk of more sanctions – and I am not even a Russian citizen anymore. I have barely spent any significant length of time in Russia in the last 25 years. I have no family, property or interests there. But the Russophobic hysteria known as "sanctions" is a problem for everyone, including people in the Russian-speaking diaspora

I have no idea whether Putin is upset about sanctions, or secretly happy that they are helping him take Fortress Russia onto a new path of fortified isolation – but I, for my part, am mighty upset. I am upset when Russian people, including those whom I once counted as friends, see it fit to take their domestic political agenda overseas by calling for sanctions on other Russian people whom I have come to respect, and stoking the Russophobic madness of certain impressionable EU and U.S. politicians. I am upset when Russia, and Russians in the West, are trash-talked with mind-boggling insane claims. I am upset when certain British politicians cowardly spew nonsense about Russia's evil, and cast suspicions on the Russian community in the UK. I am upset when I read moronic reports that claim that all Russians in London are spies. Overall, I have now become a pretty upset person, and sanctions have at least something to do with it.

2.

In the words of Dr. Seuss, it all started "way back in the day when the grass was still green". In 2014, we were practically virgins, when it came to sanctions. When the Magnitsky Act was passed in 2012, people were upset, but it didn't have a lot of practical effects. Likewise, our first reaction to Ukraine regime sanctions in 2014 was amusement. When the first list of personal U.S. sanctions related to the annexation of Crimea came out, I experienced a mixture of anxiety and incredulity all at once: long time no see, I thought. Here were all my old pals! Would the OFAC and HM Government both please note, before anything else, that I have not spoken to any of these people since early 2004; but I am also pretty sure that they haven't spoken to each other in almost as many years. And yet, here they were, all having gotten themselves into the exact same piece of trouble. It was like The Blues Brothers - *putting the band back together!*

For much of 2003, I was in Russia, where I served as press-secretary for a local politician, Dmitry Rogozin, and as communications director for the political party *Rodina (Motherland),* which Rogozin co-chaired. Rogozin was, at the time, the Chairman of the Foreign Affairs Committee of the Russian State Duma. I was there as part of a team that was put together by external consultants, and charged with making sure that the newly created *Rodina* makes it into the Duma in the December 2003 elections (which it did; we were a huge success).

Rodina embodied cognitive dissonance. Rogozin ostensibly held what I then regarded as disturbingly right-wing, conservative and nationalist views

222

(ironically, nowadays I agree with them more than I did then). The party's co-chairman, Sergey Glazyev, former minister of economic development in the Yeltsin cabinet, on the other hand, was a sort of *communist light.* His platform cheerfully included re-nationalization of natural resources (read: forcible taking of them from the businessmen who had privatized state oil and gas companies in the 1990s), and he was surrounded by a colorful posse of folks from various "proletarians of the world, unite" type groups.

Trying to tie those two sets of views together into one populist platform was quite an acid trip. I immediately dubbed the two leaders *Gena and Cheburashka,* after Soviet era cartoon characters, where the very tall Rogozin was *Gena,* the good-hearted Crocodile who walked upright, sang songs and played the harmonica, and Glazyev, a shorty, was *Cheburashka*, an unidentified small furry creature with big ears. That comparison was catchy, but not very insightful. The cartoon Gena and Cheburashka were best friends, but Rogozin and Glazyev could not stand each other. Even having them stand *next to each other* was a problem. In a memorable election night photo, in which the party leaders raised their glasses to our victory at campaign headquarters, I had to stand between them.

Post-election, the rift only intensified. The co-chairmen of the resulting Duma faction engaged in daily juvenile confrontation, enthusiastically enabled by their rivaling staff. Glazyev ended up running for President in the spring 2004 election, without the support of the party, and Rogozin went on a hunger strike to protest one of Putin's signature welfare policies. It was a mess. Before long, both *Gena and Cheburashka* were ejected from elective politics, never again to speak to each other. The Rodina faction leadership in the Duma was turned over to Alexander Babakov, a successful businessman, originally from Moldova, with extensive interests in Ukraine. Babakov was considered the principal financial backer of Rodina's 2003 election campaign. He remains in politics and made a steady career out of it; Babakov is now a member of the Federation Council, the upper chamber of the Russian legislature.

Least of all did I expect to see those three names on the same list ever again. And yet, here they were. "Jesus", – I thought. – "What have the three of them done now?" Here is the thing, though – I spent a long time looking, but I still do not have an answer to this question. I do not think a coherent answer to this question exists. Rogozin has got his weaknesses, and quick sardonic wit is one of them. I imagine he had done some talking. In the version of the sanctions list published by the UK government (which eventually adopted EU sanctions at the time of Brexit), it says that Rogozin called for the annexation of Crimea. Jesus my! Firstly, God help us all if everything that Rogozin says is going to be taken this seriously. Secondly, of course, at least half of the people in Russia, and more than half in Crimea itself, called for annexation of Crimea at that same time. Why not sanction everyone? The whole country? One certainly thinks that Rogozin may have been picked on for being a loudmouth, hardly a sound basis for government policy.

Further to that, Rogozin was a long-time diplomatic official. He had been the Chairman of the Foreign Affairs Committee in the Russian Duma, and, following a short stint in Rodina, French-speaking Rogozin was shipped off to Brussels, where he became Russian envoy to NATO, and was given the rank of ambassador. In other words, this was a man whom Russia had put forth to represent itself in foreign relations. At the time of the sanctions announcement, he was Deputy Prime Minister of Russia. It is true that he had made his name in politics, in the early days before *Rodina*, on pandering to Russian-speaking diasporas in the Baltic States, and diasporas were his theme. Perhaps, having been as appalled as the rest of Russia at the treatment that Russians in Ukraine had been subjected to, he talked. Either way, sanctioning him for nothing more than just talking was a direct and calculated way to cause offense. Offense to Russia was the only possible consequence of sanctions against Rogozin. Make no mistake that it was more or less all Russians that took offense.

Glazyev, by contrast, was an unearthed relic. Whether or not he called for the annexation, it is not clear why anyone in Russia, let alone the United States, would care what he said. The American media called him "an adviser to Putin", but I cannot find evidence that he ever was – and, knowing Glazyev personally, I find it hard to imagine. But the most bizarre aspect of the Glazyev sanctions was that he himself was Ukrainian. Glazyev was born and grew up in Ukraine, reportedly retained Ukrainian citizenship and was an active member of the Ukrainian Academy of Sciences at the time he was sanctioned. In other words, here was a fella who was sanctioned by the United States and the EU for ostensibly giving opinions about the future of *his own country*.

I had thought that this was an aberration, until I accidentally discovered that random lunch companion on the sanctions list. Unlike Glazyev, who has lived in Russia for most of his adult life and is a public Russian figure, that particular guy was *just* Ukrainian. He had no Russian citizenship at the time of sanctions – I know, because he was keen to stand in the next Russian Duma election, and was trying to obtain Russian citizenship through a repatriation program for Russian speakers. But that meeting took place in early 2020, and the dude had been sanctioned since 2015. I concede that the individual in question had been involved in the separatist movement in Ukraine; but what conceivable business is it of either the United States or the United Kingdom to sanction Ukraine's own citizens for whatever actions they took in their country's own politics? This is bizarre.

Little surprise that it all went downhill from there. Alexander Babakov, it seems, was sanctioned purely for existing. In his political career, he had been the President's representative to the diasporas, but it is not clear whether he is alleged to have made any public statements on the annexation of Crimea at all. Babakov is not one for scandalous pronouncements, and has, or used to have, substantial business interests throughout Ukraine – including, principally, mainland Ukraine. The UK government sanctions brief states now that Babakov voted for the annexation – but so did hundreds of Duma members.

I am aware, of course, that Executive order 13661, issued by President Barack Obama in 2014, which established the first Ukraine-related sanctions, designated "senior Russian government officials" as subject thereof. For that matter, I accept that Rogozin was, at the time of the enactment, such an official – but since ALL "senior Russian government officials" were not so designated, something must have led to him being singled out.

Glazyev, for his part, was never a "senior Russian government official", except during the Yeltsin administration in 1991-1993. Alexander Babakov was, at the time of the enactment, a member of the Russian State Duma. Russia has the same system of separation of powers as the United States, described by Baron de Montesquieu. The Duma is an elective legislative body and no more a branch of "government" than U.S. House of Representatives. Babakov is a Special Presidential Envoy on diaspora relations, which conceivably is what led to him being sanctioned. Yet, the status of Presidential Envoy is a decorative post, described by Transparency International as a fictional designation. The Russian Constitution does not provide any basis for existence of "special envoys". Putin could, just as well, appoint his labrador as a Special Envoy to squirrels.

225

EO 13661 also includes "persons acting on the direction of a senior government official" – so, setting aside the matter of the Executive not really being "government" (Baron de Montesquieu must be turning in his grave now), we can finally conclude that this is what "got" Babakov. But, just as in the case of Rogozin, it is still unclear why him, and what, if anything other than an insult to Russia, this action sought to accomplish. In the case of Rogozin, a boisterous and relatively popular public figure, Russian people as a whole did take offense, perhaps more so than he himself did. Babakov, by contrast, is not widely known. For some reason, someone must have wanted to offend him personally.

At the end of the day, the unhappy reunion of my estranged former bosses, Rogozin and Glazyev, on the Ukraine sanctions list sounded like a joke, and looked like a joke. Neither one of the men had ever, to my knowledge, much to do with the United States, and, both lifelong politicians and civil servants, neither has any significant financial interests. Always equipped with a quip, Rogozin made a cheerful pronouncement that the Americans would now have to use trampolines to reach the International Space Station, but otherwise I doubt that anyone noticed. Sanctions against those two – and, I suspect, Babakov as well – were about as effective for anything, as Russia's subsequent sanctions against Susan Rice. If she has an account at *Sberbank*, then we got her. Right.

In the public euphoria of 2014, the first wave of U.S. sanctions did not feel like much to ordinary Russians. The Sochi Olympics had gone well, and were, if anything, a public relations boost to Russia. Some believed that their success – admittedly measured by a lack of abject failure – justified exuberant construction expenditure and destruction of much of the natural habitat in the region. Ukraine was sad, but sadness was overshadowed by patriotic joy – Crimea was ours! Rogozin was, at one point, forced to turn around when he tried to fly over Romania, but that also sounded like a joke. Romania?! Even though the sanctions were ridiculous and unfounded, they were also pitifully stupid, so much so as not to deserve an argument. People chuckled. Even though he immediately caused controversy by promising to come back in a bomber, *Dmitry Olegovich* would simply have to stay out of Romania. Big deal.

Of course, the 2014 sanctions created problems for some lesser-known individuals on the list. A friend of mine, a high school principal on the outskirts of Moscow, had exactly the same name – including first name, patronymic and last name – as some dude on the sanctions list, that no one had ever heard of. It was not fun. But overall, those sanctions were not, for the most part, economic – they were political sanctions.

Some businesses, which the Americans Google-searched to be "Russian state-owned", ended up sanctioned. *Dobrolet*, a low cost subsidiary of *Aeroflot – Russian Airlines*, that ran cheap flights from Moscow to Simferopol in Crimea, responded to sanctions in jest. It simply wound up operations and a new airline, *Pobeda (Victory)*, was created by *Aeroflot* overnight. It acquired Dobrolet's assets and continued its operations. It does to this day. This was widely reported, and Russians sniggered. There you go, America! Take this from the same people who, at least, had reportedly thought of using a pencil in zero gravity.

In the middle of propaganda-induced jubilation, Russia's oil giant Rosneft, one of the world's largest producers of oil, was hit hard by sanctions and was forced to solicit over a trillion roubles in rescue funds, a sum even the government did not have at hand. Rosneft was, perhaps, too big to fail, and it was eventually rescued, partly through investment from various international parties, including some Qataris. Where Americans and American-friendly interests were forced, by the sanctions, to pull out of one of the world's largest oil producers, the Qataris, among other people, went in. How does that serve the interests of the United States, exactly? Had anyone thought of that at all?

Notwithstanding the very real problems related to Rosneft, in 2014 the Russian government sought to make light of the sanctions, treating them as a political stunt rather than a serious economic measure than had a chance of impacting people's lives. Everyone was told not to worry, so they didn't. Russian people believed that sanctions were a stupid, politically motivated, joke. And many also believed that they knew *whose* joke it was.

3.

Most Russians who do spend time thinking about sanctions, note that the seemingly random list of people that keep on ending up sanctioned reads like a fantasy hate list of one Victoria Nuland. Victoria Nuland is a career mid-level Department of State official, and most Americans, probably, have never heard of her. Yet, just like Jen Psaki, in Russia Nuland is a household name.

During the first Ukrainian *maidan*, the *Orange Revolution* in 2004, its main investor Boris Berezovsky, traveling as Platon Elenin, was widely reported to run point on the ground and give out coffee and provisions. Organizers openly complained that the U.S. State Department delivered only promises, while BAB delivered real money and food. By the time of the *euromaidan* in 2013, Berezovsky was dead. Not to fear – the Obama administration was in office now, and Victoria Nuland, its Department of State official for Eastern Europe, was on the ground with cookies. *Cookies from the State Department*, they were called. Nuland, cheerfully photographed on *maidan* with her bags of cookies, instantly came to embody the worst sort of U.S. meddling in foreign affairs, one that that Russians have, for years, suspected existed, but hitherto could not prove.

Victoria Nuland knew Dmitry Rogozin personally. During the Bush 43 administration, she was the U.S. envoy to NATO, and her tenure there overlapped with that of Rogozin, who arrived for his own ambassadorship in early 2008, by several months. What is it that he had done to impress her so much, we might never know – but the moment Nuland got into her first diplomatic scandal related to Ukraine in early 2014, she knew who to blame.

The leitmotif of Victoria Nuland's lifelong adventures in the East is that she is prone to be victimized by surreptitious recordings of private conversations. In early February of 2014, one such recording nearly ended her budding career. The famous leaked tape of her conversation with U.S. Ambassador to Ukraine Geoffrey Pyatt was a bombshell that laid bare the depth and audacity of the U.S. involvement in Ukraine. In it, Nuland insists that the Ukrainian soon-to-be-PM Arseniy Yatsenyuk, to whom she refers as *Yats*, is the Americans' choice for the role. Crucially, she expresses disdain for the EU, framed bluntly as "f*ck the EU".

When the fecal matter hit the fan, Nuland knew that she had only one play to keep her job. The one that always works: blame the Russians. And she already had one Russian in mind, her favorite guy: Dmitry Rogozin. It was he, she claimed, who must have ordered the call to be recorded and then leaked it, in order to undermine U.S. policy in Ukraine and manufacture an artificial rift with their core allies, the same ones she urged Pyatt to *f*ck*. Why did Nuland pick Rogozin, we will never know – maybe it was because of some old grudge from the NATO times, maybe it was because he was quick to tweet about the call. But Rogozin was, by that time, nowhere near Ukraine, or even foreign relations. Yet, the play worked. Nuland kept her job, and hapless *Dmitry Olegovich* took the top spot on her hit list.

By pure coincidence, Victoria Nuland, as of February 2014, had no love lost for Sergey Glazyev, either. Shortly before the infamous recording of the

Nuland-Pryatt phone call was released, Glazyev – who, let's remember, is Ukrainian – posited in an interview that the events in Ukraine have been largely planned and orchestrated by the United States. He claimed that the United States had spent 5 billion dollars on stoking Russophobia in Ukraine since the late 1980s, and quoted Victoria Nuland herself as a source. She was outraged. Just one day before the world was to hear her picking the next Ukrainian prime minister and vowing to *f*ck the EU*, Nuland had strong words for Glazyev. His insinuations of U.S. involvement were creative fiction – *science fiction* – she claimed. The policy of the United States in Ukraine was, according to her, absolutely transparent. The next day, when the tape came out, she blamed Rogozin for the embarrassment, but Glazyev for making her come across as a liar. Which she was.

Do you see where this is going? Had Alexander Babakov done anything to anger Victoria Nuland in 2014? Seeing as we are now in the fairyland of Victoria Nuland's imagination, I cannot fully swear that Babakov did not get sanctioned simply because Nuland Googled Rogozin and Glazyev, and found out that the three had been once connected. In all likelihood, he did also anger her somehow. Making Victoria Nuland angry is not a difficult task to accomplish.

The silly first round of sanctions took place in an innocent *far away, long ago* world. A world in which Donald J. Trump had not yet ridden down the gold escalator and announced his candidacy for President of the United States. The world where Russia was only blamed for events that took place at least somewhere near its borders. The next four years changed a lot. Trump, allegations of Russian election meddling, the Muller report, the Manafort prosecution, Parnas and Fruman.

No one cared about Crimea anymore, not really. But Victoria Nuland's life's work, the sanctions introduced by the Obama administration to punish Russia for the annexation of Crimea, were still around. Victoria Nuland, although she quit the Department of State at that time, was also around. She was making endless rounds on the speaking circuit and in the media, attempting to direct policy on Russia. She was on the lookout for new victims, and, in February 2018, a man came along who angered Victoria Nuland once again. That poor soul was businessman Oleg Deripaska.

4.

Once again, Victoria Nuland was victimized by a clandestinely recorded private conversation, but this time the conversation was not her own. It so happened, that Russian businessman Oleg Deripaska was involved in a bit of a domestic PR mishap at the time. The matter, which arguably involved lack of judgment on the part of Deripaska, was rather embarrassing for a certain mid-level government official who had been allegedly invited to Deripaska's yacht[66]. The whole thing had nothing to do with foreign relations. But the story involved, among other things, an audio recording, ostensibly made on the yacht, in which several voices, one of them allegedly Deripaska's, can be heard engaging in meaningless banter on a number of random subjects.

They were at sea, somewhere in the North, near Norway. They saw some whales, perhaps. Deripaska, in his infinite wisdom, decided to recall a misogynistic joke about Victoria Nuland. She hates Russia so much, he posited, because, in her youth, she had been stupid enough to sign up to spend a month on a Russian whaling boat in the Far East, in order to learn Russian. Imagine? A female voice interjects, giggling, to suggest that the sailors must not have been very gentlemanly to Nuland. "What, do you think she was raped?" – a male voice asks, as if the implication had not been obvious enough. That third voice is not the same one that's allegedly Deripaska's, but it isn't easy to tell right away.

The conversation supposedly took place in 2016, but only became a matter of public record in February of 2018, when Russian campaigner Alexey Navalny got a hold of it. Navalny recorded an *expose* video – targeting, notably, not Deripaska, but rather the government official allegedly present. His video, helpfully subtitled into English, included some of the recordings ostensibly made on the yacht, including the Nuland-related bit. That bit was intended for comic relief. "What was Deripaska thinking?!" – Navalny roared dramatically. There was no doubt that Victoria Nuland would see that video, and she did. How do we know? Because she responded to it.

Two weeks later, on February 21, 2018, Victoria Nuland appeared on the Deutsche Welle TV channel. She was interviewed there by Zhanna Nemtsova, daughter of late politician Boris Nemtsov, and a darling of anti-Russian emigres.

---

66 That man has since died of heart-related problems, and I see no point in mentioning him by name in this context.

Speaking to Deripaska directly, Nuland begged to differ. It was not a whaling boat, she said – it was a *fishing* boat. And she wasn't on it for one month, oh no, sir – she was there for the whole six months, and she enjoyed it very, very much. It was a pleasure. Menacing tone, poker face, stone-cold Mona Lisa smile. *Luca Brasi sleeps with the fishes.* It was a threat.

A month later, Oleg Deripaska was sanctioned by the United States, under Obama era executive orders 13661 and 13662, ostensibly for involvement in the events in Eastern Ukraine and the annexation of Crimea. Then, worldwide aluminum prices went up 40%, threatening the collapse of all industries dependent on it. Apparently, Nuland hadn't realized that Deripaska was the largest producer of aluminum in the world, outside China.

5.

I can see readers rolling their eyes at this point. There were plenty of reasons for the Deripaska sanctions, they will say, and Nuland hadn't actually been at State for a year when that happened. I am aware of many reasons *given* for Deripaska's sanctions later, yes. But none of them holds water, and most look like results of a Google search run by an intern. Indeed, Oleg Deripaska appears to have been involved in many things to do with the U.S. government, FBI, the State Department – over a number of years. But none of those things is a plausible reason for sanctions, and certainly not sanctions imposed rationally by the Trump administration. Deripaska has never been involved with the events in Ukraine and the annexation of Crimea at all – and yet that is exactly the program that he was sanctioned under.

They were vaguely renamed into something else in press-releases, but these were still the original 2014 Obama sanctions for Crimea, for which the previous lucky candidates had all been picked by Victoria Nuland. For all that we now know of how Washington operates, it is of no import that Nuland herself was, temporarily, no longer at State (she is back there now). Contrary to what he has been led to believe, it was clearly not the Trump administration that sanctioned Deripaska – it was what we now call *the permanent state*, staffed to the brim with Nuland's pals.

Various civil servants attempted to give loads of cognitively dissonant, bizarre-sounding explanations for the Deripaska sanctions in the three years since, but more often than not, it is the simplest explanation that is the right one. *Hell hath no fury like a woman scorned.* In the event, the unfortunate Deripaska became a victim of double fury – Nuland's, and that of the woman who made the ill-fated recording. I am at least 90% sure that, were it not for the whole sordid affair, Oleg Deripaska's world would be very different today.

In all likelihood, Treasury Secretary Stephen Mnuchin had no idea who Oleg Deripaska was, when he read the sanctions announcement off a piece of paper given to him in April 2018. The Trump administration, indicted by public opinion for allegedly being propped up by Russia, would grasp at any straw to prove otherwise. Sanctions against Deripaska caused significant disruption to metals markets all over the world. The government was forced to lift the restrictions from Deripaska's main businesses. Deripaska's interests had been divested from them, but that did not stop dozens of semi-literate members of Congress on both sides of the aisle, all of whom had also never heard of Deripaska before, from attacking Mnuchin for being a secret Deripaska pal, and holding secret hearings about it.

One thing was immediately certain: issues that had nothing to do with one another were being conflated into a schizophrenic mix of irrelevant innuendo, in which no one quite knew anything, but everyone heard something, and no truth was knowable because Deripaska himself, the only man who could shed light on any of it, had been banned from the United States by the sanctions themselves, despite having offered to appear before the U.S. Congress and give evidence (it would be an extraordinary offer if he really were, as described in the sanctions announcement, a "senior government official" of a foreign country).

Political considerations of the moment suggested that it would be helpful for Trump, as well as his former campaign manager Paul Manafort, then on trial on various charges principally related to tax evasion, to have Deripaska around. Although Manafort owed him money, Deripaska could conceivably be a voice of reason to dissuade at least the more sensible from a rubbish narrative that had Manafort attempting to trade some election-related "briefings" to Deripaska, ostensibly to offset the debt.

Only people who had never been near any sums of money, nor any briefings, could envision that any information Manafort could, at that point, offer, would make a dent in tens of millions of dollars that he owed Deripaska. No briefings are worth that much, and it is not clear, in fact, what information Manafort could offer that wasn't publicly knowable. The Trump campaign wasn't

232

yet the Trump administration, and the Trump campaign (nor, for that matter, the administration) never had any secrets, because they all kept leaking everything faster than they could think it, and no one, including Trump himself, ever had any idea what he would do in the next five minutes.[67]

Writing for The Hill, John Solomon suggested the alternative theory of Oleg Deripaska's persecution, which I consider second most likely. He recounted years of prior cooperation between the FBI and Deripaska, and specifically the latter's efforts, at the urging of the then-director Robert Mueller and up-and-coming agent Andrew McCabe, who had been Deripaska's direct contact at the Bureau, to negotiate with the Iranians for the rescue of former FBI agent Robert Levinson, an American citizen then missing (now presumed dead) in Iran.

Perhaps it was because the Americans had Iran sanctioned at the time, or they were not allowed to pay a kidnapping ransom with state funds, but they needed someone friendly - and with enough cash that he wouldn't miss it - to handle the whole thing. Oleg Deripaska, who ended up spending $25 million of his personal funds on the effort, was that someone. It appears to be common ground among anyone with knowledge of the story in the United States that Deripaska had been able to locate Levinson and negotiate the ransom, and it was the Department of State, then headed by Hillary Clinton, that refused to give the arrangement a go-ahead[68].

Deripaska himself always maintained, in the public interviews that I saw, that he has no gripe with the FBI, and blames only the Department of State for all his troubles. I wonder if he is being naive. If nothing else, after I had people raid my house at 6 am ostensibly in order to "talk", which is what happened to Deripaska in September 2016 in New York, I would probably lose that attitude. That is no way to "talk". You call and you make an appointment. I am not just a middle-aged lady on a rant about manners – this is about manifest hostility. When a state agency manifests hostility toward you, you thereafter regard it as hostile.

---

67 And as for mysterious "polling data", we all know how much that turned out to be worth in 2016!
68 Mueller and McCabe might have forgotten to tell Deripaska that Bob Levinson was no friend of Russia. As it turns out, the missing man had been prone to rant about malignant Russians *weaving themselves into the fabric of Western society*. A quote from his written tirade to this effect, without any reference to the ultimate fate of its author, was used as an epigraph for Catherine Belton's paranoid pasquinade *Putin's People*, which came out in 2020 and it now subject to lawsuits by multiple Russians therein variously maligned.

John Solomon's theory of Deripaska sanctions seems to imply that he was a victim of *the permanent state* within the Bureau, rather than the Department of State. Solomon points out that Deripaska, by the spring of 2018, was walking and talking evidence of a conflict of interest for Robert Mueller. Once the innuendo about Manafort's proposed "briefings" materialized in Russiagate, Deripaska's mere existence, and his prior connection to Muller and McCabe, could collapse the Mueller investigation, as well as discredit McCabe's many anti-Trump pronouncements. So, goes the thinking, the FBI got rid of Deripaska. The FBI isn't supposed to have anything do with sanctions on Ukraine at all, which were to be based only on foreign intelligence, and were left solely up to Treasury and State. If it was the Bureau, I think they would have used the Election Interference sanctions. That is why I am sticking to my original theory. But once you realize *the permanent state* exists, you see that it is all connected, so why not[69].

Whatever the real reasons, they certainly had nothing to do with ostensible reasons – and even on those, the bureaucrats were all over the place. *The permanent state* surely pulled one over on the Trump administration with this one – perhaps, at least, it taught Mnuchin to read the small print before he signs stuff. About time, considering he was a grown man, by then signing the currency itself. The Trump administration lacked the courage of their convictions, and the political power, on almost anything, and they certainly lacked both to walk back the sanctions on Deripaska. But they surely knew that they had made a mistake imposing them.

6.

Of all the physical persons – so called SDNs, specially designated nationals – sanctioned by the United States in the last 8 years, under whatever auspices, Dmitry Rogozin and Oleg Deripaska are the only two that are household names in Russia. Barack Obama's Executive Order 13661, related to sanctions on Russian activities in Ukraine and the "purported" annexation of Crimea, authorizes sanctions imposed on "senior government officials". Even

---

69 I lack the knowledge and expertise to evaluate it, but a credibly sounding theory based on lobbying from U.S.-based aluminum companies was also advanced as a possible reason for Deripaska's misfortune.

though all he does is talk, Rogozin was, at the time, a senior government official, so in that respect sanctions against him made nominal sense. They may have accomplished nothing and alienated the Russian people more than the Russian State, but sure. By applying the adjusted rules of sort-of sense that the American bureaucracy usually operates under, sanctions against Rogozin were solid. No Romania for him!

But then, sanctions against Oleg Deripaska were also brought under EO13661. EO13661 related strictly to the events in Ukraine, and authorizes only the sanctioning of senior government officials, or "people acting at direction of a senior government official". The sister directive, EO13662, was also listed on the Deripaska sanctions announcement. EO13662 are "sectoral sanctions". The Executive order lists a number of industries on which they can be imposed, once such determination is made by the Treasury Secretary. Only three industries, by way of two separate determinations, had been designated under EO 13662 by Obama Treasury Secretary Jack Lew: defense, financial and energy sectors. There were no designations under EO13662 under the Trump administration.

The designation of sanctions imposed on Deripaska lists him as being *in the energy sector*, but this is not where his main interests are. Deripaska is, principally, in metals. The metals industry, although it is listed in the body of EO13662, has never received a designation under it. Moreover, sectoral sanctions are intended for businesses, and, in practice, are imposed mainly on state-owned businesses. It is not clear that you can even sanction an individual under EO13662, whatever sector they have interests in. The reference to EU13662 on the Deripaska sanctions announcement, to me, signals that the announcement itself had been prepared in haste and by people who did not know what they were doing, even by Treasury's own standards.

Eventually someone in OFAC probably figured it out, and the EO13662 designation was quietly dropped. Deripaska appears today only on the SDN list, under EO13661. He is not sanctioned under EO13662. Whether or not sanctions against him are lawful, therefore, must depend solely on whether or not he is a "senior government official" for the purposes of EO13661.

Even amidst the madness, it is common ground that, unlike my old colleagues from *Rodina*, Oleg Deripaska is not any kind of a government official, senior or otherwise, and has never been. Yet, somehow this isn't the end of story, but only the beginning. EO13661 also refers to "people acting on direction of a senior government official" - and, to the extent that the U.S. government's position is possible to discern at all, it seems to be their insistence that Deripaska acted in the proscribed way. From disclosure to disclosure, they advance new creative theories of how exactly, when and where had Deripaska acted "on direction of a government official".

Initial disclosure of a mysterious packet that ostensibly underlined the sanctions, obtained and made public by Deripaska himself through discovery pursuant to his attempts to challenge the sanctions, is mind boggling nonsense that would not pass for a high school project. The only reason I was not utterly shocked by how ridiculous it was, is that I have seen this sort of thing before, and am starting to realize this is the government's standard form of operation (God help us all).

The disclosure did not focus on the need to prove that Deripaska was "acting on the direction of a government official" – perhaps, whoever produced it was not aware of that requirement. They did, nonetheless, take some care of proving that Deripaska was somewhat in the energy sector – by printing out numerous pages from his own website, and then impugned him for the fact that his company, GAZ, apparently manufactures most of Russia's buses. (Buses! That will not be a way to harm the ordinary Russian people at all, everyone knows that only Putin and *the oligarchs* take buses.) The rest of the dump seemed to focus on demonstrating that Deripaska was a bad person, without any reference whatsoever to Ukraine or "government officials".

The main basis for the entire thesis was the multi-page printout of the October 2008 article in The Atlantic, the focus of which was to expose the late Senator John McCain, at that time the Republican presidential nominee, for his secret connections with Russians, including Deripaska. There were pictures of McCain and Rick Gates, a longtime associate of Paul Manafort and later his co-accused, walking up the rails of some yacht. The 2006 Independence referendum in Montenegro, where Gates and Manafort worked for the Independence campaign and Deripaska apparently provided the funds, was mentioned. Since that didn't sound bad enough, assorted Internet gossip about Deripaska was thrown in.

This was to be the *October surprise* of the 2008 election, the original Russiagate. It was an early rehearsal of the *Russian collusion* trope. Seeing as The Atlantic was read only by people who were not going to vote for McCain anyway, I do not think it had much impact on the election, which McCain lost for different reasons. Seems that he didn't like the article much, or his communications with Deripaska had more to do with Montenegro, the Independence of which from Serbia, a long-time Russian ally, was the stated foreign policy goal of the United States at the time – and less with *Russian collusion*. Either way, after the 2008 election McCain seemed as irritated with Russia as ever – which was manifested, among other things, in that he became a driving force behind the Magnitsky Act.

The Department of Treasury completely failed to acknowledge the geopolitical context that had brought together Gates, McCain and Deripaska in Montenegro. Instead, they focused on the part of the article that derided Deripaska with all sorts of dirt and rumors, and were now inviting us to see the 10-year old liberal political hit job on a dead man as a record of absolute truth[70]. Things that were haphazardly thrown together by some junior hack into the October surprise in 2008, must now be true, as if passage of time made them so. Nowadays we see this all the time: one of the media writes some nonsense, then the rest keep quoting each other until it starts to sound like something that "everyone knows", even if they themselves made up the underlying "knowledge".

The other assertion in the disclosed memorandum was that Deripaska ostensibly admitted to criminal wrongdoing in his own complaint against Associated Press, which he sued for defamation. The complaint was included in *the dump* in full, and even a cursory reading of it makes clear what happened here. Being a lawsuit for defamation, the complaint necessarily restated the impugned defamatory statements that were being complained about. In a Kafkaesque twist, Treasury interns mistook them for Deripaska's own.

The contribution to the memo from the State Department made even less sense. It said that the State Department had previously denied Deripaska a visa, and, surely, there must have been reasons for that. Yeah... and, what were they? They did not go there. In the media merry-go-round, it is often possible to pinpoint the original fabrication, but with a purely bureaucratic whirlwind of self-reference, such as with the now-infamous visa refusal story, it often seems as if "decision zero" is just a notion, an empty file.

---

70 McCain was still alive at the time the sanctions against Deripaska were adopted in April, but died in August 2018, before the first evidence dump was produced by the Treasury in discovery.

The thing is, of course, that nothing of this whatsoever had anything to do with being a "government official", therefore it was entirely irrelevant to sanctions. Sanctions, which are based on executive action pursuant to the President's exclusive authority to conduct foreign relations, are not intended to be a response to allegations of criminality. If there is an allegation of criminality, it has to be dealt with through a legal mechanism that exists for that purpose. For example, if someone alleges that money laundering took place over the proceeds of which the United States has jurisdiction, the procedure is to investigate and charge criminally. Sanctions are not intended, by their design, to deal with people or matters over which the U.S. has criminal jurisdiction.

If the U.S. has no jurisdiction but has reasons to believe that criminality is in play, it can deal with it via a visa refusal – and, as we see here, often does. Sanctions are not a remedy for that. Sanctions are an economic remedy against property, and it applies only when no other remedy can, by definition, apply (in other words, the assets are clean, overseas, or both, and the individual, but for the sanctions, is admissible to the United States). Since Treasury had no proof at all, at that point, that Deripaska was a "government official", and the authors of the *first dump* clearly hadn't been told that this was something they must look for, they dumped everything they had on Deripaska. Things were being conflated, and they succeeded in confusing, at least, the man himself.

7.

Upon seeing the garbage collection of confusing, unrelated and unfounded accusations that seemed to be thrown at him, Deripaska initially attempted to embark on a charm offensive in the U.S. media. It was a mistake. He later said – also in an interview – that he had trouble finding lawyers, but you hardly need to be one in order to give yourself the most basic bit of legal advice every lawyer learns to give on the morning of their first day of law school: to stop talking.

It seems that there was no one to unpick this process for Deripaska, or to explain to him how all the various issues separated into those that were legally pertinent and those that were just noise. Deripaska had once made it into memes for his brave rebuttal of a CNN reporter, to whom he said "Get lost, please. Thank you". That was three words more than anyone else would say to a CNN reporter, and it had every potential to make Deripaska into an internet hero to the American political right. I wish he had stopped at that.

Deripaska, at that time, seemed to be handling his own PR, and he could be often seen giving interviews and speeches in English. Perhaps those close to him were reticent to tell him that, but his English is non-grammatical and non-idiomatic. I venture a guess that, like many of the Soviet men of our generation, he reads fluently, pursuant to his education and wide-ranging interests. But his speech, like that of many people in business and academia, is exactly at a level that works in business and academic settings. In those settings, a little English often goes a long way, because the speaker communicates primarily with people of comparable intelligence and knowledge, who have experience with multiple languages and meet a lot of foreigners. Any language deficiency is compensated.

When you are trying to speak to the wider public – especially TV viewers in the culturally isolated United States – that does not work. And, having hitherto only spoken on business networks to business reporters about things that only business people could understand, Deripaska did not realize that he was now speaking to a wide audience of considerably less enlightened people. Speaking to the public at large is not the same as speaking to the reporter in front of you. The public is not as smart as you, it does not have the same basic knowledge as you, and it will not give you the time of day if your tenses disagree.

The lower their level of education, the more difficulty people have understanding speakers with unfamiliar accents, even if those speakers are semantically fluent. If you not only have an accent, but also misunderstand questions put to you because you are prone to translate them literally, rather than directly take them for their culturally accepted meaning; if you disregard grammar and do not properly use tenses; if you are forced to choose words that you know instead of words that you wish you knew – then you should not be trying to clear your name on American television.

When Matthew Chance, longtime Russian reporter for CNN, asked Deripaska whether he felt that the Mueller report exonerated him, Deripaska, instead of answering *yes*, took issue with the question. It was an innocent question, put in exactly the customary form. Half of Washington DC, including President Trump, was running around at that same time, saying that Mueller report exonerated *them*. Not Deripaska. You could see on his face that he translated the word *exonerated* into Russian, where the analogous word has

239

slightly different usage. That led him to take issue with the word, because he felt it would only apply if he had been charged with a crime, which he hadn't been.

In English, of course, the word is commonly used to denote having one's name cleared. You can be exonerated in a sense that you are eliminated from a list of suspects. Deripaska did not know that. Had he simply said "yes" and smiled, that would play to CNN's multi-million domestic audience in a loop. The viewers would not remember much, but something would linger. Some guy named Deripaska – charming smile – exonerated, no matter what for. Definitely not a criminal! That would be enough. By contrast, I doubt that the attempt to take Matthew Chance up on his vocabulary aired at all. I hope it didn't.

Deripaska allowed all his interviews in English to drift toward the unspecific criminality allegations or election interference – none of which had to do with sanctions against him, but he had neither legal skills to explain this, nor rhetorical skills to change the subject. Although he is a charming and charismatic man, Deripaska was, due to his poor English, coming off on American TV as a proverbial Russian villain, exactly the person they were trying to portray him as. Trevor Noah has this famous funny bit about how Russian accents are scary, regardless of what is being said. This was exactly it. Deripaska was not helping himself, even when given a platform by journalists who already sympathized with him, such as John Solomon of The Hill.

The John Solomon interview with Deripaska for Hill TV was the worst yet, and this was the biggest pity. Krystal Ball and Saagar Enjeti, then the hosts of Rising, had the best prepared audience, which included a lot of politicians and pundits. People who influence opinion watched them – more so, than they did CNN. This was the one interview Deripaska had to do well on. He did not. "Mr. Deripaska", – said Solomon cheerfully at one pivotal moment. – "I'd like to give you the opportunity to clear this up once and for all: have you ever killed anyone, or ordered anyone to be killed?" There is only one possible answer to this question in the English language: "No, absolutely not". Even Attila the Hun, if he were alive today and spoke English, would have no problem coming up with it. I will never forget the look on Solomon's face the moment he realized that this was not what Deripaska was going for.

Deripaska was clearly confused by this question, which he did not recognize as a cue for a simple denial. He parried by saying that he did not understand what "they" (presumably, the Department of State) were taking about,

240

or where was the evidence that they relied on. It came off as an equivocation. The evidence! OMG. Who cares what exactly are they talking about? Who cares if there is any proof? This is a television interview, not a consultation with a criminal defense attorney! They are asking YOU! Did you kill anyone? No! The answer is – "No, absolutely not"! Doesn't matter what they are talking about, or whether there is any proof. Still, the answer is "no"! How bloody hard is it?! I am laughing now, but at the time I watched it, I cried. I really did. How can someone this rich and this exposed not have anyone around him who would prevent this from happening? It was a farce, and it wasn't good for the Russian cause. Here was a man who managed to get lost in translation even while supposedly speaking English![71]

8.

I do not know where they were at the time of the ill-fated Solomon interview, but Deripaska, at this stage, had lawyers. I will not comment on the suit they brought in order to challenge the sanctions, because, at the time of writing, the proceedings are still ongoing. But the lawsuit, at a minimum, caused lawyers to finally get involved in the process on the government side as well. Those lawyers, having finally realized that it was necessary to prove that Deripaska was a "government official", or acting on the behest of such, came up with an entirely new list of reasons for sanctions, that did not have anything to do with the original "reasons".

The new charges included assertions that Deripaska allegedly "admitted" (in an interview) that he had a diplomatic passport; an observation that Deripaska accompanied Putin to some high level meeting in Kyrgyzstan and appeared to "follow Putin's verbal instructions" while there; that it "had been alleged"

---

71 After this book was finished, and I was very proud of myself for killing Oleg Deripaska softly with my sarcasm, I was faced with abrupt realization that I may have been too hard on the man, after all. In an NBC interview on the eve of his first summit with President Biden, Vladimir Putin, by all means, a much savvier operator, and while speaking in Russian, made exactly the same mistake - to a much greater worldwide ridicule, of course. "Mr. President, are you a killer?", - the reporter asked, to which Putin started his reply with: "Well, listen....". Dear Lord, what is it with Russian men, specifically, that none of them can give a simple "yes" or "no" answer to a straight question, instead of, or at least BEFORE, taking issue with the question? The gist of this whole book, in large part, is that Putin hadn't killed anyone. I absolutely believe that. But I would be grateful if he bothered to deny that, as well. It's tough to defend a client who beats you to the courthouse and pleads no contest.

(nevermind by whom) that Deripaska "laundered money" for Putin "on at least one occasion" (no occasion was specified); a conclusion that Deripaska gave in to Putin's "pressure" to invest in the construction of Olympic village in Sochi, and, finally, that Deripaska allegedly told The Financial Times in 2007 that he "did not separate himself from the Russian State".

Remember, we must now evaluate these from the perspective of them purportedly being examples of Deripaska acting on Putin's "directions". They are not saying that Deripaska should not have built facilities in Sochi – the United States, of course, itself participated in the Games afterward held in those facilities. They are merely saying that he should have done it on his own initiative, not because Putin told him to. They are not saying that they are sanctioning Deripaska for the unspecified money laundering, but only for the alleged fact that he was doing it on Putin's directions. And so on. It's dangerously easy to lose sight of the distinction.

Whether Deripaska ever held a diplomatic passport, I do not know – but the Department of State should. Holders of Russian diplomatic passports nonetheless require visas to enter the United States, and if State had issued Deripaska a diplomatic visa, they would then be able to assert that as a fact, not as something they read in a newspaper – and they would most certainly not refrain from sharing the capacity in which Deripaska appeared to qualify for that visa, if, indeed, it credibly defined him as a "government official". It would be their best evidence! If they are not putting any such evidence forward, it means that it does not exist. It is my understanding that diplomatic passports and visas can be issued, in certain circumstances, to a wide variety of people, not all of whom can be defined as "government officials" or acting on behalf of such.

The media speculation about Deripaska and his alleged diplomatic passport does have origins. The origin is in the actions of the United States government itself. The United States of America, for whatever reason, had never bothered to issue Oleg Deripaska a visitor visa. Immigration law gives consular officers, who are low level officials employed by the Department of State, absolute discretion over admission or non-admission of visitors ("nonimmigrants") to the United States, and their decisions are generally non-reviewable. The little-known feature of that discretion is that admission of visitors can be barred on *reasons to believe* that the individual was connected to criminality, even if they had never been charged with a crime.

242

This feature was included in the law to give consular officers freedom over keeping away drug dealers and drug users. If the interviewee appears stoned, they could be refused. But once in a while, one zealous official that read something in a paper somewhere, or on the internet, makes a decision like this, and it lives forever. There is no forum of direct appeal, in which you can ask for proof, or an appeals process through which you can argue than no proof exists. They can simply say that you are a bad person. That's it. This is a well-known problem with U.S. immigration law, and Oleg Deripaska is, by far, not the only victim of this phenomenon. Thousands of people all over the world are trapped in the same limbo at any given time, and successful challenges are extremely rare.

The Department of State does have the power to review such a decision, but almost never chooses to, for fear of creating a precedent. According to media reports, whether true or not, Deripaska spent a lot of money trying to fix this. At one point, the debacle with Mueller, McCabe and Levinson came along, and the FBI had reportedly issued Deripaska with a special visa for cooperating witnesses. Then State intervened, and the visa was, allegedly, revoked. Deripaska's animosity toward the Department of State, and the fact that he has salacious jokes about Victoria Nuland on the tip of his tongue, all have to do with her department consistently preventing him from visiting his many homes in the United States, rather than any issues in geopolitics.

Conceivably, a diplomatic passport could be a way around that. If Deripaska had somehow procured one, he would have only done it as means to circumvent years of persecution by Nuland and Co., and finally get back into his own house. While there, he would host his old FBI pals for an unscheduled early breakfast, and, according to the FBI itself, try to dissuade them out of their early-days' delusion of Russian election interference.

In response to that, the anti-Trump *permanent state*, courtesy of Nuland's pals, hits Deripaska with sanctions – the only remedy he cannot circumvent even with a diplomatic passport – and cites that very diplomatic passport as grounds for doing so. They know that, however much Trump may want to, he will not be able to backtrack on sanctions. They have won! It's a typical circle of bureaucracy-based persecution that we have seen over and over: they deliberately create a problem out of nothing, and then blame you for taking steps to solve it.[72]

---

72 It's a non-sequitur, but this is the standard *modus operandi* of American bureaucracy on every

9.

The definition of "acting on direction of government official", when not limited to any specific time, location, or type of official involved, is so broad that it makes zero sense to ever argue that you haven't so acted. EO13661 does not even specify that the official has to be that of the Russian government. If you are driving down the road and a traffic cop waves for you to pull over, you are acting on behalf of a government official, for U.S. constitutional law purposes. On the basis of logic, the definition parses the same way – in any possible way. Is Putin's driver acting on direction of a government official? What about a waiter? How about a person who walks his dog? How about a babysitter hired by one of the 450 members of the Russian State Duma? An Uber driver? A supermarket checkout girl, whom they asked for a bag?

As to "following verbal instructions" from Putin during some meeting in Kyrgyzstan, the evidence of which I haven't seen and can't be bothered to look up, everyone should put themselves in the position of a businessman who is invited, by their country's President, to join a delegation of economic officials and business people to a foreign country for co-operation talks. Russians, in a mixture of ministers and leaders of industry, go on a lot of those. No sane person would defy their President in such a context. How would you have it happen? "Let's go", – says Putin, – "we are leaving"; and then the delegation does not leave, because its members do not want to be seen as following his "verbal directions"? That would be a real boost to the reputation of Russia and all Russians, for sure. No sane person would do anything other than follow "verbal directions" of the President of their country – whichever country it is – while on an official trip abroad.

Allegations related to Deripaska building facilities in Sochi deserve particular ridicule. Deripaska grew up in the Krasnodar region, where Sochi is

---

·level. Once I qualified as an attorney with California State Bar, officials there read my previous book, and decided, on the basis of it, that I did not meet the moral standards for being an attorney. They then canceled my license, waited a few months until my finances had turned into a complete nightmare, and subpoenaed my bank accounts. In the specialized tribunal, they did not claim that I was unfit because I had written a book. "Look at her bank accounts", they said - "she can't manage money!" Nevermind that it was them that took my license, and there was no underlying reason to have done so. I wrote at the time: *They will bankrupt you and then claim that you are financially irresponsible; they will drive you crazy and then ask questions out loud about your mental health.*

located. He considers the region home and has invested a lot there. If anyone among all the Sochi investors may have had an independent, self-formed reason to do so, it was Oleg Deripaska. In the case of Sochi, his investments were not into stadiums, but rather long-term infrastructure projects. They included hotels, housing (used as Olympic village), the Sochi seaport, and a seaside promenade. His companies built the new road along the coast, which now carries most of the traffic into, and through, the Greater Sochi area. Businesses affiliated with Deripaska also invested in Sochi airport, as well as the airport in Krasnodar, the regional capital, and a number of other airports around the country. Deripaska had a lot to do with the fact that Sochi is now a modern and pleasant holiday destination, and little with the Olympic Games themselves.

Last but not least, let's suppose for a minute, for the sake of the exercise, that Putin is prone to order people around, no matter who they are – and that many, in the moment, judge it best to comply. If you blame them for it, you are defeating the West's main anti-Putin thesis. The same thesis that provides moral justification for all of Russophobia, including these sanctions. Whenever you impugn the next proverbial Deripaska for "co-operating" or "being friendly with", Vladimir Putin, or, variously, doing what Putin told them, let alone "pressured" them to do, such as build a stadium or two, try and imagine what lack of such "co-operation" would look like. Love it or hate it, Russia respects its sovereigns, in a long list of which Putin is only one. *My way, or the highway.*

While defiance of the Executive Branch of government and disrespect of the President ran wild in the United States during the Trump years, thankfully, no one in Russia, realistically, is going to punch Putin in the face instead of building *a stadium or two*. That would be just as true if not Putin, but someone else was President, and it would be true in most other countries that do not, necessarily, subscribe to the American model of so-called government (in reality, chaos). The only way to refuse to build a stadium, would be to leave the country you love and not come back. It is not because Putin is a dictator – the people would be on his side! One must share, you will be told. Spread the wealth, or get out. To impugn one for "co-operation" is simply a euphemism for impugning one for living in Russia and not yet being completely broke, or imprisoned.

As for the alleged statement to the FT in 2007, I suspect that it has been mistranslated, or simply worded ineptly in English in the first place. What Deripaska may have been trying to say, is probably the same as me writing in this book, that Russia and I are in the same boat, or that I do not separate my interests, in terms of how Russia is viewed and treated overseas, from that of Putin or any of the so-called "oligarchs". Even if it was, as reported, given in response to a question about a possibility of expropriation, then it was probably an expression of fealty, for sure. But it would be comedy to suggest that Deripaska meant anything in the vein of Louis XIV.

On the subject of fealty specifically, 2007 was a long time ago. By Russian standards, a very long time. During Vladimir Putin's first two terms, political views and loyalties among the elites, in general, ran much higher in favor of his presidency, than they have since his return to office in 2012. I do believe, as I previously said, that Putin is still popular enough in Russia to win any election, but the margins would be smaller if that election were to be held in Moscow only, or only among the elites.

I said earlier in this book that I would have voted for Putin, had I still been Russian, if I thought that he could lose – but that is because I do not see an alternative. Many in the elites do not see an alternative either, and they also see that what the West thinks are alternatives, aren't. Russians, the elites including, universally fear the chaos of the 1990s more than they fear authoritarianism of the Soviet years. Yet, seeing no better alternative and being happy with the status quo are not the same thing. The West is shooting its own geopolitical interests in the foot by conflating the two, and failing to recognize that times, fortunes and imperatives often change beneath the surface of the same views and positions.

10.

As for poor Oleg Deripaska, trying to allege that he is *Putin's man* makes anyone in Russia laugh. Too bad the CIA is too incompetent to even know that we got Starbucks in Moscow, lest they would have probably picked up on this, too. The possible range of loyalty is wide: being loyal in a sense of not committing treason is not the same as being someone's trusted adviser or top lieutenant. Even Alexey Navalny, lately famous in the West for running around and calling for people he considers "close to Putin" to be sanctioned, does not consider Deripaska to be such a person. "Deripaska does not have any sort of exclusive relationship with Putin", – shrugs Navalny incredulously in one of his videos, commenting on the Manafort-related election interference allegations.

246

The aforementioned video, which enraged Victoria Nuland, was produced by Navalny for the purpose of alleging that the now-deceased mid-level government official, who was also present, accepted a bribe from Deripaska (which both of them denied). If Deripaska was anywhere as close to Putin as insinuated by the Americans, no one in Russia would ever suggest that he needed to bribe a mid-level bureaucrat, even if the allegation was not true.

The underlying conversations on the boat were allegedly recorded in August of 2016, a month prior to Deripaska's forced breakfast with the FBI, during which he learned about the Russian election interference investigation. In their later reports on the conversation, the FBI appeared resentful about Deripaska's outward rejection of their theory. He told them they were trying to make something out of nothing -- and, as we all know now, he was right. Yet, to the extent that there may have been interference, Deripaska would be the last man to know, because no one would tell *him*.

Ever since the failed Iran-Levinson joint venture with the FBI, Deripaska has been forever tarnished in Russia with public mistrust, as an American sympathizer. His perceived affection for America was viewed as disloyalty. When thousands of people lost jobs in his companies after the sanctions, none of them blamed Putin for failure to return Crimea to Ukraine, as the Department of State ostensibly hoped they would. Instead, they all blamed Deripaska, for getting involved with the Americans in the first place. This anger was misplaced – in a rational world, Deripaska's years of collaboration with the U.S. Government should have kept him safe from its sanctions. But that is not how Russians think.

So, what about the elephant in the room: why are we asked to believe, time and again, that, of all Russians, Oleg Deripaska is the devil incarnate? Matthew Chance posited to Deripaska in the above-mentioned CNN interview, that he heard that Deripaska was a "scary guy". John Solomon unlikely asks everyone he meets whether they had people killed. Evidently, the nameless U.S. consular officer, who denied Deripaska a visa many years ago, heard some rumors, as well. So what is so scary that it is supposed to set Deripaska aside, so dramatically, from anyone else who achieved the same success in the same line of business at the same moment in history? What *exactly* are they talking about?

Admittedly, in 1990s Russia people died prematurely, and some of those deaths benefited creations of certain fortunes. But the "aluminum wars", which

Western journalists like to mention so much, weren't actually *wars*. This wasn't the Battle of Moscow in 1941, where the carnage was so bad that we could not recover or identify the bodies. If someone died in the 1990s – even if, as Roman Abramovich put it in his testimony in *Berezovsky v. Abramovich* in 2011, "someone was killed every three days over there [in the aluminum business]", – they had names, and were, by implication, of some importance. Criminal cases have been opened for every murder, and people did, and still occasionally do, go to prison for them. Deripaska's name has only ever been mentioned in any of these cases as that of a would be victim of a failed assassination attempt.

On any sane analysis, Deripaska only survived the said "wars" by a combination of sheer luck and the fact that he was, at the onset of them, a 24-year-old nerd who had just graduated from college, in a city where he barely knew anyone (having been held back for two years by compulsory military service). He had no one behind him at the start, and grew his initial capital incrementally, by trading as a broker and investing profits in shareholdings too small to be noticed, as well as accumulating privatization vouchers. When the "wars" broke out, he was a non-party to them, and without an army.

The Western public has accepted that several fortunes – including that of Roman Abramovich – were created in Russia through loans-for-shares auctions of government property, which plausibly explains their accumulation nearly overnight. Alternative theories of Deripaska's rise are becoming invented because he did not have anything to do with loans-for-shares, and the West doesn't believe that such a fortune could have been built through wit and legwork, in what they see as too short a period of time. But that wasn't just *any* time. As someone who was around for the first part of the 1990s in Russia, I see that as entirely plausible.

As his plot for control came into view and he was noticed by the real players, Deripaska appears to have paid a certain group protection money, so as to try and avoid being killed – but in America's own frame of thinking, that makes him a victim of a racketeering scheme, not a perpetrator, and certainly not a murderer. As a shorthand for such a faulty conflation, Russians usually say "either he stole, or he was robbed", but the actual distinction is crucial. In this respect, Deripaska's associations were no different to those of many other businessmen. Boris Berezovsky, in the days before his likely self-orchestrated assassination attempt in 1994, had been known to run with even scarier people. Yet, by contrast, it did not stick to him at all.

I have come to believe that the sole reason for the lifelong derision of Oleg Deripaska by the elites and the press lies in his peasant origins, which are considerably more humble than anyone in Russia who has ever achieved comparable success. As I mentioned earlier, geographic mobility, in terms of people pulling off a move to Moscow, was negligible in the Soviet Union – and most of the post-Soviet rich, admittedly, became so because they were already there. Boris Berezovsky, Vladimir Gusinsky, Alexander Smolensky, Mikhail Khodorkovsky, Pyotr Aven and Vladimir Potanin, to name a few, are all from Moscow. Roman Abramovich was born elsewhere, but moved to Moscow in time for primary school – his speech and demeanor are distinctly Muscovite.

Dmitry Rybolovlev is from Perm, a city with population of more than a million, and both of his parents were doctors. Mikhail Fridman is from Lviv in Ukraine, a comparably large city, and his father was a laureate of the USSR State Prize, its highest civilian honor, for achievements in military science. Alexey Mordashov is from Cherepovets, a smaller but sizable town in the Northwest. His father, an electrical engineer, worked at a steel factory which his son's company now owns. Although Viktor Vekselberg is from a small town, his mother was a senior engineer at an oil refinery. Oleg Deripaska is the only one whose publicly recited childhood memories include learning to live off the land in a place too small to be on a map. His ultimate achievement is all the more extraordinary for it, but Moscow was never kind to him.

When he burst onto the scene in the early 1990s, despite his exceptional wit and superb education, everything about Oleg Deripaska seemed wrong. He made disastrous fashion choices; he talked and carried himself in a passive-aggressive simpleton manner that is peculiar to deep *provincials*. The *polite society* rejected Deripaska on instinct, not evidence. Boris Berezovsky may have been a psychopath whose acquaintance was a mortal hazard – but to Muscovites, like my mother, Berezovsky walked and talked like one of them, and it was all that mattered. Did he blow up those apartment buildings? Who cared.

One of the reasons the *intelligentsia*, BAB himself including, embraced Vladimir Putin so cheerfully as Yeltsin's possible successor, instead of discarding him for his service in the KGB, as George Soros would have them do, was the same. Although *intelligentsia* he was not, Putin exuded a decidedly big city vibe, and spoke a tolerable Leningrad variant of normative Russian. In the wake of the 1999 apartment bombings, when he delivered his famous remark about *extinguishing terrorists in the outhouse,* oft-quoted as an example of his menace, Putin did not sound scary at all. He begged pardon for his language mid-sentence, and used a French-derived word for *outhouse*.

All of these people got a break because they dressed and sounded right when the world first met them, but Oleg Deripaska did not. *There was just something wrong about him!* No one cared what happened in Siberia, but his shirts were a crime. The effects of this snobbery compounded over the years, slipping into visa decisions and sanctions, informed by rumors and attitudes of foreign reporters and diplomats, who likewise marinaded in the toxic pool of Moscow attitudes. Even now, Deripaska still can't get a break. In keeping with the Marxist paradigm, his class origins became his defining immutable characteristic.

Through enlightenment and wealth, Deripaska has put on considerable gloss over the years. You could not find fault with his style today, but his accent still kills. So much so, that it matters not that *he* hasn't[73]. In a country where privilege cannot be bought and wealth is still a curse, its once-richest man ended up on the wrong side of a class war. The *permanent class* in Moscow rendered its verdict, and then the *permanent state* in America moved in for the final blow.

The same provincial bona fides and oft-expressed disdain for Moscow that earned him the scorn of the elites, equip Oleg Deripaska with something that none of the rest of our wealthy has – a genuine ability to appeal to the population at large. In places that we can't find on maps and have never been to, he is well-liked. When he turned 50 in January of 2018, a few months before the American sanctions were imposed on him, residents of Ust-Labinsk, where Deripaska grew up, apparently honored their hometown hero by assembling themselves into a number 50, large enough to be seen from space. Most of us could never hope to be so devoutly admired by strangers.

Sanctions may yet turn out to be, in the words of Winston Churchill, a *quite effectively disguised blessing* for Oleg Deripaska.

---

73 Oleg Deripaska speaks a Southern variant of Russian, which, even though it is less distinct, comes across to a Muscovite in the same way as Southern drawl to a New Yorker, or Yorkshire to a Londoner. The variant's most defining feature is conversion of ending *v* into [u] - instead of being reduced to [f], as in normative speech. The last national-level public figure to speak Southern Russian was Mikhail Gorbachev, who is from Stavropol region, not far from Krasnodar.

Oleg Deripaska belongs to the increasingly rare breed of Russia's rich, the original businessmen who propped up Boris Yeltsin's inner circle, *the Family*. While Deripaska was a later arrival to *the Family* than others, he married into it – his ex-wife Polina, whom he was in the process of divorcing around the same time as the sanctions were imposed, is the daughter of Valentin Yumashev, close advisor and formerly chief of staff to Boris Yeltsin, and a stepdaughter to Yumashev's second wife, Yeltsin's daughter Tatiana. A journalist by prior profession with an aura of an old-fashioned good guy, Yumashev would never have married his daughter off to Deripaska in 2001, if he didn't know that Deripaska was clean – and Yumashev was in the position to *know*. Sometimes it's as easy as that.

It is common knowledge that members of Yeltsin's inner circle, Valentin Yumashev and Tatiana Dyachenko (later Yumasheva) chief among them, were instrumental in the decision to select the ascendant Vladimir Putin as Yeltsin's successor in power in 1999 (whether or not the late Boris Berezovsky played any part). Certain guarantees, including, but, conceivably, not limited to, a public guarantee of immunity for Yeltsin himself, were, probably, a part of the deal. Without speculation as to who it may have been, some businessmen in the 1990s, in all likelihood, assisted the Yeltsin family with managing their assets, and maybe even held assets for them.

The influence of *the Family* had started to wane the day Putin took office 21 years ago, and had all but evaporated by the end of his first term, let alone second term. Loyalties among the members of *the Family* were personal loyalties, they do not go with any office, and they were never supposed to. Putin has his own people, those who ascended to their current level of wealth and prominence during, and in various ways due to, his presidency. For the most part, they are a very different bunch of people, too – different background, different views, and, ultimately, a different vision for Russia. To suggest that anyone from Yeltsin's *Family* is close, or *closest*, to Vladimir Putin, or are *his men*, today, 21 years later, is absurd. Rather, there once was a time when *they* thought that he was *their man*. But that was only until he was not.

When sanctions against Deripaska were announced, some pundits were even less charitable to his standing with Putin than Navalny had been. "Putin can't stand Deripaska", – declared well-known opposition journalist Dmitry Gordon, speaking on Ukrainian TV. I think this is, probably, too strong. But I can see where Gordon is coming from. Putin always seemed to merely tolerate Deripaska, and is known to humiliate him in public. On several occasions, Putin appeared to have interfered in managerial decisions at Deripaska's businesses, ostensibly to right perceived social wrongs for public benefit. In one famous episode in 2009, Putin forced Deripaska to sign some sort of agreement in front of TV cameras, and then barked at him to return the pen.

Some people thought it was an act. One act, then another, then another - really? What man would agree to be constantly humiliated? In 2019, a full ten years after the pen incident, the FT published the aforementioned new slew of the U.S. government's ostensible explanations for Deripaska's sanctions, which included an allegation of "laundering money for Putin on at least one occasion". Deripaska immediately quipped that the man would not even trust him with a pen, let alone money.

At the time of his alleged expression of fealty to the Russian state in the FT interview in 2007, Oleg Deripaska was the wealthiest man in Russia, with estimated fortune of about $28 billion. In that sense, his wealth was systemic, and he certainly was seen as too big to fail. No one would yell at him about pens, nor would there be a pretext, because there were no wrongs to publicly right. Things were good.

Nonetheless, shortly thereafter Deripaska did, almost, fail. He lost tens of billions of dollars in the financial crisis of 2008, and never fully recovered[74]. Ten years later, just before the U.S. Treasury sanctions, he was worth, by various estimates, about $8 billion. The sanctions at least halved that, due to loss of capitalization of the companies involved and divestment of shares, agreed with the U.S. government as part of a deal to lift the sanctions from those companies.

As of December 2020, Forbes put what's left of Deripaska's fortune at around $3 billion, slightly more than 10% of what he was worth in 2007. Along

---

74 Some suggest that Putin's harsh treatment of Deripaska is an act, because the Russian government ultimately stepped in to save his business from complete failure in 2009. There were good reasons for it to do so. Deripaska, although arguably over-leveraged going into the 2008 crisis, *was* too big to fail, just like some large enterprises in the United States that were similarly rescued by the Obama administration. Deripaska's companies employed tens of thousands of people, and in addition to loss of jobs, their failure would have meant, in part, giving up considerable control of strategic industries to foreign creditors. One needed not sympathize with Deripaska in order to judge those potential outcomes unfathomable.

with divestment, he was forced to step down from management roles. He is of much less interest to Putin, and fewer people want to hear his rambling suggestions on how to improve government, economy, education and fiscal policy, just as he suddenly has much more time to give them. Deripaska is all at sea now, and passes the time sharing his passion for dogs and quantitative easing with a modest audience on Telegram.

Yet, even there he recently got in trouble. Earlier in this book, I mentioned that a famous businessman took issue with the official poverty statistics, which he thought were fudged to be too laudatory. That was Deripaska. Putin's press-secretary, Dmitry Peskov, immediately admonished Deripaska, insisting that the real numbers were not worse, but even better, if properly looked at. Deripaska did not comment, but responded by deleting the original post in its entirety, and replacing it with a chillingly cheerful assessment of the overall reduction of poverty under the steady leadership of President Putin in the last five years. Internet users immediately made fun of him for flip-flopping and not standing his ground.

It seems that Deripaska deliberately styled the replacement message to match the language and tone of propaganda pronouncements of the Soviet era, as a form of silent protest against the censorship he was being subjected to. The grave sarcasm of it all may have gone over the heads of Millennials, Americans and peasants, but anyone with a college degree who grew up in the Soviet Union could tell. I have no doubt that so could Mr. Peskov.

If you scroll back through Deripaska's other winding rants, you will learn that he is very cross with Russia's Central Bank for failure to embrace the Modern Monetary Theory, gravely concerned about climate change, supports nuclear generation of electricity, considers oil and coal relics of the past, and enthusiastically approves of COVID lockdowns. He thinks that FDR's *new deal* policies brought about the modern American prosperity and paved way for its leadership in the world. With enemies like these, who needs friends? Based on his views, I'd say the man is ready to teach at Harvard. When he is done being canceled for a sexist joke about Victoria Nuland, of course.

By the way, that cursed fishing boat was not Victoria Nuland's first experience of the Soviet Union. Prior to that, she spent the summer of 1982 as a camp counselor in Odessa, Ukraine – the same place where, in 2013, fifty people were burned alive as a result of her little victorious uprising.

11.

In September 2018, the New York Times ran a sleazy story on Deripaska and the FBI. As always, it made wide-ranging allegations against Deripaska, citing only prior, equally unfounded, allegations by other media outlets. It then implied a connection between the Deripaska sanctions, the FBI raid on his house in New York in 2016, election interference investigation and Levinson rescue effort. By that time, many media outlets had done as much – but there was something else this time. The FBI, the paper argued, was *trying to turn* Deripaska. *Turn him* into what, exactly? A frog?

The FBI is a domestic law enforcement agency of the United States of America – a country in which, coincidentally, Oleg Deripaska had barely been ever present in the preceding years. Deripaska does not live in the U.S. and, although he owns property there, had been prevented, by the same government, from keeping a home there. Meanwhile, the FBI is prohibited from investigating, or getting involved in, any foreign intelligence or international affairs. That is because we have the CIA to do that. These two agencies have different type of expertise and operate under different sets of rules.

One of the reasons the FBI could not retrieve Robert Levinson from Iran, apart from sanctions, was that it had no power to act in Iran. The CIA sent Levinson to Iran and left him there, apparently disavowed, and, since Levinson had previously been a career FBI employee, Mueller and McCabe felt bad about it and tried to arrange to have him rescued privately.

The extent to which the FBI can do anything at all overseas, is a matter of some contention. I recall watching *Catch Me If You Can* as a law student, and asking myself – wait a minute, what is Tom Hanks doing running after Leonardo DiCaprio all over France, of all places? Isn't that, hm, a foreign country? In the end, I reconciled that Frank Abagnale (played by DiCaprio in the movie) committed his crimes in the United States, and was merely on the run from the said FBI in France. I assumed that perhaps it was entitled to assist the local law enforcement in pursuing him there.

The Internet complicated jurisdictional issues between Federal agencies. By and large, the FBI had claimed jurisdiction over the matter of the so-called Russian election interference, because they regard it as a matter of hacking. Their frequent use of the term *election hacking* is not an accident – it has previously been established that the FBI has jurisdiction in the hacking of financial networks,

254

even if perpetrators are overseas, and they base their jurisdiction over the purported overseas-based election interference on this theory. For the purpose of this book, I provisionally accept that the FBI has jurisdiction over its own theories of foreign election interference, even if those theories hold that it originated overseas.

But then what? As has been established, Deripaska knew nothing about any election hacking. Other than that, the FBI has nothing to do with anything that happens in other countries, and certainly nothing to do with geopolitics, subversion of foreign regimes, foreign espionage, or anything else involving international loyalties, for the purpose of changing which someone, who is not a United States resident, could be *turned*. Coincidentally, Deripaska was in New York attending a session of the UN. What could the FBI want from him? Information on Russian mafia in Brighton Beach, because, of course, *all Russians must know each other*? And what is a domestic law enforcement agency without any foreign relations remit doing, harassing someone who, the government says, entered the U.S. as a *diplomat*?

This sort of reporting is not simply stupid, it is malignant in its intentions. It reiterates the harmful framing of Russian-American relations as a zero-sum game. According to the NYT, the disgraced British investigator Christopher Steele concluded, from public sources, that Deripaska was not *Putin's man* after all – and next, the conclusion was, he must be *turned*. As if there were only two possible states of being for a Russian person: either you are a *Putin's man*, or you are prime for treason. This denial of agency to simply be your own man is emblematic of a trend that I identify every day as the biggest threat to Russian immigrant diasporas. The idea, simply put, that all Russians are either with Putin, or against Russia itself.

When emigres and retarded "former spies" propagate the idea that all Russians who may harbor doubts about the current state of affairs in their country, are ready to support its destruction, is moronic – most people's loyalty, by definition, is to their hometown, their family, friends, and fellow countrymen, and only afterward, their State. But anyone with an IQ over 80 can see the flip side of this argument: that anyone who is not for destruction of Russia in an Arab Spring-style foreign-backed revolution, is a Russian spy. And that is, pretty much, the implication with which we all live every day. That is why the New York Times keeps writing things like that.

255

That is not, of course, the reality – most of the Russians are not so much *with Putin,* as they are with *Russia,* and it includes *the Russian state.* Putin, for all his faults, for the time being, is still the only power center that is able to unite Russia against what we all perceive as an attack – not only on Russia's sovereignty, but on its right to exist. Perhaps that will, one day, change – but most of us would do anything to make sure that it is not an externally imposed change, such as the greatest tragedy of all our lives – destruction of the Soviet Union – once was. We have all learned our lesson about external change since, and no one in Russia wants a taste of Victoria Nuland's cookies, let alone the awful *Bush legs.*

In a March 2021 meeting with Russia's top businessmen, Putin opened by saying that *sanctions were being imposed on us for no reason other than we exist, and are an attack on our sovereignty.* A very effective communicator, Putin knew who he was speaking to – not the businessmen gathered, several of whom were under sanctions, but all Russians. And they all heard him. Like that mirror, he was, once again, simply confirming what all of them already thought. Most of them hadn't stopped thinking the same thing since the 1980s: the Americans are out to get us. Now that we managed to get out of the mess they got us into last time, they are trying to get us *again.* Soviet citizens of the 1980s had a secret love affair with the idea of America, the land about which they knew nothing. Today's Russians know America better than it knows itself, and they are not buying it this time.

Writing in the Financial Times in March 2021, John Dizard pointed out that sanctions are getting out of control, their impact is beyond what was predicted, and they are unsustainable in the long term. He is right. Now that so many people and companies are on all sorts of numerous lists that tarnish their names, damage to reputations is permanent. It would be very difficult, if not impossible, to reverse the impact of sanctions, even if there was a will to do so, because re-integration of the same individuals and companies in the worldwide financial and economic networks cannot, realistically, occur – where regulation no longer prevents it, risk assessment policies of institutions forever will.

The economy and markets that have been damaged by the sanctions are currently being held together with duct tape, but the genie of havoc the sanctions wreaked is never going back into the bottle again. This, of course, removes any possible incentive for course correction on the part of Russia, the purpose for which the sanctions were ostensibly introduced. The damage cannot be fully

256

undone. The Russians know it. Putin knows it, the people know it, everyone who is under sanctions knows it. And they are all as united as ever now, digging in for the long haul.

12.

Sanctions will not cause the House of Russia to divide against itself, as its enemies hope. On the contrary, to the extent that any predicate for such division may exist, sanctions suppress it. A much smaller, weaker Iran, ruled by fanatics, survived 37 years of U.S. sanctions, albeit with assistance from the Soviet Union, later Russia. If anything, Russia can definitely help itself. The talk of the town in Moscow nowadays is all about surviving a siege – and, after all, it was Russians who survived the deadliest siege in modern history, the Siege of Leningrad during World War II. They think they can manage a nonviolent siege.

The people who are making decisions in Russia today are the same people who stood on the ruins of our way of life the last time Americans sold us a fairy tale, and they are not going to buy it, and wait for the chlorinated chicken legs, this time. The fall of the Soviet Union happened within the waking, conscious lifetime of the majority of current Russian adults. As a result of their collective lived experience through all that followed, Russians, each individually and as a group, have a higher risk tolerance than Europeans, Brits or Americans. The very idea that their lives can change dramatically does not scare them as much, because they already have, and more than once.

Everyone who built fortunes in their youth in the 1990s by sheer luck and chutzpah, always sort of knew that those fortunes can also be lost – the assumption of that risk has always been the part of the high rewards that Russian business offered. None of them is ready to die on a hill that's a pile of money somewhere; they would rather put it back when they found it – in Russia. My generation of Russians, Generation X, has seen it all, and they are now middle-aged, grumpy, and won't be manipulated.

Modern Russia is stronger and more viable than the stagnation-era Soviet Union. Not only does it produce its own oil and gas – and that for much of Europe – it also grows its own food, manufactures its own cars, buses and trains, it develops and manufactures its own medicine and vaccines. To the extent that there is something Russia does not produce, it has an almost 3000-mile long land

257

border with a country that produces most of anything, for the whole world, and will be happy to oblige.

Russians are on Telegram, the only social media platform that is not controlled from the United States. They use Yandex, not Google, for their maps, food, taxis, e-mail and disk storage. They use Huawei phones, the latter having recently introduced its own operating system instead of Google's Android. The Huawei App gallery comes with Yandex apps preinstalled. A couple of months ago, I dropped and cracked the umpteenth laptop (as I do often), and had to walk into an electronics store in Moscow and buy the cheapest laptop on offer. It was not an HP or Dell, not a Chromebook, nor anything that ran Windows. It was a Chinese brand with Linux OS. A few weeks in Russia, and you are 100% free of any hardware or software products produced by, or controlled from, the U.S.

Russia is no stranger to economic isolation. The currency system of the Soviet Union, infamously, was entirely autonomous and did not "plug", on a consumer level, into the world economy. You could not buy foreign currency and buy the same things with it abroad. Everyone in Russia is prepared now for the day when this may be a reality again. After the 2014 sanctions, when there was a brief disruption in Visa and MasterCard services, Russia announced its own payment system. It is rather ineptly called MIR (as in, *the world*), seeing as it works only in Russia. First, it sounded like a crazy idea. Then, they forced anyone in receipt of social payments to get MIR cards, and simultaneously introduced government-subsidized 10% and 20% discounts on transport and hospitality, when those are paid for with MIR cards. MIR is the most popular payment system in Russia now.

If you still want a debit card that belongs to an international payment system, any Russian bank today offers cards bearing logos of China-based Union Pay, as well as Japanese JCB. The movement to introduce a digital rouble, based on blockchain technology, has intensified. In Russia, this could now happen quickly. After all, we have Deripaska actively pushing for *economic sovereignty* that it portends, and, thanks to the U.S. Department of Treasury, the man has got lots of free time on his hands.

You can see, perhaps, why most Russians were not surprised when they heard that the EU wants to disconnect them from SWIFT, the system that enables international wire transfers. Many of them believe that they will soon have no currency that can be sent overseas anyway, or that they will be forbidden from doing so by sanctions, even if the technology is available to do so. No one around there feels like there is much left to lose in the global world. In reality, of course, there is much left to lose still, but this is not necessarily what the masses believe.

Seven years ago, when the government called for *import substitution*, a requirement that certain foods – such as, for instance, cheeses or cured ham – were produced locally, instead of imported from the EU, people laughed. There was footage of truckloads of prosciutto ham dumped at the border into the ditch. It was weird. No one understood what it was about then, but they do now. I will be the first one to admit, Russian-made Camembert was awful at first. But it's getting better, and so is Crimean wine. Russia can survive a siege and still have Camembert and wine.

13.

Yet, with all this almost-enthusiasm for the long winter, I cannot ignore the darkness that is lurking in the shadows. As a former Soviet Union citizen who dreamed of traveling the world, the Iron Curtain was the ever-present nightmare of my childhood. I could not help but see that, during the COVID-19 pandemic, the Russians jumped on the bandwagon of travel restrictions a bit faster than was necessary, and with a bit too much fervor. The phobia of being, once again, locked inside Russia one day, when it decides to draw the new Iron Curtain, is not rare among my fellow Russians. We frequently talk about it to each other. The primary reason behind my decision to renounce Russian citizenship was to have the right to British consular assistance if, and when, it happens.

My theory has always been that this would be a slow, creeping process under a pretext of some calamity or other. Epidemic, computer failure at the passport control, need to introduce new passports for some bizarre reason, you name it. When Russia shut down its airspace during COVID, it also prohibited crossing of land borders – not just for entry, but also for exit. Air borders were ostensibly open, except that there weren't any flights. You could only get out by private aircraft – that is, if you don't own a Gulfstream registered to a sanctioned entity. Then you can't use that, either. To drive the point home, the government "closed" the hitherto unmarked border with Belarus. One day, overnight, ditches were dug in the woods where it supposedly runs, to prevent surreptitious crossings. *VGTRK Rossiya* blared out creepy, long stories about dangers of foreign travel, reminiscent of *The Truman Show*.

259

A year later, there still weren't as many international flights out of Moscow as there were before COVID, and I am certain there will never be again. For six months, Russia maintained an unexplained prohibition on flights to and from the UK, where tens of thousands of Russians live or have close family members, and thousands of Russian children go to school. People who took flights from the UK back to Russia via connections in other cities were harassed upon arrival by special brigades sent to catch them and fine them. It was bizarre, and no legitimate epidemiological interest warranted that. But it chimed eerily with my prior experience that seemed designed, specifically, to intimidate Russians living in the UK and the United States.

One day a few years ago, having landed in a Moscow airport, I discovered that, without warning, banks were no longer allowed to exchange British Pound notes, and none of my foreign cards worked in Russia. I had trouble getting out of the airport, because I had only pounds with me, and no way to turn them into bus money. Then, at one time in 2020, while leaving Russia, I was taken by the Border Force into a separate room, where they confiscated my British passport and questioned me for twenty minutes, KGB style, on when, and under what circumstances, I had acquired it. This was pure intimidation, as if the message was, *don't come back.*

This happened notwithstanding the fact that I am, as the reader knows by now, a supporter of *the Putin doctrine,* and believe that *#Crimeaisours.* I, certainly, did obediently notify the Russian government of my second citizenship when the law requiring me to do so was adopted, even though I had a bad feeling about that law. I do not think this creeping Iron Curtain chimes with the Putin doctrine – which, as I understood it for years, presupposes the worldwide spread of Global Russians, world leadership on a range of topics and issues, success in international sport, stronger influence in Eastern Europe. Those are all the things that Putin we all know, or think that we know, believes in. So, what gives?

My conspiratorial fear of Russia's tendency to shut borders is so great, that I will stop short of entirely blaming sanctions for this process. Something else is going on underneath the surface, and I do not yet know what it is. But sanctions create a beautiful, effective pretext for the new Iron Curtain. One that, unlike COVID, will not go away. Our country is our castle now, and the drawbridge is going up.

14.

All of this, to me, looks like survivalism in the woods of Idaho, but on steroids and with more weapons. Russians consider the sanctions to be a *hybrid war,* not a cold war. Earlier in this book, I lamented that the patriotic surge from the Victory in WWII was finally waning, and that Russia was in desperate need of a new unifying idea. The United States, via sanctions, are delivering that idea. *With enemies like these, who needs friends?* And those of you who still think that Vladimir Putin is a killer and a despot, should consider the role that the popularity of Joseph Stalin played in the last war.

Like most people, I love my hometown, Moscow – but I am wary of Russia. I respect it, and I am in awe of it, but I also fear it. I do not think Russia is a threat to others – rather, I am afraid of what it can do to itself. It's like having a family member on suicide watch. But if you are one of those who think that Russia threatens the world, then please let's stop making it upset.

The Soviet Union did not fall because it had the Iron Curtain and the Berlin Wall. It fell when they were destroyed. Putin's Russia was not going to be the new Soviet Union, but, by forcing it to build the new Iron Curtain – *or, depending on your view, by giving it the pretext to build the new Iron Curtain –* you might just make it into one. Soviet Union 2.0 will be much improved and more sustainable.

Unlike in the original Soviet Union, no one will want to leave, because it will be populated with resentful former Global Russians, whom your endless Russiagate and Russophobic furor will push back inside its walls, because they will not want to stick around for Japanese internment 2.0, soon to be the *Russian Internment.* And behind the walls they will stay, long past the cessation of hostilities, like the proverbial guerrilla fighters in the woods, who are still derailing trains because they don't know that the war is over.

Anyone who doesn't know any better – and I don't – must now start believing that the sanctions were never intended to bring Russia around into the Western family of nations. They were intended to start a new war – the hybrid war – for the benefit of the old military industrial complex in the United States. If you, or your parents, were taught to hide under a school desk from a nuclear bomb during the Great Red Scare of 1962, then it is up to you now to prevent a permanent, non-geographic, omnipresent and neverending Cuban Missile Crisis from taking shape.

The sanctions aren't simply *not working*. They are working very well, except that they are accomplishing the exact opposite of what you were led to believe that they will. To be honest, I am not sure this process can still be stopped. But, just in case, it is time to call your congressman, your MP, your psychiatrist, your priest, your pot dealer, and everyone else you know, and tell them: the 1980s called, and they want Victoria Nuland back.

PART THREE. WHAT HAVEN'T WE DONE?

Russiagate

It was once fun to be Russian in America. You were white, and you blended in. As a diaspora, Russians are known to have a very low level of political activity in the United States, lower than almost any other immigrant group – despite the fact that Russians, on average, are better educated and speak better English than many other groups. There is a lot of talk in the diaspora now as to why – most likely, it is because Russians are enterprising by nature and tend to focus on business, while others are able to command high enough salaries professionally in finance and IT. When you are focusing on making money and succeeding at it, politics seems like a waste of time. The Soviet Union and the 1990s have not endeared politics to many Russians, either. We have now realized that, had we been more politically active for all these years, we would have been politically represented. Alas, it may be too late: we are so toxic now that people get out of elevators to avoid riding them with us.

The first signs came in 2015, when Donald Trump announced his candidacy for President. The earlier voices, suggesting that he had a lot of Russian fans, sounded as much as a joke as the Trump campaign itself did, at the time. He lived in New York and developed real estate – obviously, he knew a lot of Russians! By 2016 though, things became pretty bad – and, by 2017, they were unbearable. Most of us stopped telling anyone that we *were* Russian. "If I had ever met *a Russian*, surely I would have remembered!" – shouted Chris Matthews, himself since disgraced, on MSNBC. No one asked him the only pertinent question: if there were at least 3 million Russians in the United States, how would he have known that he met one? We are not green, do not have antennae on our heads, and most of us do not have Oleg Deripaska's scary accent. Was Chris Matthews proposing, by any chance, that we should all wear something that marks us? Perhaps a red star? It felt like it was coming to that.

That was years ago now, of course. Trump has come and gone. We have established that Putin did not say "yes, I did", Christopher Steele is an idiot, and Manafort did not offer anything to Deripaska in 2016. What, then, remains of Russiagate? Not much, according to the Muller report – except collateral damage. This damage is measured in people whose lives have been wrecked. Some have

263

been accused of crimes, however minor, or simply subjected to hysteria and hatred: Michael Flynn, George Papadopoulos, Carter Page, Roger Stone, Maria Butina, Natalia Veselnitskaya, Igor Fruman and Lev Parnas, Paul Manafort himself. Some have been victimized by arbitrarily imposed sanctions – and, a world away, thousands of innocent civilians lost jobs and livelihoods due to the near-collapse of businesses that sanctioned individuals owned. No one received any sort of apology, let alone redress.

Let's suppose that the findings of the Muller Report are broadly correct. It seems to be like that mirror from Harry Potter, in which everyone sees their most sacred desire come true. People who read the report all drew different conclusions from it. It proved a particularly challenging read for the poorly informed, the paranoid schizophrenics and everyone else at MSNBC. To the rest, the Mueller report confirmed what was already obvious to anyone who knew anything about Russia, the Russians, or international affairs: that there was no collusion between the Trump campaign and the Russian government, and no coordinated campaign by Russia to assist Trump in being elected.

Yet, the disappointed left kept pouring over the recantation of all the wishful thinking, self-aggrandizement, fraudulent misrepresentations and coincidence that plagued the Trump campaign, just as all of these things always plague any election campaign. The left kept connecting the dots with strings of red yarn, like obsessed mentally ill people do with newspaper clippings in their garages. So, what are the actual allegations of the 2016 election interference, as confirmed by the Muller report, and what, if anything, did the rest of these people do wrong? In most cases, nothing at all, or nothing of the sort of things that the media alleges they did.

The election interference allegations started with an idea – completely discredited – that President Trump was, in some way, directed by the Russians, or relying on their help to get elected. The former and the latter are not, of course, the same – nor are *the Russians* the same as *Russians*. The left is eager to claim a contradictory distinction between Putin and everyone else Russian when it suits them, and then completely lose sight of that distinction when it does not, sometimes to the effect of disenfranchising American citizens of Russian descent.

Being a spy of the Russian state is not quite the same as having some Russian *babushkas* in Florida, all of them long-time American citizens, campaign

264

for you. Many U.S. citizens and permanent residents, originally from Russia, supported Trump and were perfectly entitled to do so. Yet, CNN and MSNBC denied them that franchise. When Russian-speaking Americans in Florida organized in support of Trump, who is hugely popular in the community, they were derided as spies and Putin stooges, and fellow Americans of non-Russian descent were shamed by CNN crews for joining in. At one point, a CNN crew showed up at some poor woman's house and shamed her for aiding the "Russian operation", which was actually a local rally for Trump in Florida. During Russiagate, everyone forgot that at least three million people of Russian descent live in the United States, and it is their right to support Trump, which most of them do. The immigrant-loving establishment just did not love *these* immigrants, after all.

In their zeal, the media also forgot, it seems, that the allegedly existing meddling Russians from overseas were supposedly doing so by pretending to be *not Russians*. Meanwhile, the Russian-speaking community in Florida, which calls itself that proudly, just like the Cuban-American community does, did not hide that they were Russian. They thought they did not have to – until CNN showed up and started to tell Americans off for getting too friendly with their immigrant neighbors.

In the Russian-speaking community in the United States, there has never been a social distinction between Russians and Ukrainians, and the latter, for the most part, also support Trump. So did Igor Fruman and Lev Parnas, long-time American citizens who, as best as anyone can tell, were businessmen that donated their own efforts and funds to Trump-related causes. It has not, to the best of my knowledge, been alleged that these were not their own funds. What gives, then? What have they done? They were accused publicly of interfering in Ukraine by having a prosecutor fired, at Trump's behest. So, in summary, these are two American citizens accused of doing what the American President asked them to do. What is criminally wrong with that?

Nothing, and that is why this isn't what they have been charged with. Eventually, they were charged, I think, with making political donations in the United States in furtherance of results that coincided with the wishes of some person, or other, in Ukraine. Wait a minute! Parnas and Fruman, although American citizens, have lived and done business in Ukraine themselves. Could it be that *their own* wishes were the same, after all? If we cannot claim that they

265

funneled someone else's money as donations – and there was no such accusation – then how can we prove that they, as U.S. citizens, did not themselves wish for the election of relevant officials? We cannot. They were simply bullied for being immigrants, and for supporting Trump.[75]

To me personally, the disenfranchisement of the immigrant diasporas that thus occurred is the most troublesome aspect of it all. It is the lingering assumption, once again, that the only acceptable immigrant is either a former dissident or a proverbial Uber driver who knows nothing of politics and is not involved in it. In the United States both U.S. citizens, including those who are also citizens of other countries, and U.S. permanent residents are entitled by law to donate their own funds to political campaigns, to support and promote candidates. Collectively they are known as "U.S. persons", a term critical to both campaign finance law and sanctions law.

The phenomenon of people who have multiple nationalities is, admittedly, a phenomenon of recent decades. The idea of multiple allegiances to different states was unthinkable just a generation ago. From the perspective of the receiving countries, e.g. the United States and the United Kingdom, it can be framed in different ways. In those immigrant-receiving nations, whose policies have been written with an assumption that the persecuted will be fleeing to them, naturalization laws never required abdication of prior allegiance – and the question of *whose side would all these people take in a war*, thankfully, did not arise for many years.

The Soviet Union used to strip emigrants of citizenship, but Russia does not, so anyone who left Russia after 1991 retained theirs[76]. The post-globalization world, crisscrossed by hordes of Global Russians, contains within it numerous citizens with multiple passports and various allegiances to different countries. Often these are countries that mutually think of themselves as unfriendly to each another. In America there are, probably, hundreds of thousands of them, a lot of people simply do not realize that. Not all of them are naturalized immigrants, either – many, of course, as U.S.-born children of immigrants, who acquired U.S.

---

75 It is my understanding that eventual charges against these two included only some alleged commercial improprieties, and/or a possibly improper political donation unrelated to the presidential election whatsoever. I would not be surprised to learn that even those were concocted, as well.

76 In practical reality, it is more complex. Most of those who left in the last years of USSR also either retained Russian citizenship, or were quickly able to get it back.

citizenship by birth in the country, but their parents' citizenship, or even citizenships, through parentage. My middle daughter, born in America, is a citizen of three countries at the same time. People who are citizens of both Russia and the United States today could easily number more than a million. I would guess that the Chinese-American community could have similar numbers.

America has a bad history of paranoid political delusion in respect of immigrant communities within it. The internment of Japanese Americans during WWII is on the minds of everyone in the Russian-American community today. Most likely as a result of that internment, when U.S. citizens already in camps were asked whether they were willing to take up arms against Japan, many answered "no". They were universally American patriots going in, but the abhorrent treatment alienated them. At that time, dual citizenship was unthinkable, and most of the internees were U.S. citizens by birth.

British citizenship is my only citizenship – just as American citizenship was the only citizenship for many interned Japanese – but I will be the first to acknowledge that I would probably flee to Timbuktu if Russia and Britain were at war, as I would certainly not take up arms against either of them. If any expatriate Russians on either side of the Atlantic were willing to take up arms against Russia before Russiagate started, they certainly won't now. Quite a few people who left the Soviet Union in the late eighties have now become Russian patriots and fancy Putin. The modern equivalent of being interned in a camp in the 1940s is being ring-faced as a security threat in a company that you yourself co-founded. The result is the same.

I know people with three or four nationalities whose sanity rests, presumably, solely on the persistence of world peace. Whether the answer to this dilemma is for every country to stop immigration and pull up the drawbridge, or to stop being suspicious and afraid, and learn to live globally all together, is a question for another book. Be as it may for now, in Parnas, Fruman and many unnamed Trump rally organizers in Florida, we have U.S. citizens prosecuted and persecuted for nothing more than their national origin and political views.

In the United States, even temporary residents, including legal nonimmigrants and illegal immigrants, are perfectly allowed to campaign for political candidates and offer volunteer services to campaigns, without making financial contributions. They are also allowed to share their opinions as to which candidates they prefer to win, or information about candidates and issues (when they are physically present in the United States, they all have constitutional rights, and the First Amendment protects their right to do so).

At the time when I was yet not a permanent resident, I actively participated in Gore 2000 and Davis for California 2002 campaigns, and recall meeting Gore and attending Davis' inauguration. In hindsight, the same year that I worked for the Gore campaign, my then-husband worked directly for Vladimir Putin's first presidential campaign in Moscow. A childhood friend of mine, who was one of the managers of that campaign, went on to work for the Presidential Administration during Putin's first term (to the FBI's credit, it picked up on the latter before I did, and called me to ask when I had last heard from that friend). Just to think how much trouble with the pundits we would all have been in, on the same facts, 20 years later! Or, perhaps, none at all, seeing as those were Democratic campaigns?

In more recent years, before Russiagate prompted my own abrupt pivot to the right, I drove around with a *Bernie* sticker on my car – I had to buy one on eBay, though. It turns out you are not allowed to buy official campaign merchandise because it is considered a contribution. The sticker is still on my car, by the way. Nowadays, it keeps my tires from being slashed.

My point being, of course, that Maria Butina was perfectly entitled to the entirety of her intervention in the United States. Nothing whatsoever kept her, legally, from dating a Republican, asking Trump questions at town halls, or organizing for Russian-American gun rights cooperation. The left media spent a lot of time asking "how stupid was the NRA", but the NRA was not stupid at all – they probably had lawyers, and lawyers told them the truth: there was nothing wrong with any of it. The most vocal point of media ridicule was the very notion of gun rights in Russia, where, according to MSNBC, there were "no guns".

While it is true, of course, that you cannot buy one in the supermarket, and most of the people in Russia do not have guns, it does not mean that *there are no guns*. My father owned a registered hunting rifle in the 1980s. In the early 1990s, I myself owned what we called a "gas gun", a rather massive revolver adapted to fire gas instead of bullets. At the time, it was commonly thought of as suitable means of personal protection for young women. Moreover, it is precisely because you cannot go and buy guns freely in Russia that some people campaign for the ability to do so. Gun rights advocacy very much exists, and Maria Butina, judging by her LiveJournal feed, had been involved in it for years. It was her thing, and it was her thing before she met the Russian official at whose behest, without FARA registration, she was eventually charged with acting (an offense that would carry no more penalty than a speeding ticket, had she not been Russian). However misguided Butina's quest was, it was clearly her own.

I do not personally know Maria, but I know people who do, and, according to them, she had been enthusiastically pro-American and intent on building her future in the U.S., up until the day of her baffling arrest. As a result of her persecution, she is now back in Russia. At the time of writing, she is likely to be elected to Russian State Duma in 2021, and her Telegram feed is an embodiment of scathing anti-American sentiment. One can hardly blame her for that. But how does it help the interests of the United States? It does not.

So what, then, of Michael Flynn, Carter Page and George Papadopoulos? Flynn was, of course, guilty of the most heinous crime: he sat next to President Putin at a banquet. In the terminology used by Chris Matthews, he thereby definitely *met a Russian*. Putin assured everyone that he had not been introduced to Flynn and had no idea who it was. Predictably, that intervention didn't help – to which we will get later.

Carter Page was apparently guilty of writing a shoddy PhD dissertation, which no one read. That, anyhow, was the focus of his vilification in the media – which I took personally, ready to defend the honor of the School of Oriental and African Studies at the University of London. Its illustrious alumni include Aung San Suu Kyi and my daughter Darya, who, like my Grandpa Boris, is a Japanologist. Most Americans have never heard of SOAS, the world's pre-eminent school of oriental studies, but I knew right away that there was nothing wrong with Carter Page's PhD.

As for the rest of it, Carter Page is a victim of his own vanity. Since the Trump campaign did not know any better, numerous people showed up trying to sell their services to it. All of them greatly exaggerated their own influence, contacts and importance in the process of doing so. Hundreds, if not thousands, of Americans, Canadians and Brits work in large Russian companies at any given time. This alone does not make them intelligence assets or targets, and does not equip them with any meaningful contacts. Just walking down the street in Moscow does not magically cause you to acquire connections or imbibe intelligence. Carter Page knew nothing and no one. But he alluded to more, which people in all election campaigns do when they are hoping to get paid. That allusion backfired in step 2, when disgruntled Trump staffers started to rat on each other.

George Papadopoulos was the most hapless of the bunch (unsurprising to any Russian, given that his name, in Russian, sounds like an extended version of *popados*, slang for finding yourself in deep shit through utter misfortune). His foreign experience seems to have been limited to studying in London, and he knew neither Russian nor any Russians. In London, Papadopoulos met some extremely dodgy Maltese guy, who has since gone MIA, and an unknown Russian woman. The two somehow convinced Papadopoulos, who did not know any better, that they had connections in Russia. I can only assume that he believed them because they were not asking for money – gratuitous lying for the sake of self-aggrandizement alone is a European thing, but it is a thing. I cannot stress how far you must be from giving foreign policy advice to anyone at all if you genuinely thought that this gave you the opportunity to "set up a meeting between Trump and Putin". If Papadopoulos really told the Trump campaign that he could do it, he must have been just trying to earn himself a place under the sun.

What attracted the most media attention was the allegation, by the same shady Maltese guy, that "the Russians have dirt on Hillary Clinton" in a form of "emails". Papadopoulos proceeded to gossip about the ostensible revelation with foreign diplomats in Europe during social engagements, including the Australian High Commissioner – who, notably unlike Papadopoulos himself, notified the FBI. The emails themselves were, most likely, an invention – even if Russia did have any, this guy from Malta would not know anything about it. A lot of speculation related to those phantom Clinton emails was going around as a result of her deleting them from a private server, and Trump called mockingly for Russia to "find them". It was an easy lie to make up. In the event, no emails turned up, and the Mueller report found no evidence that Papadopoulos ever shared the rumor of their existence with the Trump campaign. He was not charged in relation to that.

For reasons unclear – probably, vanity – Papadopoulos, however, continued to insinuate to the Trump campaign that he had Russian contacts, and was ready to set up meetings. There is no evidence that he knew, or was in touch with, any Russians at all, let alone Russians from actual Russia. There is also no evidence that Paul Manafort, who took over the management of the campaign by then, took Papadopoulos seriously. The emails in which he proposed to set up meetings, however, earned Papadopoulos an investigation under FARA – the same statute as Maria Butina, but, of course, much milder consequences and a very different result overall.

At the end of the day, all of these people – my apology to them all – were a parade of clowns. They knew no Russians and very little about Russia, and were absolutely not in the position to communicate or facilitate anything. No sane Russian would have ever used them to communicate anything, either. Further, no sane FBI agent would have ever suspected that any usable information or communications were to flow through these misfits. I strongly suspect that no FBI agent did suspect anything the sort at any point. The bureau's intention toward *the clowns* must have been to scare and make an example of them. The only person they really suspected in 2016 was, as we already know, Paul Manafort. After all, Manafort and Gates both knew Russians aplenty, a fact that – as well as Manafort being on the run from Deripaska for unpaid debt – was public knowledge[77].

At the end of the day, of course, Manafort was cleared of any treasonous leanings. His undoing was tax evasion – and, apparently, the use of Telegram messaging service. The media thought that to be un-American[78].

Now onto the central allegation: the Facebook posts. When Jared Kushner summed up the allegations of election interference as "some people trolling some other people on Facebook", he was, in essence, right. An allegedly coordinated campaign of influence that trolled swaths of the American population on Facebook is the only claim against any Russians that remains standing as a result of the 2016 election campaign interference investigation in the United States. I think a lot of actual posts by Russians living in the United States, who

---

77 The other people who knew various well- connected Russians were, of course, members of the Trump family.
78 Come to think of it, they also thought his use of the app by San Francisco-based Signal was un-American. But the Feds read all of his messages, apparently, because they were saved on his device, a human error that negates the point of any encryption. Reportedly, Manafort also had his WhatsApp messages backed up onto a cloud. If anything, this lack of foresight itself proves that he was no conspirator.

were fully entitled to make them and were using equally non-grammatical English, may have gotten lumped up in it, too. I also think that a lot of various endeavors by various people from all over the world, Russians and non-Russians alike, added up to the "chatter" – the Internet being, after all, *a garbage dump*.

Nonetheless, the Mueller report tells us that a certain "troll factory" – a rented space in St. Petersburg where trained Russians pretend to be Americans to sow discord on social media, not necessarily specific to the election campaign of 2016 – was a thing. How was it such a big thing that anyone in America would be influenced by it as to their vote, is unclear. It is equally unclear whether saying stuff to people in other countries on the Internet, be it truth or lies, is in any way illegal (I do not think so). I was told by the people I trust in Russia that *the factory* was real, so I choose to believe it now, although hitherto I did not. Importantly though, there is no evidence whatsoever – and none has been alleged by Mueller – that Putin, or anyone in the Russian government, had knowledge of its existence prior to the post-election public reports and the Mueller investigation. After all, Russia is full of redundant, chutzpah-base projects that we call *samodeyatelnost*. It means people on various levels acting of their own accord for what they believe, erroneously or not, to be public good.

The most ridiculous – and the farthest from the truth – part of the Russiagate narrative in the United States can be summed up by Obama's infamous quip: "Not much happens in Russia without Vladimir Putin". This was a surprisingly stupid thing to say for Obama – who, whatever you think of him, is not. Yet one more ideological descendant of Harry Truman missed the memo that Joseph Stalin was dead. Most importantly, it bred a multitude of restatements and repeats by all sorts of pundits, the crux of the message being always the same: the Russians are disciplined, and Putin personally orders the actions of everyone who is even remotely Russian.

Everyone in his circle, everyone in Russia, and, in fact, everyone around the world who speaks Russian. We were all supposedly connected and took our marching orders from one source. At any cost, none of us was capable of independent thought or action out of our own perceived self-interest. On that last point, the enduring premise was also insulting, because it sort of implied that Putin was the only smart one, while the rest of us were incurably stupid.

Do all Russians really know each other, and do they all truly take their orders from one source? This is a fundamental misunderstanding of how Russia works. The reality is the exact opposite of this notion of everyone being an empty shell of non-opinion and indecision, waiting to receive a signal from the mother ship (e.g., Putin). I will grant you, however, that neither is it a land of pluralism.

I wrote in the prologue to this book that I do not need to have met Putin to know what he thinks – because people of similar background, informed by the same set of facts, naturally come to similar conclusions. This does not only apply to me – that's pretty much everyone in Russia. Everyone thinks that they know what Putin thinks, even though many of us can be wrong to various degrees. It is not Russians that are vessels for Putin's wisdom and directions – it is him, in a way, who is a mirror in which everyone sees themselves: their own opinions, convictions, desires. One of the secrets to Putin's popularity at home is that his public image panders to everyone's confirmation bias – everyone, that is, who thinks of themselves as a Russian loyalist.

Throw in an occasional affirmation – Putin often does speak in public and in the circles of power, and, directly or indirectly, many of us know what he thinks (or, at least, what he says). That makes us more confident in approximating the rest. The last, most crucial secret ingredient is the desire to win favor – *выслужиться* – that is the main motivator of anyone in Russia who exists at any level of any power structure. The mechanism of how favor is won is absolutely NOT waiting to be given orders and carrying them out. That way, many reason, they can be waiting forever and never be given a chance to distinguish themselves, or do so more than their nearest competitors in the quest for favor.

Conversely, you win favor by taking initiative and acting on your own, on behalf of the common good. You would usually come up with multiple ways in which to try to distinguish yourself, until some of them actually work out, e.g. until you reach some success that you can take credit for. Then, you go a level, two levels above you – and if you are high enough, maybe even to Putin – and you claim a reward, or promotion, or propose something else and solicit funding, based on what you already achieved. This is a very familiar phenomenon to anyone who operates in Russia – businessmen, mid-level politicians, PR people and everyone else near the centers of power usually make low level investments in various interventions that they think are broadly in line with the "party line", expecting to plausibly deny involvement if the interventions fail or make things worse, and to take credit for success if the same interventions end up pleasing.

Quite a lot of those projects are often bizarre, and start with one person or two people – who are nobodies with an idea – taking it to whomever they personally know, who belongs to any structure of power whatsoever. That person will either bring them to a larger player capable of bankrolling the project or bankroll it themselves. If this is just some random idea that may or may not be what is needed, or may or may not succeed, no one is going anywhere high up to seek approval for it. Firstly, you need to give the benefit of plausible deniability to the person or people higher up than you; and second, you yourself do not want to be associated with a possible failure in their eyes.

Most of those, of course, are domestic ventures, but some are not. The absolute majority of instances of "Russian interference", or other bemoaned initiatives that went South for the world to see, were very clearly such low level "why not" interventions by domestically insignificant players. The quest of Maria Butina was clearly one such instance, and the quest of Anna Chapman – if there even was ever any quest, of which I am not convinced – was another.

The West makes a crucial mistake when it assumes that Russia had initially sponsored every venture that it directly or indirectly acknowledged *post factum*. Russia would acknowledge anyone who acted initially on their own if its suits the Russian narrative, and regardless, I suspect, of whether those people want to be so acknowledged or not. It is in the nature of all geopolitical players to own success or, occasionally, indignation, but to disown failure. Sometimes it is also a genuine, even if ineffective, attempt to help. For example, as in the case of Chapman, if you are trying to prove that you are not a spy and have done, broadly, nothing you could be charged with, and then the Russian state, having never heard of you before but wishing to free you from jail, offers to accept you as part of a coincidentally happening spy exchange, your position becomes rather untenable. With friends like these, who needs enemies?

The quest of Natalia Veselnitskaya, the supposed "Kremlin-affiliated" Russian lawyer behind the "Russian adoptions" meeting in 2015 in the Trump Tower, was a particularly ridiculous example. Based on her social networks, as they have been reported, I am more Kremlin-affiliated than this woman is. At best, she could have been audaciously trying to secure sanctions-related assertions from the Trumps in order to put herself on the map back home.

274

I rather think that she was motivated by the hysteria of Russia's democratic opposition, of which the prohibition of adoptions in Russia by U.S. citizens (tied by many to the Magnitsky Act as a quid pro quo), is a pet cause. They do not care about the sanctions but use the adoption ban, usually, to paint Putin as the enemy of little children. Certainly, no one would be leading with that topic while trying to ostensibly represent him. (The most stunning in this, to me, is that the Trumps had no one in their circle who was familiar enough with Russia to have told them that before they took the meeting).

To this, critics will tell me: how can you say what you say, when this person or that person knows such and such, or worked here and there? This is the fundamental flaw in their thinking. All Russian-speaking people in the world are not connected – yet, everyone in Moscow knows each other. So much so, that these connections are meaningless. If you live in Washington, DC and are in any way involved in policy, politics, media or the non-profit sector, ask yourself: who do you know? How many people do you know who work, or have worked, for the current or previous presidential administration? As congressional staffers? How many political advisers, congressmen, past or present, have you met, or people from the security services? The answer is: a lot. It's a small town. Everyone knows each other. They know who the other person is, they have met them on some occasions, work-related or social, they may have talked to them.

It does not mean that you are *connected* to all these people that you *know* by either some sort of common interest or a scheme of influence. You may be connected to some of them, but not others; you may have been connected to some people in the past and are now their enemy. Nor does it mean that what you have to say will have any effect on any particular one of them. You know everyone, but that doesn't mean anything.

Moscow is exactly the same. Everyone who is anyone knows everyone else. I lived away from Moscow for many years and yet I still know a lot of people. I know several people who are now under personal U.S., EU and UK sanctions. I know, to various degrees, numerous people who know Putin. I know people who helped run his election campaigns and worked in his administration, as well as people who worked in a number of other government roles. I know many people who are in the Duma, and I most certainly would have been there myself, before the age of 30, if I hadn't left Russia in the 1990s. I worked for several major print and TV outlets and know many people who do, some at the top level. And even if I do not know someone, my late mother certainly did, and I can deftly explain to them who I am if I need to get their attention.

But what's the point? When you know everyone, it is as meaningless as knowing no one at all. True connections aren't built on "who you know" – that's a popular peasant myth. Not on this level, and not anymore. In the current global, internet-driven world, it is often as if you truly know, and can reach, everyone. Connections and alliances are built on shared interests, and, apart from childhood friendships and intimate relationships, are limited to the scope of those interests. When an administration has been in power for 20 years, no one in town would remain unconnected to it in some way, past or present. Yet, sometimes, past connections can hurt rather than help. If you only know one Russian person, it may be tempting for you to think – well, I know a Russian person, let me ask them this or that about Russia. But the expectation that what they tell you will be, in any way, meaningful, is just as ridiculous as asking the first random American on the street in Moscow about the inner workings of the DNC.

Asking a random person works when you are looking for common wisdom. I used to drive Uber in California sometimes, and a passenger got in one day and asked me: "what do Russians think of Gorbachev?" "War criminal", – I said, automatically. "I knew it!" – my passenger exclaimed enthusiastically, and added that such and such now owed him bet money. On the round, I think he was right to seek a wager-breaking answer to such a question from an Uber driver.

As someone who preferred Trump in the last election, it is tempting for me to write that Igor Danchenko, the Steel dossier researcher formerly of Brookings, or the then-Cyprus-based Olga Galkina who was his secondary source, were just like Uber drivers in terms of their proximity to the sort of information they were seeking. That is not entirely true. Danchenko, although irrelevant and unconnected in Russia itself, was at least a typical go-to choice of this sort of people for this type of a job. With his Russian origins, his past job at Brooking and connection to Fiona Hill, who styles herself a Russia expert, you can make it sound like he was the best Steel could get – and the *sound* of it was all that was needed. I am not overall surprised at him being chosen for the job, and no one who was *actually connected* would have agreed to do it.

To Danchenko's credit and owing to his enormous luck, his childhood friend from Perm, Olga Galkina, has held jobs in Moscow that could yield her credible connections. Based on her CV, I've probably even met her. Given that I am a sort of *Forrest Gump* of Moscow, whether one had likely met *me* is as good a measure as any of their social networks. The problem, rather, is that Forrest Gump won't be the person you would *really* be asking *about the War in Vietnam*.

Perhaps the best indictment of an idea that Russia is ruled from one source by an iron fist is provided by Masha Gessen in an afterword to a later edition of her 2012 book, *The Man Without a Face*. Masha grew up in Boston, a daughter of emigres; she is also formerly a Russian democratic opposition activist, an openly gay woman who adopted a child in Russia, a writer for The New Yorker and a friend of the Bidens. Trust her if you do not trust me.

In this later-added postscript, Masha describes how she continued to live in Russia after her excellent, but certainly not laudatory, biography of Vladimir Putin came out in the West. She had never met Putin but was afraid of retribution. She was blacklisted from the Kremlin pool, TV appearances and any meaningful journalistic accreditations in Moscow. She had assumed it was at Putin's behest, and eventually found herself editing *Vokrug Sveta* ("Around the world"), a magazine similar to National Geographic. No one ever read this magazine. It was supposed to be a safe job far away from trouble, but it was there that she was to finally face down the man of her nightmares.

At the time, Putin started to take interest in nature preservation, but many of his interventions ended up being high-profile faux pas, usually owing to the overzealousness of his minders. One day, Gessen refused to send a reporter along to Putin's yet one more wildlife venture, and was promptly fired from her job. The firing, blamed on Putin – with implied, but unexpressed, assumption that Masha's book about him had been the real reason – was covered widely by the media. A week later, Gessen was in Putin's office in the Kremlin, facing her subject for the first time in her life, scared nearly to death.

The meeting between the two immediately went not at all as Gessen expected, and was, from her perspective, underwhelming (and from his, one must think, baffling). Putin attempted to persuade Masha that his interventions in the promotion of wildlife preservation served a greater good, even if they were pathetic. He then tried to get her to stop playing a persecuted hero and agree to take her job back. He couldn't understand what got her so worked up. When she defiantly refused, Putin lost interest and suggested that they should talk later.

Gessen eventually concluded that the President of Russia was unaware of the best-selling biography of him in the English language, or that she has written it. In fact, he had no idea who she was and hadn't asked anyone prior to the meeting. Wherever the blacklisting had come from, it wasn't from Putin: *"The person I had described in [my] book – shallow, self-involved, not terribly perceptive, and apparently very poorly informed – was indeed the person running Russia, to the extent that Russia was being run"*.

The extent to which "Russia is being run" is a question on everyone's mind nowadays. In fact, we all – those who generally support *the Putin doctrine* as we, variously, understand it – hope that it is *run* to a sufficiently secure degree, and we hope so for Russia's sake. This is not to say that, having lived through such turmoil as we all have in one generation, anyone assumes that anything is what it seems. We all want to do what we can to help – but it is not by anyone's greater design that we attempt to do so, but through the strength of our own intuition. Sometimes it serves us well, and sometimes it does not.

When you consider that Vladimir Putin did not know who Masha Gessen was, it only makes sense that he – as he always maintained – also had no idea who Michael Flynn was when he sat next to him. I venture to guess that the people in charge of the seating arrangements did not know, either – to them, Flynn was probably just a man who was at the banquet alone, just like the President. Must have been convenient to seat them at one table.

If you thought, just like I did, that it was unlikely that Putin was seated next to some unvetted American at a public event, always remember that Putin was alone in a room with Masha Gessen, who, unbeknownst to him, was not just an American citizen of hostile political persuasion, but an author of an internationally best-selling *pasquinade* about him. If you assume chaos, instead of order, many things will start making much more sense.

Every Russian citizen or a Russian-speaking immigrant who made an individual decision to act at home, or intervene abroad, as *you* think, on behalf of Russia, did so purely of his or her own volition. I know this, because it also includes me: in writing this book, I am acting in the same way as described earlier in this chapter. I am doing good, as I understand it, on behalf of the diaspora – not the diaspora that the official narrative in the U.S. and the UK acknowledges, but the one that I know really exists, because I am a part of it.

In writing the book that will make sense to a Western reader and persuade anyone of anything at all, I have to sometimes acknowledge the obvious truths about Russia, and point out the weaknesses and errors. I started out wanting to make the point on behalf of the Russians and leave it at that, but the arc of this book bends toward objectivity – at least as it is perceived by me, an *a priori* subjective storyteller.

As a result, I have not the slightest idea of how this book will be received in Russia, to the extent that it will be received at all (by the Global Russians themselves and returned emigrants in the elites). I am not a Global Russian myself – I am a 1990s emigrant, who periodically comes back and marvels. My compass on Russia is off because, ultimately, I hold a Western worldview. To that point, a lot in this book is what Russians think, which may or may not be what I personally think, unless specifically so noted.

Maybe this book will make me a propaganda hero to the Russians, maybe they will label me a traitor. Those I criticize might love it, and those I laud might be nonetheless annoyed by it. If I ran the idea of this book by anyone at all who could condone it, they could just as likely condemn it. Ultimately, just like most Russians who have ever made a decision, I am informed only by the famous saying: *do what you must, and come what may*. Russia-haters might do well to keep this predicament in mind before they label me a "Putin stooge" or a "useful idiot". I might be a useless idiot after all.

During the dawn raid on Oleg Deripaska's home in New York in September of 2016, the FBI agents told Deripaska about their theory of Russian election interference, and, specifically, the hypothesis that Manafort was involved.

This was early days. Trump had not yet been elected, the transition period had not yet started, Peter Sztrok and Lisa Page hadn't yet exchanged all of their text messages, no one had yet heard of the Trump Tower meeting with Natalia Veselnitskaya, and the Obama administration hadn't yet embarked on its wiretapping of Trump campaign headquarters. At that stage, in September 2016, the existence of the election interference investigation was entirely unbeknownst to the Trump camp. It was a secret, but the FBI had no qualms about sharing it with Deripaska.

One may assume that Deripaska told relevant officials in Moscow about it. But guess what did not happen as a result of that? No one alerted Donald

Trump, and, certainly, no one alerted Paul Manafort – else, one should think, he'd have cleared his WhatsApp cloud. Isn't that alone evidence that the state of Russia was not interfering in the elections, let alone that Paul Manafort was not their agent? This lack of consequence makes all of it a self-disproving theory.

This is the point at which the Americans make their final, most daring argument. If the Russians did not help Trump win, why did Duma deputies clap when his victory was announced? If you do not know the answer to this question already, then you still do not know Russians – and, seeing as this book is drawing to a close, I have probably not done a good job explaining what we think.

Russia certainly has strategic interests at its borders, as does any other powerful sane country. Russian interference, such as it were, in Ukraine and Georgia manifests that. Russia does care about the fate of, and political leanings among, the members of its diaspora in the neighboring Baltic states, and it does attempt to execute a strategy in dealing with them.

The farther afield you go, the faster Russia's strategic interests wane. In the Middle East, we no longer really know what they are, except to not lose face again and to control the American-backed chaos. In Western Europe, it is mostly for our people to go shopping and spend time on the beaches, and to sell natural gas. Many American zealots forget that Russia provides most of Europe's fuel. It does not appear to me that Russia has any defined and coordinated strategy related to its interests in Western Europe. Rather, members of its elites, variously involved in each of those countries, each pursue their own. Often, they are conservative interests that mirror the conservative beliefs of Russians themselves.

Russia's strategic policy toward the United Kingdom is that it might as well sink to the bottom of the sea. As a country and a government, Russia cares zilch about the reputation of either itself or its emigrants in the UK, because it does not consider the UK strategically significant. We are left largely to ourselves and told in no uncertain terms that we created our own problems by choosing to live there. As far out as the UK, the attitude no longer is "let's help our fellow Russians", as it would be in Ukraine or Eastern Europe. It is "we told you these people are nuts; come home, problem solved" (expressed as "suitcase – train station – Russia" by the patriotic Russian youth brigades who picketed Berezovsky's home).

As for the United States, our tortured love, Russians have learned the hard way that they have no friends in America – no friends worth sticking up for, anyway. They would have, of course, preferred Trump over Clinton, but that was not because they liked Trump. At that point in time, they would have preferred a trained monkey over Hillary Clinton – just like many American voters did. At that moment, the Russians have just about had it with Victoria Nuland's *State Department cookies* in Ukraine, which Obama previously said was not a strategic interest of the United States, with the 2012 and 2014 sanctions, and with Clinton's pretension and incompetence. After all, this is the woman who infamously brought a specially made red button to Russia to be pushed as a photo-op to signify a reboot – *perezagruzka* – in the relationship, but it actually said *peregruzka* – overload – on the button. Initially, we were simply appalled that Clinton did not have anyone Russian-speaking on staff while trying to meddle in the Russian-speaking world, but boy, it's all been one big *overload* from there!

If you listen carefully to Russian talk shows, you will see that the elites are broadly resigned to the fact that neither Republicans nor Democrats in the United States are their friends. The madness has overcome both sides of the aisle. After all, it was the Bush administration, aided by Boris Berezovsky, that lit the fire of *color revolutions* on the *post-Soviet space* way before Victoria Nuland got her baking tray out for Ukraine. Sanctions were largely the Obama-Clinton doing, but the incompetence of the Trump administration made the situation worse, not better. Even though the U.S. Republicans were largely reserved in their anti-Russian language when the Democrats used Russiagate as a pretext to disputing the validity of the 2016 election, they are now going back to the usual Russia-bashing as well.

Just as Biden meekly posited the objective truth – that sanctions against Nord Stream 2 are futile because Germany wants the pipeline and will have it built anyway – right-wing commentators pounced on him as if Russiagate never happened. It took the FBI to explain to some particularly agitated politicians that the Russian state would not order a gang of Russian-speaking hackers to extort $5 million from a New Jersey pipeline. (Wherever you are in the world, folks, if the Russian state did break your pipeline intentionally, it would not have done so because it needed the money). In all likelihood, by the end of 2021, we may be back to a familiar pattern of anti-Russian paranoia on all sides, such a handy political device had it become. Russian analysts see it coming.

Trump was an unknown quantity, rather than something anyone desired. Everyone in Russia thought that Trump was a clown, and that was exactly why the State Duma deputies clapped upon learning the election results. The Trump victory had everything in it: the intrigue, the underdog, the amateurish nature of it all, the long odds, the chutzpah. Trump had balls, and he showed the establishment what for. He was a status quo disruptor, and Russians respect that. Trump wrote a movie ending so daring that Hollywood could have never come up with it. If Trump was possible, anything was possible. Trump was the embodiment of what we like best: *dvizhuha*. For sure, *shit was happening* now. As to what *shit* exactly that might be, the Russians, by then, did not care. America was always too far away to be among their strategic interests – and, at this point, it was too far gone for Russians to care. All they could reasonably do was be entertained.

The Russian diaspora in the United Kingdom – speaking of people from actual Russia, as opposed to immigrants from the Baltic States – is relatively homogeneous in geographic distribution and class, comprising predominantly professionals concentrated across the commuter belt around London.

By contrast, millions of Russians in the United States are as dispersed and as diverse economically as the native population. Many now fancy themselves Russian patriots as a result of Russiagate, but Motherland has no plan for them, no strategy for working with them. It makes occasional interventions on a case-by-case basis in situations when, the criteria goes, someone has got in trouble for "nothing more than being Russian", but it fosters no systemic interventions. In America, most diaspora organizations are simply redundant efforts of variably deranged fanatics, usually reduced to local cookouts and springtime *Victory mongering*.

The Russian diaspora in the United States historically votes Republican, and had done so a long way before Donald Trump became a candidate for office. The many reasons for that have nothing to do with any perceived foreign policy interests of the Russian Federation – for most of the immigrants in America, Russia is too far away to meaningfully continue to feel a part of. Some vote Republican because they are religious and socially conservative, some do because they genuinely support *laizzes-faire* economics, some – because the Republican party is the political home to many of the fringe movements that

282

reflect the diaspora's own idiosyncrasies, such as affection for guns and anti-vaccine sentiment.

Russians in the U.S. are mostly legal immigrants. They tend to be immigration restrictionists and vote on the basis of curtailing immigration, be it to reduce competition with those yet-to-arrive or due to racial discomfort toward the groups perceived as beneficiaries of open border policies. Working-class Russians in America tend to mirror the political demographics of native working-class whites. The better to do and the better educated, in an attempt to vote strategically, think of individual freedoms, lower taxes and smaller government. Just like anyone else.

The American state tends to accept Uber drivers and construction workers as blessed immigrants, treat IT professionals with suspicion, and openly target Russians that take interest in politics and policy. This reflects a complete lack of insight into diasporas. The more educated an individual is, the more independent they are in their thinking, the more selective they are as to whose authority they would recognize, and the less reliant they are on a need to belong to a group. This is basic social science. If Vladimir Putin asks me to do something, I can tell him to get lost as easily as I could any of you. But an Uber driver or a construction worker in the Northeastern suburbs of Sacramento would instantly oblige, feeling special and chosen, even if their ostensible reason for arrival in America was political asylum from *the Putin regime*.

I was in England on the day of the 2020 Presidential election in the United States. The phone rang late at night. "I have to tell you something, but you must promise to keep it a secret", – said an old friend of mine, an IT executive in the Silicon Valley. "I just voted for Trump". Excitement at the magnitude of his own mischief rang in his voice. I had always assumed this guy to be a Republican anyway – it turned out that I was wrong. A Russian immigrant of the late Soviet years, he had gone through an initial conservative stage but lately considered himself "progressive", like everyone around him in the San Francisco Bay Area.

Russiagate, COVID restrictions and the BLM riots had each done their job in changing his mind. He felt that the Russians were being persecuted without merit since 2016 and was upset that it had suddenly become unfashionable to be one. When I got back to California in March 2021, I found my friend quite content with his newfound conservatism, albeit with some doubts on abortion. He was certain it should be legal, even if undesirable, and found the position on the issue too polarized for comfort. His heroes were Joe Rogan, Ben Shapiro and Robert Rubin. He did not watch TV and did not know who Tucker Carlson was.

Yet, something caught my eye uncomfortably in my friend's office. In the break room, there now was a handmade *Free Navalny* poster, with the drawn portrait of Alexey Navalny himself. I could not imagine where would one go with such a poster, seeing as there had not been a Russian consular mission on the West Coast of the United States for years. I was told the poster had been brought in by a fellow Russian who *comes around sometimes*. Employees, comprising recent Russian immigrants, second-generation U.S.-born Russians and American nerds with no connection to Russia whatsoever, were having coffee under it.

"Do you know Navalny?" – I asked the owner of the office. "No", – he said, – "But I think it was likely that he was poisoned". "Do you think that he was, as alleged, poisoned by something called *novichok*, at the behest of the Russian government?" – I asked, my eyes widening. I did my best to make the allegation sound as ridiculous as I myself believe that it is. "I feel that I cannot rule it out", – my friend answered, stubbornly. This was an unexpected turn of events. "Well, I do know Navalny", – I said. "Let me tell you what I think". So I did. I will tell you, too.

284

The N-words: Nemtsov, novichok, Navalny

1.

It was January 23, 2005. *Bilingua* club in Moscow, which has since burned down in an unrelated incident, was partly chartered for my 30th birthday party. It was the sort of time when an era is over, and another is yet to begin. The *Rodina* election campaign was over, my book about it had just come out, my mother's house in Nikolina Gora was just finished, and, although she had stage IV lung cancer, my mother was still alive. I was hanging out with the politically-minded young people in Moscow, unsure of what to do next. Social media was not a thing yet, and, at that time, if I wanted to share an observation or opinion about something, I would simply put it in an e-mail and send to everyone I knew. It was a tribute to *echonet* newsgroups of the bygone era of the 1980s.

In Bilingua, there was a lot of talk about the future. The future was uncertain. To my left was Oleg Kashin, a young journalist from Kaliningrad, who would become a well-known political commentator and now lives in London. To my right was Lesha Navalny, chief of staff at the Moscow chapter of the pro-Western liberal *Yabloko* political party, to which former Soviet dissidents clung in despair. Lesha (short for Alexey in Russian) was a back-office operative at a quaintly irrelevant, waning organization, a small-time administrator without any political ambitions. He was unknown to the public as of yet – but that, he was telling us excitedly, was about to change.

Kashin and Navalny sat at either side of me in order to persuade me to take up using LiveJournal, an emerging platform for something they called *blogging*. "Those e-mails you keep sending everyone, they are basically a blog. You are already a blogger, you simply do not know it yet", – Kashin tried to explain. A notoriously late adopter of all technology, I was reluctant. "But I send my e-mails to people I know. Who will read my stream of consciousness there?" – I kept asking. "People will read it! Just look at me – I am popular on LiveJournal, I already have 200 subscribers!" – boasted Navalny, beaming. Kashin and I both looked at him with respect. 200 strangers reading everything you write in some journal sounded like a lot in January of 2005.

At the time, all Navalny had to say to those 200 subscribers was political gossip and housekeeping announcements on the local party business. It would be a while before that would change. I wouldn't be around for the transformation, because in October 2005 politician Boris Nemtsov, at the time leader of SPS (*Soyuz Pravych Sil – Union of Right Forces*) party, would destroy my political career before it even started, with the traitorous acquiescence of my supposed friend Alexey Navalny. I would never speak to Navalny afterward.

Throughout the spring of 2005, Navalny hung around in the non-profit that my friends and I founded. We ran a campaign for migrant rights in Moscow. Navalny, who would later style himself a Muscovite but actually grew up on a military base some miles away from the city, outside of the commuter belt, came to meetings and trolled us with what were simplistically racist views. "Why do you want to defend *the blacks*", he would say, referring to Middle Asian immigrants as "blacks" in typical Russian fashion – "I can't stand them". His declared views were strikingly different from those of Yabloko – the Western values, dissident, intelligentsia party that employed him. "I don't have any views", – he would say. "It's just a job. I am an organizer".

In the summer of 2005, I decided to run for Moscow City Duma as a single-mandate district candidate. Effectively, it meant that I had to win an election in a district of more than half a million voters. This may not sound like much, but that's nearly 10 times more than an average number of voters in a UK Parliamentary constituency. It wasn't easy. The district I chose to stand in, at the North edge of the city, included not just Sheremetyevo airport and the satellite city of Zelenograd, but also the neighborhood where I grew up. I knew it like the back of my hand, and I knew a lot of businesses and local officials there. The election was due to take place in December.

I perceived at the time that I had a problem in Moscow politics – I had been tainted by association with the right-wing nationalist politics of my recent boss, Dmitry Rogozin, whose views were not very popular in Moscow. My mother, who was huge in Moscow *intelligentsia* circles, had just died, and the bewilderment with which her friends and colleagues regarded me at her funeral highlighted the scope of the problem. Since I was good friends with Navalny, who was chief of staff of the Moscow chapter of *Yabloko*, I conceived a plan for a comeback into polite society with his assistance. Navalny brokered an agreement with Sergey Mitrokhin, at the time the chair of the party's Moscow chapter (and later the leader of the national Yabloko party). Yabloko would not field a candidate in my district and would instead support me as an independent, but aligned, candidate. I would then apply for membership in the party during the campaign and make a big deal about it, publicly confirming my democratic pro-Western beliefs.

The deal was not met with a lot of enthusiasm in my camp. My friend and mentor, the same famous political consultant who was later to tell me that I would end up with "new idiots without experience " if I fired my campaign staff, warned me not to do a deal with Yabloko. He predicted that I would be betrayed. I did not take the warning seriously. There was a territory-sharing pact between Yabloko and SPS, which was thought of as equally pro-Western and democratic. The attempts at collaboration and parity between SPS and Yabloko were painful, but my district was a Yabloko district, according to the pact. Once Yabloko did not declare anyone else by the deadline, I thought I would be in the clear for the promised endorsement.

It was nearly on the last day that I received a fateful call from Navalny, who was in ostensible alarm. Navalny informed me that Boris Nemtsov had seen that Yabloko had no candidate in my district, and was pressuring Mitrokhin to support his (Nemtsov's) young daughter Zhanna, paternity of whom Nemtsov had only recently publicly acknowledged, as a candidate, in order to give her some political training. The hard-won provisional peace between Yabloko and SPS, Navalny was apparently told, was on the cards. Having spent tens of thousands of dollars on the campaign, I was promptly dumped from endorsement. "It is nothing personal, just business", – Navalny, that little traitorous piece of shit, said to me.

2.

When the Nemtsov family bulldozered over me in my home district and my friend Lesha Navalny shamelessly betrayed me, it ended my political career in Russia. The epic feud was duly elegized by one of the emerging LiveJournal star bloggers, who retold it in poetic verse. I haven't spoken to Navalny since. By the time I was dropped from the Moscow Duma election, I was exhausted, grief-stricken at the recent death of my mother and in debt to *idiots with experience,* so the whole Nemtsov-Navalny affair barely registered with me on an emotional level. I thought that, perhaps, it was an *effectively disguised blessing.*

I never blamed Zhanna Nemtsova for her role in ending my political aspirations – at the time, she was a child, barely legal to run for office. She had never been to the district and did not know what was going on. I blamed only

287

daddy Nemtsov. The only times that I had met him in person were TV debates during the 2003 Duma campaign, where I was present for his backstage interactions with Rogozin. I remember Nemtsov as loud, brash and inconsiderate. Given the ease and lack of thought with which he later destroyed my career, I was neither sorry nor surprised when he turned up dead. It was clear that I could not have been the only one. While he had his fans among his co-workers and former staff, the real Boris Nemtsov was rude and cruel to people he did not care about. The line of those wanting him dead must have been a mile long and probably started at the nearest bar.

The implication that it led into the Kremlin, however, was the stupidest thing I ever heard. He may have been a Deputy Prime Minister of Russia briefly in the 1990s, but by 2015 Boris Nemtsov was a spent force and a man of whose existence everyone had forgotten. He no longer had any political organization behind him and had largely retired. No one cared one bit what he had to say. He was no longer a *leading opposition figure* – those laurels had, by then, been taken over by Navalny. While alive in 2015, Boris Nemtsov was no bigger a threat to Putin than your grandmother.

Yet, he was a huge inconvenience in death. Alive, Nemtsov was useless – dead, he became enormously valuable to the enemies of Russia. He was killed at a very opportune time, too – in the wake of the annexation of Crimea, when anti-Russian hysteria was at its peak, and the first wave of Ukraine-related sanctions was just being absorbed. This was a boost to Russiagate, shortly to commence, and the renaming of a piece of land outside of the Russian Embassy in Washington, DC as "Nemtsov Plaza" in 2018 was the crowning achievement of its idiocy. While not a fan of the man, on the account of all that alone I wish Nemtsov had lived – and I have no doubt that so does Vladimir Putin.

I do not know whether Alexey Navalny and Zhanna Nemtsova have ever met in person, but their ability to destroy lives in tandem when their orbits aligned persisted. In February 2018, of course, it would be Navalny that aired the tape of Oleg Deripaska telling a joke about Victoria Nuland, and then it was Nemtsova that asked Nuland to comment on that tape for Deutsche Welle TV. We may never know whether Nuland knew of the tape independently of Nemtsova. Daddy would have been proud.

After the 2005 election, I tried to forget all about it. In the spring of 2006, I took my daughters to Sochi, to which the 2014 Winter Olympics had just recently been awarded. It was my first ever visit to the town. It was March, and snow was still around. I received a call from the editor of Cosmopolitan Russia, inviting me to take part in a photo shoot for a story about young Russian female politicians. No longer intending to be one, I was nonetheless pressured by vanity into agreeing. The shoot was to be the day I got back to Moscow, and I was asked to turn up with "summer clothes", because the issue was to come out in June. I still remember trying to buy summer clothes suitable for a Cosmopolitan photo shoot, in winter, in a not yet gentrified Sochi[79]. Only when the magazine came out did I realize that it featured Zhanna Nemtsova in the same story.

3.

While I seemingly got over the 2005 fiasco, I allowed my anger at being betrayed to fester and bottle up. It was only 15 years later, when in November 2020 I watched Navalny speak at the European Parliament and call for further sanctions against Russians, that I had enough. Most of Navalny's antics had hitherto gone over my head, but that talk of more sanctions finally got to me. It had been a while since I was this angry. I called a British associate of mine, who had lived in Moscow for many years, on Telegram. "Can you believe this piece of shit?" – I screamed. "To think that I had motive and opportunity to kill the bastard 15 years ago – how different could history have been!"

Hindsight is always 20/20, I suppose. If I had put the hitherto unknown Navalny out of his misery in 2005, before he graduated from a back-office backstabber to a malignant worldwide troll, Russia would never have known how grateful it should be – so, it would have likely been me in jail all these years instead of him being in jail now. After my little "let's go back in time and kill Hitler" moment, I concluded the conversation by telling my stunned friend that "I better get on with that book I have been thinking about". A lot has happened in the six months that it took me to write this much of it, but *this is the book*. Alexey Navalny's call for sanctions moved me to finally write it.

Meanwhile, Oleg Deripaska pointed out on Telegram that calling for sanctions on Russian citizens was a crime under the Russian Penal Code.

---

79 It must have been the exhaustion of the trip that caused me to give in to having make-up applied to my face, for the first and last time in my life, during the shoot.

4.

Alexey Navalny's ascent from Yabloko's Moscow chapter to malignant troll was long and treacherous, and is worthy of a brief recount. It was during the 2005 Moscow Duma campaign for Yabloko that he found his first calling as an organizer of the electorate, rather than a party administrator. The crux of the party's campaign in the city was the fight against so-called "single point development", practiced by the government of the then-mayor Yuri Luzhkov. It meant new residential blocks of flats built in the middle of existing neighborhoods, usually in place of parks and playgrounds, and without any scaling-up of existing infrastructure.

Navalny started out on that simplistically, by instinct, when the party was short of hands. He would take a megaphone, head to a local yard or square where a "single point" construction site was identified, and call on ubiquitous *babushkas* to gather around. "What do we want? Stop the construction!" – they chanted, as passerby joined in. Unexpectedly for himself, Navalny started to gain word-of-mouth popularity in the city through his efforts. He discovered that he connected with crowds.

Soon, Lesha realized that he would miss the crowds after the election. He also realized that the Moscow *babushkas* secretly disliked *the blacks* – Middle Asian immigrants – as much as he did. Yabloko would not be on board with this, so Navalny picked up a fellow traveler – a guy named Petr Miloserdov. I knew Miloserdov because he was married to a friend of mine, who worked for the Rodina campaign – and, despite that connection, Miloserdov was also ungraciously trying to run in my district in the 2005 campaign. Miloserdov's political past was dark. Petr was a former neo-nazi who had barely managed to conceal his views and graduate to adult behavior by associating himself with the mainstream Communist Party.

Before long, Navalny and Miloserdov found each other and started running around Moscow in 2007, setting up protests against migrants. Their slogans were short and sweet: "Russia for Russians", "Moscow for Muscovites". They founded a political organization called *Narod* – The People[80]. One of the

---

80 Narod's third founder, writer Zakhar Prilepin, later became a volunteer in the civil war in Eastern Ukraine and, in 2020, leader of *Za Pravdu* political party. It was absorbed by *Just Russia* party ahead of 2021 Duma elections, making Prilepin a likely incoming Duma deputy. Meanwhile, Petr Miloserdov has been jailed for allegedly assisting another prominent nationalist in attempts to initiate a coup d'etat in nearby Kazakhstan.

key objectives of the movement was the right to own guns – while American media ridiculed Maria Butina for her crusade for gun rights in Russia, it was never mentioned that this had also been the crusade of their darling Alexey Navalny. I can only assume that the Western media is unaware of just how far Navalny was willing to go in this crusade.

Today, *Narod* is principally remembered in Russia for recording one specific promotional video. In it, Navalny demonstrates how to use a slipper to squash a cockroach, and then uses a gun to kill an intruder dressed in a cloak and turban. Ostensibly it was for gun rights, but its implications were clear: the movement was calling for an open season on Muslim immigrants. Navalny was promptly dismissed from Yabloko, whose terrified leaders distanced themselves from him[81]. The crusade was too much even for the panicked Communist Party, which fired Miloserdov.

Russian society was not ready to demand to be given guns in order to shoot Muslims, and so Navalny decided it was time to grow up and make money. As a lawyer by training, his means of choice became a form of soft extortion, affectionately called by its adepts "minority shareholder activism". This menace to business is well-known in the West: an activist, or a group, purchases a minority shareholding and uses the access rights that it gives to disrupt shareholder meetings and decision making, or files lawsuits with a view to getting paid to go away. It was not widely practiced in Russia – a gap Navalny was determined to close. During 2008 and 2009 Navalny acquired minority shareholdings in numerous Russian companies, including Rosneft and Gazprom among others.

As a "minority shareholder activist" Navalny filed dozens of lawsuits against the management of companies that failed to explain their business practices to his satisfaction, and widely publicized his efforts to his growing following on LiveJournal. Navalny's usual allegation was that the companies were operating for the benefit of majority shareholders (most often, the

---

81 When Navalny found himself in Germany in 2020 and gained traction in the EU Parliament with calls for further sanctions on Russians, well-known liberal politician and leader of Yabloko at the time of Navalny's tenure in the party, Grigory Yavlinsky, was at least as terrified as me. He wrote a well-publicized column reflecting on Navalny's true nature, but liberals were too far gone to listen, so they all ridiculed Yavlinsky instead.

government) and cheating minority shareholders out of dividends. The most notorious case concerned Rosneft, but there were many others. It was in the course of this crusade that Navalny promptly made enemies of almost everyone in the business community.

Rumors swelled around Moscow that Navalny's ostensible efforts on behalf of minority shareholders were more than a simple extortion scheme, like they usually are in the West. Navalny was, essentially, taking orders for hit jobs – business rivals, political interests and anyone else who was, for whatever personal reason, aggrieved by a company or transaction, came in with their grievance, and off Navalny went buying shares and filing lawsuits. Just like in the two embezzlement schemes in connection with which he was to be convicted later by Russian courts, Navalny was an enabler, a middleman, a messenger.

As a minority shareholder of Gazprom, Navalny undertook to challenge the amount that state-owned Gazprom paid in 2005 for the acquisition of Sibneft, the oil giant that later became Gazprom Oil. The amount was widely understood to have been the fair market price, and no one else complained about it. The author of the report on which Navalny based its fight with Gazprom was Vladimir Milov, a former energy official with various interests and feuds in the energy sector. The crusade Navalny was pursuing in his harassment of Gazprom was clearly Milov's – Navalny was only a subcontractor. This would become relevant again years later, after Milov himself would join Navalny's organization in 2018.

By the end of 2008 Navalny's once-friendship with SPS paid off, in a manner of speaking. One of the SPS co-leaders Nikita Belykh (himself currently jailed upon a conviction for corruption) was appointed governor of the Kirov region in December and invited Navalny along to assist. 2009 was a busy year: Navalny's controversial tenure in Kirov as a gubernatorial advisor took place in parallel with his crusades-for-hire against corporations in Moscow. In the event, the Kirov period gave rise to the criminal *Kirovles matter*. Navalny allegedly set up a scheme in which a state-owned enterprise, Kirovles, sold timber at a loss to a local business owned by a close Navalny associate and co-accused, Petr Oficerof. The head of Kirovles, Vyacheslav Opalev, was convicted for his part in the scheme, and so was Oficerof.

The underlying facts are not in dispute – it is rather a matter of debate, believe it or not, whether they constituted a crime insofar as Navalny's alleged

292

part in it. It does appear that the prosecution of him – which only took place after the 2012 *Bolotnaya* protests organized by Navalny in Moscow – was politically motivated. The popular belief was that the conviction was designed to prevent Navalny from running for elective office, but many agreed that it was for the better. He was given a suspended sentence which since expired. In any case, this is not why Navalny is in jail today.

Although it is true that the trial in the Kirovles matter only took place in 2012, the criminal investigation started almost immediately, in the summer of 2009, precipitating Navalny's quick exit from the regional government. In all, he barely spent four months in Kirov, and was back on his anti-corporate watch in Moscow before long.

Navalny's undoing was *the matter of Yves Rocher*, another prosecution that started in late 2012. There are two peculiar details in the case. Firstly, the prosecution commenced upon the complaint by Yves Rocher, a French company where the complainant, the head of its Russian office, was a French national without any prior connection to Russia. Suspecting him of corruption on behalf of Putin would be really bizarre. The second and more important detail was that the matter initially involved not Navalny himself but his brother Oleg. Oleg Navalny worked for The Russian Post, the country's national postal service, where he was in charge of liaison with large shippers. Yves Rocher, selling cosmetics by postal subscription, was one of the largest.

The events underlying the Yves Rocher prosecution took place between 2008 and 2011, at a time when Navalny was not yet widely known, and certainly was not regarded as any sort of an opposition politician. He wasn't a politician at all – when he was not engaged in minority shareholder hooliganism, he was busy selling state-owned timber at a loss in Kirov. It is likely, therefore, that Yves Rocher complained about the actions of Oleg Navalny in earnest. All evidence points to the fact that they were indeed victims of a delivery price-fixing scheme, in which they were forced to pay millions of roubles needlessly to an intermediary business (founded, coincidentally, by the Navalny brothers).

Much later, when they realized that the co-conspirator in the matter was now the famous political opposition activist, Yves Rocher attempted to backtrack on the complaint, yet they have never denied the veracity of the underlying allegations. The Yves Rocher official who filed the initial complaint left Moscow. Oleg Navalny went to jail. In an already familiar pattern, his more famous brother, whom the government was reluctant to jail, walked out of court with another suspended sentence. It is the alleged violation of the terms of that sentence that caused Navalny's jailing upon his return to Russia in 2021.

The 2010-2011 academic year was much quieter in Moscow: Navalny, having run out of companies he could sue, was away at Yale. When he came back, he was inspired by the theory of Western interventionism. A more sustainable business formula emerged, with or without Western assistance. Navalny realized that he did not have to sue companies or come up with any proof of his allegations about them to a judicially acceptable standard. YouTube was getting big by then, social media had blossomed, and one no longer had to create an "information point" to push their agenda to the public through the media. All they had to do was get in front of the camera and speak in flashy, catchy terms.

So Navalny did, and this indictment would be incomplete without acknowledging that he turned out to be very effective at it. He is clear, persuasive, amusing – it is rather what he chooses to say and how he frames it, and whom he speaks to, that are each a problem. Initially, his business model featured the same principle as before, negative information dumps and PR hits on people whom his customers did not like – or *he* did not like, seeing as Navalny had made an enemy of almost everyone in public life by that time.

Soon, Navalny realized that he can collect money directly from the public. I recall that he was a huge fan of the idea of public fundraising for policy and political projects even back in the mid-2000s, when fundraising was not yet a feature in public politics in Russia. Most projects used to be financed by this or that rich person, or persons, that you managed to persuade to get onboard, and direct fundraising from the public in the age before social media was thought too tedious. The public had also developed a mistrust of politicians, whom it thought secretly rich and corrupt.

Navalny was the first – and, to date, only – person to succeed at public fundraising in Russia at a grand, massive scale. He succeeded because he is a good salesman, but also because he never presented himself as a politician. His stated goals, at the time, were never to seek or take power. He immediately started to seek elective office, but ostensibly only as to indict the failings of the process, rather than to govern. People who sent him small sums did not see him as an aspiring office holder – this was, supposedly, an investigative information project, a media outlet.

The well-worn message about the 1990s privatization and vilification of the rich who benefited from it was replaced with the modern and bottomless idea that public officials were all corrupt. The difference was that with this idea Navalny could target the young – those who did not remember the 1990s and had already come to accept the Putin era as their only reality. There were many more politicians and bureaucrats than there were large businessmen, and, most importantly, you could not run out of public officials. Some of them were bound to actually be corrupt and would be thereby taken down, and new targets would take their place.

Navalny had always been devoid of any ideology, except for his deep-seated ethnic nationalism – and it seems that at Yale they finally taught him to keep that to himself. He had no ideas on improving Russia then, no policy proposals, no foreign policy goals. All he had was a message: someone is stealing from you, and they are doing it right now. The genius of this was that this message had appeal across the political spectrum: whether you were for an immediate restoration of the USSR, or for an immediate annexation of Russia by the United States, did not matter – you would not stand for being stolen from. Navalny did not have to indict the ruling party, United Russia, for its support of Putin or its policies – the best results were achieved if he branded them thieves. United Russia became "the party of thieves", "Putin is a thief" became Navalny's main slogan. After all, stories would not be juicy enough without being about Putin – although, in the event, Navalny's most famous expose would be about Dmitry Medvedev.

Navalny was making money now. It was the money he asked you to send him so that he could uncover the hidden truth about how other people stole from you. What could go wrong? A few things. Firstly, in order to produce enough juicy content to keep the donations coming in, he had to develop a loose relationship with reality. There were a lot of untruths, half-truths, and most of the rest was, just like the much later *Putin's palace* video, pure sensationalism, in which stories about nothing illegal or immoral were introduced as if they were important, cardinal revelations. Viewers get caught in juicy details and effective presentation, and never ask: *so what*? Navalny's video channel became a glorified tabloid gossip column, but thousands of young people were sending in their lunch money ostensibly to finance it.

5.

2011 was a big year for Navalny. The protests against the Duma election results in December became his first mass protests, although the point of them was lost on any adult with common sense. Navalny was right to point out that some of the local results added up to more than 100% – but, just like in the U.S. Presidential election in 2020, its many irregularities did not credibly affect the outcome. None of the smaller parties that did not make it into the Duma would have made it if the votes were counted *better*. United Russia would still win.

The problem was that Navalny did not appeal to people with common sense. Apart from various political opportunists who wanted their footage at a protest for the purpose of Western recognition, very much including the increasingly decadent Nemtsov, the call was answered by naive teenagers enamored of what they perceived as Navalny's courage and semi-senile aging *intelligentsia* who imagined this to be a sort of 1991 all over again. At that point, Navalny became a *cause celebre*. Old school dissidents hugged at the rally and felt jubilant. It was an unpermitted rally, and they were duly beaten with batons, with substantial numbers briefly detained. After the *Bolotnaya* protests, associated with Putin's election as President again, instead of Medvedev, in the spring of 2012, many participants were also slapped with criminal charges. They were mostly minor charges, but it could have a significant impact on teenagers' future lives.

Most of those in the demographic between the teenagers and the senile saw this as unethical. Navalny was using his captive audiences as cannon fodder, and it was clear that they had no idea why they were there, what the rallies were supposed to accomplish, or, crucially, who Navalny, hitherto unknown to the public at large, was. Even if they secretly believed in "Moscow for Muscovites", I doubt any of the *babushkas* would be there if they realized that this was a man whose only known political platform called for giving out guns to ethnic Russians so they could shoot Muslim immigrants.

Everything since then is history, and history repeats itself. Teenagers that went out to support Navalny's call for disorder in 2011 are now adults with mortgages and families. In the most recent round of protests Navalny's supporters, now organized and run with the benefit of Western expertise, international political clout and Western funding, brought out the kids again – and these were new kids, the generation that was too young to have been out in 2011 or remember the fiasco of the *Bolotnaya* protests. They were too young to know not only about the *Narod* movement, but also about Navalny's embezzlement convictions, or the embezzlement-related warrants out for his cheerleaders, the likes of Ashurkov and Markvo.

There are a lot of allegations abound in Russia related to shady accounting for donations received by Navalny's organization, and many accuse him and his top lieutenants of living lavishly on collections of teenager lunch money. The main reason the Russian government had to recently forbid the Navalny organization as extremist was to stop it from collecting donations.

6.

He used to be a one-man show, but the professionalization of Navalny's organization – to wit, accrual in it of some serious donation money – brought to his side a bunch of different folks in the last 5 years. They are a diverse bunch. Some, like Vladimir Milov, Navalny knew before, some were new associations. Most of these are a new generation of lieutenants, each with their own agendas and a considerable amount of personal animosities, gripes and objectives. In his popular YouTube and radio appearances, Oleg Kashin, now broadcasting from London, hinted that he now sees our old mutual pal Navalny – with whose crusades he does not agree – as a hostage of his new entourage. Kashin is right. Many of those who have known him for years see today's Navalny as a man at the center of something that is bigger than himself, and that he no longer has full control over. I agree.

Navalny was never a sound political speaker without a megaphone, and occasional glimpses into the stream of his conscience always stunned. He stunned Ksenia Sobchak when he told her that Crimea was part of the Russian Federation, but the liberal, pro-Western community took no notice. Navalny stunned French-based economist Sergei Guriev, who had reportedly written him a recommendation letter to Yale, when he told Guriev that he does not believe in legal nationality as a basis for identity – but only in ethnicity. Navalny appeared unaware that it left Guriev himself, who belongs to an ethnic minority, out of the loop for being Russian. When Guriev challenged him, Navalny's even more stunning answer was along the lines of "too bad for you, then".

The recent pronouncements made by Navalny and on his behalf in the West and in the United States are out of step with what has always been his agenda. For what it was worth, Navalny was always a Russian nationalist and, at that, a sort of a patriot. His shtick was ostensibly to stomp out corruption, not overthrow the government. A kid from a military base, a leader of angry white men against an immigrant invasion – all of his suppositions, however poorly expressed, came from the cause of Russia, not an idea of destroying Russia. The same people who gave Navalny virtual protection money to ensure their local bureaucrat was not stealing would not support him if he called upon them to overthrow the government by force, and Navalny knew it.

Destroying Russia itself was never really Navalny's thing – yet somehow, in the wake of the strange alleged 2020 poisoning attempt, while he was briefly out of commission and his many new minders stepped into the fore, this is what it has become. Ashurkov, Milov, one Leonid Volkov were all for destroying Russia in full accordance with the most extreme Western agenda. When Navalny came to and started to call for more sanctions, these words and ideas were palpably not his own. In the mere fact that he was now calling for sanctions, and in the very names Navalny was suddenly naming, animosities, grievances and talking points of Vladimir Milov, who, unlike Navalny, is a former deputy government minister and a ruthless, experienced political agitator, were reflected.

There were also obvious additions from a wish list of certain emigre Russian businessmen, who had clearly paid Navalny to say things. In a Russian Orthodox church, you can leave a donation on a plate with a note, requesting a prayer, just like you would put a coin into a song-playing machine at a bar. Navalny started to sound like he took donations with notes requesting accusations, except he was no longer on YouTube, but on the utterly unfamiliar European political stage.

It does not appear that either Angela Merkel, or the MEPs who are now ready to wage a quasi war on Russia in Alexey Navalny's name, have seen either Navalny's statements on Crimea, or his Guriev interview – or the Muslim migrant cockroach gun video, for that matter. It's on YouTube, by the way. That Navalny is a celebrity cause locally in the Silicone Valley does not surprise me: his daughter Darya Navalnaya now attends Stanford, and young people are as effective at organizing there as they are in Russia. My friend with the *Free Navalny* poster in his office kitchen, however, is the same age as Navalny and me. He had never heard of Navalny, or his videos, until recently. Yet, my friend believes that Navalny was, indeed, poisoned in 2020. Was he?

7.

Three n-words were particularly poisonous to the Russian diaspora in recent years: Nemtsov, *novichok* and Navalny. The second being, of course, allegedly the name of a poison.

The Salisbury incident, involving the first appearance of *novichok* in the attempted poisoning of defector Russian spy Sergei Skripal, has many aspects to it. As has become usual, a lot of separate issues are conflated. Tensions run high. The consequences of the incident reverberated far and wide. In the UK they were more devastating to the Russian community than the fallout from the annexation of Crimea. As a result of that polarization, the Russians have taken to denying any involvement at all. It is probably a sound legal position but it makes the opponents feel that their intelligence is being insulted. It is impossible to know – and I don't – what did or did not take place, but I will venture a guess, based on what most Russians think.

Firstly, Skripal is a former member of the Russian security services. Let's stop pretending that he was some English pensioner living peacefully in a remote village. Ostensibly, he defected, and that was, probably, his downfall. No security service in the world would look kindly upon such an act, and if they can get the person, they would. Russians are not unique in that. We have all seen spy movies. It's a thing. This industry is particularly sensitive to treason, and everyone who enters it knows that. Putin does not need to have ever heard of Skripal – and, until the incident, unlikely had. Not being a part of the security services anymore, Putin would have had no part in taking revenge upon Skripal, just like he wouldn't on Litvinenko (although my money is still on Berezovsky for the latter). If revenge of the security services is what it is – which I also doubt, as I will explain below – it would be driven by the honor code among former co-workers and superiors. On top of that, we have no idea what the focal point of Skripal's alleged defection was, and whom he may have compromised in the process. Anyhow, this would not be an act of vertical power, especially not when it concerns some guy no one heard of.

In this specific case, one good reason to believe that it was yet one more act of *samodeyatelnost* is that Sergei Skripal is alive. One thing the Russian security services could do, we must assume, is kill one hapless retired idiot. At least the assassination of Litvinenko was clean. Here, we have a huge mess, lots of collateral damage, the target alive and MIA, and a loyalist Russian citizen –

his daughter – taken hostage by the increasingly hostile British government. Whoever those mythical suspects *Petrov and Boshirov* are, they are not genius assassins. If *that* were Russian security services, Russia is in trouble.

In this case, the British government behaved – and continues to behave – in a manner at least as appalling as the would-be assassins themselves. First, the government sealed off the house, needlessly and cruelly killing Skripal's pets who dehydrated and starved to death[82]. The British government then kidnapped Yulia Skripal, who had continued to live in Russia and there was no reason whatsoever to believe that she did not wish to go on doing so. The government is holding her, almost certainly, against her will, denying the Russian authorities consular access to her. If she does want to be in England, well, have her tell us so! Show us proof of life, a hostage tape with today's newspaper, something! Of course, she does not. You are brainwashing that poor woman and have imprisoned her – and, just in case anyone doesn't know, I hear that witness protection in Britain is as much of a failure as everything else our government does. If the British government ever tells you all that it is protecting *me,* please know that it is lying, because I would rather die.

It looks plausible on the facts of the case that the would-be assassins followed Yulia Skripal from Moscow, presumably as means of locating the target. But there is no reason whatsoever to believe that she was also a target. Families are not usually targeted in such clean-up assassinations. Just let poor Yulia go! Release the women as a show of good faith, like in any hostage negotiation.

There is, of course, the unfortunate matter of the death of a local resident. My heart goes out to her. But let's acknowledge for a minute that she did not die as a result of any actions on the part of the mythical *Petrov and Boshirov* who

---

82 Much like it had killed numerous pets in the Grenfell Tower fire, whom residents were not allowed to take with them when they were rescued – no other country in the world would be that cruel to pets! I recall an article in The Guardian -where else- about a woman who "looked into her cat's eyes and thought he might never see him again". In the event, the cat survived, because the fire did not get as far as that woman's apartment. This was supposed to be a touching reunification article, while all I wanted to say was -- can we please ban this woman from owning pets for life? Are British people even human? And most of the government's inhumanity to pets is always gratuitous. Just like nothing would prevent their rescues at Grenfell, nothing prevented the police from feeding Skripal's pets and giving them water. I cried later, when I saw scenes of hurricane rescues in America, residents being lifted off roofs in helicopters with their cats in their arms.

disposed of the poison in the trash in a closed container – but those of her supposed boyfriend, who retrieved the poison from the trash and gave to his girlfriend as a gift. I can fully assure you that this is not – or hitherto was not – what Russians think of England. No one would have expected people to dig in the trash for things to give their girlfriends. The deprivation that is embedded in the premise for that chain of events, and their unpredictability, is bizarre – and, of course, no one is talking about it. In England, it is made to sound perfectly normal – yeah, he went through the trash... What do you expect Russians to make of it? *This* is supposed to be the civilized country, then? No one in Russia would give their girlfriend a present from the trash. It was entirely unforeseeable.

In order to cover up the kidnapping of Skripal's daughter and the murder of his pets and redirect the conversation away from deprivation in the local community, Britain attempted to claim the high ground on this. There was a lot of collateral damage. The hostility toward the Russian diaspora in the immediate wake of the Salisbury affair in 2018 was at its highest. No enemy of Russia could have done it better. But even if someone Russian did unsuccessfully try to assassinate Sergei Skripal, it was an honor between spies sort of scenario, and, let's admit, they were pretty rubbish at it. Let it go (after you have let Yulia go).

It would have been easier to believe the Salisbury saga if the government did not have a catchy name for the alleged poison at hand. *Novichok*? Really? In Russian, the word means *newcomer*, or *the new guy* – and, by the British government's own legend, it was nothing but. Isn't it supposed to be a part of the legacy stock of Cold War-era supplies, that thousands of rogue criminals around the world now run around with? Oh, wait, it was supposed to be, except not this one. This one has a catchy name, so it must have been the government doing it. Really, more people would believe all this if you called it C3PO.

The Salisbury saga in the UK suspiciously coincided with Russiagate in the United States. So far, we considered the 2018 wave of U.S. sanctions as a separate event, but they took place at the same time. Whoever was behind Salisbury, picked the worst possible time for Russia to have done it – which is a sure sign that it was not the Russian government. The Russian government is prone to error of judgment on occasion, but it is not, as an entity, *that* stupid. Salisbury wasn't only unprofessional, it was a geopolitical error. It was stupid, and entirely contrary to the Russian interests at that moment. *The Russians* would not have been stupid enough to fail to see that – but the British, apparently, are.

By 2020, Russiagate started to wane on both sides of the Atlantic. With the events surrounding COVID, the death of George Floyd and BLM, the focus of public debate has shifted away from Russia. How fantastically convenient for its enemies then, that something came up again. On August 20, 2020, Alexey Navalny fell ill on a flight from Tomsk, in Siberia, and the plane was diverted to nearby Omsk in order to seek medical care for him. The newest and yet most bizarre twist in Russophobic hysteria thus started to unfold.

8.

Here is my personal opinion: I do not believe that Navalny was poisoned at all. I allow for some possibility that an external interference with his health did take place. But even if he was poisoned, he certainly wasn't poisoned with something called *novichok* – and, whatever happened to him in Tomsk that day, I am 100% certain that the Russian government had nothing to do with it.

Now that I have got the main thesis off my chest, please allow me to double down on it. In all of my years of watching politics unfold, I had thought that I had seen it all, but the *Poisoning of Navalny* tops it all in absurdity. It was also poignant, because it highlighted the fact that Navalny was nearing the point of no return in his so-called career of agitation: at that moment he would be more valuable to his minders dead than he was alive. The Russian government was hitherto careful not to jail him, not even in the *Yves Rocher* or *Kirovles* cases, because he would acquire celebrity status as a result of persecution – the status which he did not have while he was walking free. Then, mysteriously, we are told that someone sprayed a hotel in Tomsk with *novichok*, and Navalny barely survived. This made him a celebrity in the West, where he was virtually unknown up until that point. This was the last thing the Russian government needed.

Would you not think that *the Russian government,* whomever exactly do you imagine that to mean, has a *modus operandi*? Everyone whom you have previously claimed the Russian government had killed within Russia, including Anna Politkovskaya and Boris Nemtsov, was shot execution-style at close range by an assassin of ethnic Chechen origin, without inflicting collateral damage or leaving forensic clues. This method virtually assures that the crime will go unsolved – a Chechen with a handgun is as close as could be to a needle in a haystack in Russia, and ethnically Russian witnesses and juries have as much difficulty with the identification of Chechens as Caucasian Americans do with African-Americans.

We had been told that *the Russian government* used polonium in London to kill Litvinenko, in order to do it in style. The assumption was that *the Russian government* was less worried about the possibility of collateral damage in London, although there was none in that case. I still think, as the readers already know, that the theatrics and timing of Litvinenko's demise point away from *the Russian government.* Yet, at least Litvinenko – and *only* Litvinenko – was dead.

What are we asked to believe in this case, exactly? Let's assume for a minute that some rogue faction in the FSB was, indeed, in possession of a substance called *novichok*, and two of its most mediocre would-be assassins had been dispatched to off Sergei Skripal with it in Salisbury, England – presumably to ensure the theatrics, as they had done in the Litvinenko case. That is the theory. Given that the poison failed to kill Skripal and inflicted disastrous collateral damage, who would be dumb enough to not only use it again, but to do it on Russia's own soil? Surely not the same *Russian government* that you are all so afraid of?

If you do not believe me, you should believe Alexey Venediktov, editor-in-chief of Echo Moskvy radio station, the same station where Masha Gessen once made fun of me for demanding that the city of Moscow stop funding the ten commandments posters with taxpayer money. Venediktov was a huge pal of my mother's, and his station is the rupor of the modern-day Russian *dissidentura*. He had met with Putin on numerous occasions and made his own judgment about Putin's view of Navalny publicly known. According to Venediktov, Putin never took Navalny seriously, considering him a small-time grifter and opportunist. When challenged on whether Navalny's rallies present a threat to the regime, Putin apparently shrugged and said that "young people would always make noise, it is in their nature". He could not care less.

If *the Russian government* wanted Navalny dead, he would be dead – not making speeches to the European Parliament or drinking tea with Angela Merkel. There is no shortage of bullets in Chechnya yet. The government would absolutely not expose residents of Tomsk to the risk of the same collateral damage that was seen in Salisbury. And, why Tomsk? Navalny lives in Moscow, a large and ethnically diverse city full of contract killers, guns and cars with untraceable plates; a city where millions of people come and go every day, and

303

where all of the hitherto unsolved contract killings that you all blame on *the Russian government* took place. Is it your theory then, that the government has gone to the trouble of doing it in Tomsk so as to make it look like local organized crime was to blame? Do you think *novichok* was a plausible means of doing it?

Just like with Nemtsov, there was no shortage of other aggrieved parties who might have preferred Navalny to be dead – and his visit to Tomsk itself was apparently connected to an "investigation" into some local concerns. Assuming that contract murders are ordered by rational people as a preventative measure, rather than in revenge, someone who feared exposure in an upcoming Navalny video as a result of that trip could have decided to have him killed. But trust me, they aren't that inventive in Tomsk, and Navalny wasn't particularly well protected. They'd have shot him or bludgeoned him to death with a rebar. There would be no room for ambiguity left. In all likelihood, the Tomsk *mafiosi*, if they were involved, would have followed Navalny to Moscow and done it there, where it could have been blamed on numerous other aggrieved parties or *the Russian government*.

9.

The rational analysis leaves two possible explanations for the events in Tomsk. First is that nothing externally inflicted happened to Navalny at all. He could have faked it, as most Russians think, or, more likely, really collapsed and became genuinely confused about it. According to Alexander Murakhovsky, the then Doctor-in-Chief at the hospital he had been taken to, Navalny's toxicology was clean, and the initial diagnosis was that Navalny collapsed from exhaustion.

Dr. Murakhovsky, who has been elevated to the post of regional health minister since, does not seem too bright an individual at first sight, judging by a more recent incident in which he managed to get himself lost in the woods for two days. Presumably inebriated at the outset, the good doctor mysteriously failed to either stay with his crashed 4×4, retrace his own tracks out of the woods, or notice a village he walked within 200 meters of at one point. Yet, despite the failure of hundreds of rescuers to find him and multiple sightings of bears in the area, the sobered-up health minister of the Omsk region did eventually walk out of the woods by himself. Perhaps, some credibility can still be given to his diagnosis of Navalny.

Murakhovsky was vilified by Navalny's clique in the West for allegedly blocking his airlifting to Germany. It does not appear that Murakhovsky was blocking it *per se* – rather, he was baffled by the demand because he did not see what could be achieved by it, since there seemed to be nothing wrong with the patient. The NHS in England routinely blocks patient transfers to other countries, including the EU, on treating doctors' whim – and has even sought to jail several sets of parents, infamously, for taking children abroad for alternative treatment.

In that vein, we now know what *was* achieved after Navalny was transferred to Germany – we were told that a trace of mysterious poison, which the politicians quickly proclaimed to have been the same as in Salisbury, was identified. The speed and precision of such an identification are highly suspect, making it a likely scenario that several things came together: Navalny did collapse from exhaustion or for yet undiagnosed health reasons, or perhaps even faked it; his collapse was seized upon by opportunistic, even if earnest, parties in Germany, including the Charite clinic, which presumably billed Navalny's sponsors for its services; the events were then seized upon by Angela Merkel, who was not aware of Navalny's Muslim immigrant shooting video, and finding of a political poison was encouraged – also raising the clinic's bill on the account of contamination, I must assume.

The second possible explanation is that this was a copycat crime, designed precisely to re-evoke the Russophobic indignation in the West post-Salisbury, and carried out by those who did not necessarily care whether Navalny ultimately survived or not, because their aims would be achieved in either case. In the last couple of years, once his organization had been taken over by the likes of Leonid Volkov, Vladimir Milov and Vladimir Ashurkov, Navalny ceased to be his own man. Previously an apolitical, and even patriotic, provocateur, a small-time grifter and opportunist who nonetheless thought Crimea was a part of Russia, Russians and Ukrainians were the same people, and Russia was *for Russians* (in a later iteration, Russian-Ukranians), Navalny was never comfortable in the West. Giving speeches against *Russian oligarchs* in Brussels – that's not Navalny, that is Vladimir Milov talking, and Ashurkov echoing him. The Tomsk incident had not only turned Navalny into a would-be martyr, but nudged him in the direction he did not appear to be previously going in. How convenient.

Navalny's collaborators have all learned the lessons of Berezovsky – political martyrdom can make a comrade more valuable to the cause dead than

305

alive. The death of Nemtsov, even though I personally think it was a result of Nemtsov's temper and unique ability to alienate people in his path, turned out to be beneficial for Vladimir Milov, who, as one of Nemtsov's last collaborators, found that a role of the mourner-in-chief yielded benefits. The same role was, of course, previously perfected by Berezovsky at the bedside of dying Litvinenko. Navalny, in the event, did not die – and was encouraged by the gang, against all common sense, to walk the path of alternative martyrdom and return to Russia, where the government was left with virtually no option other than to jail him, all the while the rest of them remained safely abroad. Navalny is second most valuable to the cause when he is in jail.

Navalny, as his own man, was always pragmatic. He had no cause. He would only return if he believed the state did not have the guts to jail him, or if rewards that were promised to him, presumably in a form of Western funding, were worth the time he would do in prison. Upon his return, Navalny appeared disoriented and acted irrationally, in one incident publicly launching a tirade of insults at a 96-year old man, causing shock to the public. Navalny was even less himself than he had been abroad. The cause goes on steered by the people who now took charge of it, over which Navalny himself has no control left. Yet, they can all gather periodically to demand his release. It is always good to have something simple to demand, something that fits on a rally poster. Browder is rather missing that with Magnitsky.

And this is, of course, the final sticking point of this debate. When I tell my friend in Silicon Valley that I do not think Navalny was poisoned by the Russian government, he asks: "Well then, this poster only says "*Free* Navalny". Do you think he should be in jail?"

10.

I know Navalny personally, and I told people that I regret not killing him myself 15 years ago. From that unique perspective, I still do not think that he should be in jail. It took me some agony to arrive at that opinion, but I shall not be taking down and secretly burning that *Free Navalny* poster in my friend's office any time soon.

For the first 45 years or so of my life, I did not know socially anyone who went to jail, anywhere in the world (not counting legal clients). I guess it is a class issue, but that simply did not happen to people in my circle. I have never been arrested and did not know anyone who has been – other than, perhaps, a few political activists who'd been picked up by riot police during rallies and then immediately released. When Petr Miloserdov, Navalny's buddy from his *Narod* movement days, was arrested, ostensibly for plotting a *coup d'etat* in Kazakhstan, it was the first time I had to ponder an idea of someone in whose kitchen I had many a cup of tea in the past doing time in prison.

Miloserdov's jailing split the polite society in Moscow. The leading voices, which ultimately prevailed, said that we should not try and stick up for him to be released, because he had been a nazi, and, more importantly, he had been implicated in domestic abuse by his ex-wife, and it was mostly understood that the allegations were true. Upon hearing of his jailing, people said – *karma is a bitch*. I admit that I ultimately joined in, and I found it surprising that the said ex-wife herself, who is also a mother of the two children they had together, seemed to be the one most disturbed by both the jailing of Miloserdov and the lack of an initiative in the community to have him freed. "Someone I used to love sitting in jail is too much", – she said. The jailing was not a vindication for any abuse she and the children may have suffered – it was, in a way, further abuse. I think it was wrong of me to fail to point out then that Miloserdov was in jail for rather dubious reasons, and that those reasons had nothing to do with whatever we, as a community, fault him for. He was released in 2019, and the issue sort of went away. And now, with Navalny, here we go again.

As a product of the dissident Soviet environment, I am no fan of any law enforcement. If someone had asked me in 1999, I would be up there with George Soros on the issue of both Putin and Litvinenko having been in the KGB, and I think that people who choose to serve in either police or federal law enforcement, in any country, are different species – *not like us*. I may have had lunch with some, but I won't sleep with one, or knowingly invite them to my kid's birthday party. The government is never your friend. Where I come from, *normal people* don't get involved in law enforcement.

The entrenched libertarian in me sees punitive incarceration as a mechanism of state control. I do not think people should be in jail unless they currently pose a danger to society. Importantly, it cannot be purely preventative either – in other words, we cannot incarcerate people simply to prevent them from doing something they have not yet done. The only people in jail should be those who we seek to prevent from repeating what they have already been convicted of doing, and only if it cannot be prevented by less restrictive means. We should, therefore, look very closely at why Navalny is in jail, and what would be the possible reasons for keeping him there.

11.

Ostensibly, Navalny is in jail in relation to the Yves Rocher matter – and let's take the conviction at face value for a minute. Firstly, of course, it's been years since the conviction, and the suspended sentence should have expired. They got him on a technicality that defies belief. Second, do we really need to put ex-government officials or founders of companies in jail in order to prevent them from embezzling again? It seems like making sure they are not in government and do not form any more companies could do the trick. Even the court in Yves Rocher did not see Navalny's involvement as worthy of incarceration at the time. We all know that is not the real reason why Navalny is in jail.

Vladimir Solovyev, one of Russia's best known and most effective TV propagandists, who is under personal U.S. sanctions, recently recounted reasons for which he thinks Navalny should stay in jail. He wrote in a Telegram post, that (and I abbreviate slightly), Navalny was in jail because he was: a fraud and an embezzler with two suspended sentences – and who knows why they were suspended; a thief, for pocketing a hundred million roubles of donations and using them to finance his lavish lifestyle; an extremist, who called upon people to engage in disorder and rioting and got children involved in committing crimes; a nazi, including his problematic 2007-era pronouncements and insults thrown upon the 96-year old veteran; a traitor to Russia, for having advised foreign states on imposing sanctions upon Russians. "You are welcome", – added Solovyev coyly at the end of the list.

This is quite a lot, and most of it is true. But none of these is ostensibly the reason why Navalny is jailed. Putting Alexey Navalny in prison supposedly for Yves Rocher, even though in reality he is there because he is a traitor to Russia and a dangerous agitator, is, in principle, no different from imposing U.S. sanctions on Oleg Deripaska ostensibly for the events in Ukraine, although in reality because he insulted Victoria Nuland and could have upended the Mueller investigation. If, like Deripaska says, calling for sanctions against Russians – as Navalny did – was a crime at that time, let's convict Navalny of that crime. But then, is jail the only effective – or even a plausibly effective – method of

308

preventing him from doing so again? He can still make statements from prison, and does. Russia is now throwing the book at Navalny; a slew of new criminal charges has been brought since he has been in jail, but they are all petty, trivial matters for which no one normally goes to jail. In that, they are no different than the numerous petty prosecutions related to the election interference investigation in the United States.

Poetic justice is not justice. We cannot go by *karma* in a society of law and order. Miloserdov's jailing on a ludicrous charge of trying to upend Kazakh politics did not deliver justice to his abused ex-wife. Paul Manafort wasn't really in jail because he cheated on his taxes, nor did he need to be in jail in order to prevent that from happening again. He was really in jail because the architects of Russiagate needed to make him look bad. Despite Manafort making away with tens of millions of dollars of his money, Deripaska did not see any poetic justice in Manafort's jailing: when asked about it in an interview, Deripaska said he felt sorry for Manafort. We do not put people in jail for debt – and, as a society of rational people, we can only stay sane if things are called by their true names and can be taken at face value.

I am personally aggrieved by Navalny, and I, too, think that he is a traitor to Russia, whether or not he has voluntarily assumed that position. Navalny also caused financial and reputation damage to many people. No jail would fix any of that now – in fact, Navalny's incarceration possibly makes it all worse. Without him, *the cause* is now entirely in the hands of people who lack Navalny's own Russian nationalism and could not care less if Russia ceased to exist tomorrow.

He is a treacherous dipshit who ended my political career and cost me tens of thousands of dollars in damage years ago, but I feel sorry for Navalny. For me, there is no poetic justice in his jailing. Having someone who sat at my right hand at my 30th birthday be imprisoned at the time of my 50th is not a remedy for any wrong he brought upon me. Looking back at the last 20 years, it only adds extra stress. Politics, money – they are all ultimately just notions, and jail is too much for offending them. On a more fundamental level, as human beings, we ought to be able to do better. So, what else could we, as a society, do with recalcitrant Navalny, to keep him from causing any more harm?

12.

Things were much simpler in the 1970s. When the Soviet government could not figure out how to deal with Solzhenitsyn, it simply put him on the plane, flew him to the FRG and dropped him off. However he poisoned the well from thereon, no one cared – Soviet citizens were not going to find out. With Navalny, we already sort of tried that – we flew him to Germany! – and, lo and behold, back he comes. The government had no option but to arrest him then – damned if they did, damned if they didn't. I thought at the time that, by arresting Navalny, the government was giving him the legitimacy he sought. It was a mistake, and one that he himself, perhaps, did not expect the government to make.

But, on some level, I can see that. The whole thing was quickly starting to prove a disaster. In Germany, Navalny called for sanctions in the European Parliament. In Russia, he would be collecting more lunch money from yet a new generation of school children, call for public unrest and publish people's illegally recorded conversations. As a civilized society, we can't have him doing any of that. If only we could get America or Germany to take him back and put him in witness protection somewhere, so he doesn't come back! The problem is, we'd need to stage an attempt on his life for this to work, and oops – someone had already beat us to it, and Germany and America did not want to keep him. So, the most logical response was – arrest him, and then sort it out.

The government has been trying to sort it out. Sort of. It declared Navalny's organization a foreign agent, prohibited its leaders – the rest of whom, notably, are all in hiding abroad and have no aspiration for political martyrdom in their leader's style – from running for office, and started an initiative to brand the organization as extremist, which would make donations to it illegal under anti-terrorism laws. This is an important step – after all, Berezovsky was only defeated as an aspiring revolutionary when he was bankrupted by his own conceit and intransigence. The problem with the latter strategy now is that children are prone to be brainwashed, and everything else Navalny had called upon them to do was already, strictly speaking, illegal. Trying to prevent him from collecting their money by criminalizing them for sending it will make a generation of criminals of a part of our youth. Instead of protecting them from bad influence, we will be alienating them with persecution. Not a perfect strategy.

When Navalny was jailed, rats abandoned ship with a vengeance – all of his remaining collaborators who were not yet in emigration having either left

Russia or denounced the organization. They continued to brood and shoot their mouths off abroad, but fewer and fewer people were sending them money from Russia. They fell back on relying on funds from the State Department, Khodorkovsky, or from whomever else it is that finances the foam-mouthed anti-Russian hysteria nowadays. As that diverse band of clowns fleeces Western emigres in his name in several countries at once, Navalny is, perhaps, safer in jail than he would be out there, lest any of them feel that his martyrdom is not sufficiently complete. Alone in a penal colony, Navalny appears rattled. Even a man on a mission would be – and this is a man who has always been without one.

In June 2012 Alexey Navalny, fresh from instigating two major rounds of protests on the Russian streets – including the infamous *Bolotnaya* protests – was elected to the board of directors of *Aeroflot – Russian Airlines*, the country's flagship air carrier, 51% of which is owned by the Russian government. He had been nominated to the post by banker Alexander Lebedev – the father of Lord Lebedev, who controls the Evening Standard and the Independent. Lebedev, who owned various interests in the airline industry, had just purchased a minority shareholding in *Aeroflot* from Roman Abramovich. Owing to Navalny's past resume of so-called shareholder activism, Lebedev seemed to hope that Navalny would shake up *Aeroflot*. There was to be *dvizhuha*.

None came. Having been brought in from the cold, Navalny took to the task with enthusiasm. He called on his social media followers to fly with *Aeroflot* and posed cheerfully with his wife for photos at banquets in the Kremlin – just as the state, which controlled the company on the board of which Navalny sat, was prosecuting him for Yves Rocher and Kirovles. His tenure as a director was conservative and uneventful. There were no exposes, no scandalous videos, no loud accusations. Nothing was embezzled or went missing. The one scandal that did take place within the company at the relevant time appeared to unfold entirely without Navalny's participation.

By then already a well-known rebel without a cause whom Berezovsky labeled a genius, Navalny suddenly acted in an entirely respectful and even somewhat trustworthy manner the moment he was entrusted with something and shown respect. This confirmed what I already knew of the earlier-edition Navalny: he always struck me as an empty set of skills in search of a project. He had no ambitions or goals. His only true ideology is disdain for migrants and ethnic minorities – beyond that, he remains as much of a blank canvass now as he

311

ever was. He doesn't care. Nothing of it is personal, it is all strictly business. This suggests that the business model could be changed once again.

Smart and capable, Navalny never really knew what – other than to shoot Muslims, apparently – he wanted. He happened to hook up with Miloserdov and Prilepin in 2007. He is a lawyer, and someone had probably asked him to sue a company or another, and he came across the idea of making shareholder blackmail into a business. Orders kept coming for a while. Then Belykh was looking for people to go to Kirov. Oleg, the brother, seemed to have a thing going on at The Russian Post, where the French could be fleeced for money. Then it turned out that people would send you money if you make sleek videos and put them on YouTube. He failed upwards overall, but Navalny did not make these things happen – rather, they happened to him. These were all chance opportunities for grift, nothing else. Navalny lived all these years like a common bandit, from heist to heist. This was a typical pattern of someone who engaged in crime because he could not get a well-paying job – and crime, even accounting for risk, pays better than menial jobs.

There was always no end and no method to Navalny's madness. I am guessing he had no real political ambitions, and no desire to govern whatsoever. Like I already noted above, he probably came back to Russia – other than for never having been a Western sort of person anyway – because he was assured that, upon serving time in jail, he would be rewarded with grants and finance that will make further grift unnecessary. If his decision-making pattern is not a strategy but a series of opportunities considered each at their own merit, then the answer to *what to do with Navalny* is the same that the American justice system had long found to be most effective in reforming ex-convicts: give him a job.

Not a job sweeping the floor in a penal colony, but a real job. He says that he wants to build a better Russia – let him take part. Just like Lebedev had him put on the board of *Aeroflot*, put him somewhere where he could use his real skills. Bring him in from the cold. Make him an offer he cannot refuse, and make sure it pays. You do not have to outbid his foreign backers – Navalny's financial ambitions do not extend beyond financing a lifestyle. Appreciation and respect, which he now feels in the West but doesn't have in Russia, will be priceless. He is a simple guy, and he is probably tired of running with traitors anyway. He needs to be given a patriotic move to make. Perhaps Russia can put Navalny in charge of immigration enforcement. Just do not give him any live ammunition.

Americans have always done it. The case in point is the story of Frank Abagnale, the notorious bank fraudster played by Leonardo Di Caprio in the movie *Catch Me if You Can*. Abagnale started forging checks because he was too young for a job and had no skills. When Tom Hanks finally caught him in France, he offered him a job at the FBI. This is a true story: real-life Frank Abagnale has long become an authority on combating bank fraud, and was the force behind legislation called Check 21 Act, which reformed the US consumer banking for the 21st century. He is not the only one – the U.S. government also routinely hires hackers, Edward Snowden being the most famous example (although probably not the one that makes my point very well, given how it turned out for the state).

In the case of Navalny, there are a lot of things the Russian government hasn't done that it should have. He himself does not require re-education, because he has no dogma. But a discreditation of Navalny does need to occur in the West, and it should have been done a long time ago. How come every member of the EU and UK Parliament, and U.S. Congress, had not yet been mailed a CD with Navalny's 2007 Muslim-shooting video, concatenated with a video of him explaining that Crimea is a part of Russia, and the tape of him explaining that states should be organized on the basis of ethnicity only? Angela Merkel, before she leaves office, must be tied to a chair and made to watch that CD on repeat, *Clockwork Orange*-style. Perhaps one lesson the European politicians who think they do not like Putin for Russia's President would learn is that they should stop signing on for causes they do not understand. You are welcome.

#JeSuisRomanAbramovich

"This man may be from Russia, but let me tell you something – he is West London through and through", – the commentator's voice on BT Sport is breaking down. It's May 29, 2021, and the UEFA Champion's League final in Porto just ended with Chelsea's victory 1:0 over Manchester City. The commentator is talking about Roman Abramovich, whose devotion to football is legendary among sporting pundits and fans. Abramovich has been popular and universally well-liked in England for the last 18 years, but Chelsea's second UEFA Champion's League victory has brought on a full-blown Abramovich personality cult in London. Too bad he is not around to enjoy it – for reasons that have never quite been made public, Abramovich had not been able to visit the country for the last 3 years.

I watched the whole game on the 29th of May – which may not sound like much until you consider that it was only the fourth football game that I watched in my entire life.[83] In keeping with the traditions of snobbery and classism, in our family popular team sports were shunned, and I proudly continued with that disinterest into my late twenties. When I was told, during the 2003 Duma election campaign in Russia, that *Abramovich bought Chelsea*, I had two questions: who is Abramovich, and how can you buy a whole neighborhood?

The first football game that I ever saw was the UEFA Champions League final in Moscow in 2008. By that time Chelsea, owing to it being owned by a Russian, was enormously popular in Russia. It was playing against Manchester United. I was in Moscow, working for *RIA Novosti* news agency. The newswire stood still as the entire newsroom gathered around the monitors.

Me and a friend and colleague of mine, whom I shall not name here so as not to share the shame of my ignorance with him, seemed to be the only two people to have never seen a game of this sport before. Crucially, neither of us knew how to tell *which one* of the teams playing was Chelsea (I hadn't moved to

---

83 Hereinafter I refer, in the British manner, to football, but it is the game that Americans call soccer. Already having finished the book, I realized that I missed one soccer game that I saw. In addition to the four games listed here, I also saw a women's soccer game, North Korea vs. USA at the 2012 Olympics. I mostly remember that Old Trafford raised the South Korean flag by mistake, and the DPRK understandably refused to play.

England yet, and did not know they were *the blues*). Even more confusingly, we could not tell which goalpost was which – goalkeepers wear a different uniform. "Do you know which ones are *our guys?"* – the colleague whispered in my ear at the start. "No idea",- I said. We knew that we could not ask anyone – betraying such ignorance would be the end of us, there and then. Yet, we were able to tell quickly, through watching the reaction of other viewers to the events on the field. Everyone on the floor was rooting for Chelsea – the devotion was the same as if it were a Russian national team. Chelsea were *our guys*.

The 2008 final was a remarkably suspenseful game, which Chelsea lost narrowly in the penalty phase under pouring rain. All of it seemed unfair and emotionally devastating. It had been another 10 years until I would dare watch two more football games during the FIFA World Cup held in Moscow in 2018. I saw first Russia, then England lose to Croatia. Football was still too emotionally difficult to bear, and I was clearly doing worse than average as a fan. Perhaps, whomever I was rooting for was bound to do better whenever I was *not* watching.

By the time of the FIFA World Cup in Russia football was firmly entwined with geopolitics. In the United States, Robert Mueller's inquiry into the 2016 election interference was in progress. Oleg Deripaska had just been sanctioned, the crisis in the world markets and the collapse of jobs and lives in Russia thus caused unfolding in the background. Russiagate was at its peak. In England, Sergey Skripal had just been allegedly poisoned, *novichok* was a household word and the media were full of paranoid anti-Russian backlash, discouraging many fans from attending the FIFA Cup matches. The same media were also full of reports from the most persistent England fans exalting Moscow's facilities in utter surprise that they hadn't all been eaten by bears. When Robbie Williams, the unlikely bard of Russia, showed the middle finger to the TV camera at the opening ceremony, he was speaking for all of us.

Just a few weeks before the FIFA World Cup opened in Russia, on May 19, 2018, the FA Cup final took place in England. This time, Chelsea beat Manchester United and took the FA Cup title. For the first time in 15 years since he bought the club, Chelsea's number one fan Roman Abramovich was not around to see the game in person – nor has he been in the three years since, as of the time of writing. It is rather lucky that they moved the 2021 UEFA Champions League final from Istanbul to Porto, rather than to Wembley. The BT Sports commentator, exalting the benefits of Abramovich's devotion to the team and the sport, had expanded on this eloquently after the game, nearly breaking down in tears. "This man loves football", – he went on, "in all of these three years, he has been on the phone every day".

I must caution that I do not know what exactly happened with Abramovich and his British visas, nor why it is that he hasn't apparently visited England since 2018. In all of my years of immigration law practice, I have not seen one single case the essence of which was correctly reported in the media, even when the immigrants themselves were a source of the reports and gave comments. Whenever reporters are trying to parse an immigration case through the prism of their own understanding, points or relevance are usually turned on their heads.

In a situation when there have not been any first-person comments by either the immigrant or the government (which would have been barred from commenting of its own accord by privacy laws), anything printed is a guess of the writer – and, in this case, most of the guessing was informed by the unfolding Russophobia. Most of what was reported does not exactly make sense to me when seen through the prism of known immigration law. In other words, I have no idea why exactly Abramovich hasn't been to England since the spring of 2018, neither do you and nor does anyone who wrote about it in the media. In all likelihood, the real reason is not at all what has been reported.

It absolutely does not matter exactly what happened, because the devil, in this case, is not in the details. The end result is what it is. In matters of immigration, just like in many others, our government has a million charming ways of alienating people and making itself unbearable to deal with. Unexplained delays, unreasonable demands, unprovoked hostility – any of this, at any point, can make anyone say: enough! The year 2018 was particularly bad in that respect for Russians in Britain. It started with Abramovich, but many followed. There was an epidemic of Russians, many of whom gave years of their lives and much of their money to Britain, saying "enough". I should know because I was one of them. In 2018 I realized that I can't stand the hypocrisy of Britain, either: and I am a British citizen *and* a paid-up member of the Conservative party, which was then in government.

I made the decision to close my long-standing immigration law practice in 2018 because it had become a bit of a farce: I started to see a long line of clients the best advice I could give to whom, from my heart, was "get out". There

316

almost aren't any immigration situations that cannot be resolved in the UK, ever. It is rather a question of sanity and perspective: is it worth it? How much of your dignity are you prepared to lose in order to cling to this wet gloomy piece of land surrounded by a cold and rough sea? What are the alternatives available to you elsewhere in the world?

Our immigration policy is written and executed on a premise that has expectations of typical immigrant decision-making absolutely backward. Broadly, the government assumes that beyond a certain number of years of residence, amount of investment and level of assimilation, it has "got you": *too heavy to carry, a pity to drop.* It thinks that if you – hypothetically – lived in England for 15 years, invested more than a billion pounds in one of its most beloved institutions, have five adult children who grew up and continue living in England, own multiple properties here, and thousands of working-class British people, literally, pray by you – well, the government then thinks that it can treat you in any shitty way because you can't just leave. You are too invested. After all, it treats millions of native-born British citizens in a shitty way every day, taking advantage of the fact that they have nowhere to go.

This is exactly the opposite of how immigrants reason. Immigration, after a first few years, does feel *too heavy to carry, a pity to drop* – but not after ten, fifteen years, and so forth. If you weigh up the circumstance of your life and decide to come to a country, make it your home, give it more than a decade of your life, the loyalty of your children – most of our adult children are forever British, mine certainly are – and, as in case of many immigrants, all of your money (or, in the case of Abramovich, some very, very substantial amounts of money), you develop certain expectations. Unlike the indigenous population, you continue to view this as an enterprise, a transaction, an unwritten contract.

You are here because you decided, at one point, that it was worth it. Perhaps you love the place, perhaps your children do, or you think it is safer for them. Perhaps, as in the case of Abramovich, you love football. There was, for each of us, something about England that we loved. The more of your life you spend, and emotions and energy you invest, in England, the more you expect for England to, perhaps, appreciate you – or at least not treat you like shit. The more you assimilate, the more you develop the ability to view the government and society critically, and the less you are willing to stand for nonsense.

The British government always assumes that it is giving immigrants a unique gift that they ought to work hard and jump through hoops to keep proving themselves worthy of. No one was ever able to explain to me: what is, exactly, the intrinsic value of that gift? Even I, an economic nobody, have not earned more money in the UK in my 13 years of residence there than I have brought in from outside and spent there. In my case, they were mere hundreds of thousands of pounds. If I imagine myself as someone who spent hundreds of millions, or a billion or two, the government is starting to look even more ridiculous.

Britain keeps telling everyone that it is a place of "investment" where people "park" their money, but Britain is an awful place to invest, and most of the money brought in is spent on goods, services and purely notional assets, such as leasehold flats. Unlike something you "park", the money we all dumped on *the Island* will not be there to drive off with when we come back. And some of us are even harassed out of coming back to check on it. What a glorious proposition! Our generation is middle-aged now, and we start seeing the time of our life as more valuable. Dignity matters more and more. Let alone that anyone who has ever had any money in the first place ought to know how to cut losses. Not only is Britain a money *shredder*, rather than a *laundromat* – it is also, in a greater sense, a state-sized Ponzi scheme.

Pray tell, how did Roman Abramovich supposedly *park* his money at Chelsea? Having bought it for circa £200 million, including debt, he invested, as I understand, way over £1 billion into facility improvements, players and numerous community initiatives. In these years, as we all gather from the media, the club experienced a legendary rise from obscurity to two UEFA championship wins and numerous other trophies, making it one of the most valuable sports brands in England. It is absolutely unique, but it does not mean it is an asset with an easily determinable value. £2 billion was mentioned in the media – but what does that mean, exactly? A sports club is not just a combination of a brand and a stadium – it is the player acquisition strategy, the now-famous manager hiring and firing, the risks taken, the expenditure on community engagement.

Clearly, Chelsea is what it is today only because of Abramovich's personal involvement with it, not because someone invested £200 million in it 18 years ago. If tomorrow there was no Abramovich and his management team running it the way they did all these years, there would not be the corresponding estimated value. An asset that has its full value only in the current owner's hands is not really an investment vessel. It is a hobby project. Money was not Abramovich's most valuable investment into Chelsea – it was, at least as much, his personal effort and his passion. He didn't give an X amount of pounds to build it, he gave it 18 years of his life. Everyone in the world of sports can see that, everyone in West London can see that, and all Chelsea fans know that. Only our government pretends not to see that.

As if there was any sort of a serious argument to be made that a football club was an investment vehicle, or a place where one could *park* their money, the recent Super League debacle settled it for good. If football clubs were tradeable assets, surely this would imply that their owners could do as they saw fit with them? The Super League made business sense, there is no question about it. In fact, I am still unsure what was so wrong with the idea in the eyes of all those fans with pitchforks – clearly, I do not know enough about the sport. But our Prime Minister – who must have watched three football games less than I have by that moment – had the best input yet. Football, Boris Johnson said, must be nationalized. *Nationalized!* Sure. That was something definitely worth leaving Russia for.

I am not one for sport, but I like opera. If I were wealthy and bought myself an opera house, not being an opera singer myself, the purpose would be two-fold. On one hand, I'd want to invest gratuitously in being able to stage perfect operas, attract bigger stars, commission new productions. I would probably believe it would make the world a better place, and I'd want to share my love of opera with the community. Perchance I'd want a place where I can force them to put on La Traviata in a modern setting, or put it on in Russian, like at the Bolshoi of my childhood. But the other critically important part of this enterprise would be that I'd want to go there and listen to the opera myself. Any number of tickets that can be sold, or increased value of the restored theater, or international acclaim for my new productions, would all be completely meaningless to me if I could not go see all of it myself. And opera, much like football on TV, isn't quite the same on Spotify, as it is in live performance. Big difference. No way would I buy an opera house that I might not be able to visit. I'd buy shares on the stock market, or invest in a commodified business. This is a difference between a hobby project and investment.

Whatever sellable value, accounting for the threat of nationalization of its industry, Chelsea FC might miraculously still have, Abramovich hasn't extracted any. He continues to spend more. Through personal expenditure, school and university tuition for five children, substantial properties, salaries for numerous staff over twenty years, service of planes... I have no idea, but I am guessing the man probably spent close to £3 billion in the United Kingdom in his lifetime – all of it being money that was infused into the UK economy, and the money he might never, really, see again. Shortly before the 2018 conundrum Abramovich was reportedly on the verge of commencing the construction of a new stadium for Chelsea, which could cost up to another £1 billion – not even thinking of jobs it would create, or joy to the community that it would bring.

How many immigrants have spent this much imported money in the United Kingdom in the entire history of its immigration system?[84] Most likely, no one else. So how come our politicians are not yet on a pilgrimage to Israel, begging Abramovich to come back with ritualistic song and dance? Instead, they pretend publicly to have no idea why Chelsea's new stadium isn't going ahead. Who knows those Russians, really? Britain has shown its worst in the aftermath of the 2018 Russiagate this side of the Atlantic. Harassment of Abramovich was followed up with the rest of us being declared spies by the Henry Jackson Society, and now we are treated to daytime Russia-bashing in Parliament in a normal course of any day. Even if they did course-correct *vis a vis* Abramovich in hope of enticing him to build the stadium, who is to say that tomorrow another toxic wind of change will not blow and they would not double down? It's not like you could put a sports stadium on Zoopla – and, by the way, the then-Mayor Johnson learned that latter point the hard way with the Stratford Olympic Park.

The intransigent self-absorption of the British elites and its politicians blinds them not only to the greater context of the world in which every immigrant compares what is available here to other countries they can live in, but also to the sentiment of their own public. Granted, football fans are working-class. But nationalization of football is not what they want. Chelsea fans like Abramovich and his special touch, and they have no wish to see the Prime Minister run their club instead. Right now, in the wake of the UEFA Champions League final, Roman Abramovich is probably the most admired man in British sport. More people would fight for Abramovich, than would for Johnson.

---

84 Mohammed al-Fayed and Rupert Murdoch come to mind, but both men made money in the UK - ultimately it would not appear that either had brought in and *shredded* nearly this much cash.

If, as the media thinks, Abramovich had a burning desire to return to the UK but something stopped him from doing so (which we do not know and I myself doubt to be the case), I would personally undertake to go down to Stamford Bridge and round up a few thousand people for *Occupy Stansted*. Let's see how long it would take, especially given that the Home Office routinely reverses immigration decisions after just one half-literate publication in The Guardian. If the government's decision making were a hurdle here, the government would be lucky that Abramovich is not a student of Saul Alinsky.[85]

Overall, 2018 and 2019 were not good years to be Russian abroad. Russiagate in the United States reached its climax, and, in the UK, the fallout from the alleged Skripal poisoning was followed by the Henry Jackson Society report and almost endless vilification of the Russians. It was not only the most famous and wealthy Russians that had problems, contrary to what the anti-Russian elites would have you believe. It was, in every possible way, all of us. I had my own share of career-shattering problems in early 2019 that connect directly to me being Russian, and they remain unresolved. Numerous others who are neither wealthy nor well-known have been accused of seemingly nothing at all and found themselves barred from countries, fired from companies they founded, or criminally prosecuted for merely being Russian.

And then, when Navalny was allegedly – although unlikely – poisoned in Russia and arrived in Germany, his sermon took a rather unusual turn. He decided, out of the blue, to appeal to foreign politicians to double and triple down on sanctions against Russians. It was clear that it was not really his project -- sanctions never were, nor was geopolitics. Vladimir Ashurkov, our fugitive embezzler on duty, out of the blue compiled a list of some sort and waved it around. Navalny later parroted it at the infamous European Parliament zoom session. No one has ever seen the rest of the "list", because he named only two names: Roman Abramovich and Alisher Usmanov. I could not believe my ears. Really? This was Lesha Navalny's idea of patriotism nowadays? It made me

---

85 One of Alinsky's famous confrontations actually involved a dispute with an administration of an airport - it was colloquially dubbed the *O'Hare shit-in*. It is famous for never coming to pass - the threat of disruption alone was enough for the administration to yield to protesters' demands. Alinsky wrote that he learned that the threat of action could be as powerful as action itself. Hm.

regret not killing Navalny in 2005, but it also puzzled me, because these two names made no sense, and even less sense when used in a sentence together. What on Earth did these two people have in common, other than they had both owned British football clubs?

I came to assume pretty quickly that the only reason Usmanov got mentioned was that he had, shortly before then, successfully sued Navalny for libel in a Russian court – consequently, Navalny owed Usmanov money. It was strictly business – or rather, petty revenge. But what on Earth did Navalny suddenly have against Abramovich? The latter had not been involved in anything in Russia for quite a long time, and has not really been a target of Navalny's attacks that I knew of. And here Navalny suddenly was, pontificating about the sale of Sibneft to Gazprom 13 years earlier to the clueless British and European MPs. What gave? It seemed unprovoked.

I haven't heard of Navalny having any problems with the Gazprom-Sibneft transaction, other than in his prior venture days when he sued Gazprom as a minority shareholder in 2008 at the bidding of Vladimir Milov. Bingo. It turns out that Vladimir Milov, once he was done playing the most grief-stricken relative at Nemtsov's grave, washed out of his other political ventures and joined Navalny's crusade, of which he quickly took primary control. Milov had long-standing beef with Gazprom – the former deputy minister for energy, he had been a crusader against the state-owned gas giant for 20 years, and vehemently criticized absolutely everything Gazprom has ever done, complaining incessantly about Gazprom's management and its internal affairs.

While in government, Milov had reportedly been an architect of plans to break up and subsequently privatize Gazprom. The winds of change blew the other way after Milov abruptly departed: not only Gazprom remained state-owned, but it became a vessel through which other assets were re-nationalized. Milov has long been as unhappy about the purchase of Sibneft and what he saw as funneling of state budget funds into Gazprom with the purpose of funding it, as he has been about Gazprom's other activities. Roman Abramovich, who happened to be the seller of Sibneft to Gazprom, was an accidental victim of Milov's conspiracy theory – it could have been anyone else. Nothing personal. Years later, once Milov was primed to take over Navalny's organization, Gazprom had already been under U.S. sectoral sanctions, so Milov decided to re-package his grudge in flashy PR-friendly terms and pick on Abramovich.

At the time when Gazprom bought Sibneft in September 2005, Alexey Navalny was nowhere near any such matters. Exactly at that same time, Navalny was busy ending my political career in the course of the 2005 Moscow City Duma elections, along with Boris Nemtsov (who would later agree to put his name on the infamous "Putin and Gazprom" report compiled by his protege, Milov). Navalny was a small-time regional administrator at Yabloko with 200 followers on LiveJournal. He drove around with a megaphone, organizing *babushkas* against single-point residential development in Moscow. He had no interest in energy affairs and no knowledge about them. It was not until he first hooked up with Milov in 2008, during the time when he was offering his services as a litigious minority shareholder to anyone who would pay, that Navalny became aware of the whole thing. He ineptly represented Milov's point of view in his own failed shareholder lawsuit against Gazprom.

On his own, Navalny could never properly explain what he thought was supposedly wrong with the 2005 sale, and cannot to this day. On his 2020 European tour, he desperately resorted to positing that Abramovich was deliberately paid more than Sibneft was worth. Navalny tried to draw childish comparisons between the amount for which Sibneft – in his words – was bought from the government in 1996, and the amount for which it was then sold back to the government in 2005. Aside from the fact that Sibneft itself was not bought from the government at all – it was later formed by combining two different companies – Navalny's bumbling sounded self-defeating to anyone who knows anything about Russian economy or business.

Firstly, assets that were privatized in the 1990s were not, in traditional understanding, businesses – they were a mixture of barely functioning dilapidated state institutions and mineral rights, all in a state of decay and disarray. The years in which they had been turned into functioning companies with efficient western-style management also saw oil prices go up quite substantially. Scores untold of Western financial managers and institutional investors were involved, and the eyes of the world's business media and analysts were on the 2005 sale. It was not exactly a secret deal. Forbes covered it head to toe. If something was wrong with the valuation, someone would have noticed. Sibneft was bought by Gazprom for approximately $13 billion. Renamed Gazprom Oil, it was valued soon afterward at $17 billion. Such was the rate of growth of oil-backed assets at the time. There is nothing there, and Navalny himself knows it. Abramovich had just become a commonplace target by then. Navalny must have thought there was no harm because he was merely bucking the trend. In more prosaic terms, it was a pile-on.

I often hear from Brits – "why are you so hung up on Abramovich, this has nothing to do with the rest of the Russians". In other words, he is one of a kind, or – give up your rich and live in peace. Except, no one in the actual diaspora of Russians living in London has ever said that to me. Not one Russian person that I know, who is assimilated to any degree at all, perceives their own interests in England to be distinct from, or not aligned with, those of Roman Abramovich. Unlike the fly-by-night "emigres" or Russians who do not actually live in the United Kingdom pontificating on this topic, everyone in London knows that diaspora is a pyramid.

Abramovich is at the top of it, because he is wealthy and well-known, and knows Putin. Ok. If we do nothing when Russia haters come for Roman Abramovich, who will they move on to when they are done with him? The tale is as old as the world. When they are done with the few super rich and people that know Putin personally, they will move on to the middle class and the people who know people who know Putin, i.e. those like myself. After us, it will be everyone else who does not picket the Russian Embassy on weekends or has societal ambitions above driving a taxi and stocking shelves – the Henry Jackson Society told us this much. Anyone who claims to not see that is a fool.

There are some Russian people who had become targets in the West, about whom I often say – well, he or she is one of a kind. There are people whose history, involvement, position are so unique that a random person in the diaspora is at no risk of ending up in their shoes. I sympathize emphatically with the plight of Oleg Deripaska *vis a vis* the United States, but there was nothing about him at all in the first draft of this book; I had reasoned that he was *in too deep*. He lives in Russia, for one, and is actively involved in its affairs. He was, at the start of the events, personally running multiple businesses that were systemic to the Russian economy and crucial to the world markets. He had a years-long history of epic political meddling, such as the orchestration of Montenegrin independence and the complex personal involvement with the FBI. He had managed to feature in an *October surprise* smear as far back as the McCain presidential campaign. Even if, as I now believe, much of what befell Deripaska,

324

in the end, had nothing to do with any of those things – which is why I wrote him into the narrative, after all – he is still in a rather unique position. I was writing from the perspective of the diaspora, and none of us is quite Deripaska, nor ever will be.

By contrast, we are all Roman Abramovich. Most of us are a less successful and a much poorer version of him, but there is nothing about Abramovich that says the rest of us could not share his fate. Abramovich has not been involved in Russian politics since 2008. He does not really live in Russia, and hadn't for years. I probably spend more time in Moscow than he does. He has not been involved in the management of any Russian-based businesses for a very long time, his existing financial investments in Russia are managed on his behalf and quite diversified. He does not control any companies, let alone industries or sectors of the economy. When he does make an appearance in public life in Russia, it is mainly to attend an exhibition, a theater play, a movie festival, or to tour a museum, usually because he had sponsored those things. Abramovich is known in Moscow nowadays mostly as a patron of the arts, and for that, he is widely admired by its rebellious creative class. He is also prone to occasionally build a hospital or two. He had recently built a large veterinary clinic outside of Moscow, and, as far as I know, a number of medical facilities in Israel, of which he is a citizen and where he has also donated to many conservative Jewish causes.

Abramovich lived in England for years. He professed affection for London in at least one rare interview. He did not need England – like most of us do not *need it*, we chose it because we, at one point, liked it there. Abramovich spent years there, his children grew up and live there. He gave his heart and years of enthusiastic stewardship to Chelsea, earning genuine love and affection of the fans, the players and most of the people in British sport. The people know when someone is for real. He is conscious of the public good. He invested huge sums and a lot of effort in the Chelsea women's team, campaigns against racism and community initiatives. During the COVID pandemic, he opened facilities to NHS workers. Abramovich is an all-round nice guy who is universally well-liked, it seems, by everyone who has met him. He does not have a scary accent, and no ominous rumors ever surrounded him.

Living in the United Kingdom for many years, most of us have been able to form an idea of what constitutes a good immigrant in terms of British societal values. Roman Abramovich ticks every box and is an apogee of that stereotype.

325

At the top of the social pyramid of the diaspora, his portrait is also a portrait of an absolutely perfect immigrant that Britain has ever professed to want. If he is suddenly not good enough – what hope, pray, is there for the rest of us? If this is the guy the British government decided to pick on, we are all doomed.

Theresa May, who was Prime Minister during the alleged Skripal poisoning, by all accounts, might not have known that Chelsea was anything other than a neighborhood. Foreign relations were not her strong suit either. She was, of course, our former Home Secretary – the one and only thing she did know anything about, was our immigration system, which was then the so-called *points-based system* (although it has never really been points-based). The points-based system was introduced in 2008, and its so-called *Tier 1* accommodated a wide range of middle to upper-class immigration, from high-skilled migrants to entrepreneurs to investors. Many of us, in the diaspora as currently constituted, are variously graduates or victims of Tier 1, and all have PTSD from it.

I completed my own UK immigration as a Tier 1 General migrant – a subcategory for high-skilled migrants, which closed almost as quickly as it opened. In the few years of its existence, its most important rules changed numerous times. If I hadn't been deeply involved in immigration policy and law my whole life, no way I'd have been able to navigate it and emerge on the other side. I later started my immigration law practice as a Tier 1 wizard. The rules were so screwed up that they required full-time expertise. Tier 1 compliance was full-time work, and grew into a whole subculture in the United Kingdom. Since 2010, the subculture's principal antagonist has been Theresa May. I may have called her something along the lines of a *non-human robot from space* on my blog on more than one occasion – although, in retrospect, she was probably more competent than all our subsequent Home Secretaries. The day in 2016 when Theresa May took office as Prime Minister was a day of mass panic in my world. People genuinely believed it was the end of the world, or at least the end of all immigration. It was with great relief that, coincidentally, I took my citizenship oath two weeks after Theresa May took office.

Given her extraordinarily long tenure as UK immigration tsar, the only thing Theresa May the Prime Minister knew about most foreign countries was that immigrants came from them. In that context, her response to the Skripal crisis was unsurprising. She said that re-evaluation needs to be taken of all

326

previously issued Tier 1 Investor visas, many of which were held by Russians. She did not elaborate on a connection she saw between the Skripal poisoning and Russian investors in the UK. It was simply the only thing she knew about Russians. The media, although without much merit, connected that to whatever visa conundrum befell Roman Abramovich shortly thereafter, reporting that he was in the Tier 1 Investor category at the time. "He is being asked to show the origins of his wealth", – the news outlets reported profoundly.

You can make almost anything sound profound, but this was, of course, utter nonsense (which is not to say that the government wasn't doing it, seeing as *nonsense* is our government's middle name). Firstly, there is nothing whatsoever unknown about the origins of Abramovich's wealth. Everyone interested knows exactly what part of it came from where and when, and there are records of that, including court records of public trials held in England. Secondly, this sort of "origin of wealth" nonsense has happened to every immigrant in England. And trust me, it is not less, but often more devastating if your finances are nothing like those of Roman Abramovich.

I don't know about Abramovich, but I was once harassed on the subject of *origin of wealth*, and oh what a spectacular wealth it was. The whole £50,000 of it – such was the cost of a studio apartment some distance from London that I was trying to buy in 2011 for my then 17-year old daughter, who was about to start university. We had just sold our main remaining residence in Russia, my late mother's house in Nikolina Gora, and, in the noble Russian tradition, the resulting proceeds were, as I previously mentioned, in cash. Actual bank-packed wads of $100 bills, in U.S. dollars. So, when Darya and I finally saw the flat we liked, and the estate agent asked for *proof of funds*, I cheerfully asked: do you want a picture of them? Cue in us being laughed all the way out of the village, and the secretary at the local solicitors' office shouting at us not to come back, very proud that she got rid of the very dangerous Russians that were about to do mischief. Darya was in tears. I felt like Ostap Bender from the *Golden Calf.*

We did eventually buy the flat, but not before overpaying dramatically for a large London-based solicitors firm, a massive overkill for the transaction to be performed, and staying an extra month at a Hilton hotel while the drama unfolded. The cultural shock that I experienced from lack of acceptance was almost as big as that which people in that small town probably experienced from seeing *Russians* for the first time in their lives. What did they think, exactly, my

327

£50,000 were? Drug money? Putin's coffers? The depth of ridicule that we had to go through was astounding. But it was, of course, perfectly normal for England, even many years before Crimea, sanctions and such like.

My numerous clients who had only had mere tens of thousands of pounds to their name had their accounts closed without warning and funds frozen indefinitely upon receiving a single transfer from Russia. For many, these were the only funds they had, and they are still fighting to get them back. The late Bob Levinson's warning was heard loud and clear. Every housewife from a provincial Russian town who sold her grandmother's apartment in order to start a new life in a land she dreamed of her entire life, only to be arbitrarily separated from all of her money, found *weaving herself into the fabric of society* cruelly difficult.

When Navalny goes and tells the EU Parliament that the conflict exists between the Russian people and the Russian state, or *the oligarchs* and the diaspora, he lies. Roman Abramovich may be at the top of the pyramid, making some things harder for him and yet others easier. But the harassment and persecution of Russians permeate all of it, and it is felt even more painfully at the bottom. If we allow this to continue, it will not end. Russia might dig a moat around and pull up the draw bridge, embracing within those who still live there – but it leaves the rest of us *weaved* hopelessly *into the fabric* of societies that suddenly, after many years of taking our money and indoctrinating our children, seek to discard us, unless we deny who we are three times, like St. Peter.

In all of the talk about "reputation laundering", we are now at the point when the British government, at least, has a reputation to launder with us, the Russian-speaking community. Those of us who lived in England for many years – in many cases, the most active years of our lives that we will not get back – those who became British citizens, those whose adult children barely speak any Russian. Many in the diaspora feel swindled. For years, money had been siphoned from them for immigration fees, IHS fees, taxes. People bought property, paid for goods and tuition, created businesses and employed workers. They brought in whatever money they could gather and spent in the UK. In return, they hoped to gain this country's love and trust, but are now getting paranoia and suspicion at levels that were unimaginable ten years ago.

We are all now Putin's stooges, spies, *mafiosi*, who, the public are told, permeated their midst with vile intentions. We are living undercover among them, *masquerading as Russians living in the UK*. Putin, for that matter, has

328

nothing to do with it personally. If one day Putin is no longer President, they will move instantly onto whomever knows the next guy. I used to vote for people I personally know in Russian presidential elections, and I once used to fancy my former boss Dmitry Rogozin as Putin's possible successor. Today, I am no longer sure that I wish for someone I know to become the President of Russia – in the antipode world that I live in, it will be no longer consistent with self-preservation. Just as well that I no longer have a say.

Let's not pretend that something profound and complicated is at play in the West, which has suddenly provided it with illuminating insight into the dangers of Russianness. People who trash talk us at daytime on the floor of Parliament in England, or people who draw up press releases in support of sanctions in the United States, and everyone in between, have no idea what they are talking about. The majority of them have never been to Russia, they have no idea what it is like, they have, like Chris Matthews, *never met a Russian*, they can't decide whether it is the evil empire, the alien mother ship that sends signals to every Russian speaker, or a *cold, vodka-soaked place*. Their spies do not know that Russians drink Starbucks and have indoor plumbing. They think that, for 75,000 people, being a Russian citizen living in the UK is *a cover*. The whole thing is a cartoon to them, or a computer game, and we are all characters in it.

To end the madness, I have a suggestion to make. How about the UK and U.S. elites revert, just for a moment, to the belief that their societies are shining cities on the hill, on which their identity has been predicated for years? Most of us first moved to those societies when they still were – and Russia, at that same time, lay in ruins. We did not come to England and America in order to *weave ourselves into the fabric of society* with malign intentions – we, the last Soviet generation, grew up with a belief, no matter how naive, that those societies were better places. We grew up fascinated by The Beatles and Sherlock Holmes, and longed for the world of American movies we watched clandestinely on rare VCRs. We stayed because we fell in love with those countries. We had thought we found our paradise. We wanted our children to play on shiny playgrounds, go to Toys'R'Us and live in a place without violent crime. We wanted to play our part in the bigger world.

Things have changed. Shining cities on the hill they no longer are. There are shiny playgrounds all over the world, and there is more crime in the United States and the UK than there is in Russia. For now. But the truth is, most of us moved next door to you, all these years ago, because we wanted to get away from Russia. We lived through turbulent times there, and did not want our children to do the same. We might love Russia and go back occasionally, but we are mindful that turbulent times could happen there again.

If someone moved to England or America, it was because they thought it would be cool to live there. If they bought a house, it was because they wanted somewhere to stay. If they sent their kid to school, it was because they wanted them to get an education. If they bought a football club, it was because they wanted to watch football games and pose with trophies. If they built an ark, it was probably because they saw the movie *2012* and wanted to stay afloat when the whole world goes to shit. And, if they wrote a book, they probably wanted to make money selling copies of it. The simple explanation is always the most likely explanation. We are not here to eat you.

Most Russians, rich and poor, will not talk about Russia's problems overseas, betray Russia or allow themselves to be used by its haters – but it does not mean that they do not see those problems themselves. The Russian people, the Russian state and the overseas diasporas are all in symbiosis – but we do not act as one. Sometimes, when our opinion differs from yours, it might not be *the word of Putin*, it might just be common sense as perceived by better-informed people with more experience of the wider world. As a result of being brainwashed by Soviet propaganda for many years, Soviet-era Russians, for the most part, are much better at thinking for themselves than the Americans and the Brits. When the time comes, that is what we will all do. Just stop patronizing us with *your* groupthink. We have had enough of that for a lifetime.

EPILOGUE

Language is a powerful tool. Something meaningless can be described as profound, something innocent can be described as menacing, failure can be made to sound glamorous. It may seem in hindsight, after 30 years, that I ultimately failed upwards, but my lifelong conquest of the world has nonetheless been a neverending failure.

She may have played dissident in the USSR, but once the political objectives of the *dissidentura* were achieved, it turned out that my mother never actually believed that America was such a great place. She met my decision to depart for the United States with 2-year old Darya in 1996 with hostility and despair. "Do you know how dangerous New York is?" – mother asked me. "You will have to carry $20 on you at all times just to make sure you have something to give to the people trying to mug you".

Funny she said that – New York was rough in the mid-1990s, but Moscow was even more so at the time. My daughter had never been out and about in the city which I had once roamed carelessly as a child, because taking the family out for a walk downtown was considered unsafe. Nor was there anywhere to go except McDonald's.

Having already determined by then that I would only live in the ever boring England *when I am old, in my forties*, I had high expectations for America. I grant my mother that New York did not meet them. Boy, was it grim and inhospitable! My contact lenses were foggy with the omnipresent moisture in the air, and no one had the time of day for me. I remember standing at the corner of Fifth Avenue and 34th street in the summer of 1996 and asking myself: what is this dystopia? What have I done and why?

The problem wasn't the size or the scale. I was an urban child, forever entwined with my hometown, Moscow – a city at least the size of New York. Midtown Manhattan was a disastrously wrong place to start, but I would later spend, overall, about seven years of my life living, working or studying in New York City, and I never quite warmed up to it. I later realized that I could never be a *New Yorker*, because, just like being *a Muscovite*, that status was a type of personality and a state of mind, not subject to acquisition at any age after early childhood. One individual can only be in symbiosis with one large city, no matter how far away from it they now live. I detest London and Paris for exactly the

331

same reasons. As Muscovites, we instinctively reject those who arrived in the city as adults[86], and, being privy to that instinct, I can physically perceive how New Yorkers, Londoners and Parisians instinctively reject me.

I later discovered the suburbs, the mountains and the shores, and warmed up to America. I brought Darya over once I found an apartment in Westfield, a nice, neat suburban town in Union county, New Jersey. A daughter of my mother's friend, who had herself left the USSR aged 3, had just moved there with her Russian husband. Westfield looked somewhat like Nikolina Gora – it had stately detached homes surrounded by land, albeit the homes were smaller and there was less land. As I was trying to deal with the implications of my disastrous decision to emigrate by avoidance, my child was expressing the uncensored truth. Darya, who had hitherto spent most of her time with grandparents and babysitters, had a full-blown panic attack when told that we shall never be going *home* again. Aged two and a half, she ran out on the street in tears, past the houses of the people whose level of relative affluence I would never reach in the United States as an immigrant single mother, screaming, in Russian: *I want to go home!*

I think now that I should have listened. Immigration became my lifelong quest and its only purpose, and that purpose eventually defeated itself. For most of my active adult life my world has become a world of borders – and most of the time I had been preoccupied with having, or being unable, to cross borders. When others have nightmares, they are of fires, tsunami and airplane crashes. My nightmares were of lacking passports and visas, being unable to cross borders, or even of being unable to find border crossings in the wilderness[87].

---

[86] This includes the city's current mayor, Sergey Sobyanin, whom we call *the deer herder*. No one in Moscow knows where the place he is from is, but we are all certain that they herd deer there. It must have been *ponayehavshie (the arrived)* that voted him in, while a slight speech impediment concealed his accent. I produced exactly one Internet meme in my lifetime, and I am very proud of it. It was a photo of Vladimir Putin standing with a puzzled expression near the Eastern end of a gigantic map of Russia. *Vladimir Vladimirovich is trying to find the hometown of Sergey Semenovich*, the caption read.

[87] Many years later, I called my immigration practice *World Without Borders*, but I can see in hindsight that it only worked ironically. As for my nightmares, being unable to find a border crossing in the wilderness is something that actually happened to me, more than once. In a twist, COVID19 made the rest of them true as well. As I am finishing this book in June of 2021, I am living, literally, in the world of my nightmares.

Twenty-one is too old to fully assimilate into any new society – I have never seen it accomplished by anyone who was transplanted anywhere past high school age. Russia of the early 1990s aged us all quicker, so my 21 years then were nothing like the 21 of any of my Western-raised children years later. I was a fully formed product and a full participant of a society that I was trying to leave behind, and my connection with it could never be properly severed.

I did not know anyone in New York and was only able to survive because a few Russians knew *me*. My 1992 book about Aquarium had sold well, and many immigrant fans of the band had a copy. Faced with the unexpected arrival of the author in the flesh, some of them went out of their way to assist me. I was offered a job at a company named Joy-Lud Distributors. It was owned by a guy called Tamir Sapir, whom, the best I can recall, I have never met in person. Principally, Joy-Lud was involved in the sale of oil that was produced by the Moscow refinery. The oil was sold by tankerload. I handled letters of credit that were offered by buyers to guarantee payment. Joy-Lud was the real reason I ended up in the MBA program, and it sponsored my first H1B visa. I was 23 years old when I left Joy-Lud in 1998, 23 years ago now.

I had forgotten all about Joy-Lud, and it ceased to exist years ago. There would be absolutely no point in mentioning any of it now, but for one unexpected twist. In 2020, The Guardian ran a particularly moronic paranoid story, ostensibly based on revelations of yet one more elderly demented ex-KGB defector. According to that story, Joy-Lud had been a KGB outfit, and its owner was a long-time KGB asset. "F*ck", – I thought. Later, I discovered that the same nonsense with the same attribution was claimed by the infamous Catherine Belton in her book "Putin's People".

I had already been equally upset by the existence of Belton's book in the first place (I thought the publishers, in this case, would know better), and the pending legal action against it by Roman Abramovich and several other wealthy Russians, variously aggrieved by different bits of nonsense in it (high-profile defamation litigation usually amplifies the impugned defamatory statements). But then I discovered that the cursed book dedicates at least as much space to claiming that everyone at Joy-Lud was KGB, as it does to Abramovich. So now I am, once again, in the notional second line behind Russophobia's named primary targets. In his legal action, Roman Abramovich, by extension, now represents me, too. What better proof that diaspora is a pyramid?

As Vladimir Putin took office and state-owned Gazprom took over NTV, expelling its owner, Vladimir Gusinsky, into emigration, my mother suddenly warmed up to America. She had been to everywhere we lived in it, and seemed to think it was, after all, a proper place to raise a family. But it was illusory, of course. Due to difficulties around my immigration status, I had not left the United States, initially, for 7 years. When Grandma Clara died in Moscow in 2001, I was not there.

I was told not to worry – Grandma Clara had dementia and would not recognize me anyway. But I did not have dementia just yet, and had virtually grown up in the care of my maternal grandparents, who always lived next door. They were the first to show up when Darya was brought home from the hospital, too. Grandma Clara died having never met her second granddaughter, who was born in the United States. This upset me. J.K. Rowling hadn't yet written the relevant chapters of the Harry Potter saga by then, but I felt as if my soul was splitting into horcruxes, like Voldemort's.

Immigration destroyed my first marriage, because I refused to return to Russia, which my husband insisted on doing. At one point, he had briefly left, and the U.S. government refused to let him back in, even though he had a relevant visa. The U.S. Embassy in Moscow, drawing on its infinite wisdom and vast local knowledge, wrote a three-page letter to the INS insisting that his employer – a well-known political consultancy that was less than one year away from successfully electing Vladimir Putin to his first term as President of the United States – *did not really exist*. They had eventually let him in, a year later, but he missed Sophia's birth and had not met her, his first child, until she was 6 months old. What sort of life was it? [88]

I like to tell people proudly that Grandma Tonya lived with us in our new house in Nikolina Gora before she died. My late mother, whose house it actually was, had refused to speak to Grandma Tonya for years and pre-emptively banned Grandma Tonya from her funeral. If I believed in life after death, I would not have dared move Grandma Tonya into my mother's former bedroom. I told the neighbors that we were looking to vindicate Grandma Tonya for the injustice of

---

[88] In a nutshell, immigration destroyed my second marriage as well. My second husband would not stay in Russia, and I could no longer return to the United States quickly, having left with what was then a patchy immigration history. A lengthy process would have to be followed.

being evicted by Uncle Yuri's family from their dacha across the street after his death. This was a concept that members of the dacha co-op, acclimated to habitual acrimony, could absorb. But it wasn't the real reason Grandma Tonya moved to Nikolina Gora.

The real reason was that we sold the apartment in Moscow in which Grandma Tonya had hitherto lived, so that I could finance my immigration to the United Kingdom. After she died, we sold the house in Nikolina Gora, too. In England, and then partly in America, all of this was simply spent. It went like water into the sand.

I think Grandpa Georgiy is right where he needs to be in his veterans' home. He could no longer live by himself, he suffers from dementia and, with his large military pension, he is extraordinarily amenable to every swindle and fraud that comes his way. He can barely walk, he can barely see, and he cannot hear. There is no way he would have survived the COVID pandemic outside of the home, or would have even lived to be as old as he is now. Russian society is not well set to accommodate 96-year olds. He had set his 9-story apartment building on fire every time he tried to boil a teapot, flooded the neighbors downstairs every time he turned the water on, and a gas explosion was just a matter of time.

Yet, none of these was the real reason he had to move. The real reason was that I, in the neverending search for *my America*, wanted to sell the apartment that he was living in so that I could pay off my LLM tuition in order to take the California Bar Exam. That was supposed to be my big break.

This was early 2018, and I, like many others, failed yet to realize the full implications of Russiagate. I passed the Bar exam – an extraordinary feat for anyone foreign-educated and doing it by self-study. But then, California Bar revoked my *positive moral character* determination and refused to swear me in. Someone from Russia had sent them an anonymous letter detailing my political history in Russia and my history of book-writing in Russian. It included a book I have previously written, a novel ostensibly based on my first seven years in the United States. No one at The Bar could read Russian, so they had to rely on the anonym's interpretation of it. The letter told them that the book mocked the United States and glorified bank fraud.

California Bar admits thousands of foreigners from all over the world every year, about whom it truly knows nothing – including Russians, of course. But I was the wrong kind of a Russian, and at a very wrong time and place to be one. They were embarrassed that they had failed to previously Google me. If they had, the anonym's actions would have been superfluous – but, as it stands, the intervention cost me hundreds of thousands of dollars and at least two and a half years of my life. I am telling myself every day, as California burns in riots and wildfires, that it was a *quite effectively disguised blessing*.

In the subsequent two years, California Bar effectuated an "evidence dump" of about 1500 pages of garbage. It included, among other things, complete printouts of everything I ever posted to any social media, printouts of all of my websites, printouts of all emails in which my name was mentioned at the Temple University law school, including emails between staff, printouts of some random pieces of media in Russian without translation, every bank and credit card statement that they could get a hold of for the last 20 years, and a complete background check on a receptionist in a mail place which I used to receive mail when I was overseas[89]. The latter was a waste of the Bar's time – the mail place dumped me immediately after having to sign for some 80 subpoenas duces tecum, some of which the Bar dispatched twice, for good measure.

They subpoenaed every bank in the Yellow Pages to see if I ever held an account there; the management of my apartment complex for the list of all visitors; Google, LinkedIn and Facebook for my emails and private messages and every IP address I ever used to access their platforms (the messages were not disclosed, but the IP addresses were). After they were done with that, they sent letters to the Department of Homeland Security and USCIS claiming that it was suspicious that I travel too much. In the course of it all they accidentally disclosed my Social Security number to several dozen parties who had no business knowing it. Anyone else want to practice law in California?

I know who wrote that letter now, even though that person had approached me using a false identity and I do not know their real one. Throughout my years in England, I had been tracked, both online and in real life,

---

89 After all that, the mere 70-something page evidence dump initially produced by U.S. Treasury on Deripaska neither surprised nor impressed me. His detractors were clearly lazier than mine, but their *modus operandi* was the same: a pile of garbage that includes a mountain of nonsense no one will ever read through, in hope that its overall disheveled appearance will somehow make the target look bad enough. More recently, I heard Lara Logan on Fox News calling this tactic "ambiguity increasing", and explaining that it was a well-known feature in information warfare.

in order to keep an eye on me. *I think* I know on whose orders. Once upon a time, a certain someone failed to see my own intervention in their career as a blessing in disguise, but I shall not name them, because it will detract from this book's narrative. After all, we are supposed to be on the same side, and it does no good for *patriots* to turn on each other. Une trêve, peut-être? Or are there, even, sides? Just like John Solomon put it in one of his columns, most things in Russia are not black and white. Russia is shades of grey all around. Oh, the things we would do to each other.

This brings me to my final and most important point. What is patriotism, what is national identity, and how do *we*, however constituted, tell who is, or isn't, on our side? I wrote earlier – more than once – that it is a mistake to consider that there are sides in Russia. There are simply people, some with allies, some without, who act in ways they consider expedient at every turn. Their interests often coincide, but that is only until they do not. There is no *higher loyalty*.

In the United States, we are used to thinking that there is a *higher loyalty*. America, Freedom, Constitution. Preservation of America as this one unique place that we all, at one point in our lives, fell in love with. Today, most Americans no longer have any system of values that binds them together. Most Russians will not besmirch Russia when overseas, but Americans would, and do. In the immigration system we are all conditioned to strive for citizenship – but what, exactly, does the concept of citizenship mean anymore? Your country used to be the object of your loyalty, but how can it be if you have two or three? Does your *higher loyalty* belong with your country of birth, or the country of your parents' birth, or the country in which you grew up, or the one to which you raised your right hand and took an oath of allegiance to?

What if the country you were born in no longer exists? What if there is more than one country in each of the last three categories? Not only do I know numerous people who have multiple passports acquired by accident of birth or in childhood, I also know people who managed to take an oath of allegiance to more than one country. The naturalization laws of neither the United Kingdom nor the United States prevent that from happening. The United States, to its credit, holds that you can self-expatriate by taking an oath of loyalty to another country, but it would work the other way around.

My middle daughter is a good example of a child of three worlds. She was born in the United States to two Russian citizens on work visas, thereby acquiring both American and Russian citizenship at birth. She had spent her early childhood and school years almost equally in Russia, the United States, and the United Kingdom, in all of which she went to school in different years. She received British citizenship by registration while still a child. When asked about her identity throughout her childhood, she always said she identified as Russian. She has barely visited Russia since starting high school in the UK, and is now very uncomfortable with it. Whenever back in America, she seems to think, at all times, that she is about to get shot.

In other words, here is a British young woman who sees both Russia and America as simply her mother's crazy ideas. Yet, having graduated from a well-known British university with a degree in International Relations, I do not think she would have had a career in the Foreign Service, being a child of two politically exposed Russians. I do not know if she would have done better at the Department of State, either. Ultimately, questions of immigration ruined her life, too – or this is the way I see it, anyway. She ended up going to medical school, which delighted her Jewish father.

The country in which I was born and raised no longer exists. Russia exists in its place, but I was 17 years old when it came into being and have barely lived in it as an adult. Symbolically, it took Russia years to stop printing passports that said *USSR* on them – but that's now gone. I do not really know or understand the Russia that exists today as well as I claim in this book that I do. Neither of my three grown children speaks my native language at any such level that permits an intelligent conversation: the oldest speaks Japanese better than Russian, and the middle one – French. The youngest is taking Spanish. And all of them read The Guardian and refuse to set foot in Russia.

Some years ago I raised my right hand and pledged allegiance to Her Majesty Queen Elizabeth II and Her heirs and descendants. Unlike some, I have only done it once in my life – and, until recently, I struggled with the meaning of that act. Much as I claim that I wish for the *Island of Doom* to sink, I guess it is only the Britishness in me talking. Being grumpy and complaining about the government are the main British national traits that I am aware of. I do not know whether Her Majesty would ever send me to war against Russia, and I would not

338

go to such, or any, war – but the reason I gave up my Russian citizenship was that I wish there to not be any ambiguity about my *higher loyalty*.

But that is not, of course, the real reason – or, at least, not the only one. The real reason for me relinquishing my Russian citizenship was that it protects my British citizenship from deprivation in case HM Government does not like this book or any of my past or future books. Deprivation became an epidemic since Theresa May's tenure at the Home Office, but is only possible if the target has another citizenship, or an automatic right to acquire one (would the Home Secretary please note that, to become a Russian citizen again, I would have to reside there for a period of time as an immigrant). In case the government of the United States, or any of its agencies, do not like my book, or any of my past or future books, my position will also be very different as a British citizen only, versus a Russian citizen. I have seen too much of that in the last three years.

And, of course, the last thing I would want would be to become the subject of the Russian government's infamous chivalry, in which it steps in to claim as its own all people accused of silly things in America who had nothing do to with the Russian government in the first place. I have seen that happen and destroy any meaningful line of those persons' defense. Renunciation of Russian citizenship also entitles me to consular protection in Russia in case the government there does not like my book, or anything else about me, as the Russian government is prone to do – and increasingly so of late. Perhaps the British government can then swap Yulia Skripal for me.

Have you spent any time of your life having to think of things like that? If no, then you know nothing about immigration, and you haven't started to imagine being Russian. I tell people that I ended my immigration law practice because rising Russophobia made it dishonest of me to facilitate Russian immigration to the UK. But this wasn't the real reason. My immigration practice had been a non-profit, and most of my clients were not Russian. The reason I no longer wanted to facilitate immigration was that I started to see a perceived need to migrate as a form of madness, and the idea that any meaningful assimilation can be ultimately achieved in the first generation – as an illusion.

From the very start in 1996, I have only survived in America because I already had a certain identity in Russia which allowed me to draw on the resources of the Russian-speaking community. I was already incurably Russian, by the time I first arrived. In England, working with and on behalf of the Russian-speaking community became my only marketable skill. People with three, four and sometimes even five passports are the norm in my life. Strangers in my only country of citizenship ask me on the train every day *how long am I here for:* hanging around with Russians so much, I re-acquired a strong accent that I previously did not have. It's a mad, mad world.

You could spend billions of pounds in England on a business you love and be revered by hundreds of thousands of its citizens, but you won't get citizenship unless you took a moronic exam with questions about Florence Nightingale and sat on *the Island* for 270 days per year. Even then, some moron would come up and say that the hitherto unknown you were just trying to *launder reputation.* You could spend many years trying to get back to your house in the United States, which you love because you are a fan of Ayn Rand, FDR, trickle-down economics and quantitative easing – all at the same time. In the process, you spend tens of millions of dollars of your own money trying to rescue a well-known American Russophobe from captivity in a third country at the request of the FBI, but in the end, you are only labeled Public Enemy #1.

Meanwhile, tens of thousands of children in Russia, China, India and other countries have now reached adulthood, who had been born in the United States to parents who then left and took the children with them. They all have American passports showing benign places of birth, like New York City and Miami, but many have never been to the country other than at the time of their birth. They did not grow up on any American street, they did not support any baseball or football team, they did not go to school with anyone, and often do not know anyone in the United States. Do they even care that it continues to exist?

Their parents may have loved the United States. Maybe they lived in the United States for years, or flew to the United States, *the shining city on the hill,* to give birth in order to give their future child a chance to attend college, live and work in America when they are an adult. But their parents may not have possibly known what the child themselves would think once they grew up entirely in Putin's Russia or Chairman Xi's China. What is the *higher loyalty* of these children? Do we really think they love America more, or present less danger to it, than Oleg Deripaska? We do not even know who they are, and how to tell them from everyone else – and we certainly know very well who *he* is, so it's quite unlikely that *he* will be able to get a job at the Department of Defense.

The current American paradigm states that every adult Russian is a threat but birthright citizenship is sacrosanct. This is putting the real world of immigration and the question of higher loyalty on its head. You are all looking for enemies in the wrong places. Navalny, for his part, does not believe that we should even have citizenship as a concept. He thinks we should all simply reorganize by ethnicity, which is obviously nazism – but I would grant him that the notion of *higher loyalty,* as it was once understood in the world, is outdated.

The idea that there are countries, comprising their citizens, in which everyone shares the same purpose and is *on the same side*, is a farce. It has not been true for years. The American political establishment was at the forefront of making a farce of the idea of citizenship since it managed to sanction a number of Ukraine's own citizens for meddling in the affairs of... Ukraine. Ukraine cheerfully joined the pile-on by sanctioning its own citizens. What does it even mean anymore to be a citizen of a country? Apparently, not much. Consequently, this paradigm can no longer be applied to determine who is, or isn't, *us* or *them*. Loyalty becomes a revolving door, like the star-off machine in *Sneetches on Beaches*. No one knows who is who, and which is which, and pretending that sometimes we do, and sometimes we don't, is the highest form of hypocrisy.

When Theresa May became Prime Minister, she said: *citizens of the world are actually citizens of nowhere.* I knew she was right because it was true about me. Just like you cannot simultaneously see across of all of time and space, you cannot spend your life living in many worlds at once. It is not life, you won't belong in any of them, and your children will hate you.

This is what has been happening to most of us so far, and it is getting worse as the many worlds we try to live in start to insulate themselves from one another. Mobility conundrums of the COVID pandemic are only a visual aide to what is happening on an economic, social and political level in each of them. Does it have to be this way? Theresa May was speaking against multi-allegiance when she said that it was not possible to be a *citizen of the world.* And what if there was *one world*? That idea is not new, U2 sang about it a long time ago.

I hesitate to say *global world,* but that is what I mean. While it took away our ability to migrate one-way and completely transition from one identity to another, globalization did give us something in return: the ability to develop common understanding and form alliances across borders. Neither Trumpism

341

nor wokeness is confined to the United States, and many other trends and ideas reverberate throughout all of the developed and developing world simultaneously.

I wrote in the Prologue that Russians of a certain age and education level were sufficiently similarly informed as to come to the same conclusions on the same observations – but it is more than just Russians now. As facts become shared across the world, so does common sense. May it be that we will not need to have the current system of loyalty anymore, and citizenship really will no longer be the principle based on which we come together and draw battle lines?

Today's world is simultaneously moving in two opposite directions. On one hand, there is a drive away from globalization and for increased insularity of nation states. The concept of *EU free movement* is dead, international travel is permanently damaged by the COVID pandemic and politicians' paranoia, Russia is digging the moat because of sanctions and threatens to build whatever-it-is-this-time (it was once socialism) *in one single country.* Last time around it meant the Iron curtain, non-convertible currency and the economy without any export and import points except the state-controlled sale of fossil fuels. Now, according to Rogozin, Russians are actually going to *build their own space station.* Hello, Robbie Williams! It will literally be a *vertical sovereignty.* This time, Russia is eerily on trend – many ostensibly free countries are doing a lot of it, too, except that they are less honest about it.

At the same time, the virtualization of the global public square that took place during the COVID pandemic has also globalized discourse in the literate world to a greater degree than was done by actual globalization. I am not thrilled about humans moving all of their interactions into virtual space – I am old enough to believe that crucial social skills will thereby be permanently lost. Nonetheless, residents – so as to avoid *the c word* – of all countries in a certain notional space occupied by civilized debate are now more aware of each other's facts and perspective, and are able to agree and align themselves with those who would otherwise be outside of their reference group, just as they lose the previously presumed shared interests with their actual physical neighbors.

It is no wonder that the world is being torn apart. Is it possible to have insular economies operating within fortified nation-state borders and, at the same time, a virtual supra-state ideological space devoid of nationally determined quasi-security interests driven by paranoia? This is a subject of much bigger debate, but the likely answer is *no* – the globalization of thought and the localization of politics and security interests are forces that pull the world in opposite directions. One will have to prevail and the other to lose.

At the time of writing, it would appear that insularity is the trend, and, although it sounds regressive, the resulting world might be more environmental, ethical and secure. But, just like 100 years ago, multiple loyalties would not be possible in that world, and paranoia will reign. I cannot fathom a safe space for diasporas, including naturalized citizens, in this brave new world. As they exist today, diasporas include within them not just the Global Russians, but Global Chinese, and *global* everyone else, to say nothing of Canadians and Mexicans when it comes to the United States. The British are quite numerous, too – and it's not been *that* long since we were the enemy. In fact, many of America's notions of citizenship and loyalty, and its toxic early-era immigration acts, came into being as means of thwarting the greatest threat of the day: a British *revanche*.

The untenable position of split loyalty is only a Russian problem because of Russiagate, but we are trying very hard to cede the top spot on the hatred pedestal of immigrant groups to the Chinese, and it can become their problem soon. There are many more of them, and, even though the rates of naturalization and nativity in the Chinese community are much higher than in the Russian one, they are easier to visually identify – in that sense, *Chinagate* will be even more toxic to the American society than Russiagate. Yet, the ultimate insularity that the conservative movement is striving for cannot be achieved without going through it. Either way, the sovereignty trend does not bode well for immigration: be it internment, ghettos, employment restrictions or demands for expression of fealty in the actual physical public square, written declarations of willingness to take up arms against your homeland – none of it will be good for anyone, and yet we are going there very fast.

I was clearly not the only immigrant Russian who realized this. In order to renounce citizenship, you have to obtain a certificate that you do not owe taxes to Russia. There is now a dedicated team dealing with the issuance of those certificates at the Russian tax service, which accepts requests for those certificates by mail from all over the world. At its odious compound at Pokhodny Proezd in Moscow, there is a large plastic clear mailbox – perhaps a decommissioned voting urn – dedicated to requests for tax clearance certificates, to be delivered by hand and international mail couriers. I saw it myself, and it was bursting at the seams.

The more global world, one in which nation-state notions of loyalties would become obsolete, had been the trend until recently. If it wins, it may achieve world peace between nations – but it will probably be a poorer, less secure and less sustainable world. You would, though, be able to live in all of it at the same time – we will all be global citizens of it, except that some will have an ark, and some will not. I am tempted by the global world, since I am already a product of that paradigm, once defined by Theresa May. I belong nowhere and my children want to have nothing to do with me.

The global world does not require that you hold, acquire, express or renounce any loyalty, and in that sense, it is not only the place to be for holders of five passports, but an answer to a conservative prayer. Only in it, as David Byrne sings, can you *form a country in your house*, where your family, your street, and your militia unit can become the basis for your loyalty instead of the nation state. Its inherent danger is that humans, being pack animals, will indeed seek to form groups on exactly the same basis as envisioned by Navalny: on an ethnic basis. Perhaps then, it is better to have a hybrid war between insular nation states than to have one between Tutsies and Hutus.

The ultimate selection of a course rests on one question that plagued humanity for ages: are we more different across nations, than we are alike? If we all shared the same facts, would we all come to the same conclusions? You be the judge now. I leave you with several excerpts from a speech made by a public figure in a public forum at one point in 2020-2021. I invite you to guess who it was – especially if you are an American conservative. You can check my website, olgachilds.com, for the right answer.

"There is a crisis of the familiar paradigm in economic development. The income gap is widening, globally as well as in individual countries. This has been happening for a while, but it is now also causing the sharp polarization of public discourse, fueling the growth in right-wing populism on one end and radicalization on both sides of the political spectrum. <...>

We can all hope that the "hot" world war is no longer a possibility, because it would mean the end of our civilization. <...>Yet, we are standing at the precipice of a systemic crisis in world development, when everyone will be fighting against everything in an attempt to attribute intrinsic crises to newly discovered "enemies", foreign and domestic. In the process, our most basic value – the nuclear family unit – will be destroyed, and individuals' basic freedoms, such as freedom of choice and right to privacy, will be trampled. <..>

344

The widening of the income gap between the rich and poor in developed countries is profound. According to the World Bank, in the year 2000 approximately 3,6 million Americans had a daily income per capita of less than 5,5 US dollars; in 2016, it was already 5,6 million people. During that same period of time, globalization led to a substantial rise in the capitalization of large transnational corporations, many of which are based in the United States. <..> But who was the principal beneficiary of the rising corporate profits? We all know the answer – the top 1% of the population. And what of the rest of the people? In the last 30 years, the income of more than half of the residents of many developed countries did not grow in real terms. Meanwhile, the cost of education and medical care increased three-fold. <...>

Some are hoping that advances in technological development will allow us to reboot the previous growth model once again. It is true that the last 20 years have laid the foundation for the so-called fourth industrial revolution, which is expected to be fueled by widespread reliance on artificial intellect and automation. COVID-19 pandemic gave a boost to these trends. However, this process will result in seismic changes in the job markets. Without serious government interventions, large numbers of people will become unemployed. Many of them will be those whom we would have lately called the middle class, the foundation of any modern society. <...>

Increased economic inequality causes the breakdown in the fabric of society, breeds social, racial, ethnic hatred. The outbursts of it can now be seen in many countries with seemingly stable social and democratic institutions. The public discontent caused by systemic social and economic problems cannot be treated symptomatically – root causes of the underlying problems need to be addressed. If the true nature of the issues that cause the social outbursts is glossed over, a serious political and social divide will remain. True reasons for public discontent lie not in declared superficial issues, but in the real problems that affect everyone – regardless of anyone's stated political preferences.

<..> Modern technological and digital giants are now playing an increasing role in social life. This has been talked about a lot, including in the context of the 2020 election in the United States. These are no longer simply large companies, in many ways they are de facto competitors of national governments.<...> Their position as de facto monopolies in their respective markets enabled them to optimize their business processes – but are these monopolies serving any public good? Where is the red line between a successful global business that meets existing demand for services and consolidates global data, and one that uses its resources to exert unprecedented control over society, undermine legitimate democratic institutions, strip individuals of free choice and freedom of speech? <...> " ***